HYPOMNEMATA HEFT 42

HYPOMNEMATA

UNTERSUCHUNGEN ZUR ANTIKE
UND ZU IHREM NACHLEBEN

Herausgegeben von
Albrecht Dihle / Hartmut Erbse
Christian Habicht / Günther Patzig / Bruno Snell

HEFT 42

VANDENHOECK & RUPRECHT IN GÖTTINGEN

RONALD MELLOR

ΘΕΑ ΡΩΜΗ

The Worship of the
Goddess Roma in the Greek World

VANDENHOECK & RUPRECHT IN GÖTTINGEN

FOR ANNE

CIP-Kurztitelaufnahme der Deutschen Bibliothek
Mellor, Ronald
The worship of the goddess Roma in the greek world:
the Rome.
(Hypomnemata; H. 42)
ISBN 3-525-25138-6

© Vandenhoeck & Ruprecht in Göttingen 1975. — Printed in
Germany. Ohne ausdrückliche Genehmigung des Verlages ist es nicht
gestattet, das Buch oder Teile daraus auf foto- oder akusto-
mechanischem Wege zu vervielfältigen.
Gesamtherstellung: Hubert & Co., Göttingen

PREFACE

Several years ago, while I was preparing a book on Dea Roma and the imperial cult in the western provinces, several colleagues suggested an introductory chapter on the origins of Roma in the Greek world. This "Introduction" grew — the process is not unknown to scholars — and I must finally present it as a monograph in its own right. I have tried to bring together the widely scattered evidence for the worship of Roma in the East and to provide some historical context for the cults and honors paid to Roma. I am greatly endebted to numerous colleagues for references and assistance of various kinds. I am especially appreciative of those who read all or part of this manuscript and provided me with their written comments and corrections: E. BADIAN; T. R. S. BROUGHTON; G. P. BURTON; G. W. CLARKE; ALBRECHT DIHLE; ERICH GRUEN; CHRISTIAN HABICHT; JOYCE REYNOLDS; and my colleagues at Stanford, A. E. RAUBITSCHEK; MICHAEL WIGODSKY; and the late T. B. L. WEBSTER. RUDOLPH ARBESMANN and FRANK C. BOURNE were most helpful in my earlier work on the imperial cult and Roma in the West. Several scholars kindly gave me permission to quote or mention unpublished inscriptions or readings: GUNTER DUNST; N. M. KONTOLEON; JOYCE REYNOLDS; and LOUIS ROBERT. T. B. L. WEBSTER provided me with his own unpublished material on personification in Greek art and literature. These scholars are, of course, not responsible for the use I have made of their advice and criticism. The manuscript was completed late in 1973, and I have been able to make only limited use of material that reached me since that time.

Most of the book was written in London. I spent much of 1970 and the academic year 1972-73 as a member of the Institute of Classical Studies — a comfortable and congenial place to work. I am immensely grateful to its Director and the successive Librarians for the opportunity to use its fine library and participate in the stimulating activities of the Institute. During those years in London I was also an honorary member of the staff of University College London. I sincerely appreciated the kindness of Professors ERIC HANDLEY and OTTO SKUTSCH and the hospitality of their colleagues.

Professor CHRISTIAN HABICHT, as an Editor of the Hypomnemata series, devoted much time to my manuscript. He also kindly sent me his paper on the Imperial cult in the Augustan age delivered at the

Fondation Hardt. Though my manuscript had been completed, I have taken some account of it in my revisions. I am grateful to Professor HABICHT and to the staff of Vandenhoeck and Ruprecht for the time and care they have lavished on this book.

My colleagues at Stanford have supported my work over the years and I should here thank the successive chairmen of the Department of Classics: BROOKS OTIS; T. B. L. WEBSTER; MARK EDWARDS; and A. E. RAUBITSCHEK. The publication of this book has been assisted by grants from the Tresidder Fund of the Classics department and from LINCOLN MOSES, Dean of Graduate Studies. Time for uninterrupted research was provided by grants from Dean MOSES and by a fellowship from the National Endowment for the Humanities.

But in these times, professional advice and financial support might not prove adequate to sustain the weary and timid young scholar. That this book was completed is due above all to my wife, Professor Anne Kostelanetz Mellor, who willingly undertook the varied roles of typist and cheerleader to bring the manuscript to completion. And so to Anne, for her warm emotional and moral support and, most of all, for herself, I lovingly dedicate this book.

RONALD MELLOR

San Francisco, April, 1975

Table of Contents

Abbreviations 9

PART I

1. The Origins of the Goddess Roma 13
2. The Evidence for Θεὰ Ῥώμη 27
   - I. Rhodes 27
   - II. Lycia 36
   - III. Cibyra 39
   - IV. Caria 41
   - V. Ionia 50
   - VI. Aegean Islands 59
   - VII. Lydia 70
   - VIII. Phrygia 74
   - IX. Aeolis, Mysia and the Troad 76
   - X. Commune Asiae (Κοινὸν Ἀσίας) 79
   - XI. Bithynia and Pontus 82
   - XII. Pamphylia, Pisidia and Cilicia 85
   - XIII. Galatia 89
   - XIV. Cappadocia 90
   - XV. Cyprus 92
   - XVI. The East 94
   - XVII. Greece 97
   - XVIII. Macedon and Thrace 107
   - XIX. The West 109

PART II

3. The Greek View of Roma 111
   - I. Epithets 111
   - II. Poems 119
   - III. Joint Cults 128

4. Honors Paid to Roma	134
I. Temples	134
II. Statues	145
III. Altars	154
IV. Sacrifices	156
V. Dedications	158
VI. Calendars	160
VII. Coins and Gems	162
5. Romaia	165
I. Athletic Contests	169
II. Musical and Dramtic Events	170
III. Gladiators and Beasts	173
IV. Joint Festivals	175
6. Officials of Roma	181
Municipal Priests	181
Other Municipal Officials	188
Provincial Officials	190
7. Roma Alone	195
Epilogue	199
Additional note: The Dedicatory Inscriptions on the Capitoline Hill	203
Appendix: Inscriptional Evidence for Roma in the Greek World	207
Index	229

Abbreviations

In epigraphical and papyrological collections, the Roman numeral following the title refers to the volume; the Arabic numerals refer to the number of the specific text. In other works, the Arabic numerals refer to pages or columns, while the sign # precedes the number of a text or coin. The sign # is also used to designate section numbers in J. & L. ROBERT's *Bulletin épigraphique*. For periodicals, I follow *L'Année Philologique*.

A. Epigraphical and Papyrological Corpora

BGU = *Aegyptische Urkunden aus den Staatlichen Museen zu Berlin, Griechische Urkunden*
CIG = *Corpus Inscriptionum Graecarum*
CIL = *Corpus Inscriptionum Latinarum*
Didyma = *Didyma* vol. II *Die Inschriften* ed. REHM (Berlin, 1958)
EHRENBERG-JONES = *Documents illustrating the Reigns of Augustus and Tiberius* ed. V. EHRENBERG and A. H. M. JONES (2nd ed., Oxford, 1955)
Ephesos = *Forschungen in Ephesos* (Vienna, 1906ff.)
IAG = *Iscrizioni agonistiche greche* ed. MORETTI (Rome, 1953)
IBM = *Ancient Greek Inscriptions of the British Museum*
ID = *Inscriptions de Délos* (Paris, 1926ff.)
IDelphes = *Fouilles de Delphes* III *Epigraphie* (Paris, 1909ff.)
IG = *Inscriptiones Graecae*
IGR = *Inscriptiones Graecae ad Res Romanas Pertinentes* ed. CAGNAT (Paris, 1911–1927)
IGUR = *Inscriptiones Graecae Urbis Romae* I ed. MORETTI (Rome, 1968).
ILLR = *Inscriptiones Latinae Liberae Rei Publicae* ed. DEGRASSI (Florence, 1957–1963)
IMagn. = *Die Inschriften von Magnesia am Mäander* ed. KERN (Berlin, 1900)
IPriene = *Inschriften von Priene* ed. HILLER V. GAERTRINGEN (Berlin, 1906)
Lindos = *Lindos Fouilles de l'Acropole* II *Inscriptions* ed. BLINKENBERG (Copenhagen, 1941)
LSAM = *Lois Sacrées de l'Asie Mineure* ed. SOKOLOWSKI (Paris, 1955)
MAMA = *Monumenta Asiae Minoris Antiqua* ed. CALDER et al. (London, 1928–1962)
Milet = *Milet. Ergebnisse der Ausgrabungen und Untersuchungen seit dem Jahre 1899* (Berlin, 1906ff.)
NS = *Nuova silloge epigrafica di Rodi e Cos* ed. MAIURI (Florence, 1925)
OGIS = *Orientis Graeci Inscriptiones Selectae* ed. DITTENBERGER
Olympia = *Olympia* V *Die Inschriften* ed. DITTENBERGER-PURGOLD (Berlin, 1896)
Pergamum = *Altertümer von Pergamon* VIII *Die Inschriften von Pergamon* I–II ed. FRAENKEL (Berlin, 1890–1895) III ed. HABICHT (Berlin, 1969)
RDGE = *Roman Documents from the Greek East* ed. SHERK (Baltimore, 1969)
Sardis = *Sardis* VII 1 *The Greek and Latin Inscriptions* ed. BUCKLER and ROBINSON (Leyden, 1932)
SEG = *Supplementum Epigraphicum Graecum*

SGDI = *Sammlung der griechischen Dialect-Inschriften* ed. COLLITZ et al. (Göttingen, 1884–1915)
Syll. = *Sylloge Inscriptionum Graecarum* ed. DITTENBERGER (3rd edition)
TAM = *Tituli Asiae Minoris*

B. Numismatic Corpora

BABELON *Coll. Wad.* = E. BABELON *Inventaire sommaire de la Collection Waddington* (Paris, 1897–1898)
BMC = *A Catalogue of Greek Coins in the British Museum*
BMCRE = *British Museum Catalogue of Coins of the Roman Empire*
ECKHEL = J. ECKHEL *Doctrina Nummorum Veterum* (Vienna, 1792–1826)
GAEBLER = H. GAEBLER *Die antiken Münzen von Macedonia und Pannonia* (vol. III of *Die antiken Münzen Nord-Griechenlands*) (Berlin, 1906–1935)
IMHOOF-BLUMER *KM* = F. IMHOOF-BLUMER *Kleinasiatische Münzen* (Vienna, 1901–1902)
MACDONALD = G. MACDONALD *Greek Coins in the Hunterian Collection* (Glasgow, 1899–1905)
MCCLEAN = S. GROSE *Catalogue of the McClean Collection of Greek Coins in the Fitzwilliam Museum, Cambridge* (Cambridge, 1923–1929)
SNG-DEN = *Sylloge Nummorum Graecorum*—Denmark
SNG-GER = *Sylloge Nummorum Graecorum*—Germany (v. Aulock collection)
WADDINGTON *Recueil Général* = WADDINGTON, BABELON & REINACH *Recueil Général des Monnaies Grecques de l'Asie Mineure* (Paris, 1904–1912; 2nd ed. vol. I—1925)

C. Books and Articles

ACCAME = S. ACCAME *Il dominio romano in Grecia della guerra acaïca ad Augusto* (Rome, 1946)
ALFÖLDI = A. ALFÖLDI *Die trojanischen Urahnen der Römer* (Basel, 1956)
BADIAN *Flamininus* = E. BADIAN *T. Quinctius Flamininus: Philhellenism or Realpolitik* (Cincinnati, 1970)
BADIAN *FC* = E. BADIAN *Foreign Clientelae* (Oxford, 1958)
BADIAN *Imperialism* = E. BADIAN *Roman Imperialism in the Late Republic* (2nd ed., Oxford, 1968)
BADIAN *Studies* = E. BADIAN *Studies in Greek and Roman History* (Oxford, 1964)
BOWERSOCK = G. BOWERSOCK *Augustus and the Greek World* (Oxford, 1965)
BRISCOE *Livy* = J. BRISCOE *A Commentary on Livy Books XXXI–XXXIII* (Oxford, 1973)
BRUNEAU = P. BRUNEAU *Récherches sur les cultes de Délos à l'époque hellénistique et à l'époque impériale* (Paris, 1970)
CAH = *Cambridge Ancient History*
CERFAUX-TONDRIAU = L. CERFAUX; J. TONDRIAU *Les Cultes des Souverains dans la Civilisation Greco-Romaine* (Tournai, 1957)
CHRIST = F. CHRIST *Die römische Weltherrschaft in der antiken Dichtung* (Tübingen, 1938)
COOK *Zeus* = A. B. COOK *Zeus* (Cambridge, 1914–1940)
CRAMPA *Labraunda* = J. CRAMPA *Labraunda: Swedish Excavations and Researches* III part 1 (Lund, 1969)
DEININGER *Politischer Widerstand* = J. DEININGER *Der Politische Widerstand gegen Rom in Griechenland 217–86 v.Chr.* (Berlin, 1971)
DEININGER *Provinziallandtage* = J. DEININGER *Die Provinziallandtage in der römischen Kaiserzeit* (Munich, 1965)

FERGUSON *HA* = W. FERGUSON *Hellenistic Athens* (London, 1911)
FORTE = B. FORTE *Rome and the Romans as the Greeks Saw Them* (Rome, 1972)
FRASER-BEAN = P. FRASER; G. E. BEAN *The Rhodian Peraea and Islands* (Oxford, 1954)
GERNENTZ = W. GERNENTZ *Laudes Romae* (Rostock, 1918)
HABICHT = C. HABICHT *Gottmenschentum und griechische Städte* (2nd ed., Munich, 1970)
HAMDORF = F. HAMDORF *Griechische Kultpersonifikation der vorhellenistischen Zeit* (Mainz, 1964)
HANSEN = E. HANSEN *The Attalids of Pergamum* (2nd ed., Ithaca, 1971)
HEINEN = H. HEINEN "Zur Begründung des römischen Kaiserkultes" *Klio* 11 (1911)
HERRMANN *Teos* = P. HERRMANN "Antiochos der Grosse und Teos" *Anadolou* 9 (1965)
HOLLEAUX *Études* = M. HOLLEAUX *Études d'épigraphie et d'histoire Grecques* (Paris, 1938–1968)
HOLLEAUX *Rome* = M. HOLLEAUX *Rome, la Grèce et les monarchies hellénistiques au IIIe siècle avant J.-C. (213—205)* (Paris, 1921)
JONES *CERP* = A. H. M. JONES *The Cities of the Eastern Roman Provinces* (2nd ed., Oxford, 1971)
JUDEICH = W. JUDEICH *Topographie von Athen* (2nd ed., Munich, 1931)
LARSEN *Rep. Gov.* = J. A. O. LARSEN *Representative Government in Greek and Roman History* (Berkeley, 1955)
LAUMONIER = A. LAUMONIER *Les cultes indigènes en Carie* (Paris, 1958)
MAGIE *AS* = D. MAGIE "Rome and the City States of Asia Minor" *Anatolian Studies presented to W. H. Buckler* (Manchester, 1939)
MAGIE *RRAM* = D. MAGIE *Roman Rule in Asia Minor* (Princeton, 1950)
MARCADÉ = J. MARCADÉ *Au Musée de Délos* (Paris, 1969)
MELONI = P. MELONI *Perseo e la fine della monarchia macedone* (Rome, 1953)
MORELLI = D. MORELLI *I culti di Rodi* (Pisa, 1959)
NILSSON = M. P. NILSSON *Geschichte der Griechischen Religion* (2nd ed., Munich, 1955–1961)
NOCK *Essays* = A. D. NOCK *Essays on Religion and the Ancient World* ed. STEWART (Cambridge, Mass., 1972)
OLIVER *Athenian Expounders* = J. OLIVER *The Athenian Expounders of the Sacred and Ancestral Law* (Baltimore, 1950)
OLIVER *Demokratia* = J. OLIVER *Demokratia, the Gods, and the Free World* (Baltimore, 1960)
PICARD *EAD* = C. PICARD *L'établissement des Poseidoniastes de Berytos* (vol. VI of *Exploration archéologique de Délos*) (Paris, 1921)
RE = *Realencyclopädie der classischen Altertumswissenschaft* ed. PAULY-WISSOWA-KROLL
RICHTER = F. RICHTER "Dea Roma" in ROSCHER *Lexikon* IV 130–164
ROBERT *BE* = J. & L. ROBERT *Bulletin épigraphique* in *Revue des Études Grecques*
ROBERT *Carie* = J. & L. ROBERT *La Carie* II (Paris, 1954)
ROBERT *EA* = L. ROBERT *Études anatoliennes* (Paris, 1937)
ROBERT *EEP* = L. ROBERT *Études épigraphiques et philologiques* (Paris, 1938)
ROBERT *Gladiateurs* = L. ROBERT *Les Gladiateurs dans l'Orient grec* (Paris, 1940)
ROBERT *Laodicée* = L. ROBERT in DES GAGNIERS *Laodicée du Lycos: la Nymphée* (Paris, 1969) 247–389
ROBERT *MG* = L. ROBERT *Monnaies Grecques* (Paris, 1967)
ROBERT *Villes* = L. ROBERT *Villes de l'Asie Mineure* (2nd ed., Paris, 1962)

ROSCHER *Lexikon* = W. H. ROSCHER *Ausführliches Lexikon der griechischen und römischen Mythologie*
ROSTOVTZEFF *SEHHW* = M. ROSTOVTZEFF *Social and Economic History of the Hellenistic World* (Oxford, 1941)
ROUSSEL *DCA* = P. ROUSSEL *Délos colonie athénienne* (Paris, 1916)
SCHMITT *Rom* = H. H. SCHMITT *Rom und Rhodos* (Munich, 1957)
SCHMITT *Antiochos* = H. H. SCHMITT *Untersuchungen zur Geschichte Antiochos des Großen und seiner Zeit* (Wiesbaden, 1964)
VALLOIS *AHD* = R. VALLOIS *L'architecture hellénique et hellénistique de Délos* (Paris, 1953)
VERMEULE *Goddess Roma* = C. C. VERMEULE *The Goddess Roma in the Art of the Roman Empire* (Cambridge, Mass., 1959)
VERMEULE *RIA* = C. C. VERMEULE *Roman Imperial Art in Greece and Asia Minor* (Cambridge, Mass., 1968)
WALBANK = F. WALBANK *Commentary on Polybius* (Oxford, 1957–1967)
WEINSTOCK *DJ* = S. WEINSTOCK *Divus Julius* (Oxford, 1971)
WILL = E. WILL *Histoire politique du monde hellénistique (323–30)* II (Nancy, 1967)
WISSOWA = G. WISSOWA *Religion und Kultus der Römer* (2nd ed., Munich, 1912)

PART I

Chapter 1

The Origins of the Goddess Roma

The figure of Roma is a familiar one in the art and poetry of the Roman Empire. She alone of the pagan gods survived the victory of Christianity. Late in the fourth century the last great pagan statesman, Symmachus, invoked Roma in his speech against the removal of the altar of Victory from the Senate[1]. He spoke in vain; paganism was finally outlawed. Yet a few decades later the Christian court poet Claudian portrays Roma summoning the emperor Honorius to his triumph in Rome[2]. Even the new Christian capital city, Constantinople, was depicted standing beside her model Roma[3]. And still today in Santa Maria Maggiore in Rome one can see a triumphal arch decorated with a mosaic depicting Roma enthroned over her temple in which Jesus is presented to the elders[4].

In these last examples Roma can hardly be called a goddess; her persona has survived though not her divinity. But the attributes of this ex-goddess remained a powerful influence on Christian thinkers: *Roma Victrix*; *Roma Resurgens*; *Roma Renascens*. The most famous persona was *Roma Aeterna*—a conception of the city and Empire which captivated philosophers and poets alike for more than a millenium[5].

---

[1] Symmachus *Relatio* 3, 9 (ed. SEECK *MGH* (Berlin, 1883) 282).

[2] Claudian *De Sexto Consulatu Honorii* 354ff.
CAMERON *Claudian: Poetry and Propaganda at the Court of Honorius* (Oxford, 1970) 363f.

[3] J. M. C. TOYNBEE *JRS* 37 (1947) 135f.; *Studies in Honor of D. M. Robinson* (St. Louis, 1953) II 261f.

[4] RICHTER-TAYLOR *The Golden Age of Classic Christian Art* (London, 1904) 314f. and plate 39.

[5] KOCH *Gymnasium* 59 (1952) 128–143; 196–209; PASCHOUD *Roma Aeterna* (Rome, 1967).

Yet Roma was more than a convenient personification, a conceit available to poets, rhetoricians and artists. Liberty and Britannia may be depicted or invoked, as Jerusalem and Constantinopolis were in the late Roman Empire. But none of these had ever been deified; none had ever been worshipped in a cult. Roma had had cults; she had been a goddess. All the conventional trappings of divinity had once been dedicated to Roma: altars, temples, festivals, sacrifices, priests. In this monograph I will examine the origin of this goddess, where, when and why she was "invented"[6], and what meaning she had for those who worshipped her.

The origins of the goddess Roma must be sought in the Greek world. Before the time of Cicero, *Roma* could not be used in Latin as a substitute for *patria*, *res publica* or *populus Romanus*. The word was not a collective but merely referred to the city itself[7]. So *Roma* could not have been understood as the deification of the Roman people in second century BC Italy. Even if the head which appeared on early Roman coinage was Rhome (which I doubt), we shall soon see that Rhome had nothing to do with the goddess Roma[8]. Roma was rather the product of the Greek mind, and we might usefully examine in some detail her first known appearance in the Greek world.

In AD 26 the Commune Asiae decreed a temple to Tiberius, Livia and the Senate. When permission had been granted to the league to build the temple, envoys from eleven cities came to Rome to plead for the privilege of constructing it. Tiberius himself listened in the Senate to the debate that narrowed the candidates to Sardes and Smyrna. The Smyrnaean emissaries, having related the many ties between their city and Rome, continued:

> seque primos templum urbis Romae statuisse M. Porcio consule magnis quidem iam populi Romani rebus, nondum tamen ad summum elatis, stante adhuc Punica urbe et validis per Asiam regibus[9].

After more than two centuries, the temple of Roma at Smyrna still served its original function: to flatter Rome and thereby secure favors for Smyrna. In this passage the Smyrnaean ambassador speaks brilliantly. He does not fawn; rather he praises his homeland by linking it to Rome's martial past. And the Senate, bored with adulation and

---

[6] The word is used by LARSEN *Mélanges Piganiol* (Paris, 1966) III 1637.
[7] KNOCHE *Gymnasium* 59 (1952) 332.
[8] I have used "Roma" for the goddess whether she is referred to as *Roma* or Ῥώμη in the source; "Rhome" to refer to the eponymous founder of Rome; and the Greek Ῥώμη without specifying whether the word refers to goddess, founder, or the city.
[9] Tacitus *Ann.* 4, 56.

appreciative of the sophistication of his flattery, turns a blind eye to his history and grants the temple to Smyrna. But the history is weak: it is true that Carthage was still standing in 195; but that strife-torn city was no great threat, least of all to Smyrna! And the implication that Smyrna built the temple of Roma in courageous defiance of King Antiochus III is a bit wide of the mark. In fact the temple was erected to encourage the Romans (who were negotiating with Antiochus) to assist the Smyrnaeans (who had already been besieged by him)[10]. But even if some senatorial pedant were to have pointed out this fact, he would rightly have been ignored. Did not Smyrna freely choose West over East ("Punica", "Asiam")? Did she not freely defy a king ("regibus")? In a single breath this shrewd emissary had touched on the twin phobias of the Roman people. He well deserved whatever honors his grateful compatriots voted him on his return.

What were the historical circumstances that led to the establishment of this first cult of Roma? By 195 Smyrna was in a difficult position. Thirty years earlier Smyrna and several other cities, including Lampsacus, had given their allegiance to King Attalus I of Pergamum[11]. Seleucid power was then at its ebb in western Asia Minor and dynastic rebellion and eastern wars subsequently kept Antiochus from reasserting his "hereditary rights" over the Greek cities. But in 197, after his Egyptian victories, he sailed to Ephesus and demanded allegiance. Most cities prudently submitted, but Smyrna and Lampsacus refused, at the instigation of King Eumenes of Pergamum. Antiochus invested the cities and they in turn appealed to Rome[12]. Lampsacus based her appeal on kinship: Rome's close ally Massilia had been founded by nearby Phocaea and, as a trump card, Rome herself had been founded by nearby Troy[13]. The Smyrnaeans had no such connection with Rome and so invented one: the deification of the city of Rome—θεὰ Ῥώμη. Not surprisingly, this cult does not seem to have spurred the Romans to immediate action on Smyrna's behalf. The Romans were still playing the game of "cold-blooded geopolitics" in the East[14]. They offered to tolerate Seleucid domination of the Greek cities in Asia so long as Antiochus withdrew from his European bases in Thrace[15]. But war finally came between Rome and Antiochus, and

---

[10] Livy 33, 38, 3–4.
[11] CADOUX *Ancient Smyrna* (Oxford, 1938) 128f.; Polybius 5, 77, 6.
[12] Livy 33, 38, 3f.; Eumenes' intrigue: Livy 35, 17, 1; Smyrnaean activity: LARSEN *Mélanges Piganiol* (Paris, 1966) 1636f., HOLLEAUX *CAH* VIII 179, 187, 206f.; contacts of Smyrnaeans and Lampsacenes with Romans: Polybius 18, 52, 1f.; Livy 34, 59, 4f.; 35, 17, 1f.
[13] *Syll.* 591 and HOLLEAUX *Études* V 141–155.
[14] BADIAN *FC* 76; he argues that, even if Rome actually desired war with Antiochus, she did not have a sufficient pretext to enlist eastern support.
[15] Livy 34, 59, 4f. as interpreted by HOLLEAUX *CAH* VIII 200.

at the peace conference of Apamea both Smyrna and Lampsacus were freed. Even if this grant of freedom was due more to Roman Realpolitik than to the temple of Roma, this young divinity was a witness to Smyrna's triumph and subsequently flourished elsewhere.

It would be misleading to view the worship accorded Roma and similar divinities as the Romans did: manifestations of the servile sycophancy of the Greeks—*adulatio Graeca*[16]. For the Greeks such cults were political and diplomatic acts, sometimes sincere, sometimes not, as is the custom in politics and diplomacy. Diplomatic acts can manifest servility in certain historical circumstances, but diplomacy as such does not imply servility. For the Greeks the cult of Roma was just such a political tool; but the Romans understood this no better than they understood other aspects of the Hellenistic world. Polybius tells us that Rome won many flatterers but few real friends among the Greek cities. Yet it would be unfair to apply Cicero's stricture that flattery does great harm to friendships to the Greeks[17]. Who can blame them? They were enthusiastic at Rome's first appearance, and some Greek cities continued to be genuinely grateful for Roman favors[18]. But many found the *amicitia* proffered by Rome something much less than true friendship. So the cult of Roma covered the entire range of political emotion: enthusiastic affection, servile flattery, gratitude, suspicion, naked fear. It was a cult based on political, rather than religious, experience.

Whence θεὰ Ῥώμη? Where did the Smyrnaeans get the idea for this divinity[19]? Greek authors had been writing about Rhome, the eponymous heroine of Rome, for centuries before cults of the goddess Roma were established. Rhome must therefore be examined as a possible model for Roma, though the origins and importance of Rhome herself are unclear. Relatively early accounts of Rhome are preserved (sometimes obviously distorted) in late and divergent sources. This is typical of foundation legends, as is also (alas!) the endless scholarly debate which ensues. Therefore I will only summarize the major versions of the Rhome-story without detailed discussion[20].

---

[16] ROBERT *CRAI* (1969) 63.
[17] Polybius 24, 10, 5; Cicero *Amic.* 91: nullam in amicitiis pestem esse maiorem quam adulationem.
[18] FORTE 24 — though the author is somewhat too credulous of public statements.
[19] I continue on the assumption that the Smyrnaeans were the first to establish a cult to Roma, though the idea of the goddess Roma may well have been circulating in the East by the late third century.
[20] PERRET *Les Origines de la Légende Troyenne de Rome* (281–31) (Paris, 1942) 398–408; MOMIGLIANO *JRS* 35 (1945) 99f. (review of PERRET); BOYANCÉ *REA* 45 (1943) esp. 283f. (review of PERRET); ALFÖLDI *Die Trojanischen Ur-*

Roma and Rhome

By the fifth century BC Greek historians clearly wanted to establish a foundation myth for the city of Rome. That their versions all looked to Troy as the origin of the eponymous κτίστης is hardly surprising. The Greeks of the West saw Rome as an originally Etruscan city whose inhabitants had come to Italy from Asia Minor [21]. Some versions trace the name of Rome back to one Rhomus—variously identified as a friend or descendent of Aeneas [22]. But that tradition does not occur before Alcimus in the fourth century and may therefore have been influenced by the Romans' own foundation myth of male eponymous twins: Romulus and Remus [23]. The eponymous Rhome first appears in the fifth century in Hellanicus' *Chronicles of the Priestesses of Argos* [24]. This version tells us that Aeneas followed Odysseus to Italy with Trojan refugees, that Rhome instigated the other women to burn the ships, thus forcing settlement of the city which was named after her [25]. The mention of Odysseus shows that the descendants of Odysseus in Italy—thought to be the Latins—had some importance in the more complete version (or in Hellanicus' source) [26]. Rhome's marriage to Latinus in later versions provides the last necessary element in a well-made story which accounts for the Trojan foundation (Aeneas), the name of the city (Rhome), the local inhabitants (Latinus, descendant of Odysseus by Circe) and the obvious fusion of Etruscan and Latin culture in early Rome by the marriage of Rhome and Latinus.

That this version is the earliest coherent one to be discovered through the haze of the fragments hardly implies that it was the original version. Rhome's act of burning the ships seems far more appropriate to the legend which identifies her as a Trojan captive being taken into slavery in Argos [27]. This version is attributed to Aristotle, but it totally rejects the Trojan origin of Rome [28]. This has been explained from a

---

ahnen der Römer (Basel, 1956) 9f.; WEINSTOCK *JRS* 49 (1959) 170f. (review of ALFÖLDI); CLASSEN *Historia* 12 (1963) 447–457; GALINSKY *Aeneas, Sicily and Rome* (Princeton, 1969) 105; 161f.; DRUMMOND *JRS* 62 (1972) 200 (review of GALINSKY). In the following notes these works will be cited by author's name alone.

[21] Herodotus 1, 94.

[22] Cf. versions of Cephelon Gergithius; Apollodorus; Alcimus—all cited in Festus 266.

[23] CLASSEN 452.

[24] This version, which is contained in Dionysius *AR* 1, 72, is generally accepted as genuine Hellanicus. Cf. BOYANCÉ 283f.; MOMIGLIANO 100; ALFÖLDI 9; GALINSKY 105; but *contra*, cf. PERRET 367f.

[25] μετ' Ὀδυσσέα is thus preferred to μετ' Ὀδυσσέως—largely on the basis of common sense; cf. BOYANCÉ 289.

[26] ALFÖLDI 9. [27] ROSENBERG *RE* I A 1077f.

[28] Aristotle's version as reported by Dionysius *AR* 1, 72. A similar version can be found in the second century historian Heraclides Lembos (*FGrHist* III

Roman desire, after their expulsion of the Etruscan kings, to reject Aeneas who had been popular with the Etruscans [29]. The Romans may well have wished to forget Aeneas, but the connection between Roman desires and Greek historical mythologizing has not been established. In other versions Rhome is married to Aeneas, Ascanius or Latinus; she is the daughter of Ascanius, Telemachus, Evander or Italus. Confusion abounds and even the founder of the city is obscure: Aeneas, Latinus or Romulus and Remus. One version neatly avoids the entire question of foundation by having Aeneas and Evander discover a city called Valentia and translate its name: Ῥώμη [30].

The diversity and confusion of the tradition make neatly schematic patterns perilous [31]. We must keep in mind the relations between Roman beliefs and policies, local Latin and Italic foundation stories, and Greek historians and chronicles [32]. But some of the pivotal sources for this study—notably Timaeus and Hieronymus of Cardia—are lost, although we are subjected to speculations on their views [33]. It is dangerous to organize the Greek fragments into competing versions solely on the basis of Roman-Etruscan relations and to use Greek historians to support theories unproven by evidence from Rome. Most notable in this regard, ALFÖLDI hypothesizes early Roman adherence to a kind of Trojan "Urmutter", Rhome, although there is no evidence for the early appearance of Rhome in Rome [34].

Clearly this Rhome was no goddess. No cult was founded in her honor and her role in the foundation of the city was often indirect. She was not even a proper heroine; almost no acts beyond the destruction of the (Argive or Trojan) ships are ascribed to her. By the standards of myth and legend, she is an unimpressive figure. Created for only one purpose—to explain the name of the city—Rhome is predictably two-dimensional. She is no "symbol" of the Roman people, only one more of those countless nymphs invented by the Greeks to explain the names of fountains, springs, wells . . . and cities [35].

C 840 F 13b; 40d). Variant versions of Heraclides are contained in Festus 269 and Solinus 1. ROSE *Roman Questions* (Oxford, 1924) 172 believes that a distorted version of Aristotle has been transmitted by Plutarch QR 6 and Dionysius.

[29] ALFÖLDI 10 followed by GALINSKY 139f.

[30] Ateius in Servius *Ad Aen.* 1, 273; "Cumaean historian" in Festus 266. The connection of the name of the city with ῥώμη (strength) is a product of later etymological speculation and cannot "explain" the name of the city.

[31] GALINSKY 187f. attempts to depict such a pattern.

[32] On local foundation stories, cf. CLASSEN 448 and DRUMMOND 200.

[33] ALFÖLDI 10 offers such speculation, which WEINSTOCK 170 rebuffs.

[34] ALFÖLDI *passim*; *contra* cf. CLASSEN 452 n. 32.

[35] STEUDING "Lokalpersonifikation" in ROSCHER *Lexikon* II 2074–2139; HAMDORF *Griechische Kultpersonifikationen der vorhellenistischen Zeit* (Mainz, 1964).

This mortal Trojan lady, Rhome, has nothing to do with the origin of the goddess Roma, the genuine deification of the power of Rome. However, there is one important overlap. The historian Agathocles of Cyzicus says that Rhome the granddaughter of Aeneas founded a temple of Fides on the Palatine [36]. Agathocles must have been writing his history of Cyzicus after the first temple of Fides was founded in Rome about 250 BC [37]. The later close connection between Roma and Fides—both on Locrian coins of 204 and in the hymn sung at Chalcis in 191 [38]—suggests that Agathocles' text should be dated about 200 or soon after when the concept of Fides was more widely known in the East [39]. Agathocles transferred the relationship between Roma and Fides to Rhome: her foundation of the temple of Fides was an act so important that the city founded subsequently was named after her. The great gap between Rhome and the later Roma is cast into sharp relief by this text. Roma was created to deal with the political reality of Roman power. Rhome seems quite out of place as the founder of a temple of Fides, that personification so full of political meaning for the contemporaries of Agathocles. Without great success, Agathocles has tried to transpose the present into the mythic past.

Roma and Tyche

The cult of Roma in the East has sometimes been treated as a manifestation of the τύχη τῆς πόλεως which was common in Asia Minor [40]. Since the most famous cult was that of the Tyche of Antioch, the first cult of Roma might be seen as Smyrna's pointed shifting of her allegiance from the Seleucids to Rome. But this is hardly an adequate explanation of the origins of the cult of Roma or its earliest manifestations—especially since the τύχη τῆς πόλεως was usually wor-

---

[36] *FGrHist* III B 472 F 5.
[37] JACOBY commentary on 472 F 5; CLASSEN 452. ALFÖLDI 12 argues unconvincingly that the story must have had an earlier origin.
[38] On the coin, see below p. 109; on the hymn, see p. 121.
[39] ALFÖLDI 12 and WEINSTOCK 171 seem prepared to accept this late date for the passage; CLASSEN 452 prefers the mid third century.
[40] RICHTER 131, the most extensive treatment of Roma, simply refers to the "Einrichtung eines Kultes der τύχη Ῥωμαίων oder der dea Roma"; a similar reference to "τύχη Ῥωμαίων oder θεὰ Ῥώμη" appears in PFISTER *RE* I A 1061; PRELLER *Römische Mythologie* (Berlin, 1883—3rd edition) 705; WISSOWA 282; CERUTI *RIL* 91 (1957) 689; CERUTI *Epigraphica* 17 (1955) 121. FRASER-BEAN 136 are more cautious: "This worship probably had its origin in the worship of τύχη τῆς πόλεως." They also discuss other influences: the ruler cult and the goddess Rhodos. Though I would prefer a different emphasis, their brief treatment of Roma (132–136) is a clear exposition of the major influences on the cult, and it is unfortunate that it has often been ignored by recent scholars: e.g. NILSSON; also LATTE in *Römische Religionsgeschichte* (Munich, 1960).

shipped in its own city. We do not find the expected phrase Τύχη Ῥωμαίων until a much later period. Moreover one of the honors most frequently paid to Roma was the creation of festivals ("Romaia") dedicated to her, but festivals very rarely honored a τύχη τῆς πόλεως [41]. There is no doubt that in later times Roma acquired the iconography of τύχη; the polos and the horn of plenty which often appeared on coins [42]. Despite these iconographic links and the connection between Roma and Fortuna Populi Romani in the Empire [43], however, the cult of the τύχη τῆς πόλεως cannot explain the deification of the city itself, the Romaia, and the early establishment of festivals to Roma in Greece where cults of τύχη τῆς πόλεως were almost unknown [44].

Roma and the Ruler Cult

The most powerful influence on the Smyrnaeans (always assuming we can believe their later assertion that they were the first to worship Roma [45], a reasonable assertion in keeping with Cicero's description of Smyrna must surely have been the cults of rulers which were so widespread in the Hellenistic age. The Hellenistic ruler cult was based on precisely the same political motivation which inspired the deification of Roma. Divine honors had been voted to Flamininus, as they were

---

[41] HERZOG-HAUSER *RE* VII A 1677 adduces only very few examples of a festival in honor of Tyche, and those were late since they were not known before the time of Aristotle: Simplicius *In Aristot. Physic.* 74 B (2, 4, 5).

[42] HOMMEL *Die Antike* 18 (1942) 139f. believes that this iconography may have derived from a famous statue of Tyche at Smyrna with polos and horn of plenty (Pausanias 4, 30). But even such an early iconographic link—which cannot be proved—need not imply that Tyche "inspired" the creation of Roma; the trappings were convenient and were used.

[43] *RIC* I 203 #40: Roma seated holding Fortuna. Roma appears with the attributes of Tyche on Greek coins: mural crown and cornucopia. On Roman imperial coinage, Fortuna has these attributes and Roma is more often a martial or maternal type. Nonetheless, they were sometimes confused; e.g. Athenaeus 8, 361F on the temple of Roma at Rome. Roma and Fortuna appear together on dedications; *CIL* VII 392: Romae Aeternae et Fortunae Reduci. Also *CIL* VII 370.

[44] RUHL in ROSCHER *Lexikon* V 1345f. Few of the cults listed for mainland Greece are cults of the τύχη τῆς πόλεως but rather of the older Tyche. NILSSON II 208 attributes the greater popularity of the τύχη τῆς πόλεως in Syria and Asia Minor to the many newly founded cities in those areas. The settlers felt remote from their old civic gods, and so sought new ones. The Semitic god of fortune, Gad, may have had some influence in Syria.

For festivals of Roma in mainland Greece, see pp. 98ff.

[45] The Smyrnaean envoy was a clever diplomat and would not exaggerate beyond the bounds of plausibility. The Smyrnaeans were warmly received by the Senate in 189—already recognized as strong supporters of Rome (Polybius 21, 22, 3). And Cicero (*Phil* XI 5) says: Smyrnam ... urbem, quae est fidissimorum antiquissimorumque sociorum. Perhaps the term "benefactor-cult", though less familiar, is more precise; see CHARLESWORTH *HTR* 28 (1935) 8f.

to many subsequent Roman officials in the East[46]. But even by 195 BC it must have been clear to the Greeks that consuls changed annually, proconsuls frequently, and that even the powerful Flamininus was responsible to the Roman Senate which could restrain his "philhellenic" impulses. Honors given to Flamininus were more spontaneous than the temple of Roma at Smyrna[47]. Smyrna was looking beyond Flamininus. Their envoys had met with the commissioners at Lysimachia; they had appeared before the Senate in Rome; they knew who had to be convinced.

Part II of this monograph will examine in detail similarities between the cult of Roma and the ruler-cults. Temples, altars, statues, and festivals (both athletic and dramatic) were dedicated to the goddess. Her name was adorned with the epithets of the kings and like them she was honored with sacrifices and honorific months; cults and priesthoods were established for her worship. Just as the cults and priesthoods of rulers occur more frequently in Anatolia and the islands than in mainland Greece, so it was for Roma[48]. For both the kings and Roma, honors in Greece proper more often took the forms of games and festivals than of actual cults and priesthoods[49]. But the essential similarity between the worship of the rulers and of Roma is the lack of any religious dimension[50]. The significance of the cults was political; the motivation was political; the desired consequences were political.

---

[46] Flamininus: BRISCOE *Latomus* 31 (1972) 32 n. 1.
RAUBITSCHEK "Sylleia" *Studies in Roman Economic and Social History in Honor of A.C.Johnson* (Princeton, 1951) 49–57. Other proconsuls: BOWERSOCK 112f.; 150f.; WEINSTOCK *DJ* 288f.; Suetonius *Augustus* 52: proconsulibus decerni solere templa. Even Cicero had difficulty preventing his own worship (*Ad Quint.* 1, 1, 26). Under the Empire, cults and festivals were dedicated to the imperial house; e.g. in Athens alone DEUBNER *Attische Feste* (Berlin, 1932) 236 records: Kaisareia Sebasta, Hadrianeia, Antinoeia, Antoneia, Kommodieia, Severeia, and Philadelpheia—this last ironically for Caracalla and Geta.

[47] On Flamininus' philhellenism, see now BADIAN's brilliant *Flamininus*, especially 54–57. Passages in Livy (33, 32; 34, 31; 34, 49–50) leave little doubt of the emotion of the Greeks. Chalcis (Plutarch *Flam.* 16) and Argos (DAUX *BCH* 87 (1964) 570) established festivals in honor of Flamininus—Titeia—with good reason. Chalcis had been sympathetic to Philip (Livy 31, 23) and later Antiochus wintered there and married a local girl (Livy 36, 11). Likewise Argos had been rather docile towards its Spartan garrison (Livy 34, 25). Yet both cities were granted freedom by the Romans: Livy 34, 25; 34, 51; 36, 11. The honors were sincere, even if only as an expression of relief.

[48] CERFAUX-TONDRIAU 171; 262. The Diadochi—especially Antigonus Monophthalmos and Demetrius Poliorcetes—were widely honored in Greece, but there were few cults of their successors: KORNEMANN *Klio* 1 (1901) 84–85; TARN *Antigonos Gonatas* (Oxford, 1913) 435 n. 9; HABICHT 79; and see below pp. 97f.

[49] See below p. 98.

[50] HABICHT 236. Use "Religious" here in its modern sense; in antiquity a far broader spectrum of social and political activity might be termed "Religion".

The use of religious forms and language to express political feelings was as disturbing to Romans of the second century as it is to modern men. Romans saw such divine honors as signs of appalling cowardice and sycophancy. Though such cults were acceptable if restricted to the East, when King Prusias of Bithynia prostrated himself in the Senate and hailed the patres as "savior gods" (θεοὶ σωτῆρες), Polybius, at least, was outraged [51]. They failed to understand that lack of a clear distinction between homage (paid to men) and worship (paid to gods) which characterizes the Hellenistic mind [52]. How important was the difference between the worship of Ῥώμη Εὐεργέτις and the honors voted to the Ῥωμαῖοι Εὐεργέται? There were differences in form, but the spirit was the same. Why should the epithet σωτήρ not be applied to Demetrius or Flamininus or Roma, the epithet ἐπιφανής to Ptolemy or Antiochus or Roma, if they merited the title more than Zeus or Apollo [53]? Hellenistic Greeks possessed a different set of categories from our own; much of their formal religious practice, whether directed at Olympian gods or at mortal rulers, had nothing to do with what we call "religious experience". For that experience they turned increasingly to the new popular philosophies and the mystery cults. It is essential to see the ruler-cults against this background. The Romans, who never understood these cults and scornfully treated them as servile manifestations of *adulatio Graeca*, eventually took over the forms to apply to their emperors and in a cruel irony of history were led to excesses of debasement and servility that eventually shocked even Greeks.

Though the ruler cult provided the necessary political model for cults of Roma, it is not a sufficient explanation. Roma was not a living man, a king honored as a god; she was the personification and deification of the Roman state, the res publica Romana (Livy 7, 6, 3). Personification had long been used as one of the principal Greek modes of apprehension. It was a direct, graphic presentation of forces, phenomena, or concepts and was therefore not amenable to explanation by systematic analysis [54]. Though places, cities or even countries, were often personified [55], Roma was not the city personified. She was

---

[51] Polybius 30, 18; Livy 45, 44, 4–20 reports Polybius. Cf. TAYLOR *The Divinity of the Roman Emperor* (Middletown, Conn., 1931) 41.
[52] NOCK *HSCP* 41 (1930) 50 (= *Essays* I 241); ROBERT *Laodicée* 321 n. 7.
[53] ROSE *JHS* 77 (1957) 340.
[54] WEBSTER *JWCI* 17 (1954) 10. I am grateful to the late T. B. L. WEBSTER for making available to me his unpublished papers on personification in Greek art and literature.
[55] HAMDORF 26 ff.; WEINIGER in ROSCHER *Lexikon* II 2074–2139, especially 2092f. Some examples: picture of Hellas and Salamis at Olympia (Pausanias 5, 11, 5); statue of Megalopolis in temple of Zeus of that city (Pausanias 8, 30, 10).

the personification (and deification) of a collective, the Roman state. Though this sort of personification would have been impossible in Latin before the first century BC, the Greeks had long used it[56]. One notable parallel to the goddess was the Demos of the Athenians with whom she was associated in a cult at Delos and even in Athens itself[57]. Literary personifications of the Athenian Demos occurred as early as the fifth century, when Demos appeared in Aristophanes *Knights*. His early appearance and subsequent popularity can be attributed both to the impropriety of using the eponymous divinity Athena as a local personification, and to the strong democratic conviction of Athens which considered the Demos the essence of the state. By the end of the third century, a cult of Demos and the Charites had been established in Athens[58]. The cult of the local Demos spread to Asia Minor and the islands, notably to Rhodes[59]. There, in addition to the Demos of Rhodes, there was also a goddess Rhodos. These cults provided a democratic equivalent to the worship of kings embodied in the ruler cult[60]. They show that we cannot narrowly ascribe the cult of Roma to the ruler cult; all these cults formed part of the growing tendency to vote divine honors for real or expected benefactions to gods, kings, republics and even to ordinary citizens.

Ordinarily the cult of the Demos of a city was only to be found in the city itself or in cities with kinship ties. For example the Demos of the Athenians was worshipped only in Athens, and on Delos after the Athenian occupation of 167. The Rhodian divinities were the unique exception. They were honored with cults in cities having only political or commercial ties with Rhodes, and these cults function as honors paid to Rhodes[61]. Not surprisingly, when Roman hegemony replaced Rhodian hegemony in the southern Aegean and Asia, honors to Roma

---

[56] The sisters in Greek and Persian dress in Atossa's dream (Aeschylus *Persae* 181f.) personify peoples rather than places. On the precise identity of the sisters, cf. BROADHEAD *The Persae of Aeschylus* (Cambridge, 1960) 78.

[57] *ID* 1877; *IG* II² 5047; ROUSSEL *DCA* 222.

[58] HAMDORF 31 places this cult in the fourth century, citing *IG* II 3, 1655. But WILHELM *Beiträge zur griechischen Inschriftenkunde* (Vienna, 1909) 76 #64 published a new fragment which definitely dates the text in the late third century. He places the foundation of the cult soon after 229 BC, following the expulsion of the Macedonian garrison. Both fragments are republished as *IG* II² 4676.

[59] Magnesia: *IMagn.* 205–208; Synnada: *MAMA* VI 380; 380A; Cos: MAIURI *NS* #443, 462; Aphrodisias: *BMC Caria* 26 #6. Cf. DEUBNER in ROSCHER *Lexikon* III 2130f. On the Demos of Rhodes, cf. LAUMONIER *BCH* 58 (1934) 351 #39; *IPriene* 124; *Lindos* 438.

[60] NILSSON II 145.

[61] FRASER-BEAN 133–134.

and to the Demos of the Romans appear. The parallels between the cults of Roma and those of Rhodos are worth pursuing [62].

Both these cults were essentially for foreign consumption: Roma was not worshipped in Rome until the time of Hadrian, nor did the Rhodians honor Rhodos. There was a cult of Rhodos on Rhodes, but it was administered by a special college—the συνθύται Ροδιασταί ἐπιδαμιασταί—made up of foreign residents on the island, which parallels the cults of Roma on Delos administered by non-Romans in collegia, both Italians and easterners [63]. Both Roma and Rhodos were joined to preexisting cults in a religious imperialism that accurately reflected the political situation [64]. Sacrifices were decreed to these new gods: to Rhodos at Cos, to Roma at Miletus, to the Demos of Rhodes at Priene, to the Demos of the Romans at Miletus [65]. Rhodos was invoked in treaties between Rhodes and the Cretan cities of Olous and Hierapytna, while Roma appeared in Rome's treaties with Cibyra and Astypalaea as well as in an oath of loyalty from Cyprus [66]. There were priests both of Rhodos and of the Demos of Rhodes. And in Minoa on Amorgus the priest of Rhodos was linked with the δημιουργός as the eponymous official, just as the priest of Roma later frequently served as the eponymous official, sometimes with the δημιουργός [67]. Honors came to the Rhodians from far afield: crowns were voted to their Demos by the Syracusans and a dedication to Rhodos has been found in the Crimea [68]. Nor did these honors disappear overnight with the

---

[62] ROBERT *REG* 46 (1933) 441 n. suggested these parallels. LAUMONIER *BCH* 58 (1934) 370 took this farther by suggesting that the Demos of Rhodes finally found its place everywhere as Roma.

[63] Rhodes: *IG* XII 1, 157; KONSTANTINOPOULOS *Arch. Deltion* 18 (1963) A I 23 #39; ROBERT *MG* 11–13; MORELLI 172. Delos: *ID* 1763; *ID* 1778; for discussion, see below p. 63.

[64] Rhodos with Helios at Stratonicea: FOUCART *BCH* 14 (1890) 365 #4; ROBERT *BE* 1965 #272. Rhodos with Helios on Rhodes: *Lindos* 140; 242; *IG* XII 1, 892 (as interpreted by HILLER VON GAERTRINGEN *ARW* 19 (1919) 285); KONSTANTINOPOULOS *Arch. Deltion* 18 (1963) A I 23 #39. Rhodos with Helios in an unknown city on Amorgos: *IG* XII 7, 493b. Rhodos and Helios in eponymous priesthood of Minoa on Amorgos: see n. 67 below. Rhodos and Helios at Astypalaea: PEEK *Inschriften von den dorischen Inseln* 43 #90.

[65] Cos: *Syll.* 1000; Priene: *IPriene* 124; Miletus: *Milet* 203.

[66] Olous: ORLANDOS *Kretika Chronika* 15 (1963) 230 = *SEG* 23 #547; Hierapytna: *Syll.* 581; Cibyra: *OGIS* 762 and see below p. 39 ff.; Astypalaea: *IG* XII 3, 173; Cyprus: *JRS* 50 (1960) 75–79 = *SEG* 18 #578 and see below pp. 92 ff.

[67] For priests at Stratonicea and on Amorgos, see n. 64 above; Minoa on Amorgos: *IG* XII 5, 38; XII 7, 245—on these see ROBERT *REG* 42 (1929) 20–32; *MG* 10 n. 4. For δημιουργός at Side, see chapter 2 nn. 393 and 452; on eponymous priests, see p. 183 ff.

[68] Syracuse: Polybius 5, 88, 8; Neapolis in Scythia: SOLOMONIK *NE* 3 (1962) 32–44—I have not seen this Russian article and rely on ROBERT *BE* 1965 #272.

decline of Rhodian power. The traditional loyalty of such cities as Cos remained strong enough to ensure the survival of the worship of Rhodos for generations after the end of Rhodian power [69].

Perhaps it was in the cult of Rhodos that Smyrna found immediate inspiration for the honors the city paid to Rome in 195 BC. Since the cults of Roma quickly became popular in areas once closely attached to Rhodes [70], I would suggest that while the ruler-cult inspired in a general way the cult of Roma, the cult of Rhodos served as a specific model.

The Greeks also paid homage to Rome through honors voted to the Ῥωμαῖοι Εὐεργέται, the Senate, the Demos of the Romans and individual Roman generals [71]. The Demos of the Romans, simply the Greek translation of *Populus Romanus*, raises a difficult problem: when the Demos is personified and deified, how does it differ from the goddess Roma who is also a deification of the *res publica Romana*. Louis ROBERT has recently distinguished the two forms of cults of cities as follows: the personified Demos is a political allegory of an intellectual sort with little mythological basis; the city itself is personified through its eponymous deity with a mythological history and genealogy [72]. While this schema can be useful, it does not seem to apply to Roma. The Demos of the Romans may be an intellectualized political allegory, but the goddess Roma surely did not draw her power from mythology or genealogy; she too is a collective, a political allegory. That ancient religion does not easily lend itself to schematization is vividly illustrated by two related inscriptions which refer to precisely the same statuette in three different ways: *urbs Romana*; ὁ δῆμος ὁ Ῥωμαίων; and Ῥώμη [73]. Yet Roma and the Demos of the Romans were far from synonymous. Roma was not merely a personification; she was a goddess with the trappings of divinity: cults, priests, temples, epithets. The personified Demos was honored with dedications and sacrifices, but there was no genuine divinity. In the rare instances of priests and cults of the Demos, he is joined with the goddess Roma and does not have independent divine status [74].

Where Roma and the Demos of the Romans seem confused in the ancient sources is in mentions of statues. One example has been given,

---

[69] FRASER-BEAN 135; 163. Also Amorgos: ROBERT *REG* 42 (1929) 32.

[70] For example, at Hyllarima in Caria a cult of the Demos of the Rhodians before 167 BC (*BCH* 58 (1934) 345f. #39; on the date, cf. 372); a cult of Roma can be found there later (*Ibid* 379 #43). See also p. 47.

[71] Ῥωμαῖοι Εὐεργέται: *IG* X 2, 1, 133; Senate: ROBERT *MG* 75–78; Demos of the Romans: cf. note 72 below; individual Romans: BOWERSOCK 150f.

[72] *AC* 35 (1966) 426 n. 1; cf. also ROBERT *Laodicée* 320–321.

[73] *Ephesos* III 27–28.

[74] *Milet* 203; *OGIS* 479.

but there are several other cases where Greek sources speak of a statue of the Demos of the Romans [75]. These must be statues of the goddess Roma; there is no evidence for masculine personifications of the Roman people, and Demoi must be masculine [76]. The only explanation I can offer for the confusion in the sources is that the distinction between Roma and the Demos of the Romans was not a matter of great concern as long as it was only a question of personification: sacrifices, dedications, and statues. But only Roma was a goddess and she alone was the antecedent of Dea Roma in the West.

As the kings and cities of the Hellenistic world lost their power to Rome, so they relinquished the cults and honors paid them by the Greek cities. If Rome had then been a monarchy, her king would have inherited these cults and festivals. But they passed to Roma, though such honors were occasionally voted to prominent Romans [77]. The advent of Empire changed the role of Roma. For a time under Caesar and Augustus her link with the imperial cult was of genuine importance; she provided a honorable precedent for their divine honors. But she soon was quite unnecessary because, after a hiatus, new Hellenistic monarchs had finally appeared to replace the Seleucids, Attalids and Ptolemies. There was no longer any political rationale for the inclusion of Roma in the imperial cult. If she remained, it was usually out of inertia and religious conservatism. At least during the reigns of Augustus and Tiberius, Roma's presence was required in the provincial cults of the emperors because these cults were more official and had more visibility in the West. And, though Roma was often kept in local cults now dedicated to Roma and Augustus, there is no reason to expect that any new municipal cults were dedicated to her; the presence of Roma in a municipal cult can be taken as evidence that the original cult antedated the Empire and was once dedicated to Roma alone. In the Empire the Greek Roma—$\vartheta\varepsilon\grave{\alpha}$ $P\acute{\omega}\mu\eta$—was a fossil; no longer living but excellent evidence of the past. Of course Dea Roma was alive and well in the West, but she is a different matter and not part of our story. Our story concerns the Roma of the Greeks, whose cult replaced those of the kings and who dutifully transmitted that preeminently political institution, the Hellenistic ruler-cult, to the Roman emperors.

---

[75] Polybius 31, 4, 4; *CIL* I² 728; see below p. 152f.

[76] HAMDORF 31f. The Demos of other cities may be represented by a male figure: e.g. Aphrodisias *BMC Caria* 29 #23f.

[77] P. Servilius Isauricus: *Ephesos* III 66; *JÖAI* 18 (1915) Beiblatt 281f.; MÜNZER *Römische Adelsparteien und Adelsfamilien* (Stuttgart, 1920) 357n. On cults of Roman magistrates, cf. BOWERSOCK 112f.; 150f.

Chapter 2

The Evidence for Θεὰ Ῥώμη

In our examination of the evidence for the worship of Roma in the Greek world, it will be most profitable to examine the evidence region by region. Though the evidence for any individual cult is often very skimpy, the evidence for cults in several cities may be complementary and thereby permit additional conclusions on the chronology of the worship of Roma. The worship of Roma can only be properly understood in the context of the political history of these cities and regions and of their relations with Rome. Therefore in each case I will discuss the necessary historical, geographical and political background. Much of this material is dependent on analyses and reconstructions by other scholars—notably HOLLEAUX, MAGIE and ROBERT—though I have usually refrained from repeating here the arguments offered by them in restoring or dating inscriptions, dating specific events, etc. For this reason I have been generous in citing detailed discussions of these problems.

I will begin with a discussion of the island state of Rhodes, whose relations with Rome are well documented; then Lycia and Caria, whose history in this period is so closely connected with Rhodes; Ionia and the islands; finally turning to the rest of Anatolia, the East, the Greek mainland, and the West.

1. Rhodes

Relations between Rome and the Rhodian republic swung from the fraternal republican alliance of 200 BC to the hatred, suspicion and fear of 167 BC. It has been said that Rhodes earned Roman enmity by remaining neutral during the war with Perseus. A more subtle analysis (Polybius' own) calls attention to Roman anger and jealousy at a Rhodian display of naval power and political independence in 177 BC[1]. A careful analysis of Roman-Rhodian relations in this period

---

[1] Polybius 25, 4–6.

will clarify the political background of the shift from cults of Rhodos to those of Roma in the cities of Caria and the nearby islands[2].

Rhodes and Pergamum brought Rome into the Second Macedonian War by alleging a Syrian-Macedonian alliance. Rome came and conquered Philip. And she perceived in Pergamum and Rhodes useful allies in the East: reliable, trustworthy (compared to her former allies, the Aetolians, nearly anyone else would have seemed reliable and trustworthy) buffer states. Since Rome's fetial law forbade offensive wars, such buffer states were a common Roman device for establishing the legal basis of future intervention[3]. Rome, Rhodes and Pergamum continued to co-operate during the war with Antiochus, and ostensibly for two decades after the war. But the post-war aims of Rhodes and King Eumenes of Pergamum clearly diverged. The king desired continued Roman presence in Asia and the Aegean far more than the Rhodians did[4]. The Greek cities given to Eumenes at Apamea were by no means unanimous in their devotion, and a resurgent Antiochus might easily crush him. On the other hand, Rhodes as a commercial power needed freedom of the seas, peace, and moderately good relations with the Hellenistic monarchs. Rome had conquered Philip and, avowing a policy of non-interference, had within a few years withdrawn all her troops from Greece[5]. Rhodes hoped for the same Roman policy in 188 BC. She simply wanted to revert to the balance of power existing before 202 BC, when she was on good terms with all the monarchs, yet was regarded by the Greek cities as the champion of Hellenic freedom. Rome obviously had little place in such plans. Since trade was her life-blood, Rhodes could not allow past enmities to affect her future commercial policy. She soon reestablished contacts with both Syria and Macedon and, in 178 or 177, a Rhodian flotilla conducted the Syrian princess Laodice on her way to her bridegroom Perseus, now the king of Macedon[6]. It was to this act and to Perseus' subsequent gift of timber for refitting the Rhodian navy that Polybius attributed the senatorial encouragement of a second revolt by the Lycians against Rhodes (which had been awarded the Lycians by the treaty of Apamea a decade earlier)[7]. With this act Rhodes asserted

---

[2] The following pages owe much to SCHMITT *Rom und Rhodos*. This comprehensive work on the relations between Rome and Rhodes is both scholarly and sensible.

[3] BADIAN *Imperialism* 4; 11. The reminder that non-annexation did not mean non-intervention is timely.

[4] Polybius 21, 19–21; especially 21, 21, 7.

[5] HOLLEAUX *Études* II 121 n. 1.

[6] Polybius 25, 4, 8–10; MELONI 123f.

[7] Polybius 25, 4–6; Livy 41, 6, 8f. wrongly places the embassy to Rome from Lycia in 178 BC. It must be 177.

her political independence—I cannot see the Rhodians innocently ferrying a queen for the fee and unwittingly incurring the wrath of Rome[8]. Rome could tolerate for a time the Delians' dedication of a statue of Laodice in 177, and their permission for Macedonian edicts to be published on the island[9]. It was the Delians' essential powerlessness that bought them a respite from Roman wrath, though they too paid for their indiscretions. The Senate correctly realized that the Rhodians were proclaiming the political independence so necessary to their survival as a major power. That could not be tolerated, and in the encouragement of the Lycians we see Rome's first overt act of hostility toward her former comrade-in-arms.

Rome's unique inability to tolerate the independent existence of other powers is well known[10]. Her rejection of traditional Hellenistic balance-of-power politics affected not only the great powers, but the smaller ones as well. Rhodes had no wish to rival Rome's hegemony, as Macedon or Syria did—yet she was inexorably crushed by Rome's policies. Rhodes' fierce devotion to her political independence was intimately linked to her commercial role, but such reasons were of little interest to Rome. The Romans had already demonstrated in their treatment of Carthage their total lack of sympathy with the problems of a state almost wholly dependent on trade. If Rhodes had indeed turned down treaties of alliance proffered by the Senate (as Polybius implies), the Senate would have been angry whatever the reasons given[11]. Rome's foreign policy is sometimes described as "pragmatic". In fact, it was "pragmatic" only in that contemporary, pejorative meaning of the word: "without principles". It is very difficult to discuss Roman policy in the East from 215 to 167 precisely because it seems so irregular. Was the philhellenism of 196 sincere? Why did the Romans not aid the Aetolians in 206? Did Rome enter the Second Macedonian War to punish Philip? If not, then why? Why did Rome mistreat Philip so outrageously after 189? Obviously the struggles of factions at Rome caused policy shifts, but it is difficult to view the ensemble as "pragmatic" diplomacy. There was too much ignorance, too much spite, too much emotion for Roman policies to be considered pragmatic[12]. Rather it was the Rhodian republic that tried to follow a pragmatic path, albeit an honorable one by the diplomatic

---

[8] GIOVANNINI *BCH* 92 (1969) 855 argues this position—to my mind, unconvincingly.

[9] Statue of Laodice: *IG* XI 4, 1074; Macedonian edicts: Polybius 25, 3, 2; Livy 42, 12, 6. On my discussion of Delos, see pp. 63 ff.

[10] BADIAN *Imperialism* 5.

[11] Polybius 30, 5, 6–8 on which much of my argument rests.

[12] BADIAN *Imperialism* 4 aptly describes Roman policy as a mixture of "petulance and arrogance"; also see BADIAN *FC* 65.

standards of the day. The Rhodians did not wish for long-term alliances. They wanted to remain in the center: usually as neutral mediators but, if necessary, as the balance of power. Such a position obviously damned them in the eyes of Rome.

The Rhodians themselves had played to Roman ignorance of Eastern affairs when they appealed for intervention against Philip to prevent a Macedonian-Syrian axis [13]. Their more genuine fear was that Philip's Aegean adventures would disrupt trade in the area. How soon the Senate realized that Eumenes and the Rhodians might have interests very different from Rome's is uncertain. Some scholars see Roman mistrust of Rhodes already present in the treaty of Apamea which gave far more land to Eumenes than to Rhodes, and in the Roman order that Rhodes burn ships captured from Antiochus while Eumenes was allowed to keep the captured elephants [14]. But Eumenes was the principal buffer against the marauding Galatians and against the possibility of a resurgent Syria. The Senate's actions were reasonable and its positive, if inconclusive, response to the Rhodian request for Soli demonstrates that as yet the Senate felt no hostility towards Rhodes [15].

But Rome soon learned of differences between their allies. Even before the war against Philip, both Rhodes and Pergamum had concluded treaties with cities on Crete [16]. This was only one among many possible points of conflict, but they remained united by their hostility to Philip and Antiochus until Rome defeated those enemies. The speed with which Eumenes and the Rhodian envoys rushed to Rome after Antiochus' defeat and the speeches they made before the Senate

---

[13] I remain convinced that the primary reason for Rome's war on Philip was the Senate's fear of a Macedonian-Syrian alliance, and Roman resentment at Philip's Illyrian policy was an additional spur to action. HOLLEAUX *Rome* 320–322 believed such an alliance actually existed, though even the "alliance" rumors which Appian *Mac.* 4 attributes to the Rhodians would have been a motive for war. Thus MAGIE *JRS* 29 (1939) 32ff. doubts the authenticity of the alliance, but considers the rumors a reason for the war. More recently, CRAMPA *Labraunda* III 1, 128–131 and SCHMITT *Antiochos* have argued forcefully for the existence of the Antigonid-Seleucid pact, but there remains no direct evidence. Polybius' use of Rhodian sources makes his treatment somewhat suspect. ERRINGTON *Athenaeum* 49 (1971) 336ff. argues against the alliance itself or even a rumor of it as causes of the Second Macedonian War. He provides a careful review of the sources, but I find his interpretation of the sources problematic and, as he says, his reconstruction is speculative. ERRINGTON's skepticism is a useful antidote to HOLLEAUX, but MAGIE's approach seems more measured.

[14] DE SANCTIS *Storia dei Romani* (2nd edition, Florence, 1969) IV 1, 250.

[15] Polybius 21, 24, 10–15. The only economic clauses in the treaty of Apamea were inserted for the benefit of the Rhodians: Polybius 21, 43, 16–17. This indicates Roman awareness of Rhodian interests.

[16] DUCREY *BCH* 94 (1970) 637f.

clarified the situation perfectly: Eumenes wanted a continued Roman presence to secure his position; Rhodes wanted to trade freely. Territorial imperialism vs. commercial imperialism. And the next decade would see these differences harden into open hostility between Rhodes and Pergamum.

At Apamea the Rhodians were given Lycia and Caria, which their embassy had not even requested. The theory that the Senate deviously trapped Rhodes into a client-patron relationship through this "gift" attributes too much prescience to the patres[17]. They may have been annoyed at the Rhodians for recalling Flamininus' pledge about the "freedom of the Greeks" and therefore granted Lycia and Caria as the price for Rhodian silence, realizing full well that Rhodian acceptance of these territories would effectively emasculate any future rhetoric about Greek freedom. Even a staunch republican like Cato— pro-Rhodian and anti-Pergamene—would have accepted such a line of reasoning. Some in the Senate certainly foresaw the future difficulties if Rhodes continued her traditional role, but that was for Rhodes to choose. Rome felt no malice or hostility towards Rhodes at this point, only that endemic wariness and mistrust of Greeks and, in the last analysis, a total lack of sympathy for any genuine Rhodian independence. That lack of sympathy is characteristic of the imperialistic streak in the Roman political personality[18].

The war with Antiochus had hardly finished when the Rhodians resumed their role of mediator. They and the Athenians tried to mitigate the anger of Marcus Fulvius Nobilior towards the Aetolians, and they carried the case to Rome[19]. Polybius interestingly reports that it was the Athenian envoy who convinced the Senate—strange indeed when Rhodes was ostensibly Rome's closest ally. Perhaps the germ of Roman resentment against Rhodes is evident here—especially in Fulvius and his allies. He must have been annoyed at Scipio's stunning victory at Magnesia and wished for a similar success. In these circumstances, the Rhodian attempt at mediation would have been particularly unwelcome to a man of his disposition. Since the Fulvian faction and its allies seem to have controlled the Senate for the next two decades, Rhodian intervention here together with Eumenes' recent warning against Rhodian ambitions may explain the growing suspicion in the Senate[20].

---

[17] WILL II 197f. makes this interesting suggestion, but wisely adds (198): "Mais il est un point auquel nul ne paraît avoir pensé sur le moment (y pensait-on même à Rome?) ...."

[18] BADIAN *Imperialism* 12.

[19] Polybius 21, 29, 9f.; 21, 31, 1f.

[20] Fulvian hegemony: BRISCOE *JRS* 54 (1964) 73ff. and *Latomus* 27 (1968) 149f. Contra, ASTIN *Scipio Aemilianus* (Oxford, 1967) 342f.

Through most of the 180's Rhodes and Pergamum kept on civil terms and provided mutual assistance: Rhodes helped against Pharnaces of Pontus, and Eumenes helped against the rebellious Lycians [21]. The open break occurred about 180 when Eumenes attempted to exercise effective control over the Hellespont [22]. Black Sea trade had long been important to Rhodes and she had on occasion used force to preserve free passage through the Hellespont: notably against the Byzantines, who attempted to impose a tax and blockade on the Hellespont in 220 [23]. In 180 trade contacts between Rhodes and Pergamum were broken off. It would be small comfort to Rome that Rhodes simultaneously found a new market in the reviving Carthaginian economy [24]. And a few years later, when Rhodes took part in the dynastic union of Syria and Macedon in the marriage of Laodice and Perseus, Rome lashed out at her. A Lycian embassy was told that Lycia was not the property of Rhodes, but only her "friends and allies". That response signalled a renewal of the recently pacified Lycian rebellion [25].

In giving Rhodes this unwelcome lesson in the concept of *Fides*, the Romans were not merely disingenuous but openly hypocritical [26]. There was no conceivable reason why the Rhodians should have understood *Fides* as the basis of their relationship with the Lycians but, even if they had, there was still no justification for the Roman response to the Lycians. The Roman answer implies that the Rhodians had been oppressing the Lycians. While it is true that the Rhodians were forcibly putting down the revolt, the Lycians seem to have revolted immediately after Apamea before any mistreatment at the hands of the Rhodians was possible [27]. The Senate's response to the Lycian ambassadors hypocritically implied that even simple loyalty could not

---

[21] Polybius 23, 9, 2; 24, 15, 13.

[22] Polybius 27, 7, 5. WILL II 243 must be correct in seeing in this episode the end of Rhodian-Pergamene co-operation. HANSEN *The Attalids of Pergamum* (2nd ed., Ithaca, 1971) 103 sees Eumenes as the aggrieved party.

[23] Black Sea trade: GRACE *Hesperia* Supplement 8 (Princeton, 1949) 183. ROSTOVTZEFF *CAH* VIII 625; *SEHHW* 673, 1483 n. 84; HILLER VON GAERTRINGEN *RE* Supp. V 785f.; Polybius 4, 37f.

[24] SCHMITT *Rom* 135; also cf. 131: Rhodian trading as far west as Spain.

[25] Polybius 25, 4–6; Livy 41, 6. This dispute was hardly "referred to Rome" (BADIAN *FC* 99). The Lycians went there of their own accord.

[26] BADIAN *FC* especially 4f. Of course the forms had not been followed between Lycians and Rhodians, but there is no doubt that it was to such a patron-client relationship that the Romans referred in their declaration of 177. The reference to the Lycians as "friends and allies" of the Rhodians does not disguise their client status: on *amicus* as a polite expression for *cliens*, see BADIAN *FC* 7 n. 1. Polybius 20, 9, 10f. explicitly states that Greeks misunderstood *Fides*.

[27] Polybius 30, 31, 4.

be demanded of allies. Polybius reports that many Romans feared that this decision was taken only to weaken Rhodes. We might further assume that at least some saw the incongruity of Rome's proclaiming such extreme freedom for allied states. Livy's more elaborate version of the Senate's response to the Lycians is so patently hypocritical that it could almost be used by the Rhodians in their own defense: "Lycios ita sub Rhodiorum simul imperio et tutela esse, ut in dicione populi Romani civitates sociae sint." [28] The reaction to this response was revolt in Lycia and incredulity in Rhodes.

The Rhodians were still a bit naive about Roman diplomatic methods. They thought the Senate had been misled by Lycian lies, so they sent an embassy to Rome to clarify matters [29]. No answer was given to their appeal, and now Eumenes openly aided the Lycians [30]. The Senate's actions naturally strengthened the anti-Roman party at Rhodes, and the renewed activity of that faction increased Roman suspicions still further in the last years before the war with Perseus [31]. From the Roman point of view the Rhodians were already "fluctuantes et imbuti Persei consiliis", but in fact the pro-Roman party retained control and remained loyal during the war, even providing limited military assistance [32]. In their usual desire for a balance of power, the Rhodians probably did not desire a massive victory either for Rome or for Perseus, but they can hardly be accused of disloyalty to Rome. When they sent ships, the Roman admiral Lucretius disdainfully sent them away. Q. Marcius Philippus, a sometime Fulvian ally, encouraged the Rhodians to mediate—it was a trap and the Rhodians fell [33]. They offered to mediate, but no more. The threatening and arrogant Rhodian ultimatum reported by Livy is inconceivable; it is clearly an annalistic invention [34]. But the offer of mediation was

---

[28] Livy 41, 6, 12.
[29] Polybius 25, 5–6.
[30] Polybius 27, 7, 6; Livy 42, 14, 8. As their denunciation of Eumenes had no effect, the Rhodians pathetically stooped to excluding him from their festival of Helios (Appian *Mith.* 11, 3).
[31] Polybius 27, 7; 27, 14; 28, 2; Livy 42, 26, 8: quoted in text.
[32] Polybius 27, 4, 9; 27, 7; Livy 42, 46, 6.
[33] Polybius 28, 17, 4: πῶς οὐ πειρῶνται διαλύειν οἱ Ῥόδιοι τὸν ἐνεστῶτα πόλεμον. The verbal similarity to Perseus' request to the Rhodians is striking: Polybius 27, 4, 5: πειρᾶσθαι διαλύειν. Polybius himself concludes that Philippus meant to trap the Rhodians. BRISCOE *JRS* 54 (1964) 69f. and DEININGER *Politischer Widerstand* 189 n. 34 accept this passage as reliable; SCHMITT *Rom* 146 n. 1 attributes it to a pro-Rhodian source of Polybius and thinks it a fabrication. I am inclined to accept the passage; Polybius, who could check the facts with Roman friends, would not be taken in by this story. BADIAN *Flamininus* passim and *Studies* 126 persuasively contends that the "new diplomacy" of Philippus had already been practiced in the East by Flamininus.
[34] Livy 44, 14, 8–9. BADIAN *FC* 100; SCHMITT *Rom* 150 n. 1.

sufficient. The unfortunate Rhodian embassy arrived in Rome just as the news of Perseus' defeat at Pydna was announced [35]. It may well have been Philippus who led the senatorial faction that called for war with Rhodes in 167 [36]. Rhodes had been drained by years of suspicion, intrigue and internal division; now she had to endure three more terrifying years. Rhodes lost not only Lycia and Caria, but even Stratonicea and Caunus, which she had not received from Rome (though the Peraea seems to have remained Rhodian) [37]. Delos was declared a free port, and thus established as a commercial rival. Rhodes was forced to beg for a treaty and finally, after a purge of the anti-Roman faction, it was granted in 164 [38]. The Rhodians learned how much must be endured to become a socius populi Romani. It surely reflects well on these proud islanders that their champions in Rome were Cato the Censor and Tiberius Gracchus the Elder, while men like Philippus were their enemies. So should we judge them [39].

This survey of Roman-Rhodian relations should make it clear that no cult of Roma could have existed at Rhodes or in Rhodian territory before 167 [40]. In cities subject to Rhodes, cults of Roma and Rhodos could not exist side by side—the political overtones of these cults

---

[35] Polybius 29, 19; Livy 45, 3, 3–6.

[36] SCULLARD *Roman Politics 220–150 BC* (Oxford, 1951) 287.

[37] On Stratonicea and Caunus, see below pp. 47ff. Freedom of Lycia and Caria: Polybius 30, 5, 12; Livy 44, 15, 1f. (wrongly dated in 169). Polybius 30, 24 (a fragment probably referring to 167) says that οἱ τὴν Περαίαν κατοικοῦν- τες were given their freedom. FRASER-BEAN 101–102 see the Peraea remaining in Rhodian hands since it is not mentioned in the Senate's decree freeing Lycia and Caria (Polybius 30, 5, 12) and since Rhodes is frequently mentioned on texts from this area dated after 167. The passage in Polybius 30, 24 may refer to the Lycians and Carians, since "Peraea" can refer to all Rhodian territory on the mainland in a general way (*Ibid.* 52–53; 122; SCHMITT *Rom* 157). The Rhodian ambassadors who lamented the loss of Stratonicea and Caunus in Rome (Polybius 30, 31) would surely have also mentioned the traditional Peraea, if it had been freed by the Senate.

It is unnecessary to accept the so-called "Prekaritätstheorie"—that is, that Rome had retained an ultimate legal authority over Lycia and Caria at Apamea, delegated her authority to Rhodes from 188 to 167, and merely revoked that delegated authority in 167. Rome's authority in 167 does not stem from any complex legal understanding; it derives from her naked military power. The "theory" serves no purpose: it does not explain 167 adequately since Rome had no authority whatsoever over Stratonicea and Caunus which were freed at that time. There is no basis for such a "theory" in the sources. See SCHMITT *Rom* 128; BADIAN *FC* 101 n. 1. What BLEICKEN *Gnomon* 31 (1959) 441 finds remarkable, is not.

[38] Polybius 30, 31, 20.

[39] SCHMITT *Rom* 152–156 with references.

[40] HOLLEAUX *Études* I 382f. places the *terminus post quem* for Romaia in Rhodes in 196. SCHMITT *Rom* 175 n. 1 prefers 164–163—contemporary with the statue of Roma; SEGRÉ *PP* 4 (1949) 74: 162 BC.

were too obvious[41]. And the Rhodians valued their political independence too much to allow a cult of Roma on Rhodes, just as they had refrained from establishing cults of the Hellenistic monarchs[42]. But we can be certain that the cult of Roma appeared in 167 or soon thereafter. Polybius recounts that when Philocrates returned from Rome bearing the news that there would be no war, a gold crown was dedicated to Roma; the cult may have been established at the same time[43]. When the treaty was granted three years later, the Rhodians erected a statue of Roma fifteen meters high in their temple of Athena[44]. Whether founded in gratitude for peace in 167 or for the treaty in 164, the Romaia became an important, if not the most important, festival at Rhodes[45]. There also seems to have been a second festival to Roma in the Rhodian town of Lindos, unless the Romaia moved among the cities of the Rhodian tetrapolis as the festival of Roma and Augustus later did among the cities of the *Commune Asiae*[46].

After the Mithridatic wars Rhodes regained Roman favor; some territory was even restored to Rhodes[47]. Later still, the Rhodians

---

[41] After the end of Rhodian power in 167, cults of Rhodos remained in cities such as Cos and Amorgos which had long had close ties with Rhodes. These might survive beside new cults of Roma, but they were pale shadows with emotional rather than political significance. See chapter 1 note 69. And of course cults might persist on Rhodes itself—*Lindos* II 438: a statue of the Demos of the Rhodians set up in AD 50.

[42] Polybius 30, 5, 6–8. The cult of Ptolemy at Rhodes goes back to the cult of Ptolemy Soter in the fourth century. But no new cults or festivals were instituted in the period of Rhodian independence. Cf. MORELLI 66–67; 171–172.

[43] Polybius 30, 5, 4.

[44] Polybius 31, 4, 4: the κολοσσὸν ... τοῦ δήμου τῶν Ῥωμαίων must be a statue of Roma. See p. 26 above and p. 152 below.

[45] *IG* XII 1, 46; 730; PUGLIESE-CARRATELLI *ASA* 30–32 (1952–1954) 252f. #3 and 5; MAIURI *NS* #18 and 34; SEGRÈ *PP* 4 (1949) 81 #2. The only mention of a priest of Roma on Rhodes is SEGRÈ *Ibid* 73f. On frequency of celebration of the Romaia on Rhodes: HOLLEAUX *Études* I 382 prefers biennial celebration; HILLER VON GAETRINGEN *ARW* 27 (1929) 353; *IG* XII 1, p. 107 and BLINKENBERG *Kgl. Danske Videns. Selskab Arch-Kunsthist.* (Copenhagen, 1938) II 4 both see the festival as quinquennial.

[46] Ῥωμαῖα restored on two texts from Lindos: *Lindos* 229 and 482. SCHMITT *Rom* 175 n.1 accepts these restorations. On *SEG* XXII 350 I restore Λ[ίνδῳ]. This restoration is not certain, but, I think, plausible. There is no other city whose name begins with Λ in which the presence of Romaia or even a cult of Roma is attested. Both HABICHT *Olympia Bericht VII* 218–223 and ROBERT *BE* 1962 #153; 1969 #270 have emphasized the likelihood of a Carian or Rhodian origin for the athlete honored by this text, Leon. The argument is on onomastic grounds. Romaia at Lindos would be consistent with the concentration of a number of games mentioned in this text in southwestern Asia Minor: Tralles, Cnidus, the Lycian koinon, and a little farther afield, Chios. For more on this text, see my discussion in *ZPE* 12 (1973) 259ff.

[47] MAGIE *RRAM* 233; 1111 n. 3.

were courted by the great figures of the civil wars for the few ships they could provide. Their checkered past must have caused some anxiety as they gave ships to Pompey, then refused him sanctuary; battled Cassius (in vain) and came, if only temporarily, into the good graces of the triumvirs [48]. Rhodes now existed only as a school of rhetoric and a vacation spot for exiled Romans. Even so Rhodes continued to bounce in and out of imperial favor: "freed" by Nero, in disgrace under Vespasian, and back in favor by the reign of Nerva [49]. Aelius Aristides told the Rhodians that their pride would cause them to loose their freedom yet again [50]. For such a proud people, this reminder of their "freedom" must have been bitter. The celebration of Romaia into the second century of the Empire was a continuing reminder of Rhodes' political insignificance [51].

II. Lycia

Lycia marks the southernmost point of the western coast of Asia, guarding the sea route from Ionia and Greece to Cyprus, Syria and Egypt. Its position and its rugged coastline were ideal for piracy, and the Lycians remained the perennial foe of the mercantile Rhodians. For military reasons, the Lycian coast was much coveted by Hellenistic princes. The Ptolemies controlled Lycia through the third century, but toward the end of the century their rule grew weaker and weaker. During his western operations in 197, Antiochus III took control of Lycia and the Lycians loyally supported him in his war against Rome [52]. As we have seen, they were given to their Rhodian enemies in 188 and the next two decades were devoted to bitter resistance to Rhodian rule. Outside support—whether occasional assistance rendered by Eumenes or the encouragement given to their embassy by Rome in 177—kept the Lycians fighting on, and they were finally freed by the Senate in 167. The Lycian cities were closely bound together in a league (κοινὸν τῶν Λυκίων; *Commune Lyciae*)—one of the oldest and strongest in Asia—which persisted into the Roman Empire. This league functioned as a genuine political and diplomatic force [53].

---

[48] Ships to Pompey: Plutarch *Cato Minor* 54; *Cicero* 38, 4. Refusal of sanctuary: Cicero *Ad fam.* 12, 14, 3. Cassius: Appian *BC* 4, 65f. Rewards from triumvirs: Appian *BC* 5, 7.
[49] Tacitus *Ann.* 12, 58, 2; Suetonius *Vespasian* 8; *Syll.* 819; MOMIGLIANO *JRS* 41 (1951) 150f.
[50] 24, 22 (ed. Keil).
[51] LINDOS 482.
[52] MAGIE *RRAM* 524; 1380 n. 30–31.
[53] DEININGER *Provinziallandtage* 69f.

Lycian League — The devotion of the Lycian League to Roma is witnessed in a famous inscription seen on the Capitoline in the sixteenth century and preserved in Renaissance copies [54]. The bilingual text records the Lycians' dedication of a statue of Roma to Jupiter Capitolinus and the Roman people in gratitude for the restoration of their freedom:

[Ab co]muni restitutei in maiorum leibert[atem]
[Lucei] Roma(m) Iovei Capitolino et populo Romano v[irtutis]
benivolentiae beneficique causa erga Lucios ab comun[i]
Λυκίων τὸ κοινὸν κομισάμενον τὴν πάτριον δημ[ο-]
κρατίαν τὴν Ῥώμην Διὶ Καπετωλίωι καὶ τῶι δήμωι τῶ[ι]
Ῥωμαίων ἀρετῆς ἕνεκεν καὶ εὐνοίας καὶ εὐεργεσίας
τῆς εἰς τὸ κοινὸν τὸ Λυκίων

This text can most reasonably be dated to 167 or soon after, and scholars had long assumed that this was the earliest possible date for a cult of Roma in Lycia: the Lycians had supported Antiochus against Rome (192–189) and had been put under Rhodian control at Apamea (188) [55]. But in 1948 G. E. BEAN published an important decree from Araxa in Lycia which mentions a quinquennial festival dedicated Ῥώμῃ θεᾷ Ἐπιφανεῖ and celebrated by the Lycian League [56]. I would

---

[54] *CIL* I² 725 = *CIL* VI 372; most recently MORETTI *IGUR* 5. For the arguments on the date of this much disputed text, see Additional Note.

[55] Antiochus' use of Lycian ports: Livy 37, 16; 37, 45, 2. Lycia given to Rhodes: Livy 37, 56, 5; Polybius 21, 24, 7.

[56] *JHS* 68 (1948) 46 #11 = *SEG* XVIII 570. BEAN prefers a date later in the second century—partially because the text mentions two celebrations of the festival to Roma and, if the first is to be dated in 189, the second must have taken place under Rhodian domination. We have already seen that cults of Roma were not established in areas under Rhodian control (cf. pp. 34ff. above), but it is difficult to imagine the Rhodians daring to abolish a pentaeteric festival of Roma which had already been founded. And the Lycians, who were in a constant state of insurrection, would hardly abandon the festival when they were still hoping for Rome's intercession. Therefore most scholars do not find the second celebration of Romaia a major obstacle, and date the foundation in 189 or 188: JONES reported by BEAN *op. cit.*; J. & L. ROBERT *BE* 1950 #183 and 1958 #462; MORETTI *RF* (1950) 326–350; LARSEN *CP* 51 (1956) 151–169; LARSEN *Greek Federal States* (Oxford, 1968) 245f.; HABICHT *Olympia Bericht VII* 221 n. 12; SCHMITT *Rom* 90.

The matter is complex. The chief arguments for the early date are: 1) the use of praenomina alone for Roman envoys cannot be attested after 170; 2) an Appius and a Publius are mentioned and the embassy of 188 contained men with those praenomina; 3) the epithet ἐπιφανής is most appropriate in 189/188 at Rome's first appearance in the area, and interestingly it is not used in the mention of the second celebration of the festival (see p. 114 below on the epithet); 4) the mention of a Moagetes of Cibyra is consonant with a date of 189/188, since the treachery of this Moagetes fits well with the debased behavior of a

now place the first celebration of this festival in 189. It was not an expression of gratitude towards Rome; it was part of a desperate attempt to win Roman favor in the months after Antiochus' defeat at Magnesia. Ἐπιφανής here was not mere convention[57]. It expressed the trauma of the Lycians at seeing their world disrupted by a remote power which suddenly and unexpectedly had defeated the great king and now threatened to hand them over to the Rhodians, their traditional enemies[58]. Above all else, the Lycians feared a Rhodian stranglehold on their ports.

Hence the flurry of diplomatic activity. Just as Lampsacus had recently appealed to Rome on the strength of the "Trojan origin" of Rome, so the Lycians had the Ilians intervene on their behalf[59]. And as Smyrna had erected a temple to Roma, so the Lycian League established this festival to Roma. Envoys were sent to the commissioners and perhaps to the Senate as well, but despite optimistic reports, all was for nought. Rome ignored these appeals, as she had ignored the earlier appeals of Smyrna and Lampsacus. Lycia would be freed only when it became advantageous to Rome[60].

The Lycians were serious in their desperation — it was not merely a diplomatic ploy. Almost immediately after Apamea they began to fight Rhodes, and their guerilla-type insurgency lasted for over twenty years[61]. Lycia held no intrinsic interest for the Romans; it was merely a pawn in the complex game with Macedon, Pergamum and Rhodes. After the Senate sympathetically received the envoys from Xanthus in 177 and criticized the Rhodians for mistreating their "friends and

---

Moagetes before Manlius Vulso in 189 (see p. 40 below); 5) a date of 167 is less plausible since the Lycian federation could not have exercised the power under Rhodian domination which the text attributes to it; Rhodes is not even mentioned in this text!

The scholars listed above place the first celebration about 189/188 (MORETTI: 187), while the second celebration in 185/184 constitutes the terminus post quem of the inscription.

On πανήγυρις as festival as well as an assembly, see p. 165 below.

[57] On this epithet see pp. 114f. below.

[58] SCHMITT *Rom* 88–89. On the traditional antipathy, cf. *Scholia in Iliadem* 5, 639 (ed. Erbse).

[59] Polybius 22, 5. There was ample time between Magnesia and Apamea in which to found the festival. The Ilians reported back (incorrectly) that their mission to Rome had been successful, so the Lycians proposed an alliance to Rhodes. All this occurred before the truth was known.

[60] Rome certainly took notice of such displays of affection or flattery (Polybius 21, 22, 3), but they only take effect when they were in line with Roman policy aims. Embassy to commissioners: Araxa decree; to Senate: SCHMITT *Rom* 89. On relations of Rome and Rhodes and their effect on Lycia: SCHMITT *Rom* 81–172; FRASER-BEAN 112–117; see above pp. 32ff.

[61] Polybius 30, 31, 4; Livy 41, 25, 8 (174 BC); Livy 42, 14, 8 (172 BC). SCHMITT *Rom* 136; FRASER-BEAN 114.

allies," the Lycian revolt broke out with renewed vigor [62]. But Rome did not support them; it was not yet time to humiliate Rhodes. Only after Pydna, when Macedon had been decisively defeated, did Rome act directly against Rhodes. Only then were the Lycians given their freedom.

After obtaining their freedom, the Lycian cities grew in power and influence. The league resisted Mithridates and even helped to defend Rhodes from his attack [63]. Sulla formally recognized the independence of Lycia, and the cities remained free until their annexation by Claudius [64]. Throughout this period of freedom Roma was honored both by the league and by individual cities. There were priesthoods of Roma even in the Empire; her cult was not invariably incorporated into the cult of emperors. Roma's survival independent of the imperial cult also occurred in Thrace, in Termessus and on Cyprus [65]. Roma was also linked with the popular goddess Leto in Romaia Letoia celebrated by the league, and priests of Roma of the league are attested in texts from Tlos, Sidyma, Oenoanda, and in Balbura as late as the third century AD [66]. Unexpectedly, Roma is absent from the imperial coinage of Lycia.

Cities — Evidence for the municipal worship of Roma is scarce in Lycia. There are only two priests of Roma, one at Trysa and the other at Aperlae [67]. This latter may have been priest of a composite cult including Roma, Zeus and Apollo. Here again, the emperors were not added to the cult of Roma.

III. Cibyra

Just to the north of Lycia, the cities of Cibyra, Bubon, Balbura and Oenoanda formed the Cibyrate Federation (often simply called "Cibyra" after its most important city). When the Romans first came to

---

[62] Polybius 25, 5, 3.
[63] Appian *Mith.* 20–21; 24.
[64] Sulla's recognition: Appian *Mith.* 61; Annexation: Suetonius *Claudius* 25; Cassius Dio 60, 17, 3.
[65] See Chapter 7 below.
[66] Tlos: *TAM* II 2, 583; Sidyma: *TAM* II 1, 223; Oenoanda: *IGR* III 490; Balbura: *IGR* III 474. These last two cities, originally part of the Cibyrate federation, were annexed to Lycia by Murena about 84/83 BC. On Romaia: *SEG* XXII 350 as restored by J. & L. ROBERT *BE* 1962 #153 (confirmed by DUNST *ZPE* 3 (1968) 141). A cult of Romaia Letoa also existed at nearby Caunus in the second century; see below p. 48. On Leto, cf. WEHRLI *RE Supp* V 555f. METZGER *RA* (1970) 321 reports a victory list of the Romaia of the Lycian League has been found at Xanthos. He tentatively dates it by letter forms to the second century BC.
[67] Trysa: *IGR* III 687; Aperlae *IGR* III 692.

Asia these wealthy trading communities were ruled by the tyrant Moagetes, whom Polybius describes as "savage and deceitful"[68]. He had begun as tyrant of Bubon, and then became the strongman of the federation. Livy recounts the story of his shameful performance before Manlius Vulso: he debasedly feigned poverty to avoid paying an "indemnity"[69]. And the roughly contemporary decree from Araxa also witnesses his treachery. Such a tyrant would surely be deposed at the first opportunity, which may have come in 189–188. His disgraceful behavior before Manlius could have been the catalyst; but whatever the immediate occasion, a tyrant who had been a vassal of Antiochus would have had to be removed by his prudent countrymen before the peace conference[70].

Cibyra became independent at Apamea, and the text of the treaty between Rome and Cibyra survives—there were once copies on the base of the statue of Roma at Cibyra and in the temple of Jupiter Capitolinus at Rome[71]. This treaty should apparently be dated to 188 or soon thereafter, though it remains a puzzle why Rome desired a formal treaty with an Asiatic state at such an early date. Yet it must have been this treaty which emboldened the Cibyrates to aid the revolt of Caunus against Rhodes in 167, and which also compelled them to return to the Romans the Rhodian fugitive Polyaratus[72]. Later in the second century dynasts regained control of Cibyra, but they were finally expelled by Sulla's legate L. Licinius Murena, who dissolved the federation, annexed the city of Cibyra to the province of Asia, and allowed some of the minor cities to form part of the Lycian League[73].

---

[68] Polybius 21, 34; on the independence of Cibyra: RUGE *RE* XI 375—not under Attalus and certainly not under Rhodes.

[69] Livy 38, 14, 3–10.

[70] There is no mention of Moagetes when in 167 Cibyra sent armed assistance to Caunus, or in the acceptance and later betrayal of the Rhodian fugitive Polyaratus. Moagetes had certainly fallen before 167, and the most likely occasion of his fall was 189 or 188.

[71] *OGIS* 762. TOYNBEE *Hannibal's Legacy* (London, 1965) II 440; FORTE 40; WEINSTOCK *DJ* 403 n. 2 all accept a date of 189 but no arguments are given. NIESE *Geschichte der griechischen und makedonischen Staaten* (Gotha, 1893–1903) III 61, 3; MAGIE *AS* 178; ACCAME 86f. all accept 188. DITTENBERGER ad *OGIS* 762; TÄUBLER *Imperium Romanum* (Berlin, 1913) 44f.; 454f. accept 167 as the *terminus ante quem*, while BADIAN *FC* 295 cannot accept a date before 167 without further evidence. J. & L. ROBERT *BE* 1950 #183 do not believe an exact date can be fixed on the basis of the current evidence. I agree, but tentatively prefer 188, after the deposition of Moagetes. Cibyran help to Caunus leads me to a date before 167, and after Apamea seems the most suitable. The letter forms and orthography of this text indicate a date in the first half of the second century.

[72] Polybius 30, 5, 14; 30, 9, 13–19.

[73] MAGIE *RRAM* 241f.; RUGE *RE* XI 375; J. & L. ROBERT *BE* 1950 #183; WILHELM *Neue Beiträge zur griechischen Inschriftenkunde* II (Vienna, 1912) 5–8.

The mention of the statue of Roma in Cibyra in the text of the treaty is evidence for an early cult of Roma—about 189. We know that a festival to Roma was eventually established in Cibyra, but that is the extent of the epigraphical evidence [74]. Roma appears on the local coinage in the reign of Hadrian and perhaps also in the third century AD [75].

IV. Caria

Caria, the southwest corner of Anatolia lying opposite Rhodes, was an important battlefield in the wars of the early second century BC. By the end of the third century Antiochus III had strengthened his hold over the loyalties of this area, conferring privileges on numerous Carian cities [76]. But he was far to the East when Philip's expedition to Caria turned against the Seleucid possessions. Philip soon returned to Macedon, but his generals retained control of much of inland Caria until the Macedonian defeat at Cynoscephalae [77]. Antiochus quickly returned to Caria and received the submission of some Ptolemaic cities as well as his own possessions. He made few demands on these cities; on the contrary, he granted concessions and for the sake of his Rhodian alliance even allowed some cities to slip under Rhodian "protection" [78]. All in vain, for it was the Rhodian fleet which defeated the Syrian navy at Myonnesus and Side in 190. The Roman armies defeated Antiochus at Magnesia-ad-Sipylum in January 189, and by the summer of the following year the Roman commissioners at Apamea had distributed the spoils of war: most of Caria was assigned to Rhodes [79]. Though Rhodian subjects in nearby Lycia were in revolutionary ferment for the next two decades, Caria seems to have remained calm. There is even some evidence that the Rhodians skillfully played on the traditional enmity between the indigenous Carians in the countryside and

---

[74] L. ROBERT has reported to me by letter that J. ROBERT in reexamining HAUSSOULLIER's squeeze of *Syll.* 1064 now places the Romaia in Cibyra rather than in Corcyra. This new reading will be published with photographic documentation.

[75] Reign of Hadrian: IMHOOF-BLUMER *KM* I 257 #28 with legend Ῥώμη Ἀδριανή and *SNG-DEN* 29 #273 with legend Ῥώμη. ROBERT *MG* 64f. has identified Roma on coins of Cibyra from the reign of Alexander Severus: *SNG-GER* 9 #3744–3746, 3737.

[76] MAGIE *RRAM* 945 n. 48 for references; SCHMITT *Antiochos* 245–248; CRAMPA *Labraunda* III i 132f. Antiochus' physical presence was not required in all cases; the action is diplomatic rather than military: see HERRMANN *Teos* 117.

[77] HOLLEAUX *Études* IV 334f.; CRAMPA *Labraunda* III i 130f.

[78] Antiochus thought he was making progress with the Rhodians by his concessions; otherwise he would hardly have suggested them as mediators during his difficult bargaining session with the Romans at Lysimachia in 195 (Polybius 18, 52, 4).

[79] Polybius 21, 24, 7.

the Greek townsmen to strengthen their own control[80]. This brief period of Rhodian control had a substantial impact on the Carian cities and their institutions[81]. But to no avail, since Rhodes lost Caria as well as Lycia by the Senate's decree of 167. Thus the cities of Caria became the loyal allies of Rome—loyal, at least, until the Mithridatic wars.

This brief sketch of Carian history in the early second century suggests three appropriate occasions for devotion to Roma: at the defeat of Antiochus in 189; at the treaty of Apamea in 188 (for the Carian cities freed at that time); and at the grant of freedom in 167. Carian cults to Roma were established by individual cities, since they had no league nor even an informal grouping. The cults of Roma therefore grew out of peculiar local circumstances, and it is useful to examine in some detail those cities which did honor to the goddess Roma.

Alabanda — The extant books of Livy contain only a single mention of a cult of Roma: at Alabanda, one of the principal cities of inland Caria with a reputation for luxury[82]. This cult, which included a temple and a festival, is also attested by epigraphic and numismatic evidence—a rare and welcome occurrence[83]. The Romaia at Alabanda was long considered the earliest example of a festival to Roma, and it remains the earliest attested by literary evidence[84]. The occasion was an embassy to Rome in 170 during which the Alabandan envoys presented a gold crown to Jupiter, contributed armor for the Roman forces in Macedon, and "templum Urbis Romae se fecisse commemoravere ludosque anniversarios ei divae institutisse". This cult has often been dated in 170 on the supposition that the Alabandans established the cult just before dispatching the embassy to Rome[85]. But surely "se fecisse commemoravere" leaves little doubt that Livy, at least, did not view the Alabandans as announcing a recent decision; they were reminding the Senate of their past loyalty.

When then was the cult founded? Since the epigraphical evidence is much later, there is no direct evidence for the foundation. Alabanda was granted special privileges by Antiochus in the third century and for a time was even called Antiochia[86]. After Magnesia the city seems

---

[80] ROBERT *Carie* 307; SCHMITT *Rom* 86; 124; 131.

[81] FRASER-BEAN 108, 130, *passim*.

[82] Livy 43, 6, 5.

[83] DIEHL-COUSIN *BCH* 10 (1886) 306f. #2; LAUMONIER *BCH* 58 (1934) 300f.; *BMC Caria* 4 #19 = *SNG-DEN* 25 #9.

[84] The θυσία established at Delphi in 189 was in honor of Roma; see *Syll.* 611 (= *RDGE* 38), and p. 37 above on the Lycian League's festival to Roma; on Chalcis, see p. 99 below.

[85] STERRET *PASA* I (1882) 25; WEINSTOCK *DJ* 403 n. 2; FORTE 54; WILAMOWITZ *GGA* 1914 98 n. 1.

[86] *OGIS* 234; HOLLEAUX *Études* III 141–157; SCHMITT *Antiochos* 281.

to have been on quite good terms with Rome. Manlius Vulso treated Alabanda as a friendly city: he captured a rebellious fortress and restored it to the city. Manlius' savage activities elsewhere distinguish this kindness all the more [87]. Alabanda had probably sent two embassies to Rome soon after Apamea, but it is uncertain what they accomplished. Still, the city was free after Apamea, though surely jealous of Rhodian domination of Caria [88]. In 170, sensing Rome's displeasure with Rhodes, Alabanda sent her embassy to the Senate and prepared for an opportunity to profit from Rhodes' misfortune (as she did a few years later) [89]. The ambassadors requested nothing from the Senate, save that their gifts be accepted as tokens of their fidelity. A measure of their success was the warmth of their reception in the Senate.

And the cult of Roma? Alabanda was free from 189 and continued to act as a free city in 170 and 167. The embassy of 170 harkens back to the foundation of the cult, and the only acceptable foundation dates are 189 (Magnesia; first embassy to Rome) or 188 (freedom from Rhodes assured). No more can be squeezed from the evidence, though I incline towards 189: after Magnesia and Manlius' assistance and before the first embassy departed for Rome. Thus the cult would be contemporary with that in Cibyra [90].

Roma is linked with the imperial cult in the two surviving inscriptions from Alabanda. Aristogenes was a priest of Roma and Augustus in the reign of Augustus himself, and his cursus also calls him priest of Ὑγίεια and of the σωτηρία of the emperor, reminiscent of the cult of Roma and Salus [91] at Pergamum. Perhaps this concern for the Emperor reflects the sufferings endured by the inhabitants of Alabanda during Labienus' depredations in Asia [92]. M. Antonius Meleagros, who was descended from a royal line, was priest of Roma and Augustus later in the Empire [93].

---

[87] Livy 38, 13, 2–4. On Manlius' activity elsewhere: Livy 38, 14, 10 (Cibyra); 38, 45–46 (Galatians). BRISCOE *Latomus* 27 (1968) 150.

[88] DIEHL-COUSIN *BCH* 10 (1886) 299 #1; HOLLEAUX *REG* 11 (1898) 258–266. On this problem most scholars follow HOLLEAUX: ROBERT in HOLLEAUX *Études* VI 21; BIKERMAN *REG* 50 (1937) 228; JONES *CERP* 53; SCHMITT 87–88; REHM *Milet* I p. 296. FRASER-BEAN 108 are uncertain, while MAGIE *RRAM* 994 n. 32 sees a short period of subjugation to Rhodes, then the second embassy and freedom.

[89] Alabanda's conquest of Rhodian land in 167 brought this jealousy into the open. Polybius 30, 5, 15; Livy 45, 25, 13; SCHMITT *Rom* 143 n. 1.

[90] On the date of this foundation, LARSEN *Mélanges Piganiol* (Paris, 1966) 1642 and *Rep. Gov.* 217 n. 26; LAUMONIER 357 n. 1 accept 189. REHM *Milet* I p. 296 prefers 188. For 170, see n. 85 above. BADIAN *FC* 295 dates the temple in Alabanda to the aftermath of the defeat of Perseus.

[91] LAUMONIER *BCH* 58 (1934) 300f. = *AE* 1935 #46. Roma and Salus: *CIL* III 399.

[92] MAGIE *RRAM* 431.   [93] DIEHL-COUSIN *BCH* 10 (1886) 306f. #2.

Mylasa — The port city of Mylasa was among the Carian cities freed at Apamea. It had been a Seleucid possession and was unsuccessfully attacked by Philip during his Carian campaign of 201 [94]. It gave formal submission to Antiochus on his return from the East in 197, but he allowed Mylasa, like his other Carian possessions, to slip under Rhodian influence in order to maintain his shaky alliance with the island republic [95]. No more is heard of the city until the Roman commissioners at Apamea freed it from tributary obligations to Rhodes [96]. No reason is given in the sources, but it is likely that Mylasa, which controlled considerable fertile land, had furnished supplies for the Roman armies. As a wealthy commercial center, Mylasa may have had a special distrust of Rhodes and asked Rome for an explicit grant of immunity. Its ambitions and hostility to Rhodes are evident in its rapid seizure of the Rhodian lands in Euromus in the revolt of 167 [97]. Mylasa's enmity towards Rhodes, if traditional, helps to explain its special mention at Apamea.

Only one text from Mylasa mentions a priest of Roma and Augustus, and even that requires some restoration. But we also have the report of the dedication from the epistyle of a temple built to Roma and Augustus [98]. That temple survived into modern times when it was seen by early travellers until Chandler reported that in 1765 it had been "recently" destroyed by the Turks [99]. Mylasa too had suffered at the hands of Labienus, and its embassy to Octavian in 31 received a favorable hearing. A letter of Octavian to the Mylasans granting some request is preserved [100]. After a few decades the temple was erected, presumably replacing a cult of Roma with the new cult of Roma and Augustus [101]. As with other cities freed at Apamea, I can only suggest that the original cult of Roma was most likely founded in 188 [102].

---

[94] Polybius 16, 24, 6–7; HOLLEAUX *Études* IV 262, 333 n. 2; CRAMPA *Labraunda* III i 124 n. 7.

[95] HILLER VON GAERTRINGEN *RE* Supp. V 791; SCHMITT *Antiochos* 281; CRAMPA *op. cit.* 133f.

[96] Livy 38, 39, 8; Polybius 21, 46, 4.

[97] Polybius 30, 5, 11–16; Livy 45, 25, 11–13.

[98] COUSIN-DIEHL *BCH* 12 (1888) 15 #4; dedication: *CIG* 2696.

[99] Early travellers: G. WHELER *Journey into Greece* (London, 1682) 275–276 (plate III 10); R. POCOCKE *A Description of the East* (London, 1745) II pt ii, 61 (plate 55); R. CHANDLER *Travels in Asia Minor* (second edition, Oxford, 1776) 186–187; E. DODWELL *Classical-Topographical Tour through Greece* (London, 1821) I 326.

[100] *Syll.* 768 (= *RDGE* 60); *RDGE* p. 311–312.

[101] It can usually be assumed that cults of Roma and Augustus of the imperial period replaced preexisting cults of Roma. See Chapter 7 below.

[102] The evidence for the cults is late, but the historical circumstances seem to me to demand devotion to Roma about the time of Apamea.

Bargylia — Just south of Mylasa on the southern side of the gulf of Iasus was Bargylia, a port held by Philip for almost five years until the Roman commissioner Lentulus freed it in the summer of 196. Philip's other Carian conquests had already been lost, so Bargylia was the last Macedonian possession in Asia [103]. The Bargylians remained free after Apamea [104]. The evidence for Roma there consists of a dedicatory inscription to a high priest of Roma and Augustus who served in Bargylia in the Flavian era [105]. At first glance, 196 seems an attractive date for the foundation of a cult of Roma, since the long-delayed liberation of the city would have produced considerable tension finally relieved in a great wave of pro-Roman sentiment. But, without more conclusive evidence, it would be rash to date any cult of Roma before that of Smyrna (195). Roman power was known in the East in the late third century, and it is likely that some thought was given to the ways of honoring this new political force. Dedications or honors to Roma would not be impossible before 195; in fact, they would not be surprising. But the primacy of Smyrna in establishing a cult of Roma is recorded by Tacitus and, indirectly, by Cicero and can hardly be ignored. Thus 189/188 seems the most likely time for the establishment of a cult of Roma at Bargylia [106].

Antiochia-ad-Mæandrum — The remaining cults of Roma in Caria can, with varying degrees of certainty, be attributed to the aftermath of the Third Macedonian War: 167 or 166. An inscription recording a treaty between Samos and Antiochia specifies that the punishment for infringement of the treaty be a fine paid to the goddess Roma at Antiochia [107]. Letter forms indicate that this text is from the early second century BC, and the editor HABICHT has dated it to c. 165. The text refers to the Romans as τ[οὺς κοινοὺς] εὐεργέτας πάντων and HABICHT has convincingly placed the establishment of the cult in the pro-Roman euphoria of 167. It is possible that Antiochia honored Roma when Manlius Vulso camped his army there in 189, though the

---

[103] Freed by Lentulus: Polybius 16, 24, 1f.; 18, 48, 2. See WALBANK II 529 and 619 on the date. All else lost: Polybius 18, 48, 1–2; WALBANK II 611.

[104] HOLLEAUX *Études* V 367; MAGIE *RRAM* 952 n. 61; 958 n. 75. SCHMITT *Antiochos* 280 is uncertain whether Antiochus regained Bargylia.

[105] HAUVETTE-BESNAULT *BCH* 5 (1881) 191f. #14. The first editor considered this priest to be connected with the provincial cult of Asia; BRANDIS *RE* II 479 and MAGIE *RRAM* 1614 prefer a local priest.

[106] It is of course possible that Smyrna's primacy derived from being the first to have dedicated a temple to Roma, rather than the first to dedicate a cult. Yet the emphasis placed on that primacy deters me from accepting this view, although the sources certainly allow it. If any cult in Asia seems likely to date before 195, the case for Bargylia is the strongest.

[107] *MDAI(A)* 72 (1957) 242–250 #65. A coin of Antiochia depicts Roma Nikephoros on the reverse with the legend Ῥώμη Ἀντιοχέων: *SNG-DEN* 25 #50.

city had supported Antiochus and had no reason to expect special consideration from the commissioners. HABICHT's date of 167 seems the most plausible [108].

Cos — Cos, situated at the mouth of the Ceramic gulf facing Halicarnassus, should be considered with Caria. It too has a history of Ptolemaic connections going back to the fourth century. But with the decline of Egypt, it turned towards Rhodes for protection and leadership [109]. The Coans supplied ships to the Romans in the war against Antiochus, and remained free after Apamea [110]. Ostensibly friendly towards Rome, Cos continued to follow the Rhodian lead and there, as at Rhodes, a vocal anti-Roman faction became prominent during the war with Perseus [111]. Cos remained formally, if unenthusiastically, loyal to Rome and, unlike Rhodes, was not sufficiently important to become involved in diplomatic manoeuvring. Thus the Coans escaped Rome's post-war wrath. The island remained free after 167 and, while still retaining her Egyptian and Rhodian connections [112], never again wavered in her loyalty to Rome. Only there did the Romans in Asia escape massacre during the Mithridatic Wars [113]. The goddess Rhodos had been worshipped on the island, and the cult remained even when Rhodes fell into disgrace in 167 [114]. By then the Coans would surely have balanced this cult with another to Roma. Games in honor of Roma, which may have been combined with Asclepieia, are attested by several inscriptions [115]. Coan loyalty to, and possibly even affection

---

[108] ROBERT *CRAI* (1969) 61; J. & L. ROBERT *BE* 1960 #318. WEINSTOCK *DJ* 403 n. 3 gives a date soon after 195 with no evidence adduced but this text; his date must be rejected. This inscription also records an increase in the lands of Antiochia—another reason for local gratitude to Roma.

[109] Diodorus 20, 27, 2; Polybius 16, 15, 4. Antiochus' intrigues on Cos: HERZOG *JDAI Arch. Anz.* 20 (1905) 11 #6. He had no discernible success.

[110] Livy 37, 11, 13; 37, 16, 2; 37, 22, 2. BIKERMAN *REG* 50 (1937) 239.

[111] Polybius 30, 7, 9–10. MELONI 316 n. 3.

[112] Ptolemy Alexander II was raised at Cos: Appian *BC* 1, 102. Egyptian treasures are deposited there: Josephus *AJ* 13, 13, 1; Appian *Mith.* 115; 117.

[113] Tacitus *Ann.* 4, 14, 2. For Coan activity during the Mithridatic Wars, see PATON-HICKS *Inscriptions of Cos* (Oxford, 1891) xxxvii–xl with sources quoted.

[114] *Syll.* 1000; on the date, see REINACH *REG* 4 (1891) 376; MODONA *L'Isola di Coo nell' Antichità Classica* (Rhodes, 1933) 74 n. 1; 46. See above p. 35 n. 41. HANSEN *Attalids* 466 points out that the Coans distributed divine honors rather freely, both to Attalids and Seleucids at the same time.

[115] *Syll.* 1066 (c. 5 AD); ROBERT *EEP* 126–128 #3 (1st century BC). ROBERT *REG* 46 (1933) 441 n. believes that the eponymous priest of Augustus (*IGR* IV 1087) on Cos indicates a prior eponymous priest of Roma—but no evidence is given. In *SEG* XXIII 212 Messene honors a victor in the Ἀσκλαπιεῖα καὶ Ῥωμαῖα. It is impossible to place these games with any certainty, but perhaps a suggestion might be offered. Romaia and Asclepieia are separately attested in four cities: Athens, Ephesus, Pergamum and Cos. It would be most likely to find the Romaia linked with the Asclepieia at Cos, since the Asclepieia were there the

for, Rome may be symbolized in the late second century sculpture group depicting Aeneas and Anchises which has been found on the island [116]. Rome found few such constant allies in the Greek world.

Hyllarima — Rhodian influence is apparent in Hyllarima in the years after Apamea: there was a cult of the Demos of Rhodes, and a Rhodian eponymous priest was used in Hyllarima to date decrees [117]. The evidence for Roma consists entirely of a dedication from the Empire: θεᾷ Ῥώμῃ καὶ Δήμῳ [118]. We might see this cult as a replacement for the Rhodian one, or at least as an attempt to balance it after 167. Cities which had honored Rhodes would surely have been expected to do at least equal honor to their new mistress.

Stratonicea and Caunus — These cities held a unique place among Rhodes' possessions in Caria. The Rhodians did not obtain Stratonicea and Caunus from the Roman commissioners at Apamea and, even in the face of Roman anger after Pydna, the Rhodian ambassadors plucked up the courage to ask to retain them [119]. In both cases the circumstances of Rhodian acquisition are hazy, but the envoys would hardly enter a baseless plea when war and certain defeat might result from it [120]. Since the Rhodians had appointed separate administrative officials for Lycia, Caria and Caunus in 188, their later protests to Rome were surely in good faith [121]. But uncovering the histories of these cities is very difficult.

Caunus had long been an "ally" of Egypt with connections going back, as so often in this area, to the reign of Ptolemy I [122]. With the decline of Egyptian power Caunus was virtually autonomous by the end of the third century. Nevertheless, the city was counted among the Ptolemaic "allies" which Rhodes protected against Antiochus' advance in 197 [123]. It was then purchased by Rhodes from Ptolemaic generals at the time of the Syrian War [124]. After Pydna, the Caunians revolted and were quickly defeated by Rhodes, but were shortly freed by a decree

---

most prominent local festival: Hippocrates *Epist.* 11 (ed. Littré IX 324f.). On joint cults and joint festivals see below pp. 128ff.; 175ff. On Asclepieia, see EDELSTEIN *Asclepius* II Testimonia (Baltimore, 1945) 556–575.

[116] FUCHS *AJA* 72 (1968) 385 gives a date of 130–120 BC.

[117] LAUMONIER *BCH* 58 (1934) 345f. #39; 372 (on the date). Rhodian influence: FRASER-BEAN 130; 132; ROBERT *EA* 514; ROBERT *Carie* 309 (Rhodian eponymous priest).

[118] LAUMONIER *BCH* 58 (1934) 379 #43.

[119] Polybius 30, 31, 4f.

[120] MAGIE *RRAM* 880 n. 73 disagrees.

[121] *Syll.* 619. ROBERT *EA* 478 points out that Caunus is geographically neither part of Lycia nor of Caria.

[122] Diodorus 20, 27, 1f.

[123] Livy 33, 20, 12; cf. BRISCOE *Livy* 287f.

[124] Appian: *Mith.* 23; cf. FRASER-BEAN 106 n. 3 on this passage. On the purchase, see Polybius 30, 31, 6 and n. 127 below.

of the Senate[125]. And so they remained until restored to Rhodes after the Mithridatic wars[126]. Obviously after 197 Caunus was increasingly dependent on Rhodes to protect her from Antiochus[127]. The fertile area behind Caunus was of great interest to Rhodes. Without a formal change in status, the city could have been freed after a Roman victory, as were Cos, Halicarnassus and other Ptolemaic allies. Despite Rhodian rhetoric about Greek freedom at peace conferences and in diplomacy, the islanders were not adverse to economically advantageous possessions. Under Rhodian control during the war and the post-war period, the Caunians had no occasion to turn from Rhodes to Rome. Their cult and festival to Roma must have been instituted at the time of their revolt in 167, or soon after the Senate granted their freedom. Their pentaeteric games, which included both athletic and dramatic contests, were dedicated to Roma and Leto: The Letoa Romaia which became in time the Letoa Kaisareia and survived at Caunus for some centuries[128].

Stratonicea was a foundation of the earliest Seleucids. Like Caunus it was regarded as a special possession by the Rhodians whose embassy of 167 told the Senate that Stratonicea had been given to them by Antiochus and Seleucus[129]. Scholarly controversy has raged about the date (or dates) of this gift[130]. It seems certain that Polybius refers to Antiochus III and his son Seleucus who would have given the city to Rhodes during a conciliatory period in 197[131]. The king had just taken Stratonicea from Philip, but we simply do not know who controlled the city before the Carian expedition of the Macedonian army[132]. Thus

---

[125] Polybius 30, 5, 11f.; 30, 21, 3; 30, 23, 2; 30, 31, 4f.

[126] Strabo 14, 2, 3; REINACH *Mithridate Eupator* (Paris, 1890) 210.

[127] HOLLEAUX *Études* V 364; MAGIE *RRAM* 946 n. 49 does not accept Rhodian control. HOLLEAUX *Études* I 418–425 has shown that the Rhodian acquisition of Caunus must have occurred between 197 and 188. He prefers 189, as do LARSEN *Mélanges Piganiol* (Paris, 1966) 1642 and WEINSTOCK *DJ* 403 n. 2. FRASER-BEAN 105–107 place it in 191 or 190, while SCHMITT *Antiochos* 280 n. 2 says we cannot tell the date; however SCHMITT *Rom* 112 n. 1: "197 BC".

[128] *JHS* 73 (1953) 32 #13 = *SEG* XII 466. Leto was popular in this area and Romaia Letoia are also found in Lycia; see above p. 39. On joint cults, see pp. 128f. below. A Rhodian text of the Flavian era provides the later name of the festival: Letoia Kaisareia; cf. PUGLIESE-CARRATELLI *ASA* 30–32 (1952–1954) 292 #66a and ROBERT *Arch. Eph.* (1966) 117.

[129] Polybius 30, 31, 6: ἐν μεγάλῃ χάριτι παρ' Ἀντιόχου καὶ Σελεύκου. Livy 33, 18, 22: recipi eam urbem (Stratoniceam) sine certamine potuisse.

[130] For a survey of the controversy, see FRASER-BEAN 102–105; BRISCOE *Livy* 283.

[131] BRISCOE *Livy* 283; AYMARD *REG* 58 (1945) xiii; J. & L. ROBERT *Mélanges Lévy* (Brussels, 1955) 563–565 n. 2.

[132] AYMARD, taking the *recipi* of Livy to refer to restoration of the city to Rhodes, suggests that Stratonicea was first given to Rhodes by Seleucus II, taken by Philip, and restored by Antiochus in 197. BRISCOE does not believe

Stratonicea as well as Caunus remained under Rhodian dominion during and after the war with Antiochus until freed by a decree of the Senate in 167 [133]. Here too there was no occasion to institute a cult of Roma before 167, but the cult must have been established in that year, probably replacing a cult of Rhodos [134]. By the middle of the second century there was already a musical competition in the city dedicated to Roma [135].

Stratonicea loyally resisted Mithridates until the city was taken, fined and garrisoned [136]. After the defeat of the Pontic armies, Rome restored the freedom and autonomy of the city and, perhaps in thanksgiving, the festival of Romaia Hekatesia was established at the sanctuary of Hecate at Lagina, a deme of Stratonicea [137]. Hecate, who once had been linked with the goddess Rhodos, is now joined with Roma, their epithets revealing the Stratoniceans' relief and enthusiasm: Ἑκάτηι Σωτείραι Ἐπιφανεῖ καὶ Ῥώμηι θεᾶι Εὐεργέτιδι. Here as elsewhere in the East the important local divinity is often joined to the cult of Roma, or later, of the emperor [138].

Aphrodisias — It is convenient to discuss Aphrodisias with the cities of Caria, though it is in a remote eastern corner not always included in Caria [139]. Aphrodisias did not become important until the first century BC, but it then developed very quickly [140]. It was occupied by Antiochus in 190, but little else is known of its early history [141]. Roma was honored there during the second century, as is shown by an unpublished inscription of a treaty between Aphrodisias-

---

that *recipi* necessarily implies restoration, and interprets the phrase of Polybius to refer to Antiochus III and his son Seleucus in 197 giving the city to Rhodes for the first time. NIEBUHR's emendation of Polybius, which is followed by the standard editions, is unnecessary: παρ' Ἀντιόχου τοῦ Σελεύκου; cf. FRASER-BEAN 104.

[133] Livy 33, 30, 11, but the context of this passage (that Stratonicea was given to Rhodes by Rome in 196) is a blatant attempt by the annalist Valerius Antias to justify Rome's interference in 167; see BRISCOE *Livy* 307–308. Decree of Senate: Polybius 30, 21, 3.

[134] Rhodos: FOUCART *BCH* 14 (1890) 365 #4; J. & L. ROBERT *BE* 1965 #272.

[135] *IGRR* IV 247. STERRET *PASA* 1 (1882) 25 proposed a date of 150 BC, which was accepted by SONNE ad *IGR*. LAUMONIER 358 prefers a date later in the second century.

[136] Appian *Mith.* 21.

[137] *OGIS* 441 (= *RDGE* 18). Lagina as a deme of Stratonicea: ROBERT *Carie* 98 n. 1; LAUMONIER 358–359. Thanksgiving: FORTE 125.

[138] ROBERT *EA* 521; LAUMONIER 30–31. A victory list of the Augustan age (*Syll.* 1066) mentions Hekatesia in Stratonicea. On the dropping of Romaia, see p. 176f. below.

[139] MAGIE *RRAM* 132; ROBERT *Carie* 17.

[140] ROBERT *EA* 338.

[141] Livy 37, 21, 5.

Plarasa, Cibyra and Tabae [142]. The dedication on that treaty is to Roma, Zeus and Homonoia—the two traditional guarantors of oaths and alliances, and the more recent, though less divine, guardian of the peace. The text is reported to be inscribed in letters of about the middle of the second century, and a date not long after 167 for the cult of Roma at Aphrodisias seems probable. But the evidence is as yet slight, and the history of Aphrodisias in the second century too little known. Otherwise, Roma only appears at Aphrodisias on a frieze on the portico, where the goddess is depicted together with the imperial family [143].

Other mentions of Roma in cities of Caria rest on dubious restorations or on insufficient evidence. The cult of the Demos of the Romans (or even of the Demos of the Rhodians) at Physcus remains a conjecture, and only a coin mentions Roma at Pedieis [144]. A dedication from Tabae is included in the group on the Capitoline, but the text is fragmentary and cannot be used to prove a cult of Roma in that city [145].

V. Ionia

The littoral and island communities of the old Ionian League reacted to Roman intervention in Asia much as did their Carian neighbors to the South. Rome appears on coins or inscriptions from ten of the

---

[142] I am grateful to Professor K. T. ERIM and Joyce REYNOLDS for notice of this text and for permission to mention it. Another text from Aphrodisias was long ago restored with a festival dedicated to Roma and Augustus. LEBAS-WADDINGTON *Voyage Archéologique en Grèce et en Asie Mineure* (Paris, 1847–1870) V 1620 c: πρὸ τῆς εἰς Ῥώμην [καὶ Σεβαστὸν ἑορτῆς, ἔχει δὲ οὗ]τος ὁ ἀγὼν τὰ ἄθλα. ROBERT *RP* 56 (1930) 30–31 correctly comments that the restoration demands very strange Greek. It must refer to some celebration before the competitors departed for Rome.

[143] VERMEULE *RIA* 54: "Roma or Virtus"; see p. 150 below.

[144] *Physcus*: FRASER-BEAN 3 #3: a dedication to Zeus, Augustus and τῷ δήμῳ τ[ῶν Ῥοδίων]. In his review, MEYER *Gnomon* 26 (1954) 473 prefers τ[ῶν Ῥωμαίων] which FRASER-BEAN had mentioned as possible. The suggestion is attractive; however, since Physcus was merely an incorporated part of one of the Rhodian cities until the Empire, the cult should thus be regarded as part of the Rhodian devotion to Roma; on its incorporation see FRASER-BEAN 97–98. *Pedieis*: BABELON *Coll. Wad.* #2523: head of a woman, laureate with legend [θεὰ] Ῥώμη ιϛ Πεδιάτων. No cult is attested at Pedieis, but Roma was worshiped Magnesia of which it was a dependent (RUGE *RE* XIX 34, 4; MAGIE *RRAM* 922 n. 13). But almost nothing is known of this Pedieis or the other one in Caria RUGE *RE* XIX 34, 3). *Halicarnassus*: *IBM* 894 mentions a temenos of Roma and Augustus in Halicarnassus. MAGIE *RRAM* 1614 would connect this with a local cult; I prefer to follow BUCKLER *RP* 61 (1935) 182–186 who sees it as a sanctuary of the cities of Asia, like the temple in Pergamum.

[145] *CIL* I² 730. See Additional Note.

twelve cities of the Ionian League—a very high proportion given the depredation of time[146]. In most of the cities the inscriptions can only be used to fix a *terminus ante quem* in the late second or first century BC. We must still explore the political and historical situation, as was done for Caria, to suggest dates for the introduction of the cults.

Ionian League — Though evidence for individual cities may be later, the Ionian League certainly sacrificed to Roma in the first half of the second century. A long inscription from Erythrae sets forth cult regulations for the league. It mentions sacrifices both to Roma and to an Attalid king (probably Eumenes II), as well as to Antiochus I on an old endowed foundation[147]. Since this text dates from the early second century, the Ionian League must have honored Roma soon after her appearance in Asia[148]. We have seen that Smyrna honored Roma in 195, and it is reasonable to see the Ionian League following the initiative of one of its member cities in honoring the new goddess.

Smyrna — In 195 Smyrna established a temple to Roma, and the *fidissimus socius* was not fickle in her devotion[149]. The Romaia were still celebrated there four centuries after the establishment of the cult[150]. The temple of Roma appeared on coins issued in Smyrna well into the third century of the Empire[151]. Through these centuries the city remained loyal: the Smyrnaeans hid Rutilius Rufus from Mithridates; they revolted against Mithridates; and rather melodramatically

---

[146] There were thirteen cities usually forming the league: Chios, Phocaea, Erythrae, Clazomenae, Priene, Ephesus, Samos, Miletus, Lebedos, Teos, Colophon, Smyrna, and Myus which in the second century belonged now to Miletus, now to Magnesia, and thus need not be counted. For evidence on this list, see MAGIE *RRAM* 867 n. 48; 868 n. 50. On the powers of the league: CASPARI *JHS* 35 (1915) 186f. There is no evidence for Roma at Phocaea or Colophon.

[147] *LSAM* #26. On kings: HABICHT 94f., especially n. 9.

[148] SOKOLOWSKI ad *LSAM* #26; HABICHT 93 date this text to the first half of the second century; KEIL *JÖAI* 13 (1910) Beiblatt 41 n. 55 places the terminus post quem in 191, but this seems too early for joint league action. Some Ionian cities remained loyal to Antiochus until Magnesia. 189 is a more reasonable terminus post quem: WILAMOWITZ-MOELLENDORFF *Abh. Pr. Akad.* (1914) 98.

[149] Tacitus *Ann.* 4, 56: templum urbis Romae. "Urbs" would not have been part of the original cult, but was added later in Latin. LARSEN *CP* 51 (1956) 168 n. 22.

[150] There were local games as well as those of the Koinon of Asia. *IDelphes* 1, 550 line 27: Ῥωμαῖα ἐν Σμύρνῃ; the κοινὰ Ἀσίας ἐν Σμύρνῃ are listed separately and one must be careful not to conflate them. See MORETTI *IAG* #81.

[151] *BMC Ionia* 299 #467 (Gallienus). Temple on *BMC Ionia* 288 #403 (Caracalla). Roma holding temple: *BMC Ionia* 286 #389f. (Julia Domna); 289 #410f. (Caracalla); 293 #434 (Julia Mammaea); 299 #467 (Gallienus). Roma seated between temples: *SNG-GER* 6 #2224 (Elagabalus). Other depictions of Roma with a legend: BABELON *Coll. Wad.* #1950; MIONNET III 1350 (Julia Domna). A portrait of Claudius with legend θεὰν Ῥώμην: McCLEAN III 152 #8299.

stripped clothes from their backs to outfit the army of Sulla[152]. We can hardly doubt this loyalty since the Senate itself was moved by it to choose Smyrna as the site of the temple of Tiberius, Livia and the Senate in AD 26. Thus Smyrna earned the coveted title νεωκόρος (temple warder) and she continued to be granted favors and privileges by later emperors[153]. The appeal of 195 was not answered immediately, but after Apamea Smyrna was free and had increased her territory[154]. The citizens of this Ionian city surely never regretted their early adherence to Roma.

Magnesia-ad-Maeandrum — Magnesia on the Maeander, though not a member of the Ionian League, is usually considered part of Ionia. In the second century BC the city was linguistically Ionian, but within the geographical confines of Caria. Magnesia sided with Philip in his Carian campaign and provided supplies to his armies[155]. The Magnesians were rewarded with some Milesian territory including Myus, thus provoking a war between Miletus and Magnesia which lasted until 196[156]. Magnesia managed to retain this land, but not for very long. A Seleucid garrison remained there during the war with Rome and only after the battle of Magnesia (ad-Sipylum) did the Magnesians (ad-Maeandrum) send envoys to the Roman commanders and surrender their city[157]. Given this historical background, it seems strange that L. Scipio gave the city freedom for her *Virtus* and *Fides*[158]. But the epigraphical evidence confirms that the Magnesians were free from Attalid control after Apamea, even if some land had to be returned to Miletus[159]. No priest or cult of Roma is attested at Magnesia, but Romaia, including both athletic and dramatic contests, were held there in the late second century[160]. Since Magnesia seems to have been

---

[152] Rutilius Rufus: Cicero *Pro Rab.* 10. Revolt against Mithridates: Appian *Mith.* 48. Sulla's army: Tacitus *Ann.* 4, 56.

[153] Temple to Tiberius: *BMC Ionia* 268 #266f. CADOUX *Ancient Smyrna* (Oxford, 1938) 239–240. Favors from emperors: MAGIE *RRAM* 1401 n.10; 1474 n.15; 632; 1492 n.7.

[154] Livy 38, 39, 11.

[155] Polybius 16, 24, 6–9.

[156] *Syll.* 588.

[157] Livy 37, 10, 12; 37, 45, 1. SCHMITT *Antiochos* 280–281.

[158] Tacitus *Ann.* 3, 62: Proximi hos Magnetes L. Scipionis et L. Sullae constitutis nitebantur quorum ille Antiocho, hic Mithridate pulsis fidem et virtutem Magnetum decoravere.

[159] Freedom: *Syll.* 679 (= *RDGE* 7); *RDGE* p. 46 n. 2; BIKERMAN *REG* 50 (1937) 238; CERUTI *RIL* 91 (1957) 709 n. 3. Loss of Myus: Polybius 21, 46, 5 says that ἱερὰ χώρα was restored to Miletus after Apamea. JONES *CERP* 53 suggests that this passage refers to Myus (or some of its lands) again changing hands.

[160] *IMagn.* 88 = *Syll.* 1079 (late 2nd BC); *IMagn.* 127 (1st BC). *IMagn.* 192 probably does not refer to Romaia; see chapter 5 n.130.

granted *amicitia* with Rome about the time of Apamea, the foundation of this festival should be placed then[161]. Surely the Magnesians would have felt an extraordinary surge of gratitude towards Rome when they were permitted to retain their freedom after such a checkered past.

Priene — Little can be said about the cult of Roma at Priene. Only a statue base with a fragmentary text mentioning a high priest of Roma and Augustus survives[162]. Priene was free before the war with Antiochus, but her activities during the war are unknown[163]. After the war the city remained free, though some land was lost to Samos as the result of mediation by Manlius Vulso[164]. In succeeding years Priene became embroiled in regional squabbles, though with little success. In its dispute with Magnesia, the Senate-appointed referee (Mylasa) gave the land in question to Magnesia[165]. In 155 Ariarathes of Cappadocia aided by Attalus II attacked Priene (unjustly, says Polybius) but Rome did not order the kings to desist until after the territory of Priene had been plundered[166]. But finally fortune smiled on Priene and in 135 the Senate reversed Manlius' earlier decision and settled a new Priene-Samos dispute in favor of Priene[167]. While Priene may have felt little enough gratitude towards Rome before 135, a cult of Roma must have existed at the time of the appeal in 155—especially since Ariarathes had already dedicated a gold crown to Roma[168]. The cult was probably established preparatory to the arbitration of Manlius in 189 or, at the latest, before the appeal to Rome in 155.

Miletus — The wealthy coastal city of Miletus was associated with the Romans in their campaigns against Antiochus[169]. The Milesians had suffered during Philip's incursions into Asia and, in the aftermath, failed to recover the lands lost to Magnesia. Their loyalty to Rome

---

[161] *Syll.* 679 line 54: ὅτε εἰς τὴν φιλίαν τοῦ δήμου τοῦ Ῥωμαίων παρεγένετο. KERN *loc. cit.* notes: Magnetes in Romanorum amicitiam pervenerunt Antiochi bello a. 190. GUARDUCCI *Epigrafia Greca* (Rome, 1969) II 377 dates Romaia to the decade after Apamea.

[162] *IPriene* 222. On the ἀρχιερεύς at the local level, see BRANDIS *RE* II 478–479; p. 186 below. At first glance this priest might seem to be eponymous. However texts from Priene attest the στεφανηφόρος as eponymous even in the late second and early first century (e.g. *IPriene* 107–112). The offices may well have been joined. But since this text was placed on the base of a statue of the emperor, the name of the priest of Roma and Augustus could reasonably be placed there even if he was not the eponymous official of the city—religious dedications in many religions are dated by the presiding cult official.

[163] *Syll.* 599—conflict between Samos and Priene arbitrated by Rhodes. All three cities are obviously independent.

[164] *Syll.* 688 (= *RDGE* 10); see also *RDGE* p. 58.

[165] *Syll.* 679 (= *RDGE* 7); see also *RDGE* p. 46f.

[166] Polybius 33, 6.

[167] *Syll.* 688 (= *RDGE* 10).

[168] Polybius 31, 32, 3; 32, 1, 1.

[169] Livy 37, 16, 2.

earned their freedom at Apamea and the restoration of some sacred lands — perhaps the same which had been lost a decade earlier[170]. For a century the Milesians were loyal to Rome and offered help to the Senate in the campaigns against Perseus[171]. An inscription from Miletus, probably to be dated about 130 BC, may mark the establishment there of the cult and festival of Roma. That the first priest of Roma would serve only a partial term of three years and eight months (instead of the usual four years) indicates either a new cult or a drastically revised one[172]. Yet it is difficult to envision Miletus free after Apamea and supporting Rome against Perseus, without some cult of Roma. Perhaps the closeness of Miletus to the Attalids may help to explain the situation. When the Ionian Koinon voted honors to Eumenes after his rebuff in Rome in 167, the king requested that the statue and crown be set up in the temenos dedicated to him in Miletus[173]. This presumably indicates that the Milesians had remained sympathetic to Pergamum in the years since Apamea. The Milesian inscription regulating the cult of Roma may coincide with the cults of Roma established in the former Attalid territories after the bequest of Attalus[174]. Perhaps the most acceptable explanation is that Miletus paid some modest honors to Roma, probably about the time of Apamea when the city's sacred lands were restored, but remained oriented towards the Attalids like the other great Ionian port, Ephesus. Perhaps after the fall of the Attalids, Miletus established a major cult to Roma and erected a Romaion; the elaborate regulations of 130 record this change. This reconstruction must remain tentative, but it does account for the known facts that Miletus was rewarded at Apamea, remained a Roman ally, yet was regarded by Eumenes as a supporter, and about 130 established or expanded the cult of Roma.

Erythrae — The local cult of Roma at Erythrae is only doubtfully attested by a restored dedication to Roma and Augustus from the

---

[170] See above n. 159.

[171] Livy 43, 6, 4; SCHMITT *Antiochos* 281.

[172] *Milet* 203. Though KAWERAU and REHM in *Milet* III 372 do not reject the possibility that the text can be dated earlier (after Pydna), REHM was later certain of a date about 130 based on the appearance of one Cratinus as στεφανηφόρος in this text. However, the question of the date cannot be considered closed. MAGIE *RRAM* 167 assumes that the text marks the establishment of the cult, but such *leges sacrae* could also accompany a reform of a cult. For Romaia at Miletus: ROBERT *BCH* 49 (1925) 232f. xi: [Ρω]μαῖα τὰ ἐμιλήτωι. Cf. also *Didyma* 339; probably 377; possibly 201. At Didyma the Romaia were joined with the Didymeia: *Didyma* 339.

[173] *OGIS* 763. 59–64. HOLLEAUX *Études* II 153f. demonstrated that the Ionian decree was passed while Eumenes stopped in Delos on his return from Rome. On the relations of Eumenes with Miletus, cf. HANSEN *Attalids* 123; 458; and especially HERRMANN *MDAI(I)* 15 (1965) 103ff.

[174] See below pp. 57f.; 71f.; 73f.

Empire [175]. But since the sacrifices to Roma voted by the Ionian League were recorded on an inscription set up in Erythrae, the local cult of Roma would probably have been established not long after — if it did not already exist. Erythrae was free of any royal control until the return of Antiochus in 197 [176]. He held the city until the beginning of the war in Asia, but in 190 the Erythraeans welcomed the Roman fleet which subsequently used the city as a base [177]. At Apamea the city was rewarded with a grant of freedom and additional territory [178]. Therefore 188 seems a reasonable date for the foundation of the cult of Roma at Erythrae, about the same time as a cult was established by the Ionian League.

Teos — The history of Teos has recently been reexamined in the light of a new inscription, and it is now clear that Teos was under the control of Antiochus as early as 204 or 203 — a Seleucid enclave in the Attalid dominions [179]. The city seems to have passed peacefully to Antiochus, perhaps through some sort of diplomatic exchange with Attalus [180]. In 193 Teos was voted ἀσυλία by the Roman Senate — with Antiochus as her sponsor [181]. The Teans supported him against Rome until forced to submit by the praetor L. Aemilius Regillus in 190 [182]. The succeeding period is more confused. After Apamea, Eumenes appears to have exercised suzerainty over the city and arbitrated a dispute between the Teans and the guild of Dionysiac artists established there [183]. In 166 Teos supported her colony, Abdera, in an appeal

---

[175] *IGR* IV 1534 = KEIL *JÖAI* 13 (1910) Beiblatt 47 #11: [ὁ δῆ]μος [θεᾶι Ῥώμηι καὶ Σε]βαστῶι Καίσαρι. For a different restoration, cf. now *Die Inschriften von Erythrai und Klazomenai* (Bonn, 1972) 131.

[176] No Ptolemaic control: HOLLEAUX *Études* III 135–136; MAGIE *RRAM* 928 n. 23; SCHMITT *Antiochos* 282–283. Attalus used Erythrae as a sanctuary from Philip in 201 (Polybius 16, 6, 5–8) so it must have been independent. On submission to Antiochus: Livy 33, 38, 1–2.

[177] Livy 36, 43, 10; 36, 45, 7; 37, 8, 5; 37, 12, 10.

[178] Livy 38, 39, 11; Polybius 21, 46, 6.

[179] HERRMANN *Anadolou* 9 (1965) 29–160. For comment on this study, see J. & L. ROBERT *BE* 1969 #495. Antiochus gets control of Teos: HERRMANN 106; peaceful acquisition of this enclave: HERRMANN 116f. Also see CRAMPA *Labraunda* III i 127f.

[180] HERRMANN 117.

[181] *Syll.* 601.

[182] Livy 37, 27–28.

[183] MEYER *Die Grenzen der hellenistischen Staaten in Kleinasien* (Zürich, 1925) 153; RUGE *RE* V A 551; SCHMITT *Antiochos* 282; HANSEN *Attalids* 96; BIKERMAN *RP* 50 (1937) 237 all see Teos under Attalid control after Apamea. The evidence is WELLES *Royal Correspondence in the Hellenistic Period* (New Haven, 1934) #53, which records the arbitration by Eumenes between Teos and the guild of Dionysiac artists established there. MAGIE *RRAM* 958 n. 75 unconvincingly sees Teos as free.

to Rome but such diplomatic autonomy does not necessarily imply freedom from Attalid control[184]. There is no ostensible reason why Teos should have acquired her freedom after the war with Perseus. Yet not long after, the Dionysiac artists fled from Teos to Attalid Ephesus, and Attalus settled them in Myonessus which might indicate looser ties between Teos and Pergamum[185]. Though a dedication from an altar of Roma and Jupiter Capitolinus found at Teos contributes little to dating the introduction of Roma in Teos, another text names a priest of Roma and Πίστις (which must refer to *Fides Publica*)[186]. This cult must have been established when freedom was granted by Rome: perhaps in 167, but more likely after the bequest of Attalus.

Ephesus — The most important city on the Ionian coast, Ephesus had been a vassal of Egypt for much of the third century[187]. But by the end of the century, Ptolemaic control was only nominal. On his return from the East in 197, Antiochus sailed to Ephesus and made it his chief naval base in the Aegean[188]. The city witnessed the king's first meeting with Hannibal, the futile negotiations of 193, and offered him refuge when he fled from Greece[189]. In spite of the naval defeats inflicted on Antiochus at Corycus and Myonnesus, Ephesus remained loyal to the king and sheltered the battered remains of the royal fleet until the end of the war[190]. After Magnesia the Ephesians sent envoys to surrender the city to the Scipios, but it was far too late to expect Roman favor[191]. Part of the Roman army wintered at Ephesus and the Scipios tarried there before returning to Rome, but the inevitable doom fell when the city was assigned to Eumenes of Pergamum as part of the settlement of Apamea[192].

Under Pergamene control Ephesus prospered. She was the chief port of Asia and became the second capital of the Attalids. But when

---

[184] *Syll.* 656. RUGE *RE* V A 551 assumes continued Tean dependence on Pergamum.

[185] Strabo 14, 1, 29. Teos' subsequent appeal to Rome tells us nothing of the *de jure* relations between Teos and Attalus. Cf. HANSEN *Attalids* 171–172.

[186] Altar: *IGRR* IV 1556 and p. 155 below. Priest: *BCH* 19 (1895) 554 text and comment. For πίστις in conjunction with Roma, cf. pp. 131ff. below. ROBERT *Laodicée* 321 n. 7 emphasizes that πίστις in such a context always refers to *Fides Publica*. A bust of Roma identified by the legend Ῥώμη appears on a Tean coin of the reign of Commodus: *SNG-DEN* 24 #499.

[187] HOLLEAUX *Études* III 135; IV 324.

[188] Polybius 18, 41a discusses the military importance of Ephesus to Antiochos. Livy 33, 38, 1f. (with BRISCOE *Livy* 320); 33, 49, 7. SCHMITT *Antiochos* 282.

[189] Hannibal: HOLLEAUX *Études* V 183. Negotiations: Livy 35, 16–17. Flight to Ephesus: Polybius 20, 8, 5.

[190] Livy 37, 30.

[191] Livy 37, 45, 1.

[192] Scipios at Ephesus: Livy 37, 45, 19; 38, 3, 1. Apamea: Polybius 21, 46, 10.

Ephesus gained her freedom remains a matter for debate and conjecture. MAGIE has suggested that Ephesus was free of Attalid control before 133, perhaps as early as the 160s[193]. But he has provided only two rather questionable bits of evidence: a dedication set up on the Capitoline in honor of the Roman people, and the independent action of the Ephesian ships against Aristonicus in 131[194]. The date of the Capitoline dedication is quite uncertain and can hardly be used to "prove" anything[195]. As for the naval activity, in the political vacuum following the death of Attalus in 133 and the bequest of his kingdom to Rome, the Ephesians would obviously have taken control of the ships of the royal navy stationed there—especially since these ships were probably manned largely by Ephesians[196]. There is no definite evidence for a free Ephesus until the end of the century, and there is no way of determining whether the city had been freed before 133, or whether its independence resulted from the death of Attalus— either from his testament or by the action of the Roman commissioners who organized the new province of Asia in, and after, 129. I am inclined to believe in one of the latter alternatives, since the Attalid kings would have had to come under very severe pressure indeed before freely granting independence to a city with the commercial and military value of Ephesus. Since there is no evidence of such pressures, the city was probably not free until the end of the kingdom of the Attalids.

A cult of Roma at Ephesus is first attested at the beginning of the first century BC, when her priest was the eponymous official there. A Sardian eponymous priest of Roma appears in the same text[197]. The existence of eponymous priesthoods of Roma both at Ephesus, and at Sardes and other Lydian cities which had been under Attalid control until 133 BC[198], further suggests that Ephesus was linked with the Attalid dominions until the demise of the dynasty, and that the Ephesians had founded a cult of Roma simultaneously with other Attalid possessions. These cults must have been founded soon after 133 BC, since it is most unlikely that cults of Roma were ever established in areas still under Attalid control. Cults of Roma were not

---

[193] MAGIE *RRAM* 955 n. 67.

[194] *CIL* I² 727; Strabo 14, 1, 38.

[195] See Additional Note.

[196] ROSTOVTZEFF *SEHHW* 807; 1522 n. 79; MCSHANE *The Foreign Policy of the Attalids of Pergamum* (Urbana, 1964) 196 n. 71. MAGIE *RRAM* 1040 n. 16 objects that ὑπὸ Ἐφεσίων could not apply to a part of the royal navy based at Ephesus. This is quibbling, and does not refute ROSTOVTZEFF.

[197] *OGIS* 437 (= *RDGE* 47). Romaia at Ephesus: *IGR* IV 1262; *Hellenica* IX 73–76.

[198] On eponymous priests of Roma, see p. 183 ff. below; in the Lydian cities, see pp. 70 ff. below.

established in Rhodes or Rhodian possessions and, though the Attalids might have been somewhat less sensitive than Rhodes on such matters, there is no evidence for the worship of Roma in the kingdom of Pergamum [199]. I proceed on the assumption that cities under the Attalids, like those under Rhodes, could not or would not worship the goddess Roma.

An Ephesian text of the first century lists the twelve annual priests of Roma who served from 51/50 to 40/39 BC and were charged with the administration of the Dionysia [200]. The Roman proconsul of 46–44, Publius Servilius Isauricus, was later added to the cult of Roma and this joint cult provided the vital link between the Hellenistic ruler-cult and the cults of Roma and Augustus [201]. After Actium Augustus permitted the Koinon of Asia to build a temple in Ephesus dedicated to Roma and Divus Julius [202]. WEINSTOCK has suggested the following development for the imperial cult in Ephesus: a temple of Roma established with the priesthood; a statue of Caesar erected in 48 with a cult after 40; the temple of 29 dedicated to Roma and Divus Julius; a new (or rebuilt) temple dedicated to Roma and Augustus and called the Augusteum [203]. This last was placed in, or adjacent to, the temenos of the Artemision by the Ephesians before 6/5 BC [204].

The Ephesians remained devoted to Roma during the Empire. Early in the second century AD a silver statue of Roma was erected at Ephesus—it was among the gifts bequeathed to the city by the Roman knight Gaius Vibius Salutaris, and is identified in inscriptions

---

[199] SCHUCHARDT *Pergamum* II p. 398 suggests that the Pergamenes may have dedicated a month to Roma in the reign of Attalus I. But the roof tiles with the letters cannot be dated securely; I prefer a much later date. See SCOTT *YCS* 2 (1931) 206 and p. 161 below.

[200] *Ephesos* II 30; on the date, see J. & L. ROBERT *BE* 1972 #388 and p. 184 below.

[201] *Ephesos* III 66; *JÖAI* 18 (1915) Beiblatt 281–282. On the connection of this cult with that of Roma and Augustus: MÜNZER *Römische Adelsparteien und Adelsfamilien* (Stuttgart, 1920) 357 n.

[202] Dio Cassius 51, 20, 6.

[203] WEINSTOCK *DJ* 403. This book tends to find precedents in the acts of Julius Caesar for all religious acts of Augustus, which exaggerates and distorts the influence of Julius.

[204] The bilingual text simply calls the building the *Augusteum* (Σεβαστῆον): *IBM* III 522. Of course Augustus preferred to be worshipped in his lifetime only in conjunction with Roma (Suetonius *Augustus* 52). *BMCRE* I Claudius #228 (= *SNG-DEN* 34 #424) may well depict the temple of Roma and Augustus at Ephesus. The legend COM·ASI could be taken to indicate that the coin depicts the temple at Pergamum, but the imperial cistophori from Pergamum show quite another temple (*SNG-DEN* 34 #419). This evidence is not conclusive, but worth attention. On these temples see pp. 140f. below. On Roma and Augustus at Ephesus, cf. *Ephesos* I p. 93; NOCK *HSCP* 41 (1930) 30 (= *Essays* I 225); PICARD *Ephèse et Claros* (Paris, 1922) 664.

both as Ῥώμη and Δῆμος ὁ Ῥωμαίων ²⁰⁵. A few generations later Roma Aeterna appears on the sculptural decoration of the great Antonine altar at Ephesus. Roma sits at the left end of the altar watching over both divine and human scenes ²⁰⁶. Finally, the Tyche of Roma and of Ephesus is mentioned in an inscription on the obverse of an intaglio from Emesa in Syria: Μεγάλη Τύχη Ῥώμη[ς] καὶ Ἐφέσου ²⁰⁷. Since this gem is not widely known, we should look at it more closely. It portrays a crescent and a star—symbols common throughout the eastern Mediterranean. CUMONT, who published it, suggested that the crescent (moon) and the star (Venus) here represent the Artemis of Ephesus and the city of Rome, though the crescent and star are also used together as a sign of eternity ²⁰⁸. Though the gem cannot be precisely dated, it was probably created after the foundation of the temple of Venus Genetrix by Julius Caesar and the subsequent promotion of that goddess by Augustus and his literary-artistic circle. (We have already seen that Julius Caesar had close ties with the Ephesians.) The sun god depicted on the reverse of this stone seems eastern and the text there has been inscribed by a quite different hand from the obverse. The gem's face was most likely inscribed at Ephesus and then carried in trade to Emesa (whose port Arados had extensive commercial links with Ephesus) where the reverse was inscribed in the local style ²⁰⁹.

Lebedos and Clazomenae — Two other cities of the Ionian League issued coinage with depictions of Roma identified by legends: Lebedos and Clazomenae ²¹⁰. But this evidence alone is not sufficient to presume a genuine cult of the goddess or a festival. We must simply record their public display of devotion to Roma.

VI. Aegean Islands

The principal Greek island communities along the coast of Asia supported Rome in the war against Antiochus. Cos, Samos, Chios and Mytilene on Lesbos all remained free after Apamea, as did most of the important Greek cities on the coast. Cos has already been discussed in the context of Caria. Since the coastal islands of Chios and Samos

---

²⁰⁵ *Ephesos* II 28: unam (statuam) urbis Romanae ... μίαν ἡγεμονίδος Ῥώμης; also see *Ephesos* II 27: εἰκὼν ἀργυρέα τοῦ δήμου τοῦ Ῥωμαίων. Both these texts obviously refer to the same statuette; see chapter 1 n. 43.
²⁰⁶ VERMEULE *RIA* 119–120.
²⁰⁷ CUMONT *Syria* 7 (1926) 347–352.
²⁰⁸ *Ibid.*; as a sign of eternity: ALFÖLDI 36.
²⁰⁹ CUMONT *op. cit.* 352. IMHOOF-BLUMER *KM* I 61 #70: a coin of Ephesus with the legend Ῥωμαίων Νείκη Τύχη Ἐφεσίων. Other coins with Roma: *BMC Ionia* 74 #213; BABELON *Coll. Wadd.* 1620; ECKHEL *DNV* II 516.
²¹⁰ Clazomenae: *BMC Ionia* 30 #113. Lebedos: *BMC Ionia* 156 #16.

were once part of the Ionian League, they should be discussed here within the context of the arrangements in Asia following the wars with Philip, Antiochus and Perseus.

Chios — Chios was an early ally of Rhodes and attempted to mediate the disputes between Philip and the Aetolians in the late third century [211]. In 201, the Chians allied with Rhodes and Pergamum against Philip and, after resisting his siege of the island, their combined fleets defeated him in the channel of Chios [212]. During the war against Antiochus, Chios was again allied with Rhodes and gave considerable assistance to the Romans who established a naval headquarters on the island [213]. Predictably, the Chians were rewarded at Apamea with confirmation of their freedom and a grant of increased territories on the mainland [214]. Honors to Roma would be an appropriate affirmation of this profitable relationship. The earliest Chian devotion to Roma is recorded in an inscription from the island first reported over twenty years ago, but only excerpts of this difficult text have been published [215]. The letter forms of this text were originally said to indicate a third century date, though on historical grounds such an early date seems unlikely [216]. Dedications and even cults to Roma could have been employed by Greek cities in the last decades of the third century; the growing power of Rome was evident to the politically perceptive, and the priority of Smyrna in honoring Roma perhaps referred to the temple rather than a cult or festival. Yet Chios could hardly have tried to mediate the war between Philip and the Roman-Aetolian alliance in 207 with a cult and festival to Roma already established on the island. We have seen that many cults and festivals of Roma were established in the years just after Magnesia and Apamea. If we place the cult on Chios in the same period, some interesting observations can be made about this inscription. It records a dedication to Roma (25: ἀνάθημα τῇ Ῥώμῃ) and there are several other references to Romans and even to a celebration of the foundation of Rome. In this light the phrase κατὰ τὸμ πολεμὸν ἐπιφανείας recalls the dedication of a πανήγυρις to θεὰ Ῥώμη Ἐπιφανής by the Lycian League

---

[211] 218: Polybius 5, 24, 11; 5, 28, 1; 5, 100, 9. 207: Polybius 11, 4, 1.

[212] Polybius 16, 2ff. HOLLEAUX *Études* IV 225 n. 4, 226f. denies that Philip took Chios as is reported in Appian *Mac.* 4, 1.

[213] Livy 37, 14, 2.

[214] Polybius 21, 46, 6; Livy 38, 39, 11.

[215] KONTOLEON Πρακτικά 1953 (1956) 270–271; KONTOLEON *Akte IV. Inter. Kong. für Gr. und Lat. Epigraphik* (Vienna, 1964) 192f. Comments made on the sections published: J. & L. ROBERT *BE* 1958 #384; FORREST in *SEG* XVI(1959) #486; WALBANK *JRS* 53 (1963) 3; J. & L. ROBERT *BE* 1965 #305.

[216] Letter forms: KONTOLEON Πρακτικά 271: first half or middle of the 3rd century BC; FORREST: late third century. Historical criteria: WALBANK and ROBERT (*apud* WALBANK); KONTOLEON *Akte* 196: after defeat of Antiochus.

immediately following the defeat of Antiochus at Magnesia [217]. The epithet recalls Rome's spectacular first appearance in Asia. At Chios, as in Lycia, there was also a πανήγυρις (6–7; 15) which was dedicated perhaps to thank the Romans for their intervention and liberality (βούλεσθαι χάριν ἀποδιδό[ναι]) and therefore assigned to Roma (5: [τῇ Ῥώ]μῃ μετὰ τὰ Θεοφάνια πομπῆς). Perhaps the Θεοφάνια which appear later in conjunction with Romaia originated here as a celebration of the ἐπιφάνεια of Roman power in the East [218]. Admittedly much of this is conjecture. All that is certain is that there was a dedication to Roma on Chios at a very early date, probably soon after Magnesia. A few later texts attest the Romaia on Chios, but there is no mention of a priest or cult in the epigraphical material [219].

Samos — Roma appears in numerous inscriptions from Samos, but nearly all date from the Augustan era. These are connected with the temple of Roma and Augustus established on Samos by 6 BC: dedications, mentions of the temple, statue bases and the dedicatory text on the architrave of the temple itself [220]. There is no evidence of a priesthood, and no conclusive evidence of devotion to Roma during the Republic [221]. However, the treaty between Samos and Antiochia-ad-

---

[217] I am grateful to Professor N. M. KONTOLEON for permission to mention this phrase, and a few other words, which are as yet unpublished. For the Lycian festival, cf. *SEG* XVIII 570 = *JHS* 68 (1948) 46 #11 and pp. 37f. above.

[218] Nothing is known of the origin of the Theophania and the suggestion that they might have been dedicated to Mithridates is effectively rebutted by ROBERT *BCH* 59 (1935) 464: a festival to Mithridates could never have been linked with Romaia. The Theophania Romaia may not be a late amalgamation of separate festivals; both titles may have been applied to a single festival from its foundation with Theophania descriptive of the circumstances of Rome's spectacular appearance in the East. Theophania appears in conjunction with Roma or Romaia only in this text and in *IGRR* IV 950. There is also mention of Theophania in ROBERT *EEP* 126f. #3 and *Syll.* 1064; [Ρωμ]αῖα in *SEG* XV 532 (restoration approved by J. & L. ROBERT *BE* 1956 #213). On Theophania, both NILSSON *Griechische Feste* (Leipzig, 1906) 472 and PFISTER *RE* V A 2133 are unhelpful.

[219] *SEG* XV 532 with discussion by ROBERT *BE* 1956 #213.

[220] Dedications: *IGRR* IV 977; 994 (restored by CURTIUS *MDAI(A)* 49 (1924) 47); and *IGRR* IV 971 + 978 (joined by PREUNER *MDAI(A)* 49 (1924) 44. Temple: *MDAI(A)* 75 (1960) 71 #1 B 15; 82 #2 (as restored by DUNST: [ναὸν τῆς θεᾶς] Ῥώμης. Statue bases: *MDAI(A)* 75 (1960) 83 n.42. Other statue bases from the temple of Roma and Augustus will be published by Dr. GÜNTER DUNST of Munich. Architrave of the temple: *IGRR* IV 975. I am grateful to Dr. DUNST for his view that this inscription belonged on the architrave of the temple, and for his opinions on the other texts listed above which he has kindly communicated to me.

[221] SCHEDE *MDAI(A)* 44 (1919) 34 #19 is the base of a statuary group of Cicero and his brother. There is room on the pedestal for another, smaller figure between them. The editor SCHEDE says "wird man an eine, vielleicht sitzende, Dea Roma denken müssen". He is relying on KORNEMANN's statement (*Klio* 1

Mæandrum of the early second century BC refers to a cult of Roma at Antiochia to which the Samians respond thus: ὅπως [δὲ οὖν πᾶσιν ἐμ]φανῆ ποιῶμεν ἣν ἔχομεν εὔνοιαν δι[ὰ] παντὸς πρὸς Ἀντιοχεῖς τ[οὺς πρὸς τῶι Μ]αιάνδρωι συγγενεῖς καὶ φίλους καὶ εὔ[ν]ους καὶ ἰσοπολίτας καὶ συμ[μάχους ὑπάρ]χοντας ἡμῶν, εὐχαρίστως δὲ διακειμένους καὶ πρὸς Ῥωμαίους τ[οὺς κοινοὺς] εὐεργέτας πάντων [222]. HABICHT has correctly pointed out that Rome stands behind this treaty [223]. It would then be strange for Samos not to have established a cult of Roma when other cities had already done so.

Moreover, Samos had much for which to thank Rome. The island was taken by Philip in 201 and received her freedom after his defeat at Cynoscephalae [224]. In the following years, when Samos and Priene revived their ancient quarrel over the Samian Peraea, the Rhodians arbitrated the conflict and decided in favor of Priene [225]. During the war with Antiochus the Samians provided a major naval base for the Romans and, after the king's defeat, Manlius Vulso reversed the Rhodian verdict and returned the Peraea to Samos [226]. So the Samians, who had of course retained their freedom at Apamea, had every reason to feel grateful to the Ῥωμαίους τοὺς κοινοὺς εὐεργέτας. This was an opportune time to establish a cult of Roma. The decree cited above implies as much [227]. They remained loyal to Rome, provided ships against Perseus, and resisted Aristonicus before being overwhelmed by him [228]. The city had been formally enrolled as a friend and ally of Rome in the second century, and was a stopping place for the greatest names in Roman history: Verres outraged the Samians by robbing the temple of Hera, and later Antony took away three famous statues by Myron; but Pompey and Julius Caesar favored the Samians, and

---

(1901) 94f.) that proconsuls and governors were deified in conjunction with Roma. But there is no evidence that the Samians "deified" Cicero; they simply erected statues to honor him and his family. There is no reason to place Roma in this group. For a detailed study of the monument, cf. DORNER-GRUBEN *MDAI(A)* 68 (1953) 63ff.

[222] HABICHT *MDAI(A)* 72 (1957) 242f. #65. See pp. 130ff. below.

[223] *Ibid.* 247; ROBERT *CRAI* (1969) 61.

[224] Polybius 3, 2, 8; 16, 2, 4; Appian *Mac.* 4, 1 (in an unreliable passage); Livy 31, 31, 4. Also see MAGIE *RRAM* 944 n.41; WALBANK II 505–506. On Rhodian protection from Antiochus: Livy 33, 20, 10.

[225] *Syll.* 599.

[226] Aid to Rome: Livy 37, 18, 9. Manlius Vulso and Peraea: *Syll.* 688 (*RDGE* 10); *RDGE* p. 56f.

[227] Freedom after Apamea: MAGIE *RRAM* 108; HABICHT *MDAI(A)* 72 (1957) 241; BIKERMANN *REG* 50 (1937) 239. The Samians' dealings with Manlius Vulso attest to their freedom. BÜRCHNER *RE* I A 2217 believes Samos was given to Eumenes at Apamea, but he adduces no evidence to support this assertion.

[228] Ships against Perseus: Livy 42, 56, 6. Resistence to Aristonicus: Florus 1, 35, 4.

Augustus brought Myron's statues back from Alexandria and restored two of them, Athena and Heracles, to the Heraeum (though he sent the statue of Zeus to the Capitol)[229].

Delos — Delos profited enormously from Roman intervention in the Greek world even if the native Delians did not. The Romans chose Delos to replace Rhodes as the principal trading depot of the Aegean. Quite appropriately, the cult of Roma flourished there. It is impossible to determine whether the worship of Roma already existed at Delos in its last period of independence after being freed from Philip in 197, or whether the cult came to the island with the Athenians in 167. To understand the presence of Roma on Delos, we must examine the history of the island in some detail.

HOMOLLE's ingenious reconstruction of Delian history in the years 197–167 was put forth nearly ninety years ago and, though it involves considerable speculation, no more convincing version has yet been proposed[230]. More recent writers have hardly discussed the question of Rome's relations with Delos between the wars with Philip and his son Perseus[231]. In brief, HOMOLLE's reconstruction is as follows.

Since the Delians had been sympathetic to Philip during the Second Macedonian War, the Romans had at first decided to grant the request of their Athenian allies that the island be "returned" to them[232]. But the Delians shrewdly submitted themselves to the Romans and thereby managed to retain their freedom and achieve a treaty of friendship (197). In the following years the Delians revived their traditional connections with Syria, receiving gifts from Antiochus III and voting honors to him and his wife (197)[233]. However once it became clear that Rome and Antiochus were enemies, Delos renewed her friendship with Rome (193). Subsequently Roman commanders in the East annually visited the island and made offerings there (192–189)[234]. Roman and Italian businessmen appeared on Delos throughout the 180s and

---

[229] Samos as "friend and ally": *Syll.* 688 (= *RDGE* 10B); Verres: Cicero *In Verrem* II 1, 19; Antony: Strabo 14, 1, 14; Pompey: *Syll.* 749; Julius Caesar: PREUNER *MDAI(A)* 49 (1924) 44; Augustus: Strabo 14, 1, 14.

[230] *BCH* 8 (1884) 84–92. ROUSSEL *Délos Colonie Athénienne* 3 n. 4 and SCHOEFFER *De Deli Insulae Rebus* in *Berliner Studien* 9 (1889) 106, 109 both express vague doubts, but finally seem to accept HOMOLLE's reconstruction.

[231] ROSTOVTZEFF *SEHHW*; BADIAN *FC*; WILL.

[232] Livy 33, 30, 10–11: adicit Antias Valerius ... Atheniensibus insulas datas Parum, Imbrum, Delum, Scyrum. HOMOLLE attempts to explain the error of Antias by suggesting that the Senate made the decision recorded by the annalist, but revoked it after the Delians submitted. I find this wholly unconvincing. BRISCOE *Livy* 308 correctly rejects the version of Antias.

[233] Presents: *ID* 396 B 49; BRUNEAU 573–583. Honors to the Seleucids: *ID* 399 A 48–49.

[234] *IG* XI 4, 756; *ID* 442 B 103–104.

Roman influence increased[235]. Finally the growing hostility between Rome and Macedon forced the Delians to choose between them, a choice they tried to avoid. They hesitated and temporized by honoring Roman leaders as well as Perseus and his family[236]. During the war both fleets operated in Delian waters and both entered the port of the sacred island[237]. After Pydna, Roman enmity turned against the Delians (just as it turned against Rhodes): they were handed over to their traditional enemies, the Athenians.

So HOMOLLE. My principal objection is to his treatment of 197: restoration of Delos to Athens swiftly followed by a treaty of friendship of 197 (renewed in 193). The donation to Athens rests precariously on an annalistic source; the treaty remains unproven[238]. Rather, the Delians simply desired to remain on good terms with Rome as well as with Syria and Macedon. But the Delians encountered the same difficulties as Rhodes: neutrality, whether for commercial or religious reasons, would not be tolerated by Rome. Significantly, the Rhodians had considerable influence at Delos at this time[239]. Perhaps their influence strengthened the Delians' resolve to remain neutral, for the Delians may have foolishly believed that they were safe enough in following the lead of Rome's oldest and most powerful Aegean ally. Bitter lessons were learned at the Romans' school. The Delians suffered a fate even worse than the Rhodians—they were handed over to Athens and subsequently expelled from their homeland. They would have found little consolation in the fact that the Romans were not motivated by greed and gained small profit from their expulsion, only

---

[235] HOMOLLE 88–89; HATZFELD *Les Trafiquants Italiens dans l'Orient Hellénique* (Paris, 1919) 28.

[236] L. Hortensius (praetor 170): *ID* 461 A a 83; Laodice: *IG* XI 4, 1074.

[237] Livy 44, 29, 1.

[238] On the annalist's version, see n. 232 above; for the "renewal" the evidence is *IG* XI 4, 756: Telemnestos, the son of Aristeides, proposes to send envoys to Rome to "renew the friendship"—τὴν φιλίαν ἀνανεω[σομένους]. I would raise the following points:
1) the meaning of ἀνανεοῦσθαι. See ROBERT *Hellenica* I 96 n.5; *RDGE* p. 98.
2) φιλίαν—this can, like *amicitia*, mean little more than diplomatic recognition (BADIAN *FC* 44 n. 3). I find it difficult to believe that the Romans would have offered a treaty to Delos in 197 (after the island's support for Philip) or in 193.
3) I consider the date of this text given by HOMOLLE—193—to be far from proven. He dates it largely on the basis of letter forms. The stemma of Telemnestos is given at *IG* XI 4, 751 and it shows that a considerable range of dates is possible.

Though none of these objections positively refutes HOMOLLE's reconstruction, taken together they lead me to doubt the existence of HOMOLLE's "traité d'amitié" of 197.

[239] ROSTOVTZEFF *SEHHW* 692.

revenge. The Delians had ample time to reflect on that during their exile in Achaea [240].

Though the Delians suffered as the Rhodians did for their neutrality in the war with Perseus, Delos had differed from Rhodes in her relations with the great powers. Whereas the Rhodian republic, fiercely proud of her political independence, resisted the trend towards sycophancy, flattery and the deification of rulers, the Delians did not. They only wanted to preserve their traditional immunity and generously bestowed divine honors on all—on Syrians, Macedonians and Romans alike. Though there is no evidence for the cult of Roma at Delos before the Athenian occupation, it is difficult to believe that islanders so free with honors would have neglected the preeminent power. In fact, there was a dedication of gold crowns to the Demos of the Romans and the Senate in 170 which surely manifests Delian uneasiness at the prospect of a Roman victory [241].

An inscription from the first year of Athenian domination (167/166) records the celebration of Romaia on Delos [242]. In fact, several Romaia may have been celebrated at different times of the year [243]. The festival became quite important on the island, and a large number of ἱεροποιοί were assigned to administer it [244]. However, it is uncertain whether this festival was first established during the period of Delian freedom, or after the arrival of the Athenian cleruchy when the cult of Hestia, Demos and Roma was founded [245]. This cult incorporated the two new masters of Delos into the traditional cult of Hestia in the prytaneum. Small chapels of the Demos (of the Athenians) and Roma were apparently added to the prytaneum [246].

Just as the Romans took over the gods of a conquered people during their early expansion in Italy, so Roman religious imperialism continued in the East. But there was a difference. Rather than taking the

---

[240] Italians and foreigners, not Romans, profited: BADIAN *FC* 101 n.1; BADIAN *Imperialism* 17f.; ROSTOVTZEFF *SEHHW* 788; HOLLEAUX *Rome* 88 n.4; HATZFELD *op. cit.* 372. Delians in Achaea: Polybius 32, 7.

[241] *ID* 465.

[242] *ID* 1950.

[243] In ID 2596, the Romaia are specified as Ῥωμαῖα τὰ τ[οῦ Ἑκα]τομ[β]αιῶνος, as though to distinguish them from other Romaia on Delos. PLASSART *BCH* 36 (1912) 399 n.3 sees more than one Romaia; BRUNEAU 445 is inconclusive. Multiple Romaia seem likely at Delos, since other festivals were also duplicated there; see p. 167 below.

[244] *ID* 2596.

[245] *ID* 1877 (129/8 BC); *ID* 2605 (158/7 BC). In a later Athenian text, there are several references to a simple priest of Roma at Delos (*IG* II² 2336). Whether this is the same priesthood mentioned earlier, or another one, is impossible to determine.

[246] ROUSSEL *DCA* 222; BRUNEAU 444; VALLOIS *AHD* I 174; see p. 136 below.

gods of an Eastern subject people to Rome, Roma invaded their sanctuaries. A marble altar to Roma appeared in the private sanctuary of the Egyptian gods at Delos—to acknowledge the kindness of the Senate and the Roman people in permitting the devotees of Sarapis to continue their cult [247]. A silver crown dedicated to Roma once reposed in the temple to Apollo where, ROUSSEL suggests, there may also have been a statue of the goddess [248]. And a fragment of a large marble table of uncertain provenance dedicated to Athena Nike and the Demos of the Romans has been found on Delos [249].

The collegia provide most striking examples of Roma's acceptance into pre-existing cults. A base in the agora of the Competaliasts records their dedication of a statue to Roma [250]. Though this college was founded by Italians, it had passed more and more into the hands of freedmen and slaves, largely oriental in origin [251]. Although Roman citizens would not have been involved in a cult to Roma at this date, the Italian members of the Competaliasts had not yet received Roman citizenship [252]. In 94, a statue of Roma was placed beside one of Fides (98/7) in a chapel built long before by a magistrate of the collegium [253].

The Koinon of the Poseidoniasts of Berytus also honored Roma. This private collegium set up a statue of Roma about the end of the second century BC [254]. This statue, which still stands on Delos [255], was added to the existing cella, and an altar to Roma was placed before it [256]. The traders of this Koinon clearly saw the advantages of Roman favor—ironically history records only the ill consequences brought on the college by this cult. In 88 the Pontic armies of Mithridates reached

---

[247] *ID* 2484; ROUSSEL *DCA* 223; BRUNEAU 446.
[248] *ID* 1450 A 119; ROUSSEL *DCA* 222 n. 7 (his date of 149 is a misprint for 140/139); BRUNEAU 445.
[249] *ID* 1807.
[250] *ID* 1763.
[251] ROUSSEL *DCA* 223; FERGUSON *HA* 400f.; FERGUSON *AHR* 18 (1912–13) 40f.; BRUNEAU 615f.
[252] On the prohibition of Romans from participation in the cult of Roma, see FERGUSON *HA* 383 n. 1; 400f.; *AHR* 18 (1912–13) 39f. A cult of Roma does not appear in Rome until the reign of Hadrian.
[253] Dates: *ID* 1763; *ID* 1761; BRUNEAU 617; FERGUSON *HA* 401; 434. On the connection of Roma and Fides-πίστις, see pp. 131ff.
[254] REINACH *BCH* 7 (1883) 465–6 dates it to the first century BC; PICARD *BCH* 44 (1920) 289 n. 1 and *EAD* VI 61f. agrees with that date and traces the type to a statue of Cleopatra of about 140 BC, which was found on Delos. VERMEULE *Goddess Roma* 103 #14A places the statue in 90 BC and provides a bibliography. More recently, scholars have rightly emphasized that the date of the introduction of the cult cannot be determined from the statue's date and remains unknown: BRUNEAU 446; 627–628; MARCADÉ 128–133.
[255] See p. 145f. below.
[256] PICARD *EAD* VI 62. Altar: *ID* 1779.

Delos, inflicted particularly heavy damage on the establishment of the Poseidoniasts, and overturned the statue [257]. Its head was probably destroyed at that time.

So at Delos Roma was accepted into several pre-existing cults; both the public cults of Hestia and Apollo and the private worship of the Competaliasts, the Poseidoniasts, and the worshippers of Sarapis. At Delos, as at Athens, the Athenians were devoted to their new protectress [258].

Mytilene on Lesbos — The evidence for devotion to Roma at Mytilene is late: the Civil War period and the early Empire. The earliest mention of Roma is in a text which decreed honors to Julius Caesar and Ῥώμη Νικηφόρος in 45 BC [259]. Otherwise only two testimonia for Roma on Lesbos remain. Diophenes, whose father Potamon was the leader of the embassy bearing honors to Julius Caesar in 45, served as high priest of Roma and Augustus late in the first century BC. He must have served at the temple where sacrifices were decreed by the Mytileneans soon after 27 BC [260]. There is also a dedication to Roma and Tiberius [261]. But even though there is no evidence for a cult of Roma at Mytilene before 45, we know that the city was on excellent terms with Rome throughout the second century. Ships were furnished for the war with Antiochus, and Mytilene retained its freedom after the war [262]. In 167 Rome destroyed the town of Antissa on Lesbos which had welcomed the Macedonian fleet into port, but the other cities of the Lesbian koinon—Mytilene, Methymna and Eresus—were not involved [263]. The most likely occasions for the establishment of the cult of Roma at Mytilene were 188 (Apamea) or 62 (restoration of its independence by Pompey) [264]. The hymn of Melinno to Roma was written in an artificial

---

[257] DURRBACH *Choix d'Inscriptions de Délos* (Paris, 1921) 199; PICARD *BCH* 44 (1920) 304.

[258] *IG* II² 2336 lists priests with Athenian names, but they are priests on Delos. See JUDEICH 94 n. 7.

[259] *IG* XII 2, 25; also *IG* XII 2, 26 (+ *IG* XII Suppl. ad 2, 26).

[260] Diophanes: *IG* XII 2, 656. Potamon is mentioned first among the members of the embassy: *IG* XII 2, 35 b 14. Decree: *IGR* IV 39.

[261] *IG* XII 2, Suppl. 9 (+ Addenda ad 9 on p. 208) = WILAMOWITZ-MÖLLENDORFF and HILLER VON GAERTRINGEN *MDAI(A)* 30 (1905) 142 #2: Ῥώμα καὶ Τε[βερίω Καίσαρι]. For such a spelling of Tiberius, see *IG* II² 3243. Worship of Tiberius: *IG* XII 2, 205; temple of Roma and Augustus: O'BRIEN-MOORE *YCS* 8 (1942) 34.

[262] Livy 37, 12, 5; 37, 21, 6. On freedom, see CICHORIUS *Rom und Mitylene* (Leipzig, 1888) 4; BIKERMAN *REG* 50 (1937) 239.

[263] Livy 45, 31, 14–15. On the Lesbian Koinon, see ACCAME *RFIC* 73 (1946) 104f. Refugees from Antissa were sent to Methymna, which was not affected. Though the Koinon implied a common military policy (*IG* XI 4, 1064), Livy makes it clear that the offence was the fault of Antissa alone.

[264] Plutarch *Pompey* 42. The Mytileneans remained loyal to Pompey, sheltered his family and offered to shelter him even after Pharsalus (*Pompey* 74).

Lesbian dialect, but I think it would be dangerous to link a poem of such contrived literary diction directly to Lesbos[265]. Unfortunately, the evidence permits no firm conclusions on the origin of the cult of Roma at Mytilene.

Melos — Cults of Roma on other Aegean islands are even more difficult to discuss fruitfully. Often only a single mention of Roma survives, and the extremely sketchy history of many of these islands provides no illuminating political context. So it is with Melos. A simple Doric text records the erection of a bronze statue of Roma[266]:

Ὁ δᾶμος ὁ Μαλίων ἐτίμασεν
τὰν Ῥώμαν εἰκόνι χαλκέαι
καὶ στεφάνωι χρυσέωι
ἀρετᾶς ἕνεκεν καὶ εὐερ
γεσίας τᾶς εἰς αὐτόν.

The text and statue should be dated to about the middle of the second century BC, sometime after the sculptor, Polyanthes of Cyrene, had been working on Delos (c. 160 BC)[267]. But far too little is known of Melian history in the late Hellenistic age to permit any hypotheses on a cult of Roma there.

Astypalaea — An inscription that was set up on the altar of Roma at Astypalaea records the treaty between that island and Rome in 105 BC[268]. There are several difficulties with this text. First, it reads πρὸς τῷ βωμῷ . . . τῆς Ῥώμης. Little can be done with the lacuna; Roma was probably joined with the cult of a popular local divinity, as was common elesewhere[269]. Secondly, the verb ἀνανεοῦσθαι may (or may not) mean "renew". There is a long and learned controversy on this point, but I would accept "renew" on historical grounds: 105 seems a very odd time to conclude a new treaty[270]. There is not much evidence for the history of Astypalaea in the second century. The island had been Ptolemaic in the third century, but was not part of the League of the Islanders[271]. There is no trace of Rhodian domination, so it was

---

[265] For my treatment of this poem, see pp. 122f. FORTE 135 sees the liberation of Lesbos by Pompey in the 60's as appropriate inspiration for the poem; I find such a late date most implausible.

[266] *IG* XII 3, 1097.

[267] See p. 151f. below.

[268] *IG* XII 3, 173 (= *RDGE* 16).

[269] *RDGE* 16; BOECKH (*CIG* 2485) long ago suggested Zeus, which seems appropriate to an altar with a treaty placed on it.

[270] *RDGE* p. 98; TÄUBLER *Imperium Romanum* (Berlin, 1913) 124f.; ROBERT *Hellenica* I 96 n. 5.

[271] FRASER-BEAN 157; OBERHUMMER *RE* II 1874.

probably free throughout the second century[272]. Though the cult of Roma may have existed earlier, the treaty is from the latter part of the century[273]. In any event, there was an altar of Roma in an honored place in the temple of Athena and Asclepius in the second century.

Iulis on Ceos — In the first century BC, the citizens of Iulis dedicated a statue to θεὰ Ῥώμη Σωτείρα[274]. Ceos, though one of the Cyclades closest to Attica, had belonged to the Ptolemaic League and later to the League of the Islanders[275]. It was probably held by Macedon around 200 and then freed by Rhodes who may have controlled it with so many other islands until 167[276]. After that time it was almost certainly under Athenian influence. The cult of Roma may stem from 167, or from the aftermath of the Mithridatic Wars.

Ios — Ios was also a former member of the Ptolemaic League which later entered into alliance with Rhodes after the decline of Ptolemaic power in the Aegean[277]. Almost nothing else is known of the island's history in the second and first centuries BC. In the last quarter of the first century, Ios set up a simple dedication to Roma and Augustus[278].

Thasos — A far more elaborate monument to Roma and Augustus was erected near the forum of the north Aegean island of Thasos. An inscription from Thasos records the dedication of a new marble pavement in the temple of Roma and Augustus[279]. The walls of this temple, now placed by scholars on the northeast side of the Agora, were filled with official documents and local correspondence with the emperor[280].

Thasos was freed from Macedonian rule by Rome in 196, and the islanders remained loyal—even holding out against Mithridates' siege. In 80, Sulla and the Senate rewarded Thasos handsomely: the city not only regained but increased its territory on the mainland. A cult of Roma might have been established during the second century, or else after the bounty of 80 BC[281].

---

[272] FRASER-BEAN 138 n. 2: autonomous coinage and no trace of Rhodian domination. *IG* XII 3, 171 records thanks from the Ephesians to the Astypalaeans for help against pirates in the late second century.
[273] FRASER-BEAN 125 n. 1.
[274] *IG* XII 5, 622: ὁ δῆμος ὁ Ἰουλιητῶν θεᾶι [Ῥώ]μηι Σωτείραι.
[275] FRASER-BEAN 156.
[276] FRASER-BEAN 157, 159; BUERCHNER *RE* XI 189. Polybius 16, 26, 10; Livy 31, 15, 8; *SEG* XIV 544. It seems likely that Rhodes lost control of the island league in 167: FRASER-BEAN 171f.
[277] FRASER-BEAN 156f.; *CAH* VIII 625; *IG* XII 5, 8; Livy 31, 15, 8.
[278] *IG* XII 5, 1013.
[279] *IG* XII 8, 380.
[280] FREDRICH *MDAI(A)* 33 (1908) 235; PICARD *BCH* 45 (1921) 105–106; DUNAND-POUILLOUX *Recherches sur l'histoire et les cultes de Thasos* (Paris, 1958) II 59; 60 n. 2.
[281] DUNAND-POUILLOUX *ibid.* II 36–55.

Paros — A fragmentary text from Paros may be concerned with dramatic performances at Romaia—whether at Paros or elsewhere cannot be determined [282]. However the restoration is too uncertain to merit detailed analysis.

Crete — The Cretans could not have greatly endeared themselves to the Romans. They allied themselves with Philip, later supported Mithridates, and nearly always harbored pirates. They beat off M. Antonius in the 70s, but were finally subjugated by Q. Metellus Creticus about 68 [283]. Roma appeared not long after on a coin of Gortyna and later on a coin of Cnossos [284]. There is no reason to believe that a cult of Roma existed on Crete before Rome conquered the island.

VII. Lydia

The empire of the Attalids of Pergamum reached both its zenith and its nadir in the second century BC. The kingdom of Eumenes II was enormously enlarged by the treaty of Apamea which brought most Seleucid territories west of the Halys river under Pergamene control. The numerous cities which were given, or confirmed in, their freedom by the treaty were the more highly Hellenized cities of the coast [285]. No city of Lydia or Phrygia is recorded as free after 188. These vast stretches of Anatolia remained subject to the Attalids until Attalus III died in 133 and bequeathed his dominions to the Roman people. Then much of this area was organized into the new Roman province of Asia.

We must therefore approach the lands of the Attalid empire differently from Ionia, Caria and the islands. Most cities of Lydia, Phrygia and Mysia shared a common fate throughout the second century. Roma is not attested in the Attalid dominions until after 129, and even then appears only infrequently. I have already suggested that cults of Roma in cities under Attalid control would have been unlikely, though not impossible [286]. But we must beware lest the paucity of evidence lead us to *ex silentio* conclusions. Excavation and epigraphical collection are not as advanced in these areas of Anatolia as in Caria, Lycia and Ionia. We must simply record the evidence for Roma that is available.

Evidence for municipal cults of Roma in Lydia, even if late and combined with the cult of emperors, points to some earlier worship of

---

[282] *IG* XII 5, 139: [ὑπ]οκριτα[ὶ ἐνίκησαν τὰ Ῥωμ]αῖα.

[283] Antonius: ORMEROD *Piracy in the Ancient World* (London, 1924) 226–227; Livy *Periocha* 97. Metellus: Appian *Sic.* 6.

[284] HEAD *Historia Numorum* (London, 1911²) 467; *SNG-DEN* 17 #398. If we accept MOMMSEN's reading of *CIL* III 4, there was a *sacerdos divi Augusti et urbis Romae* at Gortyna at the end of the second century AD.

[285] BIKERMAN *REG* 50 (1937) 236–239.

[286] See pp. 57f. above.

Roma during the Republic. The cult, priesthood and festivals of the *Commune Asiæ*, founded so deliberately in 29 BC, were quite different from these municipal cults and will be treated separately below.

Sardes — Several Lydian cities had local priesthoods of Roma in the late Republic. In some cases the priest even served as the eponymous official, most notably in Sardes, the chief city of Lydia [287]. In the mid-second century the eponymous official at Sardes was στεφανηφόρος, but by the beginning of the first century the priest of Roma served this function [288]. As at Ephesus, it seems reasonable to suppose that the priesthood of Roma was established and made eponymous about 129 BC, when Aristonicus had been defeated, Asia had been organized as a province, and Sardes had obtained her freedom. Apart from the honorific decree on the statue base of the priest Iollas, all other mentions of Roma are simply in the titulature of her priests used for purposes of dating [289]. Occasionally a co-eponymous appears: once the priest of Zeus Polieus and once the στεφανηφόρος [290]. But generally the texts simply name the priest of Roma; and even when the title is omitted and merely the name of the priest is given, there can be no doubt of his office [291]. Iteration was not unusual, and one priest seems to have served for thirteen years. Even Mark Antony served a year as priest of Roma at Sardes [292]. The use of this priest as eponymous official continued at least until the reign of Augustus and perhaps later, but there are no texts dated by an eponymous which can securely be placed in the post-Augustan empire [293]. While it is likely that the cult of Roma gave way before the imperial cult, the process does not seem to have been as universal or as rapid as scholars once asserted [294].

---

[287] On eponymous officials, see p. 183ff. below.

[288] *Sardis* 21 (150 BC); *OGIS* 437 line 91 (= *Pergamum* 268 E line 36). On the date of the latter text: ROBERT *REA* 62 (1960) 343 n.4; *RDGE* p. 259.

[289] Statue base: *Sardis* 27.

[290] Zeus: *OGIS* 437; *Sardis* 93 where the priest of Roma and the στεφανηφόρος is the same man. It is therefore difficult to say whether there were really two eponymous magistrates or whether the old title was simply added on occasion to the priest of Roma.

[291] Roma is mentioned in *Sardis* 93; 112; 113; 114; 115 (restored, but certain). No title is given for the eponymous magistrate in *Sardis* 116; 117; 118; 120-127; 129; 130; 132—all of whom Buckler-Robinson *AJA* 18 (1914) 47 accept as priests of Roma. *Sardis* 119 gives a female eponymous magistrate; possibly a στεφανηφόρος before 133 or a priestess of Roma after that date. BUCKLER-ROBINSON ad *Sardis* 119 prefer the latter, but no other priestess of Roma is known outside the imperial cult; see p. 181f. below.

[292] Iteration: *Sardis* 127; Antony as eponymous: *Sardis* 129.

[293] A priest with the name of Julius (*Sardis* 114) could hardly have served before the latter part of the first century BC.

[294] BUCKLER-ROBINSON *Sardis* p. 51; 110; 111 continuously assert that the priest of Roma could not have been eponymous after the late first century BC. However, they provide no support save another assertion (*AJA* 17 (1913) 44):

Roma continued to appear on the imperial coins issued at Sardes, identified by the legend θεὰ Ῥώμη²⁹⁵.

Thyatira — The main road north from Sardes crosses the river Hermus and its wide valley before reaching Thyatira. It was the central road junction in northern Lydia at the mid-point of the Sardes-Pergamum highway, with a major road to Magnesia and an important route north to Bithynia. Its geographical position made Thyatira a crossroads of Hellenistic kings. It was ruled by Attalus I, its lands were devastated by Philip in 201, and it fell under the control of Antiochus during the Syrian war²⁹⁶. The city returned to Attalid control after Apamea though it was occasionally invaded, by Prusias of Bithynia in the 150's and of course by Aristonicus²⁹⁷. Sometime after incorporation into the province of Asia, Thyatira established a priesthood of Roma and the priest, who also served as πρύτανις, is honored in a decree of the city²⁹⁸. A priest of Roma also appears in a text of the Augustan period as one of the eponymous officials of the city²⁹⁹. This text also records the dedication of an altar to the goddess Roma, to Augustus and to the Demos. Here the priesthood of Roma remained eponymous and was not incorporated into the imperial cult at a time when Roma and Augustus were already honored together. Roma also appears on coins of Thyatira of the second century AD identified by the legend θεὰν Ῥώμην³⁰⁰.

Apollonis — About ten miles west of Thyatira on the road to Pergamum lies Apollonis. Here too the priest of Roma appears as eponymous official on a text from the very beginning of the Augustan era³⁰¹. The priest also bears the title of στεφανηφόρος, perhaps a remnant from the earlier eponymous magistrate as at Sardes.

"we are bound to assume that in so important a city as Sardes the cult of Roma alone ceased soon after 27 BC" owing to the introduction of the cult of Roma and Augustus. They admit examples to the contrary, but ascribe them to remote areas: Phrygia, Pisidia, Cyprus, Thrace. Their generalization on this matter does not bear scrutiny; see below pp. 195ff.

²⁹⁵ *BMC Lydia* 246 #77; 249 #94.

²⁹⁶ Attalid possession: ROBERT *Villes* 34f. Philip's invasion: Polybius 16, 1, 7; HOLLEAUX *Études* IV 212; 248f. Antiochus: MAGIE *RRAM* 775 n. 81; ROBERT *Villes* 34.

²⁹⁷ Prusias: Polybius 32, 15, 10. Aristonicus: Strabo 14, 1, 38.

²⁹⁸ *IGR* IV 1228.

²⁹⁹ *IGR* IV 1304 which should be classed among inscriptions of Thyatira (ROBERT *Hellenica* VI 71).

³⁰⁰ *BMC Lydia* 294 #18. For other coins, see n. 309.

³⁰¹ *SEG* XIX 710 = HERRMANN *Denkschr. Österr. Akad.* 77 (1959) #6. The attribution to Apollonis has been accepted by ROBERT *REA* 62 (1960) 344 n. 1. HERRMANN proposes that στεφανηφορούσης should be restored at the beginning of his text #3 (= *SEG* XIX 709) and suggests that this lady may also have been priestess of Roma. But this remains conjecture.

Nysa — Just north of the Maeander, the city of Nysa geographically belongs to Caria though it must have been given to Eumenes after Apamea. It was easier for the Romans, as it is for us, to treat the Maeander as the northern boundary of Caria—however arbitrary that division really is.

There is a text from Nysa concerning the restoration of sacred books which can be dated very precisely to 1 BC [302]. In the preamble we are given the names of the priest of Roma and Augustus, the στεφανηφόρος, the Roman consuls, the γραμματεύς of the city, as well as some other officials. All these are obviously not eponymous officials at Nysa, but the listing of the priest of Roma and Augustus and the στεφανηφόρος before the Roman consuls indicates that this pair were the local eponymous officials. Since the priest of Roma and the στεφανηφόρος are linked elsewhere in Lydia for the same purpose, it is likely that they served the same function at Nysa. Eventually Augustus was simply added to the existing cult of Roma.

Hierocaesarea — Not far to the southwest of Thyatira was Hiera Kome, once a small settlement around a sanctuary of the Persian goddess and later an important city whose name was changed by Augustus to Hierocaesarea. The development of sanctuaries into commercial centers was common in Anatolia. The evidence for the priesthood of Roma is a simple dedication to Apollo set up by one Athenodorus who is identified as a former priest of Roma [303]. That Athenodorus' father is identified in the text as Mithrês, a Persian name, testifies to the city's sacred past [304]. Roma appears on the coinage of Hierocaesarea and is identified by the legend θεὰ Ῥώμη [305].

Tripolis — At the opposite corner of Lydia, far to the southeast where the Lycus joins the Maeander lies the city of Tripolis. Here the terms "Lydia" and "Phrygia" become quite arbitrary. A truncated text from Tripolis records an Apollonios who has served as στεφανηφόρος and also as priest of Roma [306]. It is unclear whether, as in Apollonis, these offices were joined or whether the priest of Roma was an eponymous official. The bust of Roma also appears on the coins of Tripolis with the legend θεὰ Ῥώμη [307].

Though cults of Roma are only attested in a handful of Lydian cities, her priests appear to have played an important local role and the

---

[302] *Syll.* 781. Another Carian city north of the Maeander was Tralles, where Roma appears only in a very dubious restoration: STERRETT *MDAI(A)* 8 (1883) 326 #9.
[303] *IGR* IV 1309.
[304] ROBERT *Hellenica* VI 29.
[305] IMHOOF-BLUMER *KM* I 173 #3.
[306] *MAMA* VI 53.
[307] *BMC Lydia* 364 #8; 367 #25; 373 #54.

priest is often eponymous. These similarities support the assumption that the cults were founded about the same time under similar circumstances. The obvious *termini* are 133 BC (Bequest of Attalus) and 98 or 94 BC (treaty dated by eponymous priests of Roma at Ephesus and Sardes). Within these limits, the most obvious time for widespread foundation of cults of Roma would be 129 or very soon after: the defeat of Aristonicus (who had little support among the Greek or Hellenized cities) and the organization of the Roman province. This would have been the psychologically appropriate moment for the priests of Roma to replace, or at least be joined with, the στεφανηφόρος as eponymous throughout Lydia[308].

There are numerous coins minted in Lydia during the Empire which portray the goddess Roma, but these alone cannot be taken to prove the existence of actual cults and priesthoods during the Republic[309].

VIII. Phrygia

Evidence for the worship of Roma in Phrygia is even sparser. The cult of the goddess does not seem to have penetrated into the highlands of Phrygia until the very end of the Republic. A few priesthoods are attested and some dedications suggest the presence of cults of Roma. But vast stretches of Phrygia remained unhellenized until long after Roman power came to Asia. The remains from Phrygia show even less cohesion than the Lydian evidence and, until further discoveries are made, one can only set forth what little evidence exists.

Apamea — The priest of Roma, who was also γραμματεύς, was here honored by the city and by the Roman residents[310]. RAMSAY has claimed that a temple of Roma existed at Apamea on the rather flimsy grounds that since a Roman calendar is known to have been set up in the city, a temple of Roma would be the appropriate home for such a text[311]. But neither priesthood of Roma nor a Roman calendar necessarily implies a temple of Roma—the priest might serve at an

---

[308] See above p. 57. See *RDGE* p. 259 n. 1 for references on the date of *OGIS* 437 (= *RDGE* 47).

[309] Coins portraying the goddess Roma (identified by a legend) were issued by Bagis (*BMC Lydia* 31 #6); Blaundus (*BMC Lydia* 56 #89); Cilbiani Inferiores (ECKHEL *DNV* III 97); Daldis (BABELON *Coll. Wadd.* 4953); Gordus-Julia (*BMC Lydia* 90 #2f.); Hermocapelia (*BMC Lydia* 99 #1f.); Hierocaesarea (IMHOOF-BLUMER *KM* I 173 #3); Mostene (*BMC Lydia* 161 #5); Sardes (*BMC Lydia* 246 #77); Silandus (*BMC Lydia* 278 #1); Stratonicea (*BMC Lydia* 284 #2); Thyatira (*BMC Lydia* 294 #18); Tripolis (*BMC Lydia* 367 #8). Roma also seems to appear on coins of Acrasus, Apollonis, Apollonos-Hieron, Attalia, Hycanis, Maeonia, Nacrasa, Philadelphia, and Sala.

[310] *IGR* IV 793.

[311] *The Cities and Bishoprics of Phrygia* (Oxford, 1895) II 377; 479.

altar of Roma set up in the temenos of another god. There is no evidence for a temple of Roma at Apamea.

Eumenia — The priest of Roma at Eumenia, Epigonos Philopatris, was honored by a dedicatory inscription erected by the city [312]. The text honoring Philopatris can be dated to the reign of Augustus, since an Augustan coin from Eumenia bears the name of the priest [313].

Apollonia — A copy of the *Res Gestae* was set up in Phrygian Apollonia on a monument which supported statues of Augustus, Germanicus, Drusus, Tiberius and Livia [314]. Yet the cult of Roma does not seem to have been immediately assimilated into the imperial cult. The two priests of Roma attested there, Olympichos and Demetrios, belonged to the same powerful family and were probably father and son [315]. Olympichos had served as ambassador to Germanicus, probably when Tiberius' heir had come to the East in 18 AD, and this text should therefore be dated to the Julio-Claudian period [316]. The son, Demetrios, probably served as priest of Roma during the reign of Claudius. The dates are uncertain, but the texts indicate that the cult of Roma in Apollonia survived for a time independent of the imperial cult.

Acmonia — An inscription from Acmonia has been restored to read ἀ[ρχιερέ]ως τῆς πό[λεως] [317]. But the restoration is dubious, and this use of πόλις for Ῥώμη is very rare. Parallels with the use of *urbs* are irrelevant. Roma does appear identified by a legend on the coinage of Acmonia, but that is not sufficient to justify postulating a cult of Roma at Acmonia [318].

Dorylaïum — Far to the north on the river Tembris near Bithynia, a dedication was erected in the first century AD to honor the goddess Roma along with the deified emperors and empresses, the deified Senate and the Roman People [319]. This text also mentions that all these "divinities" were served by a single priest.

This completes the survey of evidence for Roma in Phrygia [320], though several texts from the group on the Capitoline were dedicated by Phrygian cities and so should be mentioned briefly.

---

[312] *IGR* IV 741.

[313] *BMC Phrygia* 216 #36.

[314] *MAMA* IV 143.

[315] *IGR* III 320; *MAMA* IV 142, which gives a stemma of the family.

[316] LATTE *Römische Religionsgeschichte* (Munich, 1960) 312 n. 1 dates it to the reign of Caligula.

[317] RAMSAY *The Social Basis of Roman Power in Asia Minor* (Aberdeen, 1941) 18 #7. On πόλις, cf. n. 504 below.

[318] *BMC Phrygia* 6 #17.

[319] *OGIS* 479. On the date of this text, see BUCKLER *RP* 61 (1935) 187.

[320] Coins portraying Roma (identified by a legend) were issued by Acmonia (*BMC Phrygia* 6 #17); Aezani (*BMC Phrygia* 30 #48–49); Amorium (*BMC Phrygia* 49 #16f.); Cotiaëum (*BMC Phrygia* 158 #3); Hierapolis (*BMC Phrygia*

Laodicea-ad-Lycum — During the Republic a statue of Populus Romanus was set up on the Capitoline at Rome by the citizens of Laodicea on the Lycus river in the extreme southwest corner of Phrygia [321]. The bilingual dedication calls the Demos of the Romans both σωτήρ and εὐεργέτης. Statues of the Demos of the Romans must have been indistinguishable from those of Roma, one of which also stood on the same Capitoline monument. The epithets confirm the similarity of these representations. Laodicea had belonged to Pergamum after Apamea and little else is heard of the city until her citizens surrendered the Roman praetor after a terrible siege by the Mithridatic armies [322]. The statue and dedication in Rome almost certainly imply that a cult of Roma had already been established in Laodicea, and a late second century date would be reasonable—perhaps about 129 when the city, like Sardes and Ephesus, was given her freedom and not included in the new province of Asia [323]. Roma appeared on coins issued at Laodicea during the first three centuries of the Empire [324].

Hierapolis — Another text attributed to the same monument on the Capitoline simply reads: POPULUS IE[RAPOLITANUS ?...] [325]. Though the proposed restoration of Hierapolis, situated only seven miles down the Lycus from Laodicea, is probable enough, little more can be done with this tiny fragment. Some of the texts in this "group" on the Capitoline seem to imply cults of Roma, and Roma does appear on the coinage of Hierapolis, but nothing further can be said [326].

IX. Aeolis, Mysia and the Troad

Cyme — Much of the northwest corner of Asia Minor had become subject to the Attalids in the latter part of the third century. The Aeolian cities were temporarily occupied by Antiochus during the Syrian War, but at Apamea nearly all were returned to Attalid con-

---

232 #33); Laodicea (*BMC Phrygia* 298 #121f.); Synaus (*BMC Phrygia* 387 #1ff.); Synnada (*BMC Phrygia* 395 #20f.); Temenothyrae (Flaviopolis) (*BMC Phrygia* 410 #13f.). Roma also seems to appear on the coinage of Appia and Cadi.

[321] *CIL* I^2 728 (= *CIL* VI 374; *IGUR* 6; *ILLR* 177). On the texts set up on the Capitoline, see Additional Note.

[322] Pergamene influence: MAGIE *RRAM* 127; DES GAGNIERS *Laodicée-du-Lycos* 3. Mithridates' siege: Appian *Mith.* 20.

[323] DEGRASSI *BCAC* 74 (1954) 22 follows Mommsen ad *CIL* I^2 728 in placing it in the post-Sulla era. Moretti *IGUR* 6 agrees. MAGIE *AS* 176 n. 1 finds rather farfetched the suggestion that this text is an acknowledgment of Laodicea's gratitude for Roman forgiveness after their capitulation to Mithridates. He prefers an earlier date, when Laodicea was thanking Rome for some favor. Freedom granted soon after 129 might be such an occasion.

[324] *BMC Phrygia* 298 #121f.

[325] *CIL* I^2 729 (= *ILLR* 178).

[326] *BMC Phrygia* 232 #33.

trol. Among the fortunate few that received their formal independence was Cyme, though freedom did not preclude close ties and perhaps even a treaty with Pergamum [327]. An inscription from Cyme records an eponymous priest of Roma and Augustus between 2 BC and the death of Augustus [328]. This priesthood derived from the earlier eponymous priesthood of Roma found elsewhere in the former dominions of the Attalids. Those priesthoods seem to date from about 129 BC, but there is no reason why the independent city of Cyme could not have had an eponymous priesthood still earlier. Cyme benefited from Rome at Apamea, and three decades later the Senate forced Prusias of Bithynia to make reparations to the city for damages he inflicted while invading Pergamum [329]. There was, therefore, ample reason for the Cymeans to honor Roma in the first half of the second century. However, the lack of evidence to support an early foundation imposes caution. The priesthood is certainly republican, and not likely to have come long after the similar priesthoods in Lydia—i.e., late second century BC.

Assus — The Aeolian city of Assus also honored Roma [330]. This inscription was the base of a statue of Roma set up by the city and the resident Romans in her honor. Assus had been part of the Pergamene kingdom until 133 and, we are told, was free after Sulla's victory over Mithridates. Worship of Roma would be appropriate in Assus after 133 or after 85, but the text does not allow further specification [331].

The goddess Roma, identified by a legend, appears on the coinage of several other cities of Aeolis, Mysia and the Troad [332].

Pergamum — For the Attalid capital of Pergamum there is considerably more evidence. When Attalus III bequeathed his kingdom to the

---

[327] Polybius 21, 46, 4; 33, 13, 8; MAGIE *RRAM* 939 n. 36; HOLLEAUX *Études* V 410; 423.

[328] *IGR* IV 1302. On eponymous priests of Roma, see ROBERT *REG* 46 (1933) 441 n.; also see pp. 183 ff.

[329] Polybius 33, 13, 8.

[330] MERKELBACH *ZPE* 13 (1974) 280 has joined two texts from Assus: (a) LE BAS-WADDINGTON *Voyage Archéologique en Grèce et en Asie Mineure* (Paris, 1847–1870) 1727; (b) *Ibid.* 1034a (= *IGR* IV 250). The new text reads:

ὁ δῆμος καὶ   [οἱ] πραγματευόμενοι Ῥω[μαῖοι]
θεὰ[ν Ῥώ]μην [τ]ὴν εὐεργέτιν τοῦ κόσμ[ου]

CHAPOT *La Province romaine proconsulaire d'Asie* (Paris, 1904) 423 accepted fragment a as evidence for a priest of Roma at Assus.

[331] Freedom of Assus: *OGIS* 444; MAGIE *RRAM* 234; 1119 n. 24. About 150 BC, a citizen of Assus went to Stratonicea in Caria to judge a musical contest in honor of the goddess Roma. Stratonicea sent a crown to the city of Assus in gratitude, and a text recounting this episode is preserved in Assus (*IGR* IV 247).

[332] Perperene: *BMC Mysia* 168 #4; Pitane: *BMC Mysia* 172 #15; Ilium: *BMC Troas, Aeolis, etc.* 60 #27; Myrina: *BMC Troas, Aeolis, etc.* 139 #42; Elaea: BABELON *Coll. Wadd.* #1323.

Roman people, the capital received its freedom in his will[333]. Soon after the defeat of Aristonicus, the Pergamenes concluded a treaty with Rome and the text includes Roma among the deities to be honored with sacrifices[334]. This can be taken as evidence of a cult of Roma at Pergamum[335]. The cult would not be unexpected. Cults of Roma were being established in the former Attalid cities of Ephesus and Sardes in the years after the defeat of Artistonicus, cults whose priests were the eponymous magistrates of their cities[336]. At Pergamum too the priest of Roma may have been one of the two eponymous officials. Originally the πρύτανις was the eponymous magistrate[337], but later texts are dated by the πρύτανις and by a priest—though the full title of the priest is not given in any extant text[338]. However, coins of the imperial period bear legends giving the priest of the imperial cult as the eponymous official[339]. This indicates that the priest of Roma was the unspecified eponymous priest during the Republic, and was later replaced by the priest of Augustus.

Whether or not the priest of Roma was eponymous, the cult certainly existed before the Augustan era since the emperor is absent from the earliest mention of the priesthood. M. Tullius Cratippus, son of the philosopher who was a friend and client of Cicero, was *sacerdos Romae et Salutis*[340]. Whether this was one or two separate priesthoods cannot be said with certainty, though the wording seems to indicate a single office[341]. As elsewhere, the cult was soon linked with the imperial cult, and the son of Cratippus was a priest in this cult during the reign

---

[333] *OGIS* 338. For a full treatment of the evidence for the freedom of Pergamum, see MAGIE *RRAM* 1045 n. 34.

[334] *Syll.* 694. Though found at Elaea, the text surely is Pergamene: MAGIE *ibid.*; ROBERT *EA* 49 n. 3; WILHELM *JÖAI* 17 (1914) 18. Recently FORTE 104 n. 26 again attributes this text to Elaea or Pitane, but without argument.

[335] FABRICIUS *MDAI(A)* 38 (1913) 42. When this text was published, it was the earliest epigraphical evidence for the cult of Roma in Asia. Perhaps the sanctuary of the Attalids was used for the cult of Roma; see BOEHRINGER-KRAUSS *Altertümer von Pergamon* IX (Berlin, 1937) 84.

[336] *OGIS* 437. See pp. 183f.

[337] *Pergamum* 5 (3rd century BC); 251 (2nd century BC). See FRAENKEL in *Pergamum* II p. 207.

[338] *Pergamum* 258 and 323; KOLBE *MDAI(A)* 32 (1907) 432 #282 which ROBERT *REG* 46 (1933) 441 n. takes as evidence for the eponymous priest of Roma at Pergamum.

[339] *Pergamum* II p. 207 which gives reference to MIONNET *Description de Médailles* ... (Paris 1806–1837) Suppl. V 446 #1040.

[340] *CIL* III 399. See O'BRIEN-MOORE "M. Tullius Cratippus, Priest of Rome" *YCS* 8 (1942) 23–49.

[341] O'BRIEN-MOORE *Ibid.* 31 n. 3 comments on the reference to Roma as "Aesculapi filia" in Marianus (*FPR* p. 384). If this was an early genealogical speculation, it may have encouraged the combination of Roma and Hygieia (Salus) at Pergamum—a city especially devoted to Aesclepius.

of Tiberius: *ἱερέα διὰ γένους θεᾶς Ῥώμης καὶ θεοῦ Σεβαστοῦ*[342]. The phrase *διὰ γένους* undoubtedly refers to the father's tenure as priest in the earlier form of the cult. This emphasizes the continuity from the cult of Roma to that of Roma and Augustus.

This last inscription shows that the municipal worship of Roma did not disappear at Pergamum with the establishment of the federal temple of Roma and Augustus. Another Augustan text refers to this municipal priesthood, and Cratippus held this office after Augustus' death [343]. In the second century the Pergamenes established their own municipal games in honor of Roma and Augustus. These are quite different from the Romaia Sebasta of the Koinon of Asia which had been founded at Pergamum almost a century and a half earlier. The new *εἰσελαστικὸς* (*ἀγών*) was purely local, established by the Boule and Demos of Pergamum during the reign of Trajan [344]. Since this text is the latest piece of evidence for the municipal cult at Pergamum, we cannot tell how much longer this cult and its festival persisted [345].

X. Commune Asiae (*Κοινὸν Ἀσίας*)

The cult of Roma had existed in the East for nearly two centuries before it was officially sanctioned by the powers in Rome. In 29 BC, the cities of Asia (as well as those of Bithynia) requested permission to dedicate a temple or temples to Augustus. Exactly what was re-

---

[342] HABICHT *Pergamum* III (Berlin, 1969) p. 165 shows the relationship of the three Cratippi: 1) philosopher, friend of Cicero and father of 2) priest of Roma and Salus and father of 3) priest of Roma and deified Augustus. He convincingly restores *IGR* IV 473 (*Pergamum* 260; *MDAI(A)* 24 (1899) 178 #30):

[*Μ. Τύλλιον Κράτι*]*ππον Μάρκου*
[*Τυλλίου Κρατίππο*]*υ τοῦ τῆς πό-*
[*λεως εὐεργέτ*]*ου υἱὸν, γενό*[*με-*]
[*νον ἱερέα διὰ*] *γένους θεᾶς*
[*Ῥώμης καὶ θεο*]*ῦ Σεβαστοῦ.*

Thus there was a Cratippus, priest of Roma and Divus Augustus after AD 14 with a distinguished father (*εὐεργέτου*) who came into the priesthood *διὰ γένους*. The genealogy is now much clearer. The restoration of lines 3–5 above had been suggested with minor differences by CONZE and SCHUCHARDT (*MDAI(A)* 24 (1899) 178f.).

[343] *Sardis* 8 line 127; BUCKLER-ROBINSON *AJA* 18 (1914) 360–361.

[344] *Pergamum* 269. MAGIE *RRAM* 1296 seems to consider this festival to be provincial.

[345] A Pergamene inscription from the time of Hadrian reads (*IGR* IV 1687): *Ἰουλία Αὔλου θυγάτηρ Πώλλα βασιλὶς τῶν ἐν θεᾶι Ῥώμη(ι) ἱερῶν*. I accept the suggestion originally made by IPPEL in his editio princeps *MDAI(A)* 37 (1912) 300 that Julia Polla served as *regina sacrorum* in Rome (see also *CIL* VI 2124). This is a rare use of *θεά* modifying *Ῥώμη* used exclusively in the geographical sense; see p. 112 below.

quested is uncertain; it is clear however from Tacitus and Dio that the request was initiated by the cities [346]. Since the struggle against Antony and Cleopatra had been so recently concluded and vitriolic anti-eastern propaganda was still in the air, Augustus had to be particularly cautious in handling this request. He permitted two temples in each province: a temple of Roma and Divus Julius for Roman citizens (at Ephesus and Nicaea), and a temple of Roma and Augustus for non-citizens (at Pergamum and Nicomedia) [347]. The inclusion of Roma had ample precendent in the East (such as the priesthood of Roma and P. Servilius Isauricus at Ephesus) and her inclusion would protect Augustus against criticism of an oriental excess. As Suetonius (*Augustus* 52) says: "templa, quamvis sciret etiam proconsulibus decerni solere, in nulla tamen provincia nisi communi suo Romaeque nomine recepit". Even in this the princeps was able to find a republican preecdent.

The temple of Roma and Augustus at Pergamum chiefly concerns us here, for that sanctuary became the center of the imperial cult in the province of Asia. It also became the religious and political center of the Koinon of Asia—the organization of the cities of Asia. The Roman province of Asia was organized in 129 BC, but the first evidence of the cities of Asia acting in concert comes from the beginning of the first century BC. The cities, then calling themselves οἱ ἐν τῆι Ἀσίαι δῆμοι καὶ τὰ ἔθνη, honored the Roman proconsul Q. Mucius Scaevola by the establishment of pentaeteric games called Μουκίεια [348]. Until recently there has been a controversy whether such expressions indicated the Koinon itself, which is first attested in a rescript of Marc Antony preserved on the back of a London papyrus, or whether there was a difference between these "cities" and the organized Koinon [349]. Several years ago a decree of the Koinon of Asia was found at Aphrodisias, and

---

[346] Dio Cassius 51, 20, 6–9; Tacitus *Ann.* 4, 37: cum divus Augustus sibi atque urbi Romae templum apud Pergamum sisti non prohibuisset. Dio's word ἐπέτρεψε and Tacitus' "non prohibuisset" make clear that the request originated in the cities themselves. Cf. BOWERSOCK 116.

[347] Roma is not mentioned in Dio's account but the Tacitus passage, the statement of Suetonius (quoted above), and numerous coins depicting the temple with the legend ROM.ET.AVG.COM.ASIAE (*SNG-DEN* 34 #419) make her presence certain. We will also find similar discrepancies between literary and numismatic-epigraphical evidence in the West, at Lugdunum. See p. 196.

[348] *OGIS* 437 (= *RDGE* 47). On the antecedents of the Koinon of Asia, cf. BRANDIS *Hermes* 32 (1897) 509f.; DEININGER *Provinziallandtage* 14–16; BOWERSOCK 115f. These discussions must now be altered to incorporate the results of DREW-BEAR's analysis of the new Aphrodisias inscription: *BCH* 96 (1972) 460ff.

[349] *RDGE* 57, which BOWERSOCK *AJP* 91 (1970) 226f. recently interpreted as the earliest clear reference to the Koinon. He dated *Milet* I 2, 3 (= *RDGE* 52) to the early twenties. That must now be called into question.

the recent comprehensive publication of this text illuminates the operation of the Koinon during the Republic[350]. Here the Koinon sends an embassy to Rome to defend the interests of the inhabitants of Asia against the exactions of the publicani. The text must be dated between the reestablishment of the publicani in Asia in 80 and the abolition of the system of tax-farming by Julius Caesar in 48, and the editor DREW-BEAR reasonably places it between 80 and Lucullus' reforms of 71 — a decade of extreme difficulty for Asia. This text refers not only to the οἱ ἐν τῇ Ἀσίᾳ δῆμοι καὶ τὰ ἔθνη but the Koinon is given its proper name: τῷ κοινῷ τῶν ἐπὶ τῆς Ἀσίας Ἑλλήνων. Therefore these various locutions do not designate different political realities; rather, they are used for different purposes. The conclusion of the Aphrodisias decree makes this clear when it quotes the text to be placed on honorific statues decreed by the Koinon: οἱ ἐν τῇ Ἀσίᾳ δῆμοι καὶ τὰ ἔθνη. So these lists of the constituent parts of the Koinon are used in honorific texts; the simple κοινόν in decrees or letters.

When Octavian stopped in Asia in 30 on his return from Egypt, the Koinon was already an established organization with some mechanism for taking communal action, whether political or religious. Their desire to honor Octavian was predictable. The triumphant leader characteristically seized the opportunity to use an existing local institution to strengthen Roman control in Asia.

The Koinon assembled annually at the temple in Pergamum, and at those meetings games were celebrated in honor of Roma and Augustus: Romaia Sebasta[351]. Though ostensibly religious in character, the assembly came to play an important political role in imperial administration[352]. But Pergamum did not long remain the only center of the imperial cult of the Koinon of Asia. Other temples were soon erected elsewhere; perhaps the first was the one requested of Tiberius by the Koinon and finally, as we have seen, awarded to Smyrna in 26 AD[353]. Temples were later established in the principal cities of Asia: Ephesus, Sardes, Miletus[354]. Cities with provincial temples could be rewarded by the emperor with the title of νεωκόρος. This came to be regarded as a great distinction, and centers such as Ephesus were particularly proud that they had been so honored several times for

---

[350] Text: DREW-BEAR ZPE 8 (1971) 286f.; text with commentary: BCH 96 (1972) 443ff.

[351] Syll. 1065: [P]ωμαῖα Σεβαστὰ τὰ τιθέμενα ὑπὸ τοῦ κοινοῦ τῆς Ἀσίας ἐν Περγάμωι.

[352] DEININGER Provinziallandtage 52–60; 136–172; see also MILLAR CR 16 (1966) 389.

[353] See pp. 14f. above.

[354] For evidence, see DEININGER Provinziallandtage 37–38; ROBERT RPh 41 (1967) 46f.

their temples: *νεωκόρος τρίς*³⁵⁵. The celebrations of the festivals were eventually rotated among the major cities of Asia, though so many cities hosted the celebrations that the precise system of rotation remains obscure³⁵⁶. The essential point for our purposes is that the imperial cult and festival of the province of Asia did not remain rooted in Pergamum, but was spread among several centers, some of which had their own "provincial" temples and priests of Roma and Augustus.

Eventually the name of Roma was omitted from the temples and the games, from the titles of the priests and the hymnodes³⁵⁷. Her disappearance, or absorption into the general imperial cult, is a phenomenon we encounter elsewhere. After the Julio-Claudian emperors the balance that her name provided became far less important in the East. Later emperors were quite willing to become the complete Hellenistic prince, divine honors included. The cult of the goddess Roma in the East had always been a kind of substitution for the Hellenistic ruler cult, at times a rather clumsy one. Rome's eastern subjects would have welcomed a return to the form and nomenclature of political dependence that had been so familiar to their ancestors.

XI. Bithynia and Pontus

In 74 BC King Nicomedes III of Bithynia followed the example of Attalus of Pergamum and bequeathed his kingdom to the Roman people. Bithynia was organized as a province and in the last years of the Republic the cities began acting together in a Koinon³⁵⁸. We have

---

³⁵⁵ Ephesus: *Ephesos* II 53–56. The meaning of the title *νεωκόρος* as awarded to cities has given rise to a considerable scholarly literature. BUECHNER's 1888 Giessen dissertation *De Neocoria* was exhaustive for its time, and is still very useful. He linked the title *νεωκόρος* to the presence of provincial temples—a view forcefully argued recently by ROBERT *RPh* 41 (1967) 44–64. That seems to me to be the best interpretation of the evidence. Contra, MORETTI *RFIC* 32 (1954) 279f. argues that the title had nothing to do with the provincial cult, and in this he is followed by DEININGER *Provinziallandtage* 143 n.5.

³⁵⁶ Two annual cycles: DEININGER *ibid.* 55; MORETTI *RFIC* 32 (1954) 279f. This simple pattern of two pentaeteric cycles with eight centers is the most plausible suggested, but it still seems too perfect and makes me uneasy. MORETTI's reconstruction depends on his dismissal of Miletus from the usual list of nine provincial centers. The arguments on this point are not sufficiently compelling. More complex systems (which retain nine centers) have been proposed by MAGIE *RRAM* 1295f. n.55 and 57; BEHR *Aelius Aristeides and the Sacred Tales* (Amsterdam, 1958) 63 n.14. These are ingenious, but little more than that. I do not believe that the evidence is sufficient to take us beyond speculation on this point. *IAG* 65 seems to invalidate BEHR's suggestion.

³⁵⁷ Games: *IAG* 69; Priests: see *IGR* IV p. 640; Hymnodes: *IGR* IV 1608c; 460; Temples: *IGR* IV 39.

³⁵⁸ There is no direct evidence for the existence of the Koinon during the Republic. The authenticity of the "Greek Letters of Brutus", which attest such a Koinon, continues to be challenged; e.g. DEININGER *RhMus* 109 (1966) 356–

already seen that the Bithynians, like the cities of Asia, wished to honor the triumphant Octavian in 30 and, like Asia, they were permitted to erect temples to Roma and Divus Julius (Nicaea) and to Roma and Augustus (Nicomedia). The temple at Nicomedia was for the non-Roman population, and as in Asia soon became the political as well as the religious center of the Koinon. Coins bearing the legend κοινὸν Βειθυνίας depict the temple flanked by Roma and the personification of Bithynia [359]. Musical and athletic contests formed part of the annual festival celebrated at the temple, and the provincial assembly probably also met there though the evidence for this is much sparser than for Asia [360]. A Bithyniarch was the chief official of the Koinon, and presumably presided over the provincial cult as high priest—though there is no epigraphical mention of the provincial priest of the imperial cult [361]. The Koinon was active in the prosecution of dishonest Roman officials during the first century of the Empire, and of course Pliny mentions the *"concilium"* in his correspondence [362]. During the Empire it seems that, as in Asia, although other cities sometimes hosted the provincial games, Nicomedia remained the principal site of the festival until the third century [363].

In the organization of Roman Asia, the territory of each province might include several Koina. After Pompey's defeat of Mithridates, the kingdom of Pontus was simply joined with the existing province of Bithynia under a single Roman governor. Already during the Republic Pontus had a separate Koinon which was headed by a Pontarch [364]. But a startling indication of the close connection between Bithynia and Pontus is the inscription recording that a single man served both as Bithyniarch and as Pontarch [365]. The evidence for the Koinon and provincial cult of Pontus is even sparser than for Bithynia, and there has even been disagreement over the seat of the Koinon and over

---

372. Nevertheless, there are good reasons for accepting its existence: the parallel with Pontus; simultaneous issue of coins in the governorship of Carbo; and the request of the Βιθυνοί to honor Augustus in 29 BC. See DEININGER *Provinziallandtage* 18–19.

[359] *BMC Pontus* 105 #10; 108 #32.

[360] Games: *CIG* 1720; *IGR* IV 1645; *IG* II² 3169 line 22; *IGR* I 802; *IGR* III 370.

[361] DEININGER *Provinziallandtage* 60–61; MAGIE *RRAM* 1301 n. 62.

[362] Tacitus *Ann.* 12, 22; 14, 46. Pliny refers to the Bithynians acting in concert many times, but he only uses *"concilium"* at *Ep.* 7, 6, 1.

[363] At Nicaea in the reign of Nero: *IAG* 69. Also see DEININGER *Provinziallandtage* 61. *IG* II² 3169 (mid third century AD) still mentions games in Nicomedia.

[364] DEININGER *Provinziallandtage* 64.

[365] DOERNER *Bericht über eine Reise in Bithynien — Denkschr. Österr. Akad.* 75, 1 (Vienna, 1952) #18.

whether there might not have even been two Pontic Koina[366]. Neocaesaerea seems to have been the seat of the Koinon, and therefore of the temple of the provincial cult, but this conclusion must remain tentative until further evidence appears[367].

One of those troublesome inscriptions from the Capitoline in Rome records the dedication of a statue of the Demos of the Romans by Mithridates Philopator[368]. As with all these texts, MOMMSEN wishes to date it in the first century and has accordingly invented a Mithridates Philopator, a son of Eupator established in Paphlagonia by Sulla[369]. That seems unnecessary when there is a perfectly good Mithridates IV Philopator ruling Pontus 170–150 BC[370]. At that time the Rhodians were erecting an enormous statue of the Demos of the Romans — which obviously must have been portrayed as the goddess Roma, not as the male Demos found on the coins of some Greek cities — and rivals for the throne of Cappadocia were dedicating gold crowns to Roma[371]. Mithridates' reason for the dedication remains unknown, but after the defeat of Perseus any number of situations could have given rise to such a tribute. Until evidence for another Mithridates Philopator appears, I think it best to attribute the bilingual dedication and the statue of the Demos of the Romans to the Pontic king of the mid-second century.

But the only specific mentions of Roma in Bithynia and Pontus are on coins, beginning with an extraordinary series depicting a martial goddess (identified by the legend $Ῥώμη$) issued by eight cities immediately after Pompey's departure for Rome[372]. There has been no adequate explanation for this sudden spate of monetary issues[373]. Clearly there

---

[366] JONES *CERP* 421 n. 20; DEININGER *Provinziallandtage* 65.

[367] RUGE *RE* XVI 2411 places the seat of the Pontic Koinon in Neocaesarea where BRANDIS *RE* III 536 would place the temple. On the other hand, KEIL *CAH* XI 575 sees Amastris as the capital of Roman Pontus, the seat of the Koinon, and the location of the temple of Roma and Augustus. See *BMC Pontus* 32 #1f.

[368] *CIL* I² 730 (= *OGIS* 375). See Additional Note. The name of the king is not actually given in either Latin or Greek text, but is easily restored since this dynasty retained the name for generation after generation:

[Rex Metradates Pilopator et Pil]adelpus regus Metradati f(ilius) . . .

[βασιλεὺς Μιθραδάτης Φιλ]οπάτωρ καὶ Φιλάδελφος [βασιλέως Μιθραδάτ]ου . . .

[369] *Zeitschrift für Numismatik* 15 (1887) 207f. = *Ges. Schr.* IV 71f.

[370] *ID* 1555. Also REINACH *L'histoire par les monnaies* (Paris, 1902) 127f.; LARSEN *CP* 51 (1956) 157–159.

[371] See p. 25 above and pp. 90f. below.

[372] Amisus: Waddington *Recueil Général* I² 73 #45; Amastris: *Ibid.* 169 #22; Apamea: *Ibid.* II 249 #29; Prusa: *Ibid.* IV 576 #1; Tieium: *Ibid.* IV 617 #5; Bithynium: *BMC Pontus* 117 #1; Nicaea: *BMC Pontus* 152 #2f.; Nicomedia: *BMC Pontus* 179 #1f.

[373] MAGIE *RRAM* 400: "presumably finding a shortage of currency in low denominations, he (Carbo, Pompey's successor) encouraged the communities to

must have been considerable coordination between the cities; at whose suggestion or direction is unknown. Possibly the coinage results from some action taken by the Koina of Bithynia and Pontus. The cities had received very substantial benefits from Pompey's reorganization. They received greater local autonomy and probably controlled and taxed some of the former royal lands [374]. Pompey's successor as governor, G. Papirius Carbo whose name appears on most of these 'Ρώμη-issues, may well have been particularly popular in the province. Some years earlier he had prosecuted M. Aurelius Cotta, hated in Bithynia for his destruction of Heraclea [375]. And now Carbo put into effect the Lex Pompeia which decentralized local administration and increased the power of the Hellenized cities [376]. Since it was precisely those cities that minted the 'Ρώμη-coins, these issues might well reflect relief and gratitude. How the decision to mint these coins was taken cannot be known with any certainty, but if it was done at the instigation of the cities—which I think likely—it would be the first known action of the Koina of Pontus and Bithynia.

Roma continued to appear on the coinage of some Bithynian and Pontic cities during the Empire: Neocaesarea, Nicaea, and an unknown city in Pontus portray Roma identified by a legend, and other cities have figures resembling Roma on their coins [377].

XII. Pamphylia, Pisidia and Cilicia

Before the first century BC, Rome had little contact with southern Asia Minor east of Lycia. Cn. Manlius Vulso extorted tribute from Termessus and Aspendus after the war with Antiochus, but Roman interest then waned in the area [378]. It was largely isolated from the rest of Anatolia by the Taurus mountains, and was oriented towards the sea rather than to the cities to the north. Rome came into closer contact with the cities of southern Asia Minor only when she became con-

---

issue copper coins, and as many as eight separate places responded with coins bearing his name". Possible of course, but there is no evidence except the coins to support this speculation about the shortage of currency.

[374] JONES *CERP* 156f.; MAGIE *RRAM* 1231 n.34; KEIL *CAH* XI 578. On another concession of Pompey to these cities, see MARSHALL *JRS* 58 (1968) 107f.

[375] Dio Cassius 36, 40, 3f. Carbo's prosecution by Cotta's son reeks of a political and/or personal vendetta, *pace* MAGIE *RRAM* 400.

[376] JONES *CERP* 159 mentions that the revised constitutions of these cities would give them considerably greater autonomy. The timing of these monetary issues was clearly the result of some communal decision, perhaps also aimed at flattering the Romans at a time when Senate confirmation of Pompey's acta was seriously in question.

[377] Neocaesarea: *SNG-DEN* 18 #219; Nicaea *BMC Pontus* 155 #25; Unknown city: IMHOOF-BLUMER *Monnaies Grecques* (Paris, 1883) 464 #28. Figures which might be taken to be Roma also appear on imperial coins from Amisus, Carausus, Sebastea, Amastris, Nicomedia, and Tieium.

[378] Vulso: Livy 38, 15.

cerned with the pirates who had their lairs along that irregular coastline. At first the praetor who held the "province" of Cilicia was simply given a mandate to police the seas [379]. There is no evidence of the annexation of territory into this province until after the defeat of Mithridates by Sulla when Pamphylia and sections of Pisidia were organized into the province. But Cilicia proper was brought into the province which had previously borne its name only after Pompey's conquest of the pirates in 67 BC [380]. Subsequent administrative realignments of these areas occurred but they remained thereafter under Roman rule.

Termessus — After buying off Cn. Manlius Vulso in 189, Termessus in Pisidia was able to retain at least nominal independence almost continuously for five centuries. The city had good relations with the Attalid kings, and was later on friendly terms with Rome. Termessus resisted Mithridates, and about 68 BC her autonomy was reaffirmed by Rome through a plebiscite [381]. Antony may have assigned the city to his puppet King Amyntas of Galatia, but Termessus soon regained her autonomy and does not seem to have relinquished it again during the first three centuries of the Empire [382].

The cult of Roma was clearly of considerable importance at Termessus. There is epigraphical evidence for a number of priests of Roma independent of the imperial cult from about 160 to 225 A.D. The priests of Roma simultaneously held important municipal offices: priest of Augustus; priest of Dionysus; priest of Zeus Solymeus (patron of Termessus); and the eponymous πρόβουλος [383]. The three temples on the

---

[379] On this wider use of *"provincia"* see LEVICK *Roman Colonies in Southern Asia Minor* (Oxford, 1967) 21f.; LIEBMANN-FRANKFORT *Mélanges Renard* (Brussels, 1969) II 448f. For an earlier lengthy discussion, see MAGIE *RRAM* 285; 1163–1166 n. 14–15.

The new inscription from Cnidos may be relevant to this controversy: HASSALL-CRAWFORD-REYNOLDS *JRS* 64 (1974) 195ff. This law is dated to late 101 BC. While the text provides the first evidence that Lycaonia had been annexed by that time, the brief comment on the "province" of Cicilia (*Ibid.* 202 III 35–37) does not clearly resolve the problems surrounding its annexation. Nonetheless, this document demands more caution on Cilicia than I expressed in my comments above. Such judgments should now be held in abeyance while this new text is examined and discussed in greater detail.

[380] Appian *Mith.* 106; 108.

[381] *CIL* I² 589 = *ILS* 38. This decree recalls that Termessus was given special privileges in 91 BC. SYME *JRS* 53 (1963) 55f. dates the plebiscite to 68. See also, HEAD *Historia Numorum* (2nd edition, London, 1911) 712.

[382] Pamphylia given to Amyntas: Dio Cassius 49, 32, 3; Pisidia: Appian *BC* 5, 75. Autonomous coinage of Termessus seems to end in 39 BC: MAGIE *RRAM* 1283 n. 17. Later autonomy: HEBERDEY *Termessische Studien* — *Denkschr. Österr. Akad.* 69 (Vienna, 1929) III 66f.; *BMC Lycia* 272f.

[383] Priest of Augustus: *TAM* III 1, 110; priest of Dionysus: *TAM* III 1, 108–110; priest of Zeus Solymus: *TAM* III 1, 113–114; πρόβουλος: *TAM* III 1, 153; 156. On πρόβουλος as eponymous official, cf. HEBERDEY 127; on the temples, see LANCKORONSKI *Städte Pamphyliens und Pisidiens* (Vienna, 1892) II 48.

terrace in Termessus were perhaps dedicated to Zeus Solymeus, Roma and Augustus. The priesthood of Roma precedes all other titles in the cursus honorum, taking second place only to the eponymous πρόβουλος. Why Roma should have occupied such an important place in Termessus is a mystery. Whether the cult was founded in 189, 70 or at some other time is impossible to say. Oddly enough, even in the second century AD the priests of this important cult of Roma are not Roman citizens, while a contemporary priest of Zeus was a citizen [384]. Only after the edict of Caracalla are the priests of Roma at Termessus given Roman names [385]. Why this should have been so, and why this cult of Roma should have flourished for so long at Termessus depend on local peculiarities which we cannot now discern.

Attalia — Of the five great cities of the fertile crescent at the head of the Mare Pamphylicum (now the gulf of Antalya), three—Attalia, Side and Aspendus—show some evidence of Roma. But here the imperial cult is attested only on the local level: there are no games, no Pamphylian Koinon, no provincial cult before the time of Diocletian. Attalia was annexed into the province of Cilicia by P. Servilius Isauricus in 77 BC, and by the reign of Augustus had a large resident Roman population [386]. One text honors a priest of the goddess Roma ἀρχηγέτις and Drusus, and perhaps the epithet ἀρχηγέτις indicates that Roma served Attalia like the κτίστης of old, i.e., that a Roman colony had been founded in the city [387]. The priestess of the cult of Roma and Livia was a Roman citizen, and her son was destined to become a governor under Claudius [388]. Two dedicatory inscriptions—one set up by the city and the other by the city together with the resident Romans—honored S. Valerius Flaccus who had served twice as priest of Roma [389].

---

[384] *TAM* III 1, 52.
[385] Greek names on *TAM* III 1, 16 (161–169 AD) and *TAM* III 1, 787 (180–200 AD), but a Roman name on *TAM* III 1, 108.
[386] Cicero *De Lege Agraria* 1, 2; 2, 19. On the Romans resident at Attalia, cf. *SEG* VI 646 and the recent scholarship: LEVICK *op. cit.* 107f.; LEVICK-JAMESON *JRS* 54 (1964) 101f.
[387] *SEG* XVII 582; ROBERT *BE* 1948 #229; and see PACE *ASA* 3 (1916/20) 12. LEVICK *op. cit.* 127; LEVICK-JAMESON *op. cit.* 102. The argument against colony status is strongly put forward, but *IGR* III 785 with its reference to Attalia as κολω[νία] cannot so easily be dismissed merely by citing a few instances where the distinction of *colonia* has been wrongfully assumed in the late Empire. BROUGHTON *TAPA* 67 (1935) 22f. has argued for a Roman colony of the Augustan age in Attalia, and he is followed by ROBERT *BE* 1948 #229; BOWERSOCK 64 n. 3. There are problems on either side, but I think the evidence accords more easily with the view that Attalia was an official colony, though there may have been Roman traders resident there long before the official designation.
[388] Priestess: *SEG* II 696; on the son, M. Calpurnius Rufus, see BOSCH *Belleten* 11 (1947) #10; ROBERT *BE* 1948 #229; LEVICK *op. cit.* 107f.
[389] City: *SEG* XVII 577; City and resident Romans: *SEG* XVII 578.

The priesthood of Roma must have existed during the Republic, but the evidence does not allow us to determine when it was established.

Side — The great mercantile rival of Attalia was Side, also on the gulf of Antalya. Even though it assisted Antiochus, the city was free after Apamea [390]. It later formed part of the province of Cilicia until it was given by Antony to Amyntas together with other areas of Pamphylia and Pisidia [391]. A series of inscriptions from Side, published in 1965, show that the priesthood of Roma was an important office in that city [392]. In fact it seems to have been frequently (if not invariably) linked with the δημιουργός, the eponymous magistrate of Side [393]. In these texts the imperial cult is quite separate from the cult of Roma, though the priest of Roma sometimes held the priesthood of Augustus at the same time [394]. No date has been attributed to these texts, and there is no way to date the introduction of Roma to Side—though 189/8 would be plausible. Roma appears on a coin of Side of the reign of Caracalla, and on a later coin of Aspendus together with the personified Aspendus [395].

Antiochia-ad-Cragum — Moving still further to the East, there is a dedication honoring a priest of Roma from Antiochia-ad-Cragum in Cilicia Tracheia [396]. ROBERT has shown that this text is in fact an elegaic couplet, but it cannot be dated [397]. So little is known of Antiochia that we can only record the text without making suggestions about the cult of Roma there.

Anazarbus — At the eastern end of the province in Cilicia Pedias, a text to honor Domitian was set up in Anazarbus about AD 92 [398]. The two dedicants, L. Valerius Niger and L. Valerius Varus Pollio, are both identified, as at Side, as former δημιουργοί and priests of Roma. The cult of Roma might perhaps be dated to Augustus' stay in Cilicia in 19 BC when Anazarbus took the name of Caesarea. But since the cult of Roma is quite separate from the cult of the emperors, it probably

---

[390] Antiochus' ally: Livy 35, 48, 6; 37, 23, 3. Freedom: Appian *Lyb.* 123; Maccabees I 15, 23; BIKERMAN *REG* 50 (1937) 239.

[391] *BMC Galatia* p. xviii; 2 #1–7.

[392] BEAN *The Inscriptions of Side* (Ankara, 1965) 111; 112; 127; 183; 186; 189.

[393] On δημιουργός as the eponymous official at Side, cf. *BGU* III (1903) 887; J. & L. ROBERT *BE* 1951 #219. Since the publication of the new texts from Side, it is clear that *BGU* 887 must be restored ἐν Σίδῃ ἐπὶ δημιουργοῦ ἱερέως [θεᾶς Ῥώμης] since this priesthood was held by the δημιουργός in virtually all cases. For another δημιουργός and priest of Roma who possibly served at Side, see n. 452 below and *ZPE* 13 (1974) 277ff.

[394] BEAN *op.cit.* 111.

[395] Side: IMHOOF-BLUMER *KM* II 339 #19a; Aspendus: *BMC Lycia* 109 #104.

[396] BEAN-MITFORD *Journeys in Rough Cilicia in 1962 and 1963* — Denkschr. Österr. Akad. 85 (Vienna, 1965) 34 #36. On ἱερῆα, see p. 181 below.

[397] J. & L. ROBERT *BE* 1967 #623.

[398] *JÖAI* 18 (1915) Beiblatt 55.

goes back to the Republic, perhaps to Pompey's revitalization of this area after 67 BC when he repopulated cities ravaged by Tigranes[399]. At that time many cities honored him as their saviour, and it would have been an appropriate time to honor Roma as well.

XIII. Galatia

In the second century BC the Romans first came into contact with the Gauls of Asia Minor. Rome, absorbing Greek prejudice, regarded them as little more than savages. The Gauls were massacred on Cn. Manlius Vulso's vicious rampage through Asia in 189, so that their land might more easily be plundered[400]. Later they were supported, freed or betrayed by Rome as pawns in her elaborate political intrigues with the dynasts of Pergamum, Pontus and Bithynia[401]. But after Mithridates' treacherous murder of their leaders in 88, the Galatians remained steadfast allies of Rome[402]. Following four decades of domestic assassination and complex foreign intrigues with the great dynasts of the Roman civil war, the death of King Amyntas in 25 led Augustus to annex Galatia as a province to which Marcus Lollius was dispatched as the first governor[403]. The non-hellenized Galatians had few cities, so Lollius had to select a remnant of Persian rule as capital of the new province, the fortress of Ancyra.

The focal point of Roman presence in Galatia was the temple of Roma and Augustus in Ancyra. There the provincial assembly met; there the annual games were celebrated. But this temple is most famous for what it contained—the most complete text of the *Res Gestae* we have[404]. Augustus' memoires were inscribed on the inner walls of the temple. Strangely enough, the other two texts of this invaluable work come from cities which may also have fallen within the sphere of the Galatian Koinon: a Latin text from the temple of Roma (?) and Augustus at Antiochia-near-Pisidia[405], and a Greek text from Apollonia[406]. Why this important document has been pre-

---

[399] Anazarbus-Caesarea: Pliny *HN* 5, 22; *BMC Lycaonia* 31f. Pompey: Appian *Mith.* 96; 115; Dio Cassius 36, 37, 5–6; Strabo 8, 7, 5; 14, 3, 3. *IGR* III 869 describes Pompey as κτίστης.

[400] Polybius 21, 37–39; Livy 38, 17–27. Criticism of Vulso: Livy 38, 45, 2f.

[401] Pergamum: Polybius 30, 1, 3f.; 30, 28. Bithynia: Polybius 30, 30; 32, 1, 5f. Pontus: Polybius 24, 14f.

[402] Appian *Mith.* 46.

[403] MAGIE *RRAM* 459; 1318 n. 26–27.

[404] On the date of the Galatian Koinon, see DEININGER *Provinziallandtage* 20 n. 5 for a survey of the scholarship. The date of the temple has been disputed, but an Augustan date seems most likely; see pp. 144f. below.

[405] RAMSAY *JRS* 6 (1916) 108f. RAMSAY *ibid.* 105 has argued that the text was carved on the wall of the temple of Roma and Augustus at Antiochia; he presents no evidence.

[406] See *MAMA* IV p. 50 and above p. 75.

served in this area and nowhere else in the Empire remains a puzzle. It is possible, perhaps even likely, that the *Res Gestae* was set up elsewhere in bronze (as at Rome) which has perished[407]. But why should Galatia have been different? There has been much discussion of the relative influence of Roman elogia and eastern traditions of royal autobiography on Augustus' *Res Gestae*[408]. Perhaps in unhellenized Galatia, the eastern tradition of massive, autobiographical inscriptions also provided a model for the manner of setting up such texts. The *Monumentum Ancyranum* was probably set up not by Roman administrators but by the Galatian Koinon as a cult act, much as the publication of the Julian calendar in the province of Asia was regarded as an act of the imperial cult[409].

The cult of Roma and Augustus was administered for the Galatian Koinon by a high priest, who also served as Galatarch, the chief secular official of the Koinon[410]. Inscriptions show that a priest could serve more than once[411], and also that the incumbents were not necessarily drawn from the very small hellenized minority but were men with Gallic names[412]. The festival celebrated to honor the imperial cult further reveals the unhellenized character of Galatia and the imperial cult there. Beast hunts and gladiatorial combats already took place at Ancyra by the reign of Tiberius[413]. Later, of course, the Greeks themselves became fond of these events[414]. But for the early Empire, Galatia was unique: aping the model provided by the Asian Koinon but in a different, unhellenic spirit. As elsewhere, the temple of Roma and Augustus appears on the coinage, both on the issues of the Koinon and on those of Ancyra herself[415]. Another coin of Ancyra portrays a bust of Roma identified by the legend $\vartheta\varepsilon\grave{\alpha}\ \mathcal{P}\acute{\omega}\mu\eta$[416]. All this conscious imitation of Greek coinage, cults and institutions was a considerable impetus to the eventual hellenization of Galatia.

XIV. *Cappadocia*

The remote and mountanous land of Cappadocia was controlled by the Ariarathid family for more than two centuries. The Persian satrap, Ariarathes, managed to withstand Alexander's invasion and, though

---

[407] Suetonius *Augustus* 101: indicem rerum a se gestarum, quem vellet incidi in aeneis tabulis, quae ante Mausoleum statuerentur.

[408] On the models for the *Res Gestae*, see GAGÉ *Res Gestae Divi Augusti* (Paris, 1950²) 31f.; MOMIGLIANO *The Development of Greek Biography* (Cambridge, USA, 1971) 92f.

[409] DEININGER *Provinziallandtage* 68.

[410] High priest as Galatarch: *OGIS* 540; DEININGER *Provinziallandtage* 43–50.

[411] *OGIS* 540.

[412] ROBERT *Gladiateurs* #86 (better text than *OGIS* 533).

[413] ROBERT *Ibid.*   [414] See below pp. 173ff.

[415] *BMC Galatia* 6 #8f.; 7 #3f.   [416] MCCLEAN III 316 #9195.

he himself was killed in the anarchic wars following the death of Alexander, his descendants retained control of Cappadocia. They were soon acknowledged as "kings", though they remained clients of the more powerful Seleucids. So the troops of Ariarathes IV loyally fought on the side of Antiochus against the Romans at Magnesia[417]. By betrothing his daughter Stratonice to Eumenes II, Ariarathes secured a powerful ally in the Roman camp and Cappadocia was accepted into "friendship" with the Roman people[418]. The king provided assistance to Rome in the war against Perseus, and Ariarathes V succeeded his father to the throne in 164/3[419]. The Galatians brought charges against the new king to the Senate, but he was exonerated and the "friendship" was renewed[420]. There followed a period of turmoil, an age which the sources do not clarify. The king's brother, Orophernes, revolted with the support of Demetrius of Syria, and the rivals both sent to Rome crowns of gold coins dedicated to Roma in an attempt to influence senatorial opinion[421]. The Senate seems to have remained curiously inactive, while Ariarathes was first deposed (with Syrian help) and finally reinstated (with Attalid support). Whether encouraged or chagrined by Roman non-intervention, Ariarathes and his ally Attalus II attacked Priene where Orophernes had deposited his treasury. Polybius calls the attack unjust, but Rome did not deter the kings until after the territory of Priene had already been plundered[422]. Rome's policy during this entire episode seems curious, but that may be due to the incompleteness and confusion of our sources. (The order of the fragments of Polybius on this matter is disputed.) The Cappadocian kings did remain loyal to Rome: Ariarathes V died fighting Aristonicus who might have been expected to appeal to the Cappadocians. The dynasty was finally exterminated near the end of the century with the murders of Ariarathes VI and Ariarathes VII at the instigation of Mithridates[423].

It is important to appreciate the enormous cultural gap between the inhabitants of Cappadocia and their rulers. The people were backward, chiefly shepherds and horse breeders. They were still unhellenized at the end of the Republic—Strabo records only two cities in all of

---

[417] Livy 37, 31, 4; 37, 40, 10; Appian *Syr.* 32f.

[418] Livy 38, 37, 5f.; 38, 39, 6; Polybius 21, 41, 4–7.

[419] War against Perseus: Livy 42, 29, 4; Ariarathes V: Polybius 31, 3, 1f.; Livy *Periocha* 46.

[420] Galatian complaints: Polybius 31, 2, 13; 31, 3; 31, 8. I have accepted BRISCOE *Historia* 18 (1969) 56–57 for the ordering of the Polybian fragments concerning Cappadocia in books 31 and 32. Also see Diodorus 31, 28f. and Appian *Syr.* 47.

[421] Ariarathes: Polybius 31, 32, 3; 32, 1; Orophernes: Polybius 32, 10, 4.

[422] Polybius 33, 6; Diodorus 31, 32.

[423] REINACH *Trois Royaumes de l'Asie Mineure* (Paris, 1888) 30–55.

Cappadocia (Tyana and Mazaca) and says that Cappadocian remained the dominant language, a language that survived into the late Empire[424]. Yet the Ariarathid kings and princes were highly hellenized. Ariarathes V was an enthusiastic philhellene, and was even made a citizen of Athens. His brother Orophernes is accused by Polybius of introducing the elegant debauchery of Ionia into his homeland[425]. This difference of orientation might explain the royal honor to Roma in diplomatic transactions, but the absence of any cult of Roma in Cappadocia itself. The population could hardly have understood, or responded to, such an institution.

In the first century a Cappadocian noble, Ariobarzanes, was put on the throne by the Senate. He and his family ruled uneasily with sporadic interruptions until deposed by Antony in 36. One of these kings set up a dedication on the Capitoline in Rome, though nothing more than the king's name is preserved[426]. Here too, if there was a dedication to Jupiter and the Roman people, it was a product of the Hellenistic diplomacy of the Cappadocian ruling class. There was almost certainly no local cult of Roma.

XV. *Cyprus*

The island of Cyprus remained under Ptolemaic control from the beginning of the third century BC until its annexation by Cato in 58 BC. There does not seem to have been any occasion in early contacts between Rome and Cyprus suitable to the establishment of a cult to Roma, so the cults and festivals probably first appeared after annexation in the last years of the Republic[427]. Two fragmentary dedicatory texts of the Koinon of Cyprus honor priests of what seems to be a cult of Roma and the Divi[428]. These are probably priests of the provincial cult. If the cult of Roma and Augustus had not existed during the lifetime of Augustus (which seems unlikely), it would surely have been established when the Cypriots in their oath of allegiance to Tiberius pledged to vote honors to the goddess Roma[429]. One element in such honors was certainly a provincial cult and festival of Roma and the emperor.

---

[424] Strabo 12, 2, 7; JONES *CERP* 175–176.

[425] Ariarathes: Diodorus 31, 19; *Syll.* 666; Diogenes Laertius 4, 65. Orophernes: Polybius 32, 11, 10.

[426] *CIL* I² 731. See Additional Note.

[427] On earlier relations, see HILL *A History of Cyprus* (Cambridge, 1949) I 190–206.

[428] MITFORD *Opus. Arch.* 6 (1950) 74 n. 7: [ἀρ]χιερέα τῶν [Σεβαστῶν κα]ὶ τῆς [Ῥώμης?]. *Ibid.* 75 n. 1 (= *IGRR* III 961): [ἀρ]χιερα[σ]αμένου τ[ῶ]ν Σεβαστῶν [καὶ τῆς Ῥώμης]?

[429] MITFORD *JRS* 50 (1960) 75–79.

Other epigraphical evidence seems to indicate that local cults of Roma also existed, but since these texts are fragmentary the priests mentioned might actually have been serving the provincial cult. A text from Citium honors a man who was priest of Roma and agonothete at the quinquennial festival[430]. Since another text from Citium shows that this festival was a local one, it seems reasonable to assume the same for the priesthood. A new text from Kourion also honors a priest of Roma and this too might be interpreted as a local priesthood, since the provincial priest served in a cult of Roma *and* the Divi[431]. Since all four inscriptions mentioning priests of Roma are fragmentary, these suggestions must remain tentative until new evidence is published.

Roma's presence on Cyprus manifests itself in two additional ways. The month Romaios, which was named after Roma not Rome, can be found in two Cypriot calendars of the Augustan period[432]. And the oath of the Cypriots to Tiberius calls as a witness "everlasting Roma": τὴν ἀέναον Ῥώμην[433]. And later in the text, as I have already said, the Cypriots promise to vote honors to Tiberius, Roma and the imperial family.

So, in the early years of the Empire Roma was honored on Cyprus by cults and games, and she was enough of a religious presence to be mentioned in oaths and calendars. The cult of Roma seems to have remained even after the cult of the emperors arose[434]. But the texts are too fragmentary to be certain, though elsewhere Roma did occasionally survive separate from the imperial cult[435]. Roma does not appear on the coinage of the island.

---

[430] HOGARTH *Devia Cypria* (London, 1889) 109 #28 — dated by MITFORD *BSA* 42 (1947) 229 n. 118 to 1–50 AD. Other texts referring to games at Citium: CESNOLA *Cyprus* (London, 1877) 431 #344 (dated by MITFORD *BSA* 42 (1947) 229 n. 118 as "late") and *IGR* III 1012 (221 AD).

[431] MITFORD *Inscriptions of Kourion* (Philadelphia, 1971) #77. MITFORD 146 says that this cult of Roma alone is at variance with normal Cypriot usage. This seems overly bold, since the only examples of normal usage are both restored (see n. 428 above).

[432] BOLL *Cat. cod. astrol. Gr.* II 139f. Also see DOMASZEWSKI *Abhandlungen zur römischen Religion* (Leipzig, 1909) 234–236; HEINEN 166 n. CHAPOT *Mélanges Cagnat* (Paris, 1912) 75 suggested 15 BC as the date for the introduction of this calendar, since in that year Augustus restored Paphos after a destructive earthquake (Dio 54, 23, 7). On these calendars, see SCOTT *YCS* 2 (1931) 207–219; LAFFI *SCO* 16 (1967) 42–46; SAMUEL *Greek and Roman Chronology* (Munich, 1970) 183–186; and p. 161f. below. LAFFI 45 provides an extensive bibliography on the earlier calendar.

[433] Editio princeps: MITFORD *JRS* 50 (1960) 75–79. Also see WEINSTOCK *MDAI(A)* 77 (1962) 306–325. On the eternity of Roma, see my Epilogue.

[434] MITFORD *JRS* 50 (1960) 78; *Opusc. Arch.* 6 (1950) 75.

[435] Examples can be found at Eumenia and Apollonia in Phrygia, Termessus in Pisidia, Lycia and Thrace; see also note 294 above. The late survival of Roma independent of the imperial cult will be discussed in Chapter 7, pp. 195ff.

XVI. The East

As a result of Pompey's eastern wars, Syria and Judaea, the last possessions of the house of Seleucus, came under Roman domination. As might be expected, there was little or no concern with Roma before that time. Even after Roman hegemony, only the barest scattering of evidence for Roma in the East occurs. As we saw in Cappadocia, in unhellenized areas the use of Roma remained purely diplomatic or symbolic — a concern only of the local rulers and the Roman Senate or dynasts [436].

Syria — The only honors paid to Roma in Seleucid Syria resulted from the complex diplomatic activities of Demetrius I of Syria (162–150). About 160, the king's envoy, Menochares, brought to Rome the murderers of the Roman senator Cn. Octavius together with a gold crown dedicated to the personified Roman People. We are also told that during the Cappadocian civil war in the 150s, Demetrius was allied with Orophernes and sent Miltiades to Rome to lend diplomatic support. Since we are told by Polybius that Miltiades was utterly unscrupulous and was willing to promise anything to gain a diplomatic objective, he may have dedicated a crown to Roma as did his ally Orophernes [437]. It is readily apparent that there was no cult of Roma in Seleucid Syria, at most some honors voted for diplomatic purposes.

In 47 BC Julius Caesar, on his way home from Egypt, founded a Kaisareion in the former Seleucid capital of Antioch. And in that building, the Byzantine historian Johannes Malalas tells us, Caesar set up a bronze statue of the Tyche of Rome [438]. Whether Caesar was following the hallowed model of the Tyche of Antioch, or whether Malalas (or his source) has interpreted a statue of Roma in terms familiar to Antioch, we cannot tell. But Caesar was sensitive to local practice, and he probably would have adapted the eastern worship of Roma to make it more intelligible to the Antiochians. His impulse to associate himself with Roma provided a model for other Kaisareia, as well as for the temples of Julius and Roma at Ephesus and Nicaea.

Judaea — After Actium, Augustus confirmed Herod the Great as king of Judaea, and was honored in return with the great new city and port of Caesarea. The city and its temples clearly manifest Herod's Hellenic pretensions. A temple of Augustus was built on a hill overlooking the port, and monumental statues of Roma and the emperor

---

[436] Among the group of dedications to Jupiter and the Roman people on the Capitoline, there is a fragment with the name of C. Julius Ariobarzanes. His exact position is far from certain — though he might be king of Media Atropatene or son of a king of Armenia Maior. See DEGRASSI *BCAC* 74 (1954) 33–34 and Additional Note.

[437] Polybius 32, 10. On Menochares, see Polybius 32, 2, 1.

[438] Malalas p. 216, 17–21 (ed. Dindorf); SJÖQVIST *Opus. Rom.* 1 (1954) 91–95.

were placed there by Herod [439]. Josephus reports that the statue of Roma actually rivaled that of Hera at Argos. Though Josephus calls it the νεὼς Καίσαρος, the statues indicate that the temple was dedicated to Roma and Augustus, like those in Pergamum and Nicomedia some years before. After twelve years of construction, the city was dedicated in 10 BC with an enormous festival. These shows and games were continued as a quinquennial event, probably dedicated both to Roma and Augustus. Roma appears on the coinage of Caesarea in the late Empire, and a figure resembling Roma is also found on the coinage of other cities of Palestine [440].

Herod also rebuilt the city of Samaria, dedicating it to the emperor and renaming it Sebaste. Here too, as Josephus tells us, Herod built a temple to the emperor; and the probability is that, as at Caesarea, it was dedicated to both Roma and Augustus [441].

Cyrene — By the will of Ptolemy Apion, Cyrene was bequeathed to the Roman people in 96 BC. It was organized as a regular province in 74, and was later joined with Crete for administrative purposes [442]. Antony gave it to his daughter, Cleopatra Selene, in the Donations of Alexandria, but after Actium it was reannexed and rejoined with Crete.

The evidence for Roma in Cyrene is very scanty, and there is no positive evidence for any cult before the Empire. The most notable mention of Roma is a large architectural inscription from the north

---

[439] Josephus *BJ* 1, 21, 7: ἐν δ'αὐτῷ κολοσσὸς Καίσαρος οὐκ ἀποδέων τοῦ Ὀλυμπίασιν Διός, ᾧ καὶ προσείκασται, Ῥώμης δε ἴσος Ἥρᾳ τῇ κατ' Ἄργος. Josephus *AJ* 15, 9, 6: κἂν τῷ μέσῳ κολωνός τις, ἐφ'οὗ νεὼς Καίσαρος ἄποπτος τοῖς εἰσπλέουσιν ἔχων ἀγάλματα, τὸ μὲν Ῥώμης, τὸ δὲ Καίσαρος. On dates, see MARCUS ad Josephus *AJ* 15, 9, 6 (Loeb edition, vol. 8 p. 165); HEINEN 155; SCHALIT *König Herodes* (Berlin, 1969) 421f.

[440] Josephus *AJ* 16, 5, 1; HEINEN 164. For the coinage of Caesarea: MACDONALD *Greek Coins in the Hunterian Collection* (Glasgow, 1905) III 277 #8—but HILL *BMC Palestine* 31 #147 is less certain seeing "Athena or Roma". Others of Caesarea with the same type: *BMC Palestine* 34f. #169; 177; 202; 213. Also Eleutheropolis: *BMC Palestine* lxvi; Aelia Capitolina: *BMC Palestine* 91 #54; Tyre: *BMC Phoenicea* 287 #454; 292 #480. See general comments by Hill: *BMC Palestine* xxiii. Roma at Philippopolis in Arabia: *BMC Arabia* 42f. #1; 4; 10.

[441] On renaming Samaria: Josephus *AJ* 15, 8, 5; Temple: *AJ* 15, 9, 6. On this temple at Samaria, see CROWFOOT-KENYON-SUKENIK *The Buildings at Samaria* (London, 1942) 123–127.

[442] OOST *CP* 58 (1963) 12ff. has shown that the Senate had little to do with Cyrene even after the bequest of Apion. Finally motivated by financial difficulties at Rome, the Senate sent P. Lentulus Marcellinus as quaestor pro praetore in 75/74. BADIAN *JRS* 55 (1965) 120 suggests that Lentulus was sent to exploit the royal estates rather than to organize the province, and that Cyrene probably owes its real organization to Pompey. See also REYNOLDS *JRS* 52 (1962) 101f.

stoa of the agora which honored Zeus Soter, Roma and Augustus [443].
It dates from the reign of Augustus, perhaps soon after the Edicts of
Cyrene (7/6 BC). Another monumental (though very fragmentary)
text of the early Empire referring to Roma was found on the outer
wall of the Kaisareion [444]. Perhaps a statue of Roma had been placed
in the Kaisareion as at Antioch and Caesarea. Otherwise there is little
evidence for Roma in Cyrene: a late (and very dubious) inscription and
some coins [445]. However excavations continue in Cyrene, and at least
one unpublished text mentions the goddess Roma [446]. Perhaps more
evidence will be forthcoming.

Egypt — Egypt obviously remained under Ptolemaic rule until the
death of Cleopatra in 30 BC. Julius Caesar had founded a Kaisareion at
Alexandria in 48 BC, but it is unlikely that Roma was joined with him
as in the precincts of Antioch and Caesarea [447]. Roma was unknown in
Egypt, and there was no reason to introduce her while the conqueror
willingly accepted the divine honors given to the Pharaohs, Alexander
and the Ptolemies. Roma was a substitute for the Hellenistic ruler
cult, and where that cult could be directly and unashamedly transferred from kings to dictators and emperors, the goddess was unnecessary [448]. It seems unlikely that Roma was honored there before
the Empire. The earliest definite evidence for Roma in Egypt is the
letter which Claudius sent in 41 AD to the Alexandrians [449]. In it he
refused divine honors for himself, and ordered them instead to dedicate
the golden statue of the Pax Augusta Claudiana to the goddess Roma.
It is unclear from the letter whether a cult of Roma already existed in
Alexandria, but if not one must then have been instituted. Roma had
not appeared on the coinage of Alexandria through the reign of
Claudius, but she appears very frequently after 56 AD. At first the

---

[443] *SEG* IX 127—now superseded by GASPERINI apud STUCCHI *L'Agora di Cirene* (Rome, 1965) 219: Ζηνὶ σωτῆρι καὶ Ῥώμ[αι αἰωνίαι (?) καὶ . . . .]αι καὶ Σε̣[βαστῶι θεῶι? Καίσαρι?]. On the date, see GASPERINI apud STUCCHI 220.

[444] REYNOLDS *PBSR* 26 (1958) 159 #1: [ὑ]πὲρ Ῥώμας [. . . REYNOLDS offers some examples of possible restorations: αἰωνίας διαμονᾶς or καὶ Σεβαστῶν διαμονᾶς. GASPERINI *QAL* 6 (1971) 13 prefers a 2nd century date.

[445] *SEG* IX 277 (+ addenda where REHM's restoration of [Ῥώ]μη is reported). This suggestion is almost certainly incorrect. Coins: *BMC Cyrenaica* ccxi— mention of a helmeted female head with the legend: ΙΜΩΡ. No date is given for this coin. A similar head is to be found on a republican coin (*BMC Cyrenaica* 113 #1) and may be Roma.

[446] I am indebted to Miss Joyce REYNOLDS of Cambridge for a report of this text which seems to mention the goddess Roma and Tiberius.

[447] On the Caesareum at Alexandria, see Malalas p. 217, 5–7 (ed. Dindorf); SJÖQVIST *Opus. Rom.* 1 (1954) 86f.; WEINSTOCK *DJ* 82; 297.

[448] BELL *Cults and Creeds in Graeco-Roman Egypt* (Liverpool, 1953) 56.

[449] BELL *Jews and Christians in Egypt* (London, 1924) 24 Papyrus #1912. 34ff.

goddess was clearly identified by a legend, but after Vespasian the legend does not reappear. VOGT identifies Roma on several dozen Alexandrian issues through the reign of Diocletian[450].

As might be expected, outside the hellenized city of Alexandria there is almost no evidence of Roma. The conservative nature of Egyptian religion makes it very unlikely that the cult of Roma and Augustus ever achieved acceptance outside Alexandria[451]. A papyrus from the mid third century includes an addition or gloss between the lines identifying one Kallistos as a δημιουργὸς θεᾶς Ῥώμης[452]. It seems unlikely that he would have served in that office in Egypt, if that office ever even existed. He was probably a δημιουργός and ἱερεὺς θεᾶς Ῥώμης in some Asian city, perhaps Side, and the scribe has conflated the two offices. Roma occurs nowhere else in published papyri[453].

XVII. Greece

The epigraphical evidence for the cult of Roma on the Greek mainland is quite different from the evidence for Asia and elsewhere. The mainland texts usually attest only festivals to Roma; there is relatively little evidence for priesthoods, cults, altars and temples during the Republic. This situation may partially result from the haphazard ravages of time in pre-selecting our evidence, but a more interesting explanation suggests itself: Roma is a descendant of the Hellenistic

---

[450] *BMC Alexandria* #159; 198; 211; 240; 241; VOGT *Die Alexandrinischen Münzen* 8–14, and from Vespasian to Diocletian, 18–177.

[451] BLUMENTHAL *Archiv für Papyrusforschung* 5 (1913) 327; HEINEN 142 n. 1.

[452] *BGU* 937. This text concerns the sale of a slave; the document records the buyer, the seller, the witness, the slave (one Karon of Pontus), and the previous owner: [. . .] tilius Kallistos. Kallistos is glossed as δημιουργὸς θεᾶς Ῥώμης καὶ γυμνασίαρχος. Since the office of δημιουργός is otherwise unknown in Egypt and the slave Karon comes originally from Asia where δημιουργοί were common, it seems likely that Kallistos came from Asia. But even in Asia there is no evidence for a δημιουργὸς θεᾶς Ῥώμης though the δημιουργός and the ἱερεὺς θεᾶς Ῥώμης are sometimes the same man, as at Pamphylian Side where he was the eponymous magistrate (see p. 88 above). I suggest that the seller of Karon, to add respectability to the pedigree of his slave, had the scribe gloss the name of Kallistos with impressive, foreign titles which were compressed into δημιουργὸς θεᾶς Ῥώμης—an otherwise unattested and intrinsically improbable title. See my discussion in *ZPE* 13 (1974) 277ff. There I try to show that Side's reputation as slave market and the extensive trade contacts between southern Anatolia and Egypt make plausible the suggestion that Kallistos served as eponymous magistrate—δημιουργός and ἱερεὺς θεᾶς Ῥώμης—at Side.

[453] *BGU* 895 as extensively restored (see *Berichtigungsliste* . . . ed. Preisigke) seems to mention Roma—but the restorations are very questionable. Also, *Fouad I University Papyri* (ed. CRAWFORD; Alexandria, 1949) 10 line 7 reads:]δος Ῥώμης and βασιλίδος Ῥώμης has been suggested. Crawford thinks the restoration improbable. In any case, that restoration would refer to the city of Rome proper; see *IG* XIV 830 and *ASA* 3 (1916–1920) 149 #84; WÖRRLE *Chiron* 1 (1971) 332f.

ruler-cults, and these cults differed noticeably between Greece and Asia. Quite simply, the Antigonids were worshipped far less often in Greece than their counterparts were elsewhere. The theory that the ruler-cult was "oriental" and therefore repugnant to the Greeks has long been disputed [454]. The roots of the ruler-cult have been traced back to early Greek religion and literature. In any case, the dichotomy between "Greeks" and "orientals" is spurious [455]. As we have seen, the cities of the Asian littoral were Greek cities, speaking Greek and inhabited for the most part by Greeks, not hellenized barbarians.

The mainland Greeks were no more reluctant to give divine honors than their Ionian cousins; it was the Antigonids who differed from other Hellenistic dynasties. The Macedonian monarchy, transformed elsewhere, had at home remained quasi-constitutional. Thus the Antigonids were well aware that they could never be accepted as god-kings in Macedon, and their relutance to be deified in their own domains was communicated to the cities of Greece [456]. (When Antigonus I and Demetrius Poliorcetes were so honored, the dynasty had not yet established itself in Macedon.) So we find honors voted, statues erected and festivals established in the name of Macedonian kings, but only rare instances of a formal permanent cult [457]. This attitude permeated Greece during the third century; thus in the second and first centuries it was natural that Roma also be honored with dedications and festivals but rarely with a priesthood.

Earlier I attempted to deal with groups of cities in an area with a common historical experience, e.g., Lydia or Caria. This provided a larger corpus of material with which to assess Rome's relation to the area and the cult of Roma in it. That method would not prove very useful for mainland Greece. The policy of individual cities is far too idiosyncratic and, where there supposedly was a common policy (e.g., Achaean League), there is very little evidence. I will therefore treat the evidence for each city separately, though after 146 BC such discrimination becomes almost unnecessary. At that time, whether a city was subject to the Roman governor of Macedon or was nominally "free", its dependence on Rome was clear. Honors paid to Rome (and Roma) then became indiscriminate, and little can be deduced from them. The common motivation of sycophancy inspired all.

---

[454] CERFAUX-TONDRIAU 263f.

[455] TAEGER *Charisma* (Stuttgart, 1957) I 11–168.

[456] JOUGUET *L'impérialisme macédonien et l'Hellénisation de l'Orient* (Paris, 1926) 339f. followed by NOCK *HSCP* 41 (1930) (= *Essays* I 250); also BRISCOE *Livy* 151; 214.

[457] TAEGER *op. cit.* 354–355; compare the meager honors listed on these pages with those given to the Seleucids, Ptolemies and Attalids: pp. 287–351. Also see chapter 1 n. 48 above.

Euboean Koinon — The earliest honors paid to Roma in Greece proper were in the Euboean city of Chalcis. Chalcis—one of Philip's "fetters of Greece"—had been freed by Rome in 196, but a Roman garrison had remained. In 194 Flamininus went personally to Chalcis to remove that and the other Euboean garrisons and, as Livy says, "conventum ibi Euboicarum habuit civitatium"[458]. Flamininus, adhering to the general Roman policy of encouraging local federations, revived the long dormant Euboean League[459]. At the same time, perhaps at the same meeting, this Koinon of the Euboeans instituted Romaia as a federal festival which was celebrated in Chalcis, the chief city of the Koinon. Later it can be found among the pan-hellenic festivals on victory lists[460].

Chalcis — However sincerely these honors were given at the time, they were quickly forgotten in the presence of Antiochus' army a few years later. At first Chalcis, aided by other Euboean cities, refused entry to the Great King—a remarkably bold decision given his near mythic European reputation. But when he returned with greater forces, the Chalcidians relented and Antiochus was admitted by all the Euboean cities[461]. After Antiochus' defeat at Thermopylae and flight to Ephesus, Chalcis again faced Roman wrath. Plutarch's account of this episode is amusing, but hardly to be taken at face value[462]. He portrays the consul Manius Acilius Glabrio as angry with the Chalcidians, not for admitting Antiochus, but for allowing him to marry a young girl of the city during his stay there—especially shocking since

---

[458] 34, 51, 1.

[459] LARSEN *Greek Federal States* (Oxford, 1968) 405; WALLACE *The Euboean League and its Coinage* (New York, 1956) 39; GEYER *RE* Suppl. IV 194. The concerted action of the Euboean cities, first in rebuffing Antiochus and finally in admitting him, is strong evidence that the League had already been reconstituted. WALLACE uses coins to prove this.

[460] On the federal nature of the festival, see *IG* XII 9, 899b. ROBERT Ἀρχ. Ἐφ. (1969) 44–49 has recently treated this festival with an exhaustive review of previous scholarship. Though the foundation date of the festival cannot be fixed with absolute certainty, 194 is the most probable date. Other texts demonstrate the panhellenic nature of the games: *Syll.* 1064 (Halicarnassus); *Hesperia* 15 (1946) 224 #51 (correcting *IG* II² 3153) (Athens); *IG* VII 48 (Megara); *ID* 1957 (Delos).

[461] Unity of Euboeans: Livy 35, 38; Antiochus rebuffed at Chalcis: Livy 35, 46–47; Occupation of Euboean cities: Livy 35, 51, 9–10.

[462] *Flamininus* 16. Appian *Syr.* 21 simply says that Acilius pardoned the Chalcidians. Perhaps Flamininus claimed credit locally for the reprieve (or he may have intervened in a less dramatic way); Plutarch would have heard the embroidered local version on his own visit to Chalcis. The picture of Acilius as a sacker of cities should not surprise us in Plutarch; Acilius had allowed his troops to ravage the lands of Coronea—a mere ten miles from Plutarch's home at Chaeronea (Livy 36, 20, 3). Here too there would have been a local tradition accessible to Plutarch.

the king was over fifty years old! It was clearly the Boeotian moralist more than the Roman general who was scandalized at the king's nymphophilia. Whatever the nature of Flamininus' intervention, the Chalcidians were certainly immensely grateful to him. The city dedicated a gymnasium and a Delphinium to him; a priesthood was established and a hymn was composed to honor him. The hymn recalls the games dedicated to Roma only three or four years before by all the Euboeans, but the focus remains Flamininus—the special friend and patron of Chalcis. It was with sincerity that they called him σωτήρ [463].

Delphi — At least one Romaia in Greece—the one held at Delphi—was established in the aftermath of Thermopylae. During most of the third century, Delphi and much of central Greece had remained under Aetolian control: not only the city, but even the sanctuary of Apollo and the Amphictyonic League. In the months after Thermopylae, while operating against Aetolian strongholds in central Greece, Acilius freed Delphi from Aetolian control and promised in a letter to support the Delphians' attempt to preserve the ancestral laws and autonomy of the city and the sanctuary [464].

Delphi was not disappointed. In 189 the city sent an embassy to Rome to seek official confirmation of their freedom and autonomy. A senatus consultum was passed which granted their request, and that document has been preserved [465]. However, on their return journey the Delphic ambassadors were killed. Later in 189, another embassy was sent to Rome to announce the establishment of Romaia at Delphi and request Roman assistance against the murderers of the ambassadors—suspected to be Aetolians [466]. Since the sacrifices and games dedicated to Roma — τόν τε ἀγῶνα τὸν γυμνικὸν καὶ τὴν θυσίαν ὑπὲρ ἡμῶν (Ῥωμαίων) —were announced in Rome by the second embassy, these honors must have been voted to Roma during 189 in response to the senatus consultum rather than as a result of Delphi's original liberation [467].

Two subsequent texts of the mid second century refer to the θυσία τῶν Ῥωμαίων but there are no unambiguous references to later celebra-

---

[463] *Flamininus* 16. Flamininus did seem to have a special relationship with Chalcis: Livy 34, 51, 1; 35, 49, 6; 36, 31, 5 (back in Chalcis after Thermopylae). On the paean, see p. 121 below.

[464] Livy does not specifically mention Acilius at Delphi, though 36, 35, 6 indicates that the Roman army was based for a time in Phocis in late 191. Acilius' letter was written before he left Greece in April 190: *Syll.* 609–610 (*RDGE* 37).

[465] *Syll.* 612 (*RDGE* 1).

[466] *Syll.* 611 (*RDGE* 38)—a letter of the consul C. Livius Salinator to the Delphians, which recounts the background of the incident.

[467] Livius' letter was written between October 189 and early February 188: he mentions the siege of Same as being in progress, and we know that the city fell before the end of January 189. See *RDGE* pp. 227–228; HOLLEAUX *Études* V 280–281.

tions of the festival at Delphi[468]. It is possible that new Romaia were never established, but that a celebration of the regular Pythian games was specially dedicated to Roma or the Romans with new sacrifices which continued to be performed. If the Romaia were separate, it is reasonable to suppose that they soon were overshadowed by the Pythia and so remained local and inconsequential.

Athens — Athens won her independence from Macedon in 229, and it was only with great difficulty that the city managed to preserve her neutrality through the Social War and the First Macedonian War[469]. But by the end of the third century the Athenians, to protect themselves against Philip V, joined the anti-Macedonian alliance comprised of Rhodes, Attalus and Rome. Though her military resources counted for little, Athens was a welcome member of the alliance for the city still held a moral and cultural preeminence among the cities of Greece.

The Athenians' enormous enthusiasm for their allies is evident in the account by Polybius of Attalus' arrival in Athens just before the outbreak of the war[470]. In addition to his exceptional public and official welcome, his name was added to the list of Attic heroes and one of the tribes was named *Attalis* in his honor. Since Polybius says that Attalus was voted honors rarely bestowed on benefactors and there was later a priest of Attalus at Athens, a cult and priesthood of Attalus were probably established during that visit[471]. The Rhodians were also honored: their ambassadors were lavishly feted, the city was voted isopolity with Athens, and the Demos of the Rhodians was honored with a crown. Less is said about Athenian actions towards the Romans save for the general demonstration of Athenian φιλανθρωπία towards the Roman legates. Yet honors parallel to those voted to Athens' Pergamene and Rhodian allies might well have been decreed at the same time to the goddess Roma, the Demos of the Romans or to the Ῥωμαῖοι Εὐεργέται. A newly published inscription seems to attest sacrifices in Athens to the Demos of the Romans as early as 184/3, and Roma may also have been given a cult (or at least sacrifices) in Athens

---

[468] θυσία τῶν Ῥωμαίων: *IDelphes* 1, 152; *SGDI* 2680.
Romaia: 1) *IDelphes* 1, 549: Ῥω[μαῖα] on a victory list, but the games were not necessarily at Delphi.

2) SEGRÉ *PP* 4 (1949) 81 #2 (Rhodes): a victor in Romaia, but it is unclear whether the festival was celebrated at Delphi or on Rhodes.

[469] Social War: FERGUSON *HA* 248f. Against Athenian participation in the First Macedonian War and Livy's (29, 12, 14) inclusion of Athens in the Peace of Phoinike, see HOLLEAUX *Rome* 259f. and McDONALD *JRS* 27 (1937) 181f. Contra, cf. BALSDON *JRS* 44 (1954) 32f.

[470] Polybius 16, 25–26. Cf. also Livy 31, 14, 11f.
[471] Priest of Attalus: *IG* II² 5080.

during those first two decades of the second century which saw many cults of Roma established [472].

Though Athens remained on friendly terms with Rome after the defeat of Philip in 197, there was for a time a strong anti-Roman faction in the city led by the philosopher Apollodorus who sympathized with King Antiochus [473]. Eastern kings had honored Athens and been generous to her; perhaps those in Apollodorus' movement feared the passing of the era when the city's political impotence could be assuaged by such lavish reinforcement of her sense of intellectual and cultural superiority. In any case, the faction never came to power and the leaders fled the city. That was the last crisis for a century in Athens' relations with Rome. Since the keystone of Athenian foreign policy was a deep distrust of Macedon [474], she never wavered in the war against Perseus, not even when other Greek cities were negotiating with him. Consequently, Athens was one of the few Greek cities in full favor with the Romans after Pydna, and the Athenians cynically made the most of this opportunity. They requested (and received) Haliartus, Delos and Lemnos, and sent out cleruchies to these last two former possessions [475]. Athens was in a fever of nostalgia and narcissism: the cleruchies recalled the great Athenian Empire of the fifth century. Rome came more and more to fill the role of the Hellenistic kings who had honored Athens with gifts, buildings and flattery, and who were in turn rewarded with honorific decrees, statues and festivals [476]. If Roma had not been worshipped in Athens earlier in the century, her cult must have been established soon after Pydna. Romaia were being celebrated in Athens by the 150s [477], and we can assume that not only the festival but also cults, priests and statues of Roma existed in Athens in those excited days of reborn imperialism after 167 [478].

Roma also found her way into the peculiarly Athenian cult of Demos and the Graces (Charites) [479]. The cult was originally established in the

---

[472] TRAILL *Hesperia* 40 (1971) 308 #9; ROBERT *BE* 1972 #106.
[473] Livy 35, 50, 3–4. Cf. DEININGER *Politischer Widerstand* 89f.
[474] Livy 41, 23, 1: Athens refused to admit Macedonians within her boundaries.
[475] Polybius 30, 20.   [476] DEUBNER *Attische Feste* (Berlin, 1932) 235f.
[477] *IG* II^2 1938. The dates suggested for this text vary from 160 to 150. *IG*: c. 150; HATZFELD *BCH* 36 (1912) 193: 160; FERGUSON *HA*: 296: before 153; FERGUSON *Klio* 8 (1908) 341: 152/151. M. THOMPSON *The New Style Silver Coinage of Athens* (New York, 1961) 605–606 argues that a coin independently confirms the date of 152/151 for this text. This has been accepted by MERITT *The Athenian Year* (Berkeley, 1961) 187–188, but LEWIS *CR* 12 (1962) 292 challenges her chronology.
[478] If the worship of Roma had not arrived in Athens before 167, the goddess may have come to the city through its Delian cleruchy. Cf. MARCADÉ 336.
[479] Demos, Roma and the Graces: *IG* II^2 5047; 3404 (as restored). The restoration of *IG* II^2 3547 τὸν ἱερέα συγκλή[του Ῥώμης] καὶ Δήμου καὶ Χαρίτω[ν] seems strange, though it was accepted by ROUSSEL *DCA* 381 and others. Most recently

late third century to commemorate the liberation of Athens from Macedon, so Roma's acceptance into the cult was bitterly ironic[480]. Roma probably entered this cult sometime between 167 and the first appearance of her portrait on Athenian coinage about 90[481]. Through this period Athens saw the rise of oligarchic control sympathetic to, and fostered by, Rome[482]. Yet an anti-Roman, democratic faction survived awaiting an opportunity for a popular uprising. That opportunity came in 88 when, inspired by Mithridates early success, the city rose against Roman control and declared for Mithridates[483]. In this case, the cleavage in Athenian society was largely along class lines with the upper classes closely allied with Rome[484]. But the last great anti-Roman movement in Greece came to little; in spite of courageous resistance the Athenians were soon overwhelmed by Sulla's troops. The pillage of their city in 86 taught the Athenians a sad lesson about the protection afforded by their cultural heritage in a world in which the self-interest of a barbarian super-power determined all.

We must ask to what degree the goddess Roma was modelled on the most famous city-goddess, Athena. The question is apposite; the answer seems far from certain. My own view is that Athena had little, if

MAAS *Die Prohedrie des Dionysostheaters in Athen* (Munich, 1972) 109 rejects this restoration. σύγκλη[ρον] seems to me to be more appropriate, though it is unlikely that the priesthood was assigned by lot. While the completion of συγκλη[. . .] remains questionable, the restoration of 'Ρώμης seems to be demanded by the καί before Δήμου. ROUSSEL *DCA* 381 dates this text to 34/33 BC and uses it to show that Roma was incorporated into this cult before the establishment of the cult of Roma and Augustus.

On the foundation of the cult of Demos and the Graces, see p. 23 above. I do not accept *IG* II² 2336 as evidence for a priesthood of Roma in Athens. The priests listed in that catalogue were Athenian cleruchs at Delos, and the priests of Roma served the cult of Roma on Delos; cf. JUDEICH 94 n. 7; BRUNEAU 137.

[480] FERGUSON *HA* 457 in a refreshing lapse of scholarly propriety comments on this: "and into the house of Athena, and even into the shrine of the *Demos* and *Graces*, *Roma* had come as mistress, bringing with her new ways and new orders, and yielding her favors to a few renegades only . . . . the foreign harlot".

[481] FERGUSON *HA* 366 places her entrance into the cult in the second century; OLIVER *Demokratia* 107 thinks it occurred in the reign of Tiberius, which is certainly too late. For coins with Roma, see THOMPSON *op. cit.* 359ff. where she dates the earliest appearance of Roma to 123/122 BC, but LEWIS *CR* 12 (1962) 292 places this issue 30–35 years later.

[482] FERGUSON *HA* 427f. speaks of an "oligarchic revolution" but more recent scholars see the process as a gradual consolidation of oligarchic control; see also BOWERSOCK 100f.; ACCAME *Dominio* 165f. Sulla restored this oligarchic constitution during his stay in Athens in 84 (Appian *Mithr.* 39).

[483] Pausanias 1, 20, 5; DEININGER *Politischer Widerstand* 245.

[484] BOWERSOCK 102f. For the sources of this episode, cf. BOWERSOCK 102 n. 2; 103 n. 1.

any, influence on the early cults of Roma in Asia. Roma is not a citygoddess, but rather a descendant of the Hellenistic kings. Yet Athena must have had some impact on the view of Roma in Athens or Athenian territories. There she is depicted on the coinage as an Athenatype, and such a connection may well have extended to Delos after Athenian reoccupation [485]. Thus the Athenians could honor themselves while honoring Roman power: Roma presided over her empire as once did Athena in the Parthenon with the imperial treasury at her feet. A simplistic parallel, but one that would have considerable appeal for a proud, but dependent, people. But the Athena-Roma parallel seems to go further. The Romans themselves found it attractive and it was in such a guise that Roma often appeared on Roman coinage [486]. The associations of Roma with Athena/Minerva served the purpose of transporting Roma away from the realm of deification to that of deity. And the arts of Athena, both martial and pacific, would have appealed to Rome. The pretensions of the newly hellenized ruling class in Rome would have been flattered by such associations. So in Athens and Rome these two very different kinds of godhead were associated, sometimes explicitly but more often implicitly. But that should be seen as part of the employment of Roma, rather than a reason, or cause, for her creation.

Roma was later linked to Augustus in a joint cult in which they shared a common priest. That priest of Roma and Augustus had a reserved seat bearing his title in the theater of Dionysus, though a separate seat designated for the priest of Demos, the Graces and Roma testifies to the continued existance of the older cult [487]. Though scholars have suggested that there were possibly several temples of Roma and Augustus, only the round temple on the Acropolis is generally accepted [488]. This temple was probably built in the decade after 27, and it has been suggested that there might be some connection between the temple and Augustus' reported anger towards the Athenians in 21/20 [489]. We might well think that the Athenians built this little temple in the shadow of the Parthenon to expunge once and for all the memory

---

[485] Roma as Athena-type in Athens: THOMPSON *op. cit.* 359f. #1110f.
[486] See p. 163ff.
[487] *IG* II² 5114; 5047.
[488] On this temple, see pp. 139f.
[489] On the date of this temple, see GRAINDOR *Athènes sous Auguste* (Cairo, 1927) 150; JUDEICH *Topographie* 256. FORTE 171 suggests the connection between this temple and Augustus' anger with the Athenians reported by Dio 54, 7 and Plutarch *Reg. et Imp. Apophth.* 207 F. On the decoration, see BOETHIUS and WARD-PERKINS 378. There may also have been a separate cult of Roma and Augustus in the lower city, since the phrase ἐπ' ἀκροπόλει is omitted from the priest's title on the seat in the theater of Dionysius (*IG* II² 5114). On this separate cult, see THOMPSON *Hesperia* 35 (1966) 182f.

of their hospitality towards the tyrannicides and later towards Antony. But it can only remain a pleasant surmise; no definite evidence exists to date the temple more precisely.

Other Honors to Roma — Less than a generation intervened between Pydna and the final reduction of Macedon, which was followed immediately by the conquest of Greece. The Achaean War ended in 146 with the sack of Corinth and the dismemberment of the Achaean League. The protracted scholarly debate over the status of the Greek cities in 146 is of little concern to us here [490]. BADIAN states the case succinctly: "Henceforth all allies — 'free' or 'federate' — are clients, in the sense that their rights and obligations are in practice independent of law and treaties and are entirely defined and interpreted by Rome." [491] Since virtually all Greek cities, free or federate, had equal reason to honor Roma (even though they might hate Rome, though this would depend on the class and economic interests of individual Greeks), discussion of the individual policy of each city would not be profitable. I will simply survey games and cults in Greece which were dedicated to the goddess Roma.

In addition to the Romaia established at Delphi, Chalcis and Athens in the early second century, there were several other cities in which Romaia were added during the second century to a preexisting local festival: Pytheia-Romaia at Megara; Dia-Aianteia-Romaia at Opus in Locris; and the Poseidaia-Romaia at Antigonia (formerly Mantinea) [492].

A text from Aegina mentions Romaia joined together with Aiakeia and Dionysia [493]. Since there were also sacrifices to Apollo and Roma, there may have been a cult of Roma on Aegina by this time. The origin of the cult and festival on the island probably goes back to the second century BC.

An Athenian inscription of the second century BC reports that Athens sent theoroi to the panhellenic festival of the Erotideia-Romaia at Thespiae in Boeotia [494]. But other evidence for this festival is late, when the festival had become the Kaisareia-Erotideia-Romaia [495].

---

[490] ACCAME *Dominio* 1–15 shows that there was no province of Achaea established in 146: some cities were under the governor of Macedon; the others retained their "freedom".

[491] *FC* 114.   [492] *IG* IV² 629.   [493] *IG* IV 2 (69 BC).

[494] *IG* II² 1054. On the date, see ROESCH *Thespies et la Confédération Béotienne* (Paris, 1965) 227.

[495] *IG* VII 2517–2518. Two other fragmentary texts seem to refer to these games: PLASSART *BCH* 50 (1926) 447 #87; PLASSART *BCH* 82 (1958) 158 #9 (+ comments by J. & L. ROBERT *BE* 1959 #189). *IG* II² 3153 mentions Romaia which were once placed in Thespiae, and the text was so restored. But MERITT has published new fragments which disprove that interpretation: *Hesperia* 15 (1946) 224 #51.

Another panhellenic festival in Boeotia was the Amphiaraia in Oropus, which dated back to the fourth century. The epigraphical evidence is very detailed and includes a letter from the consuls of 74 recounting the immunities and privileges given to Oropus by Sulla in 86. The letter also exempts the Oropians from the exactions of the publicani[496]. Sulla helped the Oropians celebrate games and sacrifices ὑπὲρ τῆς νίκης καὶ τῆς ἡγεμονίας τοῦ δήμου τοῦ Ῥωμαίων. Thus the festival became the Amphiaraia-Romaia though it seems to revert to its original title of Amphiaraia during the Empire[497]. No other instances of Romaia in mainland Greece are firmly attested[498].

There is little evidence of priesthoods, temples or formal cults of Roma in Greece proper. The Eleians set up a statue of Roma at Olympia[499], but we hear of no buildings dedicated to Roma (except the temple to Roma and Augustus in Athens). There is only one attested priest of Roma in Greece who is unconnected with the imperial cult: Titus Flavius Polybius who was honored by a decree of his home city of Messene in 257 AD[500]. Polybius was also honored by a decree of the Achaean Confederacy—whatever that meant in 257 AD!—so he might have been priest of Roma at Messene, at Olympia or perhaps at an Achaean city[501]. There are also several priests of, and dedications to, Roma and Augustus. A text from Exarchos in Phocis records the dedication of a statue of Caligula to the goddess Roma[502]. Elsewhere there are cases where there seem to be separate priesthoods of Roma and of the imperial family, with both positions occupied by a single incumbent[503]. And there are dedications

---

[496] *IG* VII 413 (= *RDGE* 23 = *Syll.* 747).

[497] *IG* VII 416; 419; 420; *IPriene* 232–233; *Syll.* 1064 (Halicarnassus). *SEG* VI 727 (Perge in Pamphylia) had been restored Ἀμφιάραα (κ)[αὶ Ῥωμαῖα ἐν Ὠρωπῷ], but BEAN *Belleten* 22 (1958) 53f. has seen an α and so restores Ἀμφιάραα ἄ[νδρας στάδιον] in this imperial text. On the addition of Romaia to the Amphiaraia, see MOMMSEN *Hermes* 20 (1885) 274. On the reversion to the simple Amphiaraia during the Empire, see DEUBNER *Attische Feste* (Berlin, 1932) 229; see also pp. 177f. below.

[498] *Syll.* 1064 line 7: Ῥωμαῖα τὰ ἐν Κε[ρκύρ]αι. L. ROBERT has informed me that J. ROBERT has restudied the squeeze of the text and believes this text refers to Romaia in Cibyra. I am grateful to the ROBERTS and accept their judgment on this text. See note 121 above.

[499] *Olympia* 317.

[500] *Olympia* 486. An inscription from Methone was restored by TOD *JHS* 25 (1905) 41 #1: [ἱερε]ὺ[ς]? Ῥωμαίων Γ. Ἰουλ. Φιλιπ ... [ἱερέ?]ως Ῥωμαίων υἱός. The restoration of KOLBE in *IG* V 1, 1417 seems far more plausible: [ἱππεὺς] Ῥωμαίων ... [ἱπ]πέως Ῥωμαίων υἱός.

[501] *Olympia* 487.

[502] A report of this text is given by KLAFFENBACH *SB Akad. Berlin* 1935 705–706. To my knowledge, the complete text has not yet been published.

[503] *IG* V 1, 500; 525 (Sparta). Also from Laconia, a coin with the head of Roma bears the legend Ῥώμα: *BMC Peloponessus* 128 #68. Also see *IG* V 1, 1172

at Hypata and Thespiae [504]. Priesthoods and dedications may mention the emperor, co-rulers, or the larger imperial family under a variety of titles.

XVIII. Macedon and Thrace

The goddess Roma was linked in a joint cult with Zeus Eleutherios in several Macedonian cities. Since Julius Caesar, Augustus and their successors were often linked with Zeus Eleutherios, at first sight the Macedonian cults might seem to be variants of the worship of Roma and Augustus [505]. But there are difficulties. An unpublished text from Petres (EDSON reports) attests a cult of Roma and Zeus Eleutherios long before the Empire [506]. We should therefore try to find during the Republic a common point of origin for the cults at Abdera, Aenos, Maronia, Petres and Thessalonika [507]. The defeat of Philip VI - Andriscus might be an appropriate occasion on which to honor Roma, but it is difficult to see the particular relevance of Zeus Eleutherios [508].

(Gythium): ἱερέα (θεᾶς Ῥώμης) κ[αὶ ἀρχιερέα] τοῦ τῶν [Σ]εβαστῶν [οἴκου]. This suggestion is not contained in the text of *IG*, but in the index p. 348 ad ἱερεύς.

[504] *IG* IX 2, 32 (Hypata): [θεᾷ Ῥ]ώμῃ δὲ κα[ὶ] θεοῖς Σεβαστοῖς. JAMOT *BCH* 26 (1902) 298 #17 (Thespiae): Γένει Σε[βαστοῦ] καὶ ῾Ρώμηι. PLASSART *BCH* 50 (1926) 394 #14 (Thespiae): θεοῖς Σεβαστοῖς καὶ τῷ Οἴκωι Σεβαστο[ῦ καὶ Ῥώμηι?].

A text from Thisbe in Boeotia is intriguing: Γένει Σεβαστῶν καὶ τῇ πόλει (*IG* VII 2234). The similarity with the dedication from nearby Thespiae is striking, and might suggest that πόλει here stands for Ῥώμῃ. But such an interpretation seems unjustified. πόλις usually refers to the local city rather than to Rome. Though there are occasional examples of πόλις used for Rome (e.g., Epictetus 1, 10, 5), the usage is almost unknown in inscriptions. πόλις used for θεὰ Ῥώμη is not attested, despite RAMSAY's interpretation of a fragmentary text (p. 75 above). The editors of *IG* VII are correct in taking πόλει as Θίσβη (see *IG* VII index, p. 757) as it is clearly intended in other texts from Thisbe (e.g., *IG* VII 2240).

A Neronian coin from Corinth bears the head of Roma with the legend ROMAE ET IMPERIO. (*BMC Corinth* 71 #73; *SNG-DEN* 15 #248–249).

[505] RAUBITSCHEK *AJA* 49 (1945) 128f.; ROBERT *CRAI* (1969) 50; WEINSTOCK *DJ* 140f.; ROBERT *Epigramme Grecque* Entretiens Hardt XIV (Geneva, 1968) 190 n. 2.

[506] EDSON *HSCP* 51 (1940) 131 n. 6; 134.

[507] Abdera: PICARD-AVEZOU *BCH* 37 (1913) 138f. #42; Aenos: ROBERT *BE* 1972 #275 (priest). The text was originally published by TAŞLIKLIOĞLU *Trakya' da epigrafya araştirmalari* (Publications of the University of Istanbul) II (1971) p. 3. (Non vidi.); Maroneia: *IGR* I 831 (priest); BABRITSAS *Arch. Delt.* (1965) 484 #4 and DAUX *BCH* 92 (1968) 926f. (votive altar); Petres: An unpublished text (Saloniki Museum #1281) cited by EDSON *op. cit.* 131 n. 6, which he dates before 100 BC; Thessalonika: *IG* X 2, 1, 32.

[508] EDSON linked this cult of Roma with coin issues bearing the head of Roma: *BMC Macedon* 18 #72–74. These coins were dated to the time of Andriscus. On the connection of Roma and Zeus, see pp. 129ff. below.

Andriscus was no tyrant; he was a timely embodiment of Macedonian discontent. And it would be a strange time to speak of freedom, since Macedon was now about to come under direct Roman rule for the first time. Even sycophancy should bear some relation to political reality. A cult of Zeus Eleutherios would have been more meaningful after 167, when Macedon, though defeated, was ostensibly being given its "freedom" from the Antigonids and organized as four independent republics [509]. Macedonian coins bearing the head of Roma have recently been dated to 168/7, which supports the conclusion that these cults of Roma and Zeus Eleutherios were established in the period immediately after Pydna [510]. Abdera would have found Zeus Eleutherios especially appropriate, since at about that time Abdera was attempting to persuade the Romans to restore some of their ancestral lands taken by King Cotys of Thrace [511].

The priesthood of Roma and Zeus is thus attested from five Macedonian cities, and in Abdera the priest was the eponymous official. In Maronia the epithet Eleutherios was omitted from the name of Zeus, both in the title of the priest and on the votive altar of Zeus and Roma recently discovered in that city. In Thessalonika, in addition to the priest of Roma and Zeus Eleutherios, there was also a priest of Roma and the Ῥωμαῖοι Εὐεργέται. This cult must be dated before 95 BC, and the aftermath of the defeat of Andriscus seems the most plausible occasion [512]. Εὐεργέται was justified only in that Macedon was spared the treatment which was meted out to Epirus two decades earlier by Aemilius Paullus. Roma continued to appear relatively frequently on the coinage of the Macedonian cities throughout the Empire [513].

The Macedonian Koinon was centered at Beroea, perhaps because that was the first city to surrender to Rome in 168 [514]. There is no evidence for this institution until the Empire, when a provincial high priest of the imperial cult is attested who also served as Macedoniarch [515]. The similar cults of Roma and Zeus Eleutherios are perhaps evidence of co-operative action taken by the Macedonian cities as early as the second century BC. But little more can be said.

---

[509] LARSEN *Greek Federal States* (Oxford, 1968) 295–300.

[510] MACKAY *Museum Notes* (1968) 5–13 followed by NICOLET *RA* (1971) 359. For the coins, see n. 508.

[511] *Syll.* 656; ROBERT *CRAI* (1969) 43. For recent treatments of this (unsuccessful) embassy to Rome, cf. HERRMANN *ZPE* 7 (1971) 72ff.; CONDURACHI *Latomus* 29 (1970) 581ff.

[512] Priesthood of Roma and Ῥωμαῖοι Εὐεργέται *IG* X 2, 1, 32; 133; 226. Mention of Ῥωμαῖοι Εὐεργέται in 95 BC: *IG* X 2, 1, 4; cf. p. 129.

[513] Amphipolis: GAEBLER II 39 #61–62; Edessa: *BMC Macedon* 39f. #20f.; Thessalonika: *BMC Macedon* 371 #50.

[514] DEININGER *Provinziallandtage* 91f.

[515] *IG* X 2, 1, 163; DEININGER *Ibid.* 93.

Two priests of Roma are also attested from the remote regions to the north of Macedon[516]. Both priests served during the Empire—one in the third century—but the emperor was not included in these cults at Odessus and Nicopolis. Since Thrace did not become a province until 45 AD, Roma was probably not included in the imperial cult of the provincial Koinon[517]. During the Empire, Roma can also be seen on the coinage of several cities in Thrace and along the Black sea littoral[518].

XIX. The West

Though there is a substantial amount of evidence attesting θεὰ Ῥώμη throughout the Greek world, almost none comes from Greek cities in the West. The only positive evidence for Roma in Magna Graecia is the didrachm from Locri Epizephyrii which portrays the seated personification of Roma crowned by the personified Fides[519]. The two figures are labeled Ῥώμη and Πίστις. This coin has sometimes been dated to the aftermath of Pyrrhus' invasion of Sicily, sometimes to the second Punic War[520]. I find the latter date more probable; specifically 204, when the Senate punished Pleminius against whose savage activity the Locrians had appealed: "ad vos vestramque fidem supplices confugimus"[521]. It would then seem that the earliest known deification of Roma occurred at Italian Locri—even before the temple at Smyrna. But we have already seen that the deification of Rome was possible by the end of the third century, perhaps even at Athens[522]. Deification, dedications and sacrifices would likely have preceded the temple of 195 and these would have been appropriate at the time in areas of Italy liberated from Carthaginian control. So I would interpret this Locrian coin as the earliest expression of the Greek phenomenon of the deification of Roma—a phenomenon which had traveled to Locri from the East.

Later dedications and statues of Roma were set up on the Capitol by Greek cities and Eastern kings[523]. But these can hardly be interpreted

---

[516] Nicopolis: *IGR* I 589; Odessus: *IGR* I 1439.

[517] DEININGER *Provinziallandtage* 96 f.

[518] Bizya: *BMC Thrace* 89 #7; Philippopolis: MACDONALD *Hunterian Coll.* 744 #5a; Tomi: PICK-REGLING *Die Antiken Münzen von Dakien und Moesien* (Berlin, 1898–1910) II 661 #2515.

[519] *BMC Italy* 365 #15.

[520] MOMMSEN's early date for this coin is still accepted by ALFÖLDI; the later date has been defended by MATTINGLY *NC* 17 (1957) 288; THOMSEN *Early Roman Coinage* (Copenhagen, 1957–1961) II 155f. follows the date of MOMMSEN while rejecting his reasons. Also cf. *CIL* X 16.

[521] Livy 29, 6–21; especially 29, 18, 19; cf. also Diodorus 27, 4, 1.

[522] See pp. 45; 101 above.

[523] See Additional note; also cf. pp. 37f.; 153.

as evidence for the worship of Roma in the West, and this material has already been discussed in the treatment of the various cities and kingdoms which sent them to Rome.

Finally, the most important Greek agonistic festival established in Italy is called in one text Ἰταλικὰ Ῥωμαῖα Σεβαστὰ ἰσολύμπια [524]. The festival was established in 2 AD as an Italian counterpart to the Romaia Sebasta of Pergamum [525]. But there is doubt whether this festival was actually dedicated to Roma. Rather, the original title seems to have been Σεβαστά and the games were thus celebrated in honor of the emperor alone [526]. It is possible that Ῥωμαῖα, like Ἰταλικά, serves merely as an epithet [527]. I find it unlikely that these games were dedicated to both Roma and Augustus.

*

This concludes our survey of the evidence for the goddess Roma in the Greek world. I have attempted to place the Greeks' devotion to Roma within the appropriate political and historical context. In Part II of this monograph I will attempt to analyze the various manifestations of Roma and her cult.

---

[524] *IG* XIV 748; cf. also the very fragmentary *IGR* I 448.

[525] GEER *TAPA* 66 (1935) 216 argues this date. On the connection with the festival in Pergamum, cf. ROBERT *Epigramme Grecque* Entretiens Hardt XIV (Geneva, 1968) 263; *AC* 37 (1968) 409. Also cf. BOWERSOCK 83f.

[526] On the name, cf. ROBERT *Epigramme* 263; 286; *AC* 37 (1968) 408f.; *CRAI* (1970) 9.

[527] On the possible force of such an epithet, cf. ROBERT *RP* 84 (1958) 25; NOCK *HSCP* 41 (1930) 59 (= *Essays* I 248) which discusses this use of Augustus and Σεβαστά.

PART II

Chapter 3

The Greek View of Roma

θεὰ Ῥώμη was a surrogate for the Hellenistic ruler-cult: perfectly understood by the Greeks, scorned and ignored by the Romans. By the time the ruler-cult was accepted by the Romans, the emperor had become the object of the cult and Ῥώμη was superfluous. As a result, Roman literary sources hardly discuss Ῥώμη save for a few surviving panegyrics. Plutarch has left us no essay on the goddess, and the Christian apologists found her worthy neither of exposure nor of denunciation[1]. All the known evidence for the goddess deals specifically with her priests, cults and festivals rather than with herself. So the Greek conception of Roma must be inferred from the titles and epithets bestowed upon her, from poetic references to her, and from the nature of the other divinities with whom she was joined in cults or dedications.

I. Epithets

In Greek poetry, especially oral poetry, epithets are stock adjectives used to modify the names not only of gods and heroes, but also of animals, places and even inanimate objects. Outside poetry, epithets were usually reserved to gods and men of distinction. Some were used to honor gods; others to honor men; and still others were applicable to both. In addition, certain proper epithets were reserved to particular gods (e.g. Apollo Pythios) since these epithets often identified specific cults or guises of the god. All Greek gods seem to have had at least one such proper epithet, but the deified Hellenistic rulers had none; epithets applied to one of them were applied to many. And so it is with

[1] This is also true of the ruler cult; no treatise or extensive treatment by ancient scholars is known; cf. HABICHT 129 ff.

Roma. Her epithets are common ones, and we can therefore draw from them no detailed, distinctive picture of Roma. Yet the fact that she inherited these rather weak epithets from Hellenistic kings and passed them on to the Roman emperors places the goddess in a certain historical perspective, and confirms her descent from the Hellenistic ruler cults.

The epithets given to Roma in poetic texts are frequently problematic. The poets used Ῥώμη in many different senses—as goddess, mortal, apostrophe, abstraction—and these cannot always be distinguished. We will therefore examine first the epigraphical and numismatic evidence, and discuss the poetry later.

Θεός — The word most commonly associated with Roma in inscriptions is θεά[2]. It appears in dedications as well as in the titulature of priests[3]. No pattern is discernible for its inclusion or omission. The word is hardly surprising, but it is important to emphasize that this Ῥώμη is a divinity and must be sharply distinguished from the Trojan lady of the same name. Merely the occasional use of θεά would not suffice to establish her divinity, for the word can be used purely subjectively, "a god from any point of view". Such usage is partly rhetorical and partly the result of a the personal approach to divinity that was common in antiquity[4]. Yet when applied to Roma over and over again in formal decrees, the epithet must have had real force. θεὰ Ῥώμη was worshipped with temples, festivals and priesthoods; her divinity is incontestable. Indeed, the epithet stuck so closely to Roma's name that it was later inappropriately appended when only the name of the city was intended[5].

θεός had been a common epithet in the Hellenistic ruler cult, and was later used in the various components of the Roman imperial cult. Not only the emperor and his family, but even the Senate and the Demos of the Romans were so honored[6].

Σωτήρ — Roma is given this epithet on the base of a statue of the goddess which the city of Iulis on Ceos set up in the first century BC[7]. The epithet had a long history. By the fifth century BC it was already used both as the standard epithet of Zeus and as a title of honor for

---

[2] θεός as epithet in ruler cult: HABICHT 156 n. 75.
[3] *OGIS* 533.
[4] NOCK "Notes on Ruler-Cult I–IV" *JHS* 48 (1928) 31 (= *Essays* I 145). In a similar way, Philo *De vita Moysis* I 158 calls Moses θεὸς καὶ βασιλεύς.
See also HABICHT in *Le culte des soverains dans l'empire Romain* Enteretiens Hardt XIX (1973) 43.
[5] *IGR* IV 1687; *IBM* 894 where θεὰ Ῥώμη is in opposition to πατρίς. On πατρίς as Roma, cf. ERIM-REYNOLDS *JRS* 59 (1969) 58; for Cicero's idea that every Roman has two patriae (his birthplace and Rome) see *De Legibus* 2, 5. Also cf. WÖRRLE *Chiron* 1 (1971) 332f.
[6] *OGIS* 479.   [7] *IG* XII 5, 622.

mortals. And it continued to be applied both to gods and to mortals: the Septuagint assigned it both to God and to individual leaders, and in the Christian fourth century AD σωτήρ was used both for Jesus and for mere magistrates[8]. The title never implied divinity as such[9]. σωτήρ can describe a deity, but it denoted his function rather than his spiritual nature. The function of the political σωτήρ was to bestow integrity and prosperity (σωτηρία) on the community. Thus both Roma and a mere priest of Roma were called σωτῆρες[10]. The epithet came to Roma from Hellenistic kings, especially from Ptolemy I[11], and was used of Flamininus by the Chalcidians. In a quite staggering anachronism Dionysius of Halicarnassus reports Tarquin as saying that a good king will be called σωτήρ and εὐεργέτης[12]. And so they were, Hellenistic princes and Roman emperors alike. But if Julius Caesar, Augustus and their successors carried this epithet, so did their subordinates[13]; the double meaning of the term persisted until the late Empire[14].

σωτήρ is not easily translated into Latin—now *salus*, now *conservator* was used[15]. In a bilingual text from Laodicea the Demos of the Romans is called σωτῆρα καὶ εὐεργέτην—translated by the phrase *Salutei fuit, Benefici*[16].

Εὐεργέτης — This epithet was often linked with σωτήρ, whether in honoring Hellenistic kings or ordinary men[17]. But even more than σωτήρ, εὐεργέτης refers to the realm of mortal benefaction[18]. Long the standard term for the benefactor of a city, εὐεργέτης was a title rarely given to gods and an altogether less dramatic word than σωτήρ[19]. When applied to the Ptolemies and the Seleucids, it referred to their civic benefactions rather than to their divinity[20]. And Roma inherited this usage of the word. So, like σωτήρ, εὐεργέτης was used for her priests as well as for Roma. A statue of Ῥώμη θεὰ εὐεργέτις still stands on Delos and one of Roma εὐεργέτις τοῦ κόσμου once stood in Assus[21].

---

[8] Nock "*Sôtêr* and *Euergetês*" in *Essays* II 720–735 is essential. On Jesus, cf. Nock *Early Gentile Christianity* (reprint, New York, 1964) 35f. (= *Essays* I 78).
[9] Nilsson II 184f.; 390f. See also Habicht (n. 4 above) 97.
[10] *IGR* IV 741; cf. Nock *Essays* II 728 for other examples.
[11] Pausanias 1, 8, 6; for other references to Hellenistic kings, cf. Habicht 156 n. 76.
[12] *AR* 4, 32, 1.
[13] Julius Caesar: *Syll.* 760; other evidence in Raubitschek *JRS* 44(1954) 65f. Augustus: *IGR* III 719. On others, see Nock *Essays* II 728–729.
[14] Nock *Essays* II 734–735. [15] Oxé *WS* 48 (1930) 38ff.
[16] *CIL* I² 728. [17] Oehler *RE* VI 978ff.
[18] Nilsson II 183.
[19] Nock *Essays* II 725; Robert *Le Sanctuaire de Sinuri près de Mylasa* I *Les Inscriptions Grecques* (Paris, 1945) 23.
[20] Habicht 156 n. 77.
[21] *ID* 1778. On the statue at Assus, cf. Merkelbach *ZPE* 13 (1974) 280.

In 81 BC the Stratoniceans dedicated a festival to Ἑκάτη σωτείρα ἐπιφανής and Ῥώμη θεὰ Εὐεργέτις [22]. But here the epithets divide too neatly; they are arranged more for grace and symmetry than for context. If ever it was appropriate to apply the more powerful adjectives of σωτήρ and ἐπιφανής to Roma, it was in the immediate aftermath of the defeat of Mithridates. Another statue of Roma on Melos had been erected in the second century ἕνεκα εὐεργεσίας, but we do not know any particular Roman kindness that inspired this tribute [23].

Again, like σωτήρ, εὐεργέτης was sufficiently weak not to offend Christians when associated with mortals [24]. Philo applied it to God, but it by no means implied divinity [25]. In Thessalonika, Roma was linked in a cult with the Ῥωμαῖοι Εὐεργέται which clearly did not affirm the divinity of each and every Roman [26]. εὐεργέτης was essentially a compliment, not a divine honor [27]. Any confusion over this distinction is our own and stems from a modern reluctance to pay compliments to a god. The ancients did so with alacrity.

Ἐπιφανής — By contrast the epithet ἐπιφανής is a peculiarly religious term. It came into the ruler cult from the East; we first encounter it as an epithet of Ptolemy V [28]. It is difficult to determine the reason for the epithet in this case: it may be a translation of a standard Egyptian epithet or it may refer to a specific event. Of course the events which it commemorated—ἐπιφανεῖαι—were usually military.

Antiochus IV adopted ἐπιφανής, and it then became a conventional epithet of Hellenistic kings and spread to the dynasties of Bithynia, Cappadocia and Commagene [29]. The tradition was eventually passed on to the rulers of Rome; Julius Caesar was quite plausibly honored by the Koinon of Asia as θεὸς ἐπιφανής [30]. Of course it continued to be applied to emperors and their families [31]. The Latin equivalent is used by Horace in his fifth Roman ode—"praesens divus"—and later Pliny called Trajan: "deus manifestus ac praesens" [32]. But here the sense of a continuing benevolent presence is emphasized, and the earlier connection with a dramatic epiphany has disappeared.

---

[22] *OGIS* 441.   [23] *IG* XII 3, 1097.   [24] Nock *Essays* II 734.

[25] *De Sobrietate* 55; Nock *HSCP* 41 (1930) 53 (= *Essays* I 244) shows that divine honors given to εὐεργέται do not imply deification.

[26] *IG* X 2, 1, 31–32; 133; 226.

[27] This despite Germanicus' edict to the Alexandrians (Ehrenberg-Jones 320 B) which describes σωτήρ and εὐεργέτης as ἰσόθεος. On this, cf. Nock *Essays* II 724–725.

[28] *OGIS* 90. 5; Nock *JHS* 48 (1928) 38–41 (= *Essays* I 152–156).

[29] Pfister *RE Supp* IV 308 argued for a Seleucid origin for this epithet, but Nock *JHS* 48 (1928) 38 n. 87 (= *Essays* I 152 n. 87) questions that assertion. On the spread of this epithet, cf. Pfister 306.

[30] *Syll.* 760.   [31] Pfister *op. cit.* 307.

[32] Horace *Carmina* 3, 5, 2; Pliny *Panegyricus* 1.

Though the force of ἐπιφανής seems to apply to Roma rather than to Hecate in the Stratonicean festival, the epithet directly modifies Roma only once. It was an occasion when the full literal force of the term would have been intended. The Lycian Koinon dedicated a festival to Roma as θεὰ ἐπιφανής, probably just after the great Roman victory at Magnesia early in 189 BC[33]. The sudden and successful appearance of Roman power in Asia gives genuine meaning to the epithet, which probably brought to mind Apollo's famous epiphany which saved Delphi from the barbarians less than a century earlier[34]. This literal interpretation of the Lycians' use of ἐπιφανής is supported by the phrase κατὰ τὸμ πολεμὸν ἐπιφανείας in the unpublished Chian text from the early second century[35]. Theophania is also mentioned in the same text, seemingly in direct connection with Roma [τῇ Ῥώ]μῃ μετὰ τὰ Θεοφάνια πομπῆς. Perhaps the well-known festival of Theophania on Chios should therefore also be dated to the period just after the Syrian war[36].

But if this early use of ἐπιφανής has direct historical relevance, it seems to have become formulaic or at least much weakened by the time of the Empire. It is even applied to the Senate in one Asian inscription[37], where it is difficult to determine whether it refers to an actual victory of Senatorial forces during the Civil Wars or is used merely as general term of praise (as it would soon be applied to the imperial family)[38]. By the first century AD the word seems to have lost its connotative force, except in Jewish and Apostolic writers[39] who of course were drawing not on the current use of the word, but on its frequent appearance in the Septuagint where the early Hellenistic meaning was preserved[40].

In fact all the terms so far discussed—θεός, εὐεργέτης, σωτήρ, ἐπιφανής—were applied not only to the Hellenistic kings, the goddess Roma and the Roman emperors, but also to Jesus in the New Testament. It would be misleading to see this as a simple continuum, however, for the writers of the New Testament were obviously greatly influenced by the Hellenistic Greek version of the Old Testament and other products of Hellenized Judaism.

Νικηφόρος — This epithet was generally less common than those already discussed. It derives from the cult statues of gods who carry a miniature statue of Victory (Νίκη) in their hands, beginning with the

---

[33] BEAN *JHS* 68 (1948) 46 #11. See above page 37f.
[34] LARSEN *CP* 51 (1956) 155.
[35] See above pp. 60f. [36] See above p. 61 n. 218.
[37] ROBERT *Hellenica* VI 50 #15. [38] *IGR* III 680; *CIG* 4240d.
[39] Josephus *AJ* 2, 16, 2; for Christian uses, cf. PFISTER *RE* Suppl. IV 321f.
[40] For the many uses of forms of this word in the Septuagint, cf. HATCH-REDPATH *A Concordance to the Septuagint* (Oxford, 1897) I 537–538.

Olympian Zeus and Athena Parthenos of Phidias[41]. Eventually other divinities were so depicted and, by transference, the title was appropriated by Hellenistic kings. Antiochus IV of Syria was given the epithet on coins which show Zeus, seated, holding a Nike[42]. About 60 BC, the coinage of Bithynian and Pontic cities portrayed the goddess Roma holding a Nike and seated on a pile of armor—a type frequently used for Athena[43]. Later the epithet was taken less literally: Victory was personified as a bringer of victory rather than as the bearer of a miniature statue. And the single epigraphical reference to Roma as νικηφόρος should be taken in this less literal sense, for it occurs on a dedication to Roma and Julius Caesar after the victory over Pompey[44]. Roma Victrix later became a common coin legend where Roma is pictured holding a Nike[45], and emperors holding a Nike appear on coins from the reign of Nero onwards[46].

Ἡγεμών — This only occurs with Roma on an imperial text from Ephesus where ἡγεμὼν Ῥώμη describes a statuette which is elsewhere called *Urbs Romana* and the Demos of the Romans[47]. The word was never a true epithet and, though it could be used as a name for the emperor that would be translated *Princeps*, it had nothing to do with the ruler cult[48]. It seems likely that this single use of ἡγεμών with Roma derived from the more common noun ἡγεμονία. The use of ἡγεμονία for political supremacy was common from the time of Herodotus, and Sulla himself told the Oropians to join Romaia to their own Amphiaraia because of the victory and ἡγεμονία of the Roman people[49]. Since these are Sulla's own words, we should see *imperium* behind ἡγεμονία—an equivalence confirmed by the *Res Gestae*[50]. The Greeks, true to their fashion, even personified ἡγεμονία on their coinage and there is a dedication to Nerva, the Senate and the ἡγεμονία of the

---

[41] WEINSTOCK *DJ* 100; in general cf. HÖFER "Nikephoroi Theoi" in ROSCHER *Lexikon* III. 358f.

[42] *BMC Seleucids* 36 #22; also used of Ptolemies: *OGIS* 89. 3; 168. 48.

[43] E.g., *BMC Pontus* 152 #2f.; see above pp. 84f. Roma Nikephoros also appears on a coin of Alabanda with the legend θεὰ Ῥώμη: *BMC Caria* 4 #19.

[44] *IG* XII 2, 25; 26 Supp.

[45] CICHORIUS *MDAI(A)* 13 (1888) 58 connected this epithet with the "Roma Victrix" coins of the younger Cato—an assertion repeated by HÖFER *op. cit.* 359. No references are given. I do not think that Sydenham *The Coinage of the Roman Republic* (London, 1952) 176 #1053 can be so interpreted since the legend "Roma" appears on the obverse, and "Victrix" with a statue of Victory on the reverse. This imitates his father's coinage (*Ibid.* 83 #596). Since other issues of both father (*Ibid.* 83 #597) and son (*Ibid.* 175 #1052) carry "Victrix" but not "Roma", the two legends can hardly be connected. Later "Roma Victrix" became a popular theme in literature; cf. Ovid *Fasti* 4, 389.

[46] WEINSTOCK *DJ* 101.   [47] *Ephesos* II. 28.

[48] *Res Gestae* 13.

[49] *IG* VII 413 (= *RDGE* 23).   [50] *Res Gestae* 27.

Romans[51]. And in the first century of the Empire, the eternal quality of the ἡγεμονία was a common Greek expression of belief in the eternity of Roman power—*Aeternitas imperi Romani* in the West[52].

Ἀρχηγέτης — This epithet was usually associated with heroic or divine founders of cities, such as Heracles at Sparta[53]. The epithet was applied to Roma only at Attalia where θεὰ ἀρχηγέτις Ῥώμη had a cult, confirmed by the titulature of both a priest and a priestess[54]. The title was applied to Roma at Attalia because an official Roman colony was established there in the Augustan age. Therefore Roma served Attalia as ἀρχηγέτις (like a κτίστης)[55].

Ἀέναος — Perhaps the most familiar epithet of Roma in antiquity was *Aeterna*—and so she was called into the Middle Ages[56]. But it is extremely difficult to determine whether this idea originated in the Hellenistic East or in Rome itself. Traditionally, certain kings possessed eternal power—the Ptolemies were called αἰωνόβιοι[57] and the subjects of Attalus III prayed that the gods preserve his royal rule from harm εἰς τὸν ἅπαντα αἰῶνα[58]. Already in the second century BC the idea of the eternity of Roman power can be found in the Greek world. Melinno and Lycophron gave poetic voice to it. After Magnesia the idea spread that Rome was the "fifth empire" which would succeed the four great empires of the East and would endure forever[59]. This idea reached Rome by 170 BC, and its widespread currency in the East is witnessed by the fierce attacks on it in anti-Roman oracular and apocalyptic writings which continue in an unbroken line from the second century, through the time of Mithridates[60] to the Christian attacks on Roman power. It was in such a context that a Roman legate set up at Eleusis a statue of Aion εἰς κράτος Ῥώμης.

---

[51] DREXLER in ROSCHER *Lexikon* I 1877. Dedications: *IGR* IV 1195.

[52] *Syll.* 818: διαμονῆς τῆς Ῥωμαίων ἡγεμονίας; *IGR* IV 661: τῷ αἰῶνι τῆς Ῥωμαίων ἡγεμονίας; cf. WEINSTOCK *MDAI(R)* 77 (1962) 314–315.

[53] Xenophon *Hell.* 6, 3, 6.

[54] *SEG* II 696; XVII 582.

[55] On the colony at Attalia, see above pp. 87f. κτίστης was used of Hellenistic kings, as Antiochus IV (*OGIS* 253); cf. also BOEHRINGER-KRAUSS *Altertümer von Pergamon IX Das Temenos für den Herrscherkult* (Berlin, 1937) 93. It was from these Hellenistic rulers that Augustus inherited this title: GRANT *From Imperium to Auctoritas* (Cambridge, 1945) 356; 368.

[56] PASCHOUD *Roma Aeterna* (Rome, 1967) passim.

[57] *OGIS* 90.4; 168.58.   [58] *OGIS* 332.30f.

[59] For Melinno and Lycophron, see pp. 120 ff. On the myth of four empires, cf. SWAIN *CP* 35 (1940) 1–21.

[60] SANFORD *AJP* 58 (1937) 437–456; FUCHS *Der geistige Widerstand gegen Rom in der antiken Welt* (Berlin, 1938) passim.; 87f. discusses Roma Aeterna as a *Nomen Blasphemiae* to Christian writers. Most furious attacks: Daniel 2, 37f.; 7, 17ff.; *Oracula Sibyllina* III; Antisthenes story in Phlegon *Mirabilia* III—all 2nd century BC.

But in Rome itself the idea of the eternity of the city also had a long history, perhaps originating as Livy claims in the Gallic invasion[61]. In Rome, the Palladium and the fire of Vesta were long associated with the eternity of the city[62]. Even though the general idea of the eternity of Roman power was current in the East in the second century, it was not specifically identified with Roma. But Vesta's guarantee of eternity to the city was eventually expressed as Urbs Aeterna, Roma Aeterna, and Aeternitas Augusti[63]. Of all the aspects of the cult of Roma and of the emperors, it is perhaps the idea of eternity which derives most from the native Roman tradition[64].

The only clear example of a Greek version of the epithet *aeternus* is in the oath taken at the accession of Tiberius preserved on a text from Cyprus[65]. Included among the divinities to whom the oath was sworn is ἀέναος Ῥώμη. But ἀέναος had not previously been used to mean "eternal" and the usage is clearly a translation of the Latin *Roma Aeterna*. Other texts from the early empire also refer to the eternity of Roman power, but no others directly connect eternity with θεὰ Ῥώμη[66].

Σεβαστός — Other epithets of Roma in the Empire are simply taken from Hellenistic imperial titles. As we would expect, Ῥώμη Σεβαστή was used on priestly titles from Termessus, and on coins as well[67]. L. ROBERT has shown that many personifications were called *Augusta* or Σεβαστή both in inscriptions and on coins[68]. An even more specific epithet appears with Roma on a coin from Cibyra: Ῥώμη Ἁδριανή[69]. But since Hadrian had brought the cult of Roma to Rome and had built her great temple there, the conjunction is not surprising.

Πόλις — Roma in Latin is frequently modified by *Urbs*, even when the goddess Roma is intended[70]. And *urbs* alone can stand for the goddess, as in references to the Templum Urbis for the temple of Roma and Venus. Yet in Greek, πόλις does not replace θεὰ Ῥώμη[71], though

---

[61] 5, 7, 10.
[62] KOCH "Roma Aeterna" *Gymnasium* 59 (1952) 130 ff.; 196 ff.
[63] I am preparing a study of Vesta and Roma.
[64] CHARLESWORTH "*Providentia* and *Aeternitas*" HTR 29 (1936) 131.
[65] MITFORD *JRS* 50 (1960) 75–79.
[66] For texts on eternity of Roman power, see WEINSTOCK *MDAI(R)* 77 (1962) 314 f. Two texts from Cyrene have been restored in such a way that they refer to the eternity of Roma. These editions are standard: GASPERINI apud STUCCHI *L'Agora di Cirene* (Rome, 1965) 219: Ζηνὶ σωτῆρι καὶ Ῥώμ[αι αἰωνίαι(?)]; REYNOLDS *PBSR* 26 (1958) 159 #1: [ὑ]πὲρ Ῥώμας [αἰωνίας διαμονᾶς] or [καὶ Σεβαστῶν διαμονᾶς]. REYNOLDS merely offers these restorations as suggestions. Cf. now GASPERINI *QAL* 6 (1971) 13.
[67] *IGR* III 440–442; *TAM* III 1, 112–114. Coins: *BMC Macedon* 371 #50.
[68] *RP* 84 (1958) 25. [69] IMHOOF-BLUMER *KM* I 257 #28.
[70] E.g. Tacitus *Ann.* 4, 56.
[71] RAMSAY *The Social Basis of Roman Power in Asia Minor* (Aberdeen, 1941) 18 #7 is a terribly corrupt text: ἀ[ρχιερέ]ως τῆς Πό[λεως]. Even if this restora-

it serves as an epithet on a few coins. There are coins from Pontus with the legend Ῥώμη πόλις and some from Nicaea with the legend Ῥώμην μητρόπολιν[72].

Βασιλεύς — One epithet or title which Roma might be expected to have inherited from the ruler cult is βασιλεύς. Cognate forms of βασιλεύς occur in Melinno and the Oracula Sibyllina in connection with the goddess Roma, but she is never modified by the epithet[73]. When βασιλίς is used with Ῥώμη, it applies only to Rome, the city in Italy. So we have men who served as ambassadors εἰς τὴν Βασιλίδα Ῥώμην[74] and a Pisidian who died ἐν τῇ Βασιλίδι Ῥώμῃ[75]. The phrase occurs in other documents and always clearly refers to the geographical location[76]. Only in a famous passage of Dio does it seem possible that βασιλίς is applied to the goddess Roma—where the spectators in the circus in December AD 196 unexpectedly acclaimed Ῥώμη (instead of the emperor Severus) as βασιλίς and ἀθάνατος[77]. But this is hardly a genuine use of the Greek epithet; Dio is merely translating the shouts of *Roma Domina* and *Roma Aeterna* that rang through the circus.

II. Poems

Ῥώμη is used in a variety of ways by Greek poets and historians. Until the time of Cicero the Latin *Roma* could be used only for the physical city on the Tiber; no metaphorical or derived meanings were possible[78]. But Greek was far more flexible—so much so that the use of Ῥώμη in poems can sometimes be ambiguous. Here are the principal meanings of Ῥώμη:

1) the physical city itself[79];
2) metaphorically for the Cives Romani—whether living in Rome or not[80];

---

tion were correct, which I doubt, the assumption that πόλις refers to Roma is quite unfounded. An inscription from Trysa (*IGR* III 687) ending γενόμενον ἱερέα Ῥώμης πόλεως? θεοῖς is ambiguous. Cf. chapter 2 n. 504.

[72] Amisus in Pontus: WADDINGTON *Recueil Général* I² 77 #67c; Nicaea in Bithynia: *BMC Bithynia* 155 #25.

[73] Melinno 5–6: σοὶ μόνᾳ, πρέσβιστα, δέδωκα Μοῖρα κῦδος ἀρρήτῳ βασιλῆον ἀρχᾶς. Oracula Sibyllina III 46: Ῥώμη βασιλεύσει. See below n. 97.

[74] BEAN-MITFORD *Journeys in Rough Cilicia 1964–1968* Denkschr. Öster. Akad. 102 (Vienna, 1970) #1; 13.

[75] *ASA* 3 (1916–1920) 149 #84.

[76] *IG* XIV 830; *IMagn.* 180; also cf. WÖRRLE *Chiron* 1 (1971) 330f.

[77] 76, 4. Cf. J. GAGÉ *Basiléia* (Paris, 1968) 244–5; 261 n. 59 on this text.

[78] KNOCHE *Gymnasium* 59 (1952) 329f.

[79] E.g. Dionysius Periegetus *Orbis Descriptio* (MÜLLER *GGM* II 124) 354: θύμβρις, ὃς ἱμερτὴν ἀποτέμνεται ἄνδιχα Ῥώμην.

[80] E.g. Crinagoras *A.P.* IX 291; Pseudo-Scymnos *Orbis Descriptio* (MÜLLER *GGM* I 205) 231f.

3) the physical area under the power of the Senatus Populusque Romanus [81];

4) the eponymous Trojan, Rhome, who was responsible in some way for the foundation and naming of the city [82];

5) the goddess Roma—the personification and deification of the Roman people [83].

Of course these categories are not exclusive, nor do all cases fit easily into one or another of these five meanings. But this list is useful in alerting the unwary to the variety of Greek usages, and specifically to the distinction between the Trojan eponymous heroine, Ῥώμη, and the goddess Roma. These two ladies have only one essential thing, besides their name, in common: both were invented by Greeks. In all other things — model, motivation for existence, transferral to Italy — they remain quite unconnected. Rhome has already been discussed and dissociated from the goddess Roma. Here we are concerned solely with Roma.

As Roman power became established in the East, Rome was glorified, and occasionally vilified, by poets and historians [84]. Her most notable surviving eulogists from the second century BC are Melinno, Lycophron, and Polybius, while the Oracula Sibyllina attacks her. Few writings survive from what must have been an immense mass of material. Vast numbers of hymns, for example, were sung at local celebrations and festivals all over Greece and Asia, but only one from Chalcis survives. Instant panegyric is rarely great poetry and presumably the mediocrity and topicality of this literature accounts for its loss. Even Melinno's poem was preserved only through the mistake of Stobaeus who, thinking it to be a panegyric to strength (εἰς ῥώμην), included it in his anthology περὶ ἀνδρείας. To generalize from these few remnants of an enormous poetic corpus requires temerity, yet perhaps a single observation will be forgiven. This poetry treats Roma and Roman power wholly within the traditional formulations of Hellenistic court poetry. The poets do not discuss the actual Rome and her unique policies, morality and constitution. Polybius and his successors do deal with that historical reality and from it create highly individual mythologies of Roman power [85]. But the poets were the captives of tradition

---

[81] E.g. Antipater of Thessalonika *A.P.* IX 297, 5: Ῥώμην δ' Ὠκεανῶι περιτέρμονα πάντοθεν.

[82] E.g. Plutarch *Romulus* 1.

[83] Plutarch *Flamininus* 16; Nonnus *Dionysiaca* 41, 389–390. All these texts are discussed below. To distinguish between 4) and 5), I will use the common spelling Rhome for the Trojan girl and Roma for the divinity.

[84] Cf. GERNENTZ *Laudes Romae* (Rostock, 1918); FUCHS *Der geistige Widerstand gegen Rom in der antiken Welt* (Berlin, 1938).

[85] PASQUALI "L'idea di Roma" *Enciclopedia Italiana* XXIX (Rome, 1936) 910–911; BENGTSON *Gymnasium* 71 (1964) 150f.

in diction, in imagery and in general attitude. And I believe that this poetry, rather than Polybius' penetrating analysis, accurately represents the popular Greek conception of Rome as a traditional Hellenistic "kingdom".

A Paean sung by the girls of Chalcis in 191 BC to honor T. Quinctius Flamininus is the earliest extant poem to mention the goddess Roma[86]:

Πίστιν δὲ Ῥωμαίων σέβομεν
τὰν μεγαλειοτάταν ὅρκοις φυλάσσειν
μέλπετε, κοῦραι,
Ζῆνα μέγαν Ῥώμαν τε
Τίτον θ' ἅμα Ῥωμαίων τε
πίστιν· ἰὴ ἰὲ Παίαν·
ὦ Τίτε σῶτηρ.

The poem twice praises the πίστις of the Romans which should be seen as the *Fides Publica*. The references to Roman *Fides* are particularly appropriate for Chalcis. After Flamininus' declaration of freedom in 196, Roman garrisons remained at Philips' three "fetters of Greece": Demetrias, Acrocorinth, and Chalcis[87]. The Aetolians launched a propaganda campaign against Flamininus and Rome which focussed on Roman retention of these fortresses[88]. But in 194, after a dramatic new announcement by Flamininus at Corinth, all the garrisons were withdrawn[89]. Flamininus remained the patron of Chalcis even after the city unwillingly became the winter headquarters for Antiochus. The poem focusses on *Fides* and Flamininus' rule but Zeus and Roma are also hymned by the girls. The Roman insistence on *Fides* has clearly made an impression at Chalcis since the Greeks of themselves did not deify πίστις[90]. Although Jupiter Capitolinus did not usually appear to the Greeks to be a satisfactory symbol of Roman dominion, it is possible that the term μέγας Ζεύς was an attempt to translate Jupiter Optimus Maximus and thus put Chalcis under the protection of the chief god of the Romans[91].

The most famous poem honoring Roma is a panegyric of five Sapphic stanzas ascribed to the poetess Melinno of Lesbos[92]. There is no inde-

---

[86] Text from POWELL *Collectanea Alexandrina* (Oxford, 1925) 173. Poem is in Plutarch *Flam.* 16. For a paean to Seleucus I sung in Erythrae about 280 BC, cf. POWELL 140.
[87] Polybius 18, 45, 5–6; Livy 33, 31, 11.
[88] Polybius 18, 45, 1f.
[89] Livy 34, 49–51.
[90] See below p. 131.
[91] Jupiter as a symbol: NILSSON *MDAI(R)* 48 (1933) 255f. (= *Opuscula Selecta* II 518f.); cf. p. 130. μέγας Ζεύς as Jupiter: KNOCHE *Gymnasium* 59 (1952) 325.
[92] DIEHL *Anth. Lyr. Gr.* II 315–316.

pendent evidence for Melinno, and the artificial language of the poem contains elements of different dialects and cannot be identified with a particular region[93]. BOWRA's literary analysis establishes parallels and models for many of the images and formulae[94]. If not a great poet, Melinno was a skillful and learned one. The poem includes several elements of historical interest to our examination of the goddess Roma.

> χαῖρέ μοι Ῥώμα, θυγάτηρ Ἄρηος,
> χρυσεομίτρα δαΐφρων ἄνασσα
> σεμνὸν ἅ ναίεις ἐπὶ γᾶς Ὄλυμπον
> αἰὲν ἄθρυστον.
>
> σοὶ μόνᾳ, πρέσβιστα, δέδωκε Μοῖρα
> κῦδος ἀρρήκτω βασιλῆον ἀρχᾶς,
> ὄφρα κοιρανῆον ἔχοισα κάρτος
> ἀγεμονεύῃς.
>
> σᾷ δ' ὑπὰ σδεύγλα κρατερῶν λεπάδνων
> στέρνα γαίας καὶ πολίας θαλάσσας
> σφίγγεται· σὺ δ' ἀσφελέως κυβερνᾷς
> ἄστεα λαῶν.
>
> πάντα δε σφάλλων ὁ μέγιστος αἰὼν
> καὶ μεταπλάσσων βίον ἄλλοτ' ἄλλως
> σοὶ μόνᾳ πλησίστιον οὖρον ἀρχᾶς
> οὐ μεταβάλλει.
>
> ἦ γὰρ ἐκ πάντων σὺ μόνα κρατίστους
> ἄνδρας αἰχματὰς μεγάλους λοχεύεις
> εὔστοχον Δάματρος ὅπως ἀνεῖσα
> καρπὸν ἀπ' ἀνδρῶν.

Roma is here called the daughter of Ares and her characteristics are those of an Amazon. Her military domination is repeatedly emphasized in the imagery: ἄνασσα; δαΐφρων; ἀγεμονεύῃς; σφίγγεται; κυβερνᾷς; σφάλλων. *Roma Martia* is followed by *Roma domina* in the second line; both these images became common topoi in Augustan poetry[95].

There are several indications in the poem that Roma appears in the trappings of Hellenistic kingship. She is called by the more feminine form ἄνασσα[96], and the κῦδος which she is given by Fate is de-

---

[93] FORTE 135 would like the poem to refer to Pompey's liberation of Lesbos, but essentially gives no cogent reason.

[94] *JRS* 47 (1957) 21–28.

[95] Roma Martia: e.g. Ovid *Tristia* 1, 8, 24; GERNENTZ 82. Roma Domina: e.g. Horace *Odes* 4, 11, 43; GERNENTZ 125; HOMMEL "Domina Roma" *Die Antike* 18 (1942) 125–158.

[96] ἄναξ used by Theocritus 17, 135 of Ptolemy; used of emperors in *IG* IV 1475. Paean of Bassus Lollius *A.P.* IX 236 calls Rome κόσμου παντὸς ἄνασσα πόλις.

scribed as βασιλῆον[97]. Other motifs also derive directly from Hellenistic panegyric. The third stanza stresses Roma's control over both land and sea — a well-known formula for expressing hegemony[98] which had been employed by Theocritus and Callimachus to praise the Ptolemies[99]. It was later applied to Pompey[100], and Augustus himself included the phrase *terra marique* in the *Res Gestae*. Another important Hellenistic motif is αἰών — the eternity which is predicted for Roman rule. This is the first extant attribution of eternity to Roma; of course it later became her most noteworthy attribute[101]. Here, it derives from the attribution of eternity to the Ptolemies and Attalids[102]. In the first century BC the Roman legate Q. Pompeius Bithynicus set up a statue of Aion in Eleusis εἰς κράτος Ῥώμης[103] and later αἰών (or αἰώνιος) was often used in connection with the power of the emperors[104].

Roma has been sent to rule by Fate or *Μοῖρα* (where Polybius would use τύχη); her role will be both eternal and thereby unique (μόνα is used three times). Perhaps we have in this poem a reflection of the Eastern belief discussed above, the belief that a fifth great empire would follow the four traditional empires or monarchies of the East and would rule forever[105]. This idea seems to have been circulating in the East soon after Magnesia (190) and even entered Rome by about 170. This emphasis on the uniqueness of Roman power reflects the belief, also held by Lycophron, that Rome's power somehow differed from that of other Hellenistic kingdoms[106].

When was this poem written? It has been dated to every period from the fourth century BC to the Empire but these extremes are clearly untenable. The imperial date is based solely on metrical grounds: that the poem should be placed between Horace and Statius[107]. But the

---

[97] *Oracula Sibyllina* III 46: Ῥώμη βασιλεύσει. FRASER *Ptolemaic Alexandria* (Oxford, 1972) I 708 dates Book III to second century BC, though at II 990 n. 219, he dates this passage to the age of Augustus when the original introduction to Book III was reworked or replaced.
[98] MOMIGLIANO *JRS* 32 (1942) 53–64; Cf. LYCOPHRON 1229 on the Romans.
[99] *Idylls* 17, 91–92; *Hymns* 4, 165–168.
[100] *OGIS* 56.
[101] First used by Tibullus 2, 5, 23: *urbs aeterna*; GERNENTZ 46.
[102] *OGIS* 90.4; 168.48. Cf. WEINSTOCK *MDAI(R)* 77 (1962) 313; INSTINSKY *Hermes* 77 (1942) 326.
[103] *Syll.* 1125. On date, see MILTNER *RE* XXI 2061; WEINSTOCK *op. cit.* 313 (75/74 BC). It is difficult to interpret Ῥώμη in this text. While a Roman would not be expected to employ Ῥώμη for the Roman state at this early date, the mention of θεὰ Ῥώμη by a Roman citizen would be even less acceptable. Therefore I take it as equivalent to κράτος Ῥωμαίων or κράτος δήμου Ῥωμαίων.
[104] INSTINSKY *op. cit.* 327f.
[105] SWAIN *CP* 35 (1940) 1–21.
[106] CHRIST 181.
[107] USENER *RM* 55 (1900) 290.

poem can hardly be imperial and not mention the Emperor. In any case, the metrical arguments are themselves doubtful [108]. A date much before 200 is not possible in the East, and I do not think this poem could have been written in the West [109]. The learned poem of Melinno is Alexandrian in inspiration, but could have been written almost anywhere. The Hellenistic motifs are more appropriate to Asia or the islands than to the West. Scholars generally agree that the poem was written before the time of Sulla [110]; recent scholars prefer the early second century [111]. That accords well with the popularity of cults and festivals of Roma in Asia and the islands during the second century. The poem seems to be an early and rather pedantic attempt to fit Roma into the mold of the Hellenistic ruler cult.

Despite its brevity, this little poem impressively encapsulates the themes of Roman rule found in later Latin poetry [112]: Roma's domination over the world, the religious and national aspects of her rule, and Roma's transcendance of physical and temporal boundaries. Only the divine, eternal ruler is missing. But the power of the state is already personified and deified; from here it is only a short step to the poetic treatment of the emperors.

An elegy of Alpheius of Mitylene warns Zeus to lock the gates of Olympus against Roma [113]:

κλεῖε, θεός, μεγάλοιο πύλας ἀκμῆτας Ὀλύμπου·
φρούρει, Ζεῦ, ζαθέαν αἰθέρος ἀκρόπολιν·
ἤδη γὰρ καὶ πόντος ὑπεζεύκται δορὶ Ῥώμης
καὶ χθών, οὐρανίη δ' οἶμος ἔτ' ἐστ' ἄβατος.

Again Roma is portrayed as possessing dominion over land and sea, and a wry warning is given to Zeus that heaven alone remains unconquered. The poem closely imitates one by Alcaeus in praise of Philip V of Macedon [114]:

---

[108] BOWRA *JRS* 47 (1957) 22.

[109] OLDFATHER *RE* XV 523 suggests on the basis of the name in an epigram of Nossis of Locri (*A.P.* VI 353) that the poem was written in the West. This evidence carries no weight.

[110] W. VON CHRIST *Geschichte der griechischen Literatur* (Munich, 1920) II i, 325–6 (1st BC); WILAMOWITZ-MOELLENDORFF *Griechische Verskunst* (Darmstadt, 1958—reprint) 128 (between 133 and Sulla); MOMIGLIANO *JRS* 32 (1942) 54 n. 12 (130–115 BC); CHRIST *Dichtung* 181 (c. 200 BC).

[111] BOWRA *op. cit.* 28; SCHUBART *Philologus* 97 (1948) 319–320 (soon after 168); BENGTSON *Gymnasium* 71 (1964) 154 (168–146 BC).

[112] The classic treatment of these themes is by CHRIST.

[113] *A.P.* IX 526; GOW-PAGE *The Greek Anthology: The Garland of Philip* (Cambridge, 1968) I lines 3528–3531.

[114] *A.P.* IX 518. MOMIGLIANO *JRS* 32 (1942) 54 has shown that Alcaeus' poem should not be taken as derisory of Philip; cf. also GOW-PAGE *The Greek Anthology: Hellenistic Epigrams* (Cambridge, 1965) II 9.

*Μακύνου τείχη, Ζεῦ Ὀλύμπιε· πάντα Φιλίππῳ
ἀμβατά· χαλκείας κλεῖε πύλας μακάρων.
χθὼν μὲν δὴ καὶ πόντος ὑπὸ σκήπτροισι Φιλίππου
δέδμηται· λοιπὰ δ᾽ ἃ πρὸς Ὄλυμπον ὁδός.*

This earlier poem also contains the "land and sea" motif; the poem of Alpheius departs in no way from the established Hellenistic pattern. Attempts to find precise historical allusions in a conventional poem of this sort are doomed to failure[115]. Since there is no external evidence for Alpheius and the internal evidence is so unsatisfactory, the poem cannot be dated with conviction: the early Empire seems most probable[116].

The Oracula Sibyllina reflects both the Jewish and the Christian opposition to Roman rule in the East. But these texts are so highly rhetorical that they undermine any attempt to discern the actual nature of the goddess Roma. Ῥώμη often merely signifies the Imperium Romanum; for example, Ῥώμη collects the taxes of Asia[117]. Even the many direct personifications of Roma must be treated with great care. Of all these texts, the passage in Book VII 108–113 most clearly refers to Roma:

*Ῥώμη καρτερόθυμε, Μακηδονίην μετὰ λόγχην
Ἀστράψεις ἐς Ὄλυμπον. θεὸς δέ σε πάμπαν ἄπυστον
Ποιήσει, ὁπόταν δοκέῃς πολὺ κρεῖσσον ἐς ὄμμα
Ἑδραία μίμνειν. τότε σοι τοιαῦτα βοήσω.
Ὀλλυμένη φθέγσῃ λαμπρόν τοτε καὶ μαρμαῖρον.
Δεύτερά σοι, Ῥώμη, μέλλω πάλι δεύτερα φωνεῖν.*

Here we again see Roma reaching to Olympus—if only with the brilliance of her renown. But it is difficult to take this as a general reference to the goddess since this book abounds with apostrophes of cities and provinces. Some are even given epithets, usually extremely conventional ones like τλήμων[118]. The context of this book, and the others as well, makes it nearly impossible to relate this personified Ῥώμη to the goddess Roma—even when the image or epithet is a striking one[119]. The polemical nature, highly emotional tone, and late date of many of these documents make them unreliable evidence for examining the Hellenistic Ῥώμη.

---

[115] Cf. Gow-Page *Garland* II 426 for criticism of Rossbach.

[116] *Ibid.* II 425.

[117] *Oracula Sibyllina* III 350.

[118] Corinth (60); Syria (114); and Antioch (IV 140). Personifications in this book: Rhodes (1); Delos (4); Cyprus (5); Phrygia (12); Colophon (55); Tyre (62) etc.

[119] ὑψαύχενε Ῥώμη—XII 230; VIII 37; χηρεύσει Ῥώμη: XII 227; Ῥώμη αὐτὴ συλήσασα πολυκτέανον κατὰ δῶμα: IV 145–6.

The same is true of the brief passage in the Dionysiaca of Nonnus, a Christian epic poet of the fifth century [120]:

Σκῆπτρον ὅλης Αὔγουστος ὅτε χθονὸς ἡνιοχεύσει,
Ῥώμῃ μὲν ζαθέῃ δωρήσεται Αὐσόνιος Ζεὺς
κοιρανίην

Roma figures prominently in late Latin literature [121] and these texts, rather than the continuous Greek tradition, could well have been the inspiration of such late references to Ῥώμη.

Ῥώμη also figures in two poetic inscriptions. One is a straight-forward elegiac couplet honoring a priest of Roma which is found in Cilician Antioch [122]:

Τειμοκράτην ῥητῆρα θεᾶς Ῥώμης ἱερῆα
  στῆσε φίλη θυγάτηρ χρηστότατον πατέρα.

The other is an extremely fragmentary text from Demetrias in Thessaly which OLIVER prints and translates as follows [123]:

γί]νατο μ[ὲν Δει]δίος σε, δαϊ[κ]ράντειρα δὲ Ῥώμ[α
ἦ]ρεν ἐπ[ὶ κλεινὸν μ]υριοτευχὲς ἕδος,
Ὦ]λιε

"Didius begot you, but war-powerful Rome, O Aulus,
raised you to a seat attended by 10,000 armed men."

But this text is very corrupt and, short of the reference to Roma with an appropriate epithet, not much else can be established about the first couplet [124].

In other poems, both Republican and imperial, the personified Ῥώμη is hardly the goddess. Let me simply offer a few examples from different periods.

1) Pseudo-Scymnos *Orbis Descriptio* 231–234 (130–110 BC) [125]:

Ἐν τοῖς ἔθνεσι τούτοις δὲ Ῥώμη 'στὶν πόλις
ἔχουσ' ἐφάμιλλον τῇ δυνάμει καὶ τοὔνομα,
ἄστρον τι κοινὸν τῆς ὅλης οἰκουμένης,
ἐν τῇ Λατίνῃ

---

[120] 41, 389–391.
[121] Cf. PASCHOUD *Roma Aeterna* (Rome, 1967).
[122] BEAN-MITFORD *Journeys in Rough Cilicia* 1962–1963 — *Denkschr. Öster. Akad.* 85 (Vienna, 1965) 34 #36; J. &. L. ROBERT *BE* 1967 #623.
[123] *IG* IX 2, 1135 revised by OLIVER *GRBS* 8 (1967) 237–239.
[124] J. &. L. ROBERT *BE* 1968 #313.
[125] MÜLLER *GGM* I 205. On date, cf. PARETI *Saggi di Storia Antica e di Archeologia* (Rome, 1910) 133–153.

2) Crinagoras *A.P.* IX 291 5–6 (early Empire)[126]:
οὐδ' ἦν Ὠκεανὸς πᾶσαν πλήμυραν ἐγείρηι
οὐδ' ἦν Γερμανίη Ῥῆνον ἄπαντα πίηι,
Ῥώμης δ' οὐδ' ὅσσον βλάψει σθένος, ἄρχι κε μίμνηι
δεξιὰ σημαίνειν Καίσαρι θαρσαλέη.

3) Dionysius Periegetus *Orbis Descriptio* 353–356 (2nd AD)[127]:
Θύμβρις ἐϋρρείτης, ποταμῶν βασιλεύτατος ἄλλων,
Θύμβρις, ὅς ἱμερτὴν ἀποτέμνεται ἄνδιχα Ῥώμην,
Ῥώμην τιμήεσσαν, ἐμῶν μέγαν οἶκον ἀνάκτων
μητέρα πασάων πολίων, ἀφνειὸν ἔδεθλον.

Obviously all these refer not only to the city itself, but also to the personified Roman people. Even the rather literal Dionysius passage contains the phrase μήτηρ πασάων πολίων[128]. But such personification is not necessarily a Hellenistic deification. Two different traditions survived: deification patterned on the Hellenistic ruler cult and personification of the traditional Greek type. If in a given text these two seem to intermingle, on a conceptual level each has its particular rationale and its own set of models. And both appear frequently in Latin poetry—from the Augustan age until the end of the Empire in the West.

Perhaps there are even allusions to the cult of Roma in the attack on the Roman Empire in the Apocalypse of St. John. The Apocalypse was addressed to seven cities of Asia—Smyrna, Ephesus, Laodicea, Philadelphia, Pergamum, Thyatira, and Sardes—most of which had cults, festivals or even temples dedicated to Roma at the time St. John was writing. He calls the Roman Empire a beast, and laments that the beast is worshipped: καὶ προσκυνήσουσιν αὐτὸν πάντες οἱ κατοικοῦντες ἐπὶ τῆς γῆς (13:8). Another beast (which seems to refer to local administrators) is responsible for making all adore the first beast (13:12). The portrait of a great, wealthy city as a whore goes back to the Old Testament where Tyre and Nineveh are so depicted. Babylon was, of course, the archetypical city of decadence and immorality and so when John sees a woman riding on the beast, her name is written on her forehead: ΒΑΒΥΛΩΝ Η ΜΕΓΑΛΗ (17:5). This woman is Rome herself: καὶ ἡ γυνὴ ἣν εἶδες ἔστιν ἡ πόλις ἡ μεγάλη ἡ ἔχουσα βασιλείαν ἐπὶ τῶν βασιλέων τῆς γῆς (13:18). The client kings who had slept with her will weep for her (18:9)—an appropriately bitter comment from a Jew. Finally John saw a holy city replacing Rome: a new and beautiful Jerusalem (21:10f.).

---

[126] Gow-Page *Garland* II 237–8 suggest 16 BC and 15 AD as the most likely dates for this poem; see also Christ 191.

[127] Müller *GGM* II 124.

[128] Roma as mother was popular with later poets; cf. Christ 87; Gernentz 127 f.

Like the Oracula Sibyllina, the emotional vision of the Apocalypse defies easy analysis. There are allusions to the worship of the Roman Empire, as well as the overt personification of the city itself. John was certainly aware that Roma was worshipped, but it is difficult to say whether her cult (as distinct from the general imperial cult) is actually alluded to in this book.

Of course neither the tradition of deification nor that of personification referred to the real Rome analyzed by Polybius and Poseidonius. Ῥώμη was not really Rome at all—in poetry as in cult she was simply the Hellenistic ruler made over in a new guise. And as the ruler cult before and the imperial cult to follow, this cult was empty of any religious content[129]. These cults existed for political reasons, and political institutions have rarely been the subject of great poetry.

III. Joint Cults

Since the conqueror often significantly influences the religious practices of the conquered through assimilation, syncretism or simple borrowing, religious changes can be important indications of new political relationships. During Roman expansion in Italy, the Romans gallantly provided an opportunity for the gods of their opponents to change sides, although the Italic and Etruscan divinities were Romanized in the process[130]. Here religious assimilation mirrored Roman political expansion and the incorporation of Italian peoples into the Roman political, cultural and linguistic sphere.

The process was very different in the East. In the second and first centuries BC the Romans did not assimilate the Greeks; they merely imposed their military dominion on the Greek cities of Europe and Asia. Acceptance (or at least acknowledgment) of that dominion was reflected in Greek religious practice; a "sacred link" binding the conquerors and the conquered was forged[131]. Greek contact with the religious practices of Anatolia and the far East had prepared them to welcome new gods easily.

The Greeks still had to choose which god to take from Rome. Every Greek city had a patron deity, but Rome did not. Jupiter Optimus Maximus on the Capitoline was the most exalted Roman divinity, but to the Greek mind he was in no way special. He was only the familiar Zeus transplanted to Rome, hardly distinctive enough to be the imperial god of Rome's new empire as Athena Parthenos had been for Athens' island empire in the fifth century[132]. So it was the goddess

---

[129] NILSSON *MDAI(R)* 48 (1933) 256 (*Opuscula Selecta* II 518f.).
[130] BASANOFF *Evocatio* (Paris, 1947) 207f.
[131] CHAPOT *La province Romaine proconsulaire d'Asie* (Paris, 1904) 419.
[132] NILSSON *MDAI(R)* 48 (1933) 255–256 (= *Opuscula Selecta* II 518f.).

Roma modeled on the Hellenistic ruler cult who became the imperial deity of Rome. She copied Roman political imperialism by invading the sanctuaries of other gods.

Most of these invasions tell us little about Roma. If she shared a cult or festival with Leto, it is hardly revealing since Leto was a prominent divinity in southwestern Asia[133]. An altar of Roma in the Delian Serapaeum only shows that the members of that sacred college wished to honor her[134]. Roma personified the power of the new mistress; she could be taken into cults, sanctuaries and festivals throughout the Greek world. These unions were political, not religious, acts.

However, a few patterns do become clear as we survey the cults in which Roma became a joint partner. The political nature of the cult is emphasized. The worship of Roma becomes one of several honors paid to the Romans as benefactors. Thus, Roma is worshipped alongside Flamininus at Chalcis and in a cult of P. Servilius Isauricus at Ephesus[135]. There was a priesthood of Roma and the Ῥωμαῖοι εὐεργέται in Thessalonika[136]; and sacrifices and other honors were paid both to Roma and the Demos of the Romans by the Milesians[137]. Such benefactions were personified in the cult of Roma and Salus at Pergamum. Later of course, Roma was linked to the honors paid to the imperial family. In all these the political aspect of the cult predominates.

Roma was also linked with divinities who exemplified benefactions received from powers other than Rome. For example, on Delos co-ordinate honors were paid to both dominant forces. There Roma and the Demos of the Athenians were incorporated with Hestia into a joint priesthood. The chapels for Roma and Demos added to the prytaneum of Delos may have been a symbolic incorporation of the twin masters of Delos[138]. Perhaps the marble table dedicated to Athena and the Demos of the Romans also testifies to the linking of Rome and Athens as the protectors-benefactors-conquerors of Delos[139]. In Athens, Roma is linked with the Demos of the Athenians in the precinct of Demos, the Charites and Roma at the base of the Kolonos Agoraios[140].

The divinity most often joined with Roma in the East was Zeus in his various manifestations: Zeus Eleutherios, Zeus Ktesios, Zeus Polieus, Zeus Kapetolios, Zeus Solymeus and Zeus Patroos. At times the linkage of Zeus and Roma resulted from the mere joining of the new power to the pre-eminent local divinity. For example, a priest at

---

[133] *SEG* XXII 350.
[134] *ID* 2484. Nock *HSCP* 41 (1930) 1–62 (= *Essays* I 202–251). Chapot *op. cit.* 419ff. is more credulous about the enthusiasm shown for Roman gods, including Roma (423f.), by Greeks and the association of them with Greek cults.
[135] *Ephesos* III 66.   [136] *IG* X 2, 1, 31–32; 133; 226.
[137] *Milet* I 7, 203.   [138] *ID* 1877; 2605; see above p. 65.   [139] *ID* 1807.
[140] *IG* II² 3404; 3547; 5047; 4775(?); also cf. above pp. 23; 102f.

Termessus served both Roma and Zeus Solymeus, but Zeus Solymeus (named after Mount Solymos in Pisidia) had long been the patron divinity of the city[141]. No special meaning should be imputed to such a link[142]. But the association of Zeus with Roma occurs too frequently to be ignored. Though the Greeks found Jupiter Capitolinus an inadequate symbol of Roman power, they were well aware of the important political functions that he performed for the Romans: the triumphator assumed the garb of Jupiter, and Jupiter was the securer of oaths and treaties which were kept on deposit in or around his temple on the Capitol[143].

The Greeks saw Jupiter Capitolinus, not as chief god of Rome, but as the guardian of oaths and treaties[144]. Greek copies of treaties mention that they will be set up on the Capitol, and Greek cities and kings set up dedications on the Capitol[145]. It was with this function of Jupiter that the Greeks associated the goddess Roma. The Teans brought the god to the East, and set up an altar to Roma and Zeus Kapetolios[146] while the Lycians dedicated a statue of Roma to Jupiter on the Capitol itself[147]. But usually Roma fulfilled Jupiter's functions in the East by herself. While one copy of a treaty was set up on the Capitol, another was displayed locally, perhaps on an altar or statue of Roma or set into the wall of her temple[148]. A Pergamene treaty, to be erected on the Capitol and in the local temple of Demeter, was celebrated by sacrifices voted to Roma[149]. Even cities making a treaty among themselves might quite rightly include Roma since Rome was often called upon to enforce such treaties. Samos and Antiochia specified that the sanction for infringement of their treaty would be a staggering fine of 20,000 drachmas to be paid to the treasury of the goddess Roma[150]. A second-century treaty between Aphrodisias and her neighbors included a dedication to Zeus, Homonia and Roma—all guarantors of oaths and treaties[151].

When the emperors were later joined in cults with Roma, they often took over the characteristics of Zeus. From the second century BC Roma had been worshipped in association with Zeus Eleutherios; later

---

[141] *TAM* III 1, 113–114.   [142] Cook *Zeus* II 973 n. 1.

[143] Polybius 3, 26, 1 and Walbank I 353f.; cf. Aust in Roscher *Lexikon* II 723–4 for sources.

[144] See above note 132.

[145] Treaties: *OGIS* 762; *IG* XII 3, 173; *Syll.* 694. Dedications: cf. Additional Note; *CIL* X 16.

[146] *IGR* IV 1556; also Jupiter Capitolinus at Smyrna (*CIG* 3153) and Nysa (*CIG* 2943).

[147] *CIL* VI 372.   [148] See note 145 above and chapter 2 n. 280.

[149] *Syll.* 694.   [150] Habicht *MDAI(A)* 72 (1957) 242f. #65.

[151] See chapter 2 n. 142. Roma is also invoked in the Cypriot oath to Tiberius: *SEG* XVIII 578.

emperors were assimilated to Zeus Eleutherios [152]. Augustus was also assimilated to Zeus-Patroos and Roma was sometimes joined with this assimilated Augustus-Zeus [153]. Diophenes of Lesbos served as high priest of Roma and Σεβαστὸς Ζεὺς Καῖσαρ Ὀλύμπιος [154]. The emperor took over from Jupiter the god's function as a *pignus* not only of oaths and treaties but also of the stewardship of the Roman Empire (*pignus imperi Romani*) [155]. Jupiter had long ago promised to Aeneas *imperium sine fine dedi* [156], but this guarantee was supplanted by that of Roma Aeterna and the Aeternitas Augusta.

In 191 BC the Chalcidian paean to Flamininus had linked Roma, μέγας Ζεύς and the πίστις of the Romans [157]. πίστις was often joined with Roma in the Greek world. The Greeks had never seriously personified πίστις [158] and this is surely a translation of the *fides publica* of the Romans [159]. Similarly, Zeus Pistios is a translation of Dius Fidius [160].

The Romans themselves liked to trace the genealogy of *Fides* to the very beginning of their city—or rather, to a time immediately after Romulus' treacherous treatment of the Sabines and their women [161]. Numa was said to have founded the cult of *Fides* and even to have erected a sacrarum [162]. For the Romans, *fides* was not merely a legal term. *Fides* had moral and religious overtones deriving from its association with oaths [163] and the Romans regarded themselves as the most scrupulous oath-keepers. Their scorn for Carthaginian faithlessness resounds in Livy, just as Cicero and Polybius held the Greeks in condescending contempt for the same fault. Whatever the origins of *fides*, the Romans became actively aware of its international implications in the third century [164]. It was by then a useful tool in diplomatic confrontations with Carthage and the eastern kings. About the middle of the third century, A. Atilius Calantius built and dedicated a temple of *Fides Publica* near the temple of Jupiter Optimus Maximus on the

---

[152] ROBERT *CRAI* (1969) 50; *Epigramme Grecque* 190 n. 2; RAUBITSCHEK *AJA* 49 (1945) 130 n. 7.
[153] BUCKLER *RP* 61 (1935) 177f.
[154] *IG* XII 2, 656.
[155] Livy 26, 27, 14; Ovid *Fasti* 3, 72.
[156] Vergil *Aeneid* 1, 279–280   [157] Plutarch *Flamininus* 16.
[158] Theognis 1135—but in a passage full of personifications and there is no evidence of subsequent tradition; HEINZE *Hermes* 64 (1929) 163f. On the differences between πίστις and *Fides*, cf. BECKER *Reallexikon für Antike und Christentum* (s.v. *Fides*) VII 810.
[159] ROBERT *Laodicée* 321 n. 7.
[160] COOK *Zeus* II 724f.
[161] On *Fides*, cf. BOYANCÉ *Études sur la Religion Romaine* (Paris, 1972) 91–133; BADIAN *FC* 1–14; HEINZE *Hermes* 64 (1929) 140–166.
[162] Livy 1, 21, 4; Dionysius Hal. *AR* 2, 75; Plutarch *Numa* 16.
[163] HEINZE *op. cit.* 140f.; BADIAN *FC* 2; 10; BOYANCÉ *op. cit.* 91–103.
[164] WISSOWA 134.

Capitol[165]. Remember that around the same time, this founder's kinsman, Atilius Regulus, enacted perhaps the most heroic example of *Fides Romana* by returning to Carthage and certain death rather than breaking his word[166]. The temple of *Fides Publica* became a depository of foreign treaties and was used for meetings of the Senate[167].

Perhaps the tradition that Numa had erected an earlier sacrarum grew up at this time. We should recall that Agathocles' version of the Rhome legend, written in the later third century, tells us that Rhome founded a temple of *Fides* on the Palatine[168]. By that time, *Fides* played an important role in Roman relations with Greek cities in Sicily, and various versions of her early establishment in Rome were obviously circulating[169]. By the second century, the Numa version seems to have been accepted as the most plausible.

The earliest certain connection between *Fides* and Roma is the didrachm from Locri Epizephyrii which portrays a personified *Fides* crowning the seated personification of Rome[170]. The figures are labeled Πίστις and Ῥώμα[171]. Though the date of this coin has been the subject of controversy[172], I prefer to date it in 204 when the Locrians complained against the cruelty of Pleminius and appealed to Rome's *Fides*[173]. That episode can hardly be ignored in dating the coin.

Soon after this, the Chalcidians were honoring the πίστις of the Romans along with Zeus, Roma and Flamininus. What did they think they were celebrating? Did the Greeks understand *Fides*-πίστις? It is difficult to believe that they did—since the concept confused most Roman subjects[174]. To come *in fidem* did not entail a treaty, nor entitle one to support against attack. To *venire in fidem* was voluntarily to become dependent upon the Romans, to relinquish all rights but with the expectation that the Romans would act morally. The Twelve Tables condemned the patron who abused his trust; clearly, *fides* in-

---

[165] Foundation: Cicero *De Nat. Deorum* 2, 61; Location: Pliny *HN* 35, 100; Cicero *De Officis* 3, 104; WISSOWA 133–134.

[166] Horace *Carmina* 3, 5.

[167] Appian *BC* 1, 16; Valerius Maximus 3, 2, 17; 6, 6, 1.

[168] JACOBY *Fr gr Hist* 472 F 5; CLASSEN *Historia* 12 (1963) 452 on the date. Cf. also p. 19 above.

[169] ALFÖLDI 11f.   [170] *BMC Italy* 365 #15.

[171] ALFÖLDI 11 remarks on the "Latin form" of ῥώμα: The form is hardly Latin; but rather the predictable form for a city whose dialect was in the Locrian group of North-west Greek. Texts from the archives of the temple of Zeus at Locri recently published by DE FRANCISCIS in *Klearchos* confirm the dialect and make it clear that the form ῥώμα was to be expected; cf. *Klearchos* 3 (1961) 17f.; 4 (1962) 66f.; 6 (1964) 73f.; 7 (1968) 21f.; 9 (1967) 157f.

[172] See Chapter 2 n. 520 above.

[173] Livy 29, 18, 19; Diodorus 27, 4, 1.

[174] BADIAN *FC* 129: "In the West, as in the East, clientela baffled the non-Romans..." Cf. Polybius 20, 9, 10f. The literature on the meaning of *Fides* is vast.

volved a moral sanction[175]. But equally clearly, enough leeway existed to cause confusion among clients and to preserve Rome's diplomatic flexibility. Rome might defend whomever she wished. The celebration of πίστις which we find in several Greek cities seems a bit misplaced. Yet the Greeks had no other way of symbolizing that loyalty and protection they hoped Rome would provide.

The association of Competaliasts at Delos had set up a statue of πίστις in 98 and a few years later added one of Roma to the same chapel[176]. The dedications of both these statues survive although the statues have perished. πίστις also appears without Roma — an imperial text from Rhodes refers to her as a goddess[177]. Naturally, the concept of *Fides* became less important to the subject people as they achieved more stable relations with Rome while it became simultaneously more important to imperial propagandists. Octavius had bound Italy to him in 32 by an oath that was recorded on coins with the image of clasped hands over the legend *Fides*, and his successors continued to propagate this image[178].

A text from Teos records that Straton was a priest of Roma and πίστις, which surely refers to *Fides Publica*[179]. We have already seen the connection of Zeus with Roma at Teos and of Zeus, Roma and πίστις at Chalcis. Just as Jupiter and *Fides* protected Roman oaths at home and kept treaties in their temples[180], so Roma functioned in the East. It was a political triumvirate. To the Greeks, Roma and *Fides* were by nature political gods, and Zeus' political and legal attributes were emphasized in this association. All of Roma's partners in Greeks cults — not only Zeus and *Fides*, but Flamininus, Roman benefactors, Salus, the Athenean Demos — draw attention to her fundamentally political nature. These cults have everything to do with politics, little to do with religion. Roma's cults, like her epithets and panegyrics, establish her as an essential link in the political tradition stretching from the successors of Alexander to the successors of Julius Caesar. And that is how her Greek subjects saw the goddess Roma.

---

[175] VIII 21: Patronus si clienti fraudem fecerit, sacer esto.

[176] *ID* 1761; see above p. 66.

[177] CONZE *Archäologische Zeitung* 36 (1878) 163. The altar or sanctuary of πίστις at Athens is only attested by a Hadrianic, and rather unreliable, source: Diogenianus 2, 80 in *Corpus Paroemiographicorum Graecorum* I. Cf. HEINZE *op. cit.* 164 n.

[178] BOYANCÉ "La Main de Fides" *Études* 121-133; oath to Octavian: *Res Gestae* 25; HERRMANN *Der römische Kaisereid* (Göttingen, 1968) 78-89. On the use of the oath after Augustus, cf. HERRMANN 99ff.

[179] *BCH* 19 (1895) 554. On πίστις as *Fides Publica*, cf. ROBERT *Laodicée* 321 n.7; BOYANCÉ *Études* 95 n.3.

[180] MOMMSEN *G.S.* III 303-309. For Roma and Jupiter in the Empire: cf. BEAUJEU *La Religion Romaine à l'apogée de l'empire* I (Paris, 1955) 136.

Chapter 4

Honors Paid to Roma

I. Temples

The most visible manifestation of devotion to a divinity is the temple built in his or her honor. Yet we know of few temples built to Roma before she was associated with Julius Caesar and Augustus. Far more is known of her priests and festivals than of her temples. This may be due to the nature of our epigraphical evidence: victory lists and honorific decrees. But it is hardly surprising that few temples to Roma were built, since temples were by far the most expensive honor that could be paid to a god. Relatively few temples were erected in honor of Hellenistic kings; their cults were more often centered in the municipal gymnasium[1]. Roma too was honored in the gymnasium at Miletus while her temple was under construction[2], as she presumably was in other cities where she did not have a temple.

The temple (ναός) was located in an area (τέμενος) sacred to the goddess. In earlier times, the τέμενος might have been only an open space or a sacred grove but in the Hellenistic age, it designated a space which enclosed a shrine, altar or temple[3]. The ἱερόν is more ambiguous. Usually, ἱερόν seems to denote a temple or at least a cult building, yet other texts distinguish ἱερόν both from τέμενος and from ναός[4]. Appropriately equivocal modern translations might be "sanctuary" or "Heiligtum". ἱερόν is understood with terms like Heraion, referring to temples of Hera[5]. So too ἱερόν is understood with Ptolemaion, Romaion, Kaisareion and Sebasteion, but we cannot simply assume that these are temples[6]. Sjöqvist has shown that a Kaisareion was a much larger architectural complex which included a temple of Caesar[7]. The Ro-

---

[1] Habicht 143f.
[2] *Milet* I 7, 203.
[3] Sjöqvist *OR* 1 (1954) 91.
[4] Pausanias 5, 6, 4; Plato *Laws* 6, 758 E.
[5] *L-S-J* ad loc.
[6] *IGR* IV 292.39ff. calls the Diodoreion a τέμενος within which a temple was built.
[7] Sjöqvist *op. cit.* 86ff.

maion grew out of the same Hellenistic tradition which lies behind the Kaisareion. It refers not to a temple alone, but to a sacred enclosure that contained, among other things, a temple or at least an altar of Roma.

More than a dozen temples are known to have been dedicated to Roma in association with Caesar or Augustus, but only a few to Roma herself. Only two of these temples—at Mylasa and Ancyra—remained standing into modern times; most of the others cannot even be located. Since a general discussion of these temples is therefore impossible, I will simply attempt to describe briefly each of them.

Smyrna — The *templum urbis Romae* was erected here in 195 and was the first dedicated to the new goddess[8]. A number of coins issued at Smyrna in the second and third centuries of the empire variously show Roma holding a tetrastyle temple, Roma seated between two tetrastyle temples, or a temple identified by $P\omega$[9]. All the temples pictured on these coins are tetrastyle, but there is no certainty that they depict the original temple of 195 or a later replacement[10].

Alabanda — Sometime before 170 BC, the Alabandans established a *templum urbis Romae* together with a general festival to the goddess[11]. Like so many others in Caria this temple and cult were probably established soon after the battle of Magnesia in which Manlius Vulso had assisted the city by capturing and restoring a rebellious fortress[12].

Miletus — The regulations promulgated for the cult of Roma at Miletus specify that the dedication to Roma which had taken place in the gymnasium should be held in the Romaion when the temple of Roma was completed[13]. The text implies that the sanctuary was already under construction. The cult, priesthood and temple of Roma at Miletus were clearly established at some point after the Milesian Romaia. This festival was probably instituted soon after Apamea; the cult set up and the regulations enacted either after Pydna or after the defeat of Aristonicus in 130 BC[14].

Delos — While altars and statues of Roma appeared in various other sanctuaries at Delos, there is no evidence of a temple of Roma. After Roma and Demos were joined to the cult of Hestia, chapels were added

---

[8] Tacitus *Ann.* 4, 56.
[9] Roma holding temple: *BMC Ionia* 286 #389f.; 289 #410f.; 293 #434. Roma seated between temples: *SNG-GER* 6 #2224. Tetrastyle temple with $P\omega$: *BMC Ionia* 288 #403.
[10] If the temple had been replaced or restored before 26 AD, the Smyrnaeans would have mentioned it in their plea before the Senate. The ἱερὸν Καισαρῆον mentioned in *CIG* 3276 from Smyrna may have been this early temple converted to the imperial cult, the temple of 26 AD, or some later temple.
[11] Livy 43, 6, 5.
[12] Livy 38, 13, 2–4. See pp. 42f. above.
[13] *Milet* I 7, 203.
[14] See pp. 53f. above.

to the Prytaneum where the traditional cult of Hestia resided[15]. But archaeologists disagree on how Hestia and her new partners were accommodated, whether in three chapels[16] or with Hestia in a larger room flanked by two small chapels[17]. Roma and Demos must have been added to the cult of Hestia soon after the Athenians' arrival in 167, and physical changes to include the new cult may have followed soon after.

A statue of Roma seems to have shared with Fides a chapel in the Agora of the Competaliasts[18]. The chapel had been built long before but inscriptions show that the statues of Roma and Fides were not placed there until the first decade of the first century BC[19].

Termessus — There is no direct evidence for a temple of Roma at Termessus, but one of the three unidentified temples on a prominent terrace of the city has been attributed to the goddess[20]. Since Roma occupied an important position in Termessus until the third century AD, it seems reasonable to identify these three temples with that goddess, Augustus and Zeus Solymeus, the patron of the city.

*

There is no evidence of other temples built to Roma before her association with Augustus in the imperial cult. But several of the temples of Roma and Augustus can be taken as replacing earlier temples of Roma—especially when there is evidence for a pre-existing cult of Roma under the Republic.

Mylasa — Evidence exists only for the cult of Roma and Augustus and for the temple that was created there in the reign of Augustus[21]. Cults of Roma flourished in Caria in the second century BC and the new cult of Roma and Augustus probably replaced a cult of Roma founded after Apamea. Though Strabo describes the city as rich in temples, we cannot say for certain whether there was an earlier temple of Roma[22]. The temple of Roma and Augustus seems to have been a quite extraordinary temple with a unique history. It survived into modern times where it impressed WHELER (1682) and POCOCKE (1745), but disappointed CHANDLER (1765) since it had been transformed into a Turk's harem. Since this is a rare example, I will quote the texts:

---

[15] See p. 66 above.
[16] *DCA* 222.
[17] VALLOIS *AHD* I 174 offers this as one of several suggestions. Also see BRUNEAU 444.
[18] BRUNEAU 617; FERGUSON *HA* 401; 434.
[19] *ID* 1761; 1763. On πίστις—Fides, see pp. 131f. above.
[20] LANCKORONSKI *Städte Pamphyliens und Pisidiens* (Vienna, 1892) II 48.
[21] See p. 44 above.
[22] STRABO 14, 2, 23.

1682 AD. "The first Antiquity was a fair Temple of Marble, with an Inscription on the Front, shewing that it was built in Honour of Augustus Caesar, and to the Goddess of Rome."

"It had twenty two pillars about it; but the Front only is now standing."[23]

1745 AD. "But the great curiosity of Melasso is a temple which was built to Augustus and Rome, and is a most exquisite piece of architecture; a plan and view of it may be seen in the fifty-sixth plate. The temple itself was very small: In the front there is a portico of the composite order, and on the other three sides an Ionic colonade. At the entrance of the temple, on each side of the door, there is a foundation of large stones, on which probably there were pedestals for the statues of Augustus and Rome. The pillars are fluted, and the temple is raised on a basement, the cornish of which is only to be seen; there is also a sort of plinth about it that ranges round like a step, and has three faces like an architrave, as it appears at A; every particular pillar has likewise a plinth, and the base is fluted, as mentioned above. The frieze is adorned with tripodes, bulls heads, and pateras; the cornish and the pediments at each end are very richly ornamented with carvings. What the architect seems to have designed as an ornament to the building, may be rather looked on as a bad taste, that is, putting the composite order on the front, when the other three sides are Ionic. The capitals are indeed fine, except that the curled leaves, and the abacus seem rather to project too far at the corners, in proportion to the size of the capital. About two feet below the capital there are four festoons round the shaft; but what is most peculiar, and has the worst effect, is a work like a capital on the base of the pillar, the shaft resting on it in a sort of socket, from which the leaves turn outwards; this is executed in a particular manner, as may be seen in the drawing. The top of the leaves are broken, from which one might at first conjecture that the pillars had fallen down, and had been set up again on old capitals, but by examining the work, I saw that the pillars were made so originally. This building, when Christianity prevailed, was doubtless converted either into a church or some other public building; for on the stones of the temple I saw several defaced inscriptions with the cross on them."[24]

1775 AD. "MYLASA or Mylassa was the capital of Hecatomnus, king of Caria, and father of Mausolus. It has been described as situated by a very fertile plain, with a mountain rising above it, in which was a quarry of very fine white marble. This being near, was exceedingly convenient in building, and had contributed greatly to the beauty of the city, which it is said, if any, was handsomely adorned with public edifices, porticoes, and temples. The latter were so numerous, that a certain musician entering the market-place, as if to make proclamation, began, instead of (Ἀκούετε Λαοί) Hear ye People, with (Ἀκούετε Ναοί) Hear ye temples. . . .

Our first enquiry was for the temple, erected, about twelve years before the christian era, by the people of Mylasa to Augustus Caesar and the goddess Rome; which was standing not many years ago. We were shown the basement, which remains; and were informed,

---

[23] WHELER-SPON *A Journey into Greece* (London, 1682) 275–276.

[24] POCOCKE, *A Description of the East and some other Countries* (London, 1743–1745) II 2, 61.

the ruin had been demolished, and a new Mosque, which we saw on the mountainside, above the town, raised with the marble. The house of a Turk occupying the site, we employed the Hungarian to treat with him for admission; but he affirmed we could see nothing; and added, that there was his Haram or the apartment of his women, which was an obstacle not to be surmounted. It had six columns in front, and the whole number had been twenty two."[25] The dedication to Roma and Augustus has only survived in the reports of these travellers.[26]

Ephesus — The cult of Roma at Ephesus was probably established in the years following the bequest of Attalus[27]. The priest of Roma served as an eponymous official at Ephesus, and later the Roman proconsul of 46–44, P. Servilius Isauricus, was added to the cult of Roma[28]. Ephesus shows the clearest historical development of the cults of Roma: first, Roma alone; then Roma and Isauricus; then the provincial temple of Roma and Julius Caesar (29 BC); and finally, by 5 BC, a municipal cult of Roma and Augustus[29]. The cult of Roma was important at Ephesus and a temple of the goddess is likely. In 29 BC, the province of Asia was permitted by Augustus to erect a temple to Roma and Divus Julius for the use of Roman citizens of the province[30]. The local Greek population would have wanted a temple of their own, and indeed by 6 BC the Ephesians had built a temple of Roma and Augustus in, or adjoining, the precinct of the Artemesium[31]. Other centers of the provincial cults of Roma and Augustus later acquired temples, priests and occasional celebrations of the festival to Roma and Augustus. Ephesus could not yet have had its provincial temple in 26 AD when it was vying in Rome for the temple of Tiberius, Julia and the Senate[32]. But an Ephesian temple is depicted on an imperial cistophorus issued at Ephesus during the reign of Claudius with the legend ROM. ET. AUG. COM. ASI[33]. However, these coins which depict this temple as having only two corner columns can hardly be seen as accurate representations.

Samos — By 6 BC a municipal temple to Roma and Augustus stood on Samos, but the precise date of its dedication remains unknown[34]. In 29 BC Octavian entered his fifth consulship on Samos and restored to the Heraeum statues removed by Antony, but he did not restore the

---

[25] CHANDLER *Travels in Asia Minor* (2nd edition, Oxford, 1776) 186–187.
[26] *CIG* 2696.   [27] See p. 57f. above.
[28] *OGIS* 437 (= *RDGE* 47); *Ephesos* III 66.
[29] WEINSTOCK *DJ* 403; see chapter 2 n.203.
[30] Dio Cassius 51, 20, 6.
[31] *IBM* 522. On this temple, cf. NOCK *HSCP* 41 (1930) 30 (= *Essays* I 225); PICARD *Ephèse et Claros* (Paris, 1922) 664.
[32] Tacitus *Ann.* 4, 56.
[33] *BMCRE* I Claudius #228. Also cf. chapter 2 n.204.
[34] HERRMANN *MDAI(A)* 75 (1960) 83; see pp. 61–62 above.

freedom of the island. Freedom was only restored to the Samians during the winter of 20/19 BC when the emperor passed some months there [35]. That seems a particularly apt moment for the Samians to join Augustus to their cult of Roma and erect a temple, though the cult might be placed during his earlier visit since it was at the same time that the imperial cult was established by the Asian and Bithynian Koina. By 5 BC marble stelae were being set up beside the Romaion Sebaston of Samos, and the dedications to Roma and Augustus found on Samos were probably once placed in the sanctuary of these gods [36].

Athens — The little round temple dedicated to Roma and Augustus on the Athenian Acropolis is attested by its dedicatory inscription [37]. Built of Pentelic marble, it was situated about sixty feet east of the Parthenon. Its nine Ionic columns formed a circle twenty-five feet in diameter, but there does not seem to have been an inner wall enclosing a cella [38]. The decoration and detail, influenced by the Erechtheum, are in the archaizing style common in the Augustan age [39]. The monopteros plan of the temple was probably inspired in part by the temple of Vesta at Rome, and the Acropolis temple may well have included an altar of Livia, Julia and Hestia, since an inscription tells us that such a cult existed on the Acropolis [40]. Since no earlier worship of Hestia on the Acropolis is attested, it is natural to associate this cult with the only other center of the imperial cult on the Acropolis, the temple of Roma and Augustus. In my earlier discussion I have already agreed with GRAINDOR's dating of this temple between 27 BC and 18 BC [41]. I do not believe that present evidence permits a more precise dating.

Roma and Augustus may well have been worshipped in the lower city of Athens, but there is no evidence of a temple. THOMPSON has recently connected two cellas in the Annex to the Stoa of Zeus in the Athenian Agora with the imperial cult [42]. He suggests that one room was dedicated to Augustus, but hesitates to attribute the other to

---

[35] Cassius Dio 54, 9, 7. Cf. HERRMANN *Ibid.* 88.

[36] Stelae: *Ibid.* 71 #1 A 15; 82 #2 where Dr. G. DUNST has very plausibly restored ναός. Dedications: statue bases dedicated by the Demos (*Ibid.* 83 n. 42). I am grateful to Dr. DUNST for information on unpublished Samian texts.

[37] *IG* II² 3173.

[38] BINDER *Der Roma-Augustus Monopteros auf der Acropolis in Athen und sein typologischer Ort* (Karlsruhe, 1969) 73ff.

[39] BOETHIUS and WARD-PERKINS *Etruscan and Roman Architecture* (London, 1970) 378.

[40] Vesta Temple: GRAINDOR *Athènes sous Auguste* (Cairo, 1927) 153–155; Altar: *IG* II² 5096.

[41] GRAINDOR *op. cit.* 150; cf. pp. 104f. above.

[42] *Hesperia* 35 (1966) 180ff. is doubtful about Roma; THOMPSON-WYCHERLEY *The Athenian Agora XIV The Agora of Athens* (Princeton, 1972) 103 say only that a "Roman imperial abstraction" belongs in the cella.

Roma since she was already worshipped in the sanctuary of Demos, the Charites and Roma nearby at the foot of Kolonos Agoraios. Yet Roma remains the most reasonable divinity to be associated with Augustus in such a cult. We should recall that in addition to the seat for the priest of Demos, the Charites and Roma, there was also a seat in the theater for a priest of Roma and Augustus with no mention of ἐπ' ἀκροπόλει which is included in the priest's title on the dedication of the round temple[43]. Roma may well have shared the Annex with Augustus.

No other temple or shrine of Roma has been identified in the lower city, but if the suggestion that the Roman Agora was in fact a Kaisareion has merit[44], that complex of buildings may have contained an altar, statue or temple of Roma.

Thasos — At Thasos in the northern Aegean, a dedicatory inscription tells us that a Thasian couple had donated a new marble pavement for the temple dedicated to Roma and Augustus[45]. The temple, which was located on the northeast side of the Agora, served as a public record office for Thasos[46]. The walls were filled with official documents and copies of local correspondence with the emperor. Whether this temple succeeded an earlier one dedicated to Roma is unknown.

Lesbos — The Mytileneans either built a temple to Roma and Augustus or, more likely, installed Augustus in an earlier temple of Roma. The temple at Mytilene was completed while the temple authorized to Pergamum in 29 BC was still being built; the Lesbians were very quick to honor Augustus after Actium[47].

*

In 29 BC Augustus permitted the Asian and Bithynian cities to erect temples to himself and Roma at Pergamum and Nicomedia, and temples of Roma and Divus Julius at Ephesus and Nicaea[48]. Little more is heard, either in coins, inscriptions or literary sources, about the temples to Roma and Julius. Presumably the temples were soon rededicated. But the temples at Pergamum and Nicomedia survived and, as we have seen, the festivals associated with them took on a political dimension.

Pergamum — The temple of Roma and Augustus at Pergamum was the center of the imperial cult in Asia and the meeting place of the

---

[43] *IG* II² 5047; 5114.
[44] RAUBITSCHEK-BENJAMIN *Hesperia* 28 (1959) 85.
[45] *IG* XII 8, 380.
[46] DUNAND-POUILLOUX *Recherches sur l'histoire et les cultes de Thasos* (Paris, 1958) II 59; 60 n. 2. See page 69 above.
[47] *IGR* IV 39; O'BRIEN-MOORE *YCS* 8 (1942) 34 n. 40.
[48] Cassius Dio 51, 20, 6–9.

Koinon of Asia [49]. The precinct served as a repository for decrees of the Koinon, letters from Rome and decrees honoring provincial priests or other officials of the Koinon, with stelai set up in the temenos or even in the temple itself [50].

This was the only temple of the province of Asia for more than half a century (29 BC–26 AD) and so the officials of the Koinon gathered there [51]. We have already discussed the title νεωκόρος awarded to a city that had a provincial temple of the imperial cult. Of the temple at Pergamum we have no direct archaeological evidence. However, a large number of coins minted at Pergamum depict the temple of Roma and Augustus. Cistophori of the reign of Augustus show on the reverse a hexastyle temple on a podium of five steps with acroteria on the top and at the corners of the pediment; ROM. ET. AUGUST. on the entablature and COM. ASIAE in the field [52]. The temple on these coins is well drawn and the many dies agree even on the details, so this may well be a realistic portrayal of the temple. On later coins of Pergamum, Roma appears crowning Augustus in front of a temple with four pillars [53]. Since a similar temple with Zeus and Trajan appears on the obverse, it seems likely that the legend θεᾷ Ῥώμῃ καὶ θεῷ Σεβαστῷ simply refers to the divinities rather than to the building. It is much vaguer than the hexastyle temple which, with its dedication on the entablature, clearly portrays a specific monument.

There is no evidence for a municipal temple of Roma and Augustus. After the fall of the Attalids, the sanctuary of those kings would logically have been transferred to Roma, and finally to Roma and Augustus [54]. Such a temple would have remained municipal, but no evidence survives.

Nicomedia — Like the temple at Pergamum, the temple of Roma and Augustus at Nicomedia became both the center of the imperial cult and political focal point of the Bithynian cities. The temple appears on a number of coins, usually with the legend κοινὸν Βιθυνίας [55]. The coins agree in portraying an octastyle temple with three steps,

---

[49] Tacitus *Ann.* 4, 37.
[50] *IBM* 894. *OGIS* 458.29 mentions a decree of the Koinon of Asia set up ἐν τῶι ναῶι and another decree set up on a white stele in the temenos of Roma and Augustus (*OGIS* 458.63–64). LAFFI *SCO* 16 (1967) 55; 66 makes clear that these allusions are to the temple at Pergamum. RAMSAY *CB* 475 had unconvincingly linked them to a supposed temple in Apamea.
[51] See p. 81 above; p. 190f. below.
[52] SUTHERLAND-OLCAY-MERRINGTON *The Cistophoroi of Augustus* (London, 1970) 77–78 #479–535; plates 32–34.
[53] *BMC Mysia* 142 #263.
[54] Cf. chapter 2 n. 335.
[55] *BMC Pontus* 105 #10ff.; 106 #12; #17 (Ionic); 107 #28 (Corinthian). Perhaps an earlier temple was built after the reorganization of Pompey.

though they differ on details of pediment decoration or, more surprisingly, on the order employed by the architect. Other coins show a dystyle temple with the figures of Roma, Hadrian and Bithynia on the porch, but these columns clearly could not support the roof and thus cannot be an accurate representation of any temple [56]. Unfortunately, the evidence permits no further conclusions.

Nicaea — Only the passage in Dio attests the temple of Roma and Divus Julius which the Bithynian Koinon erected in Nicaea [57]. There is no evidence for any other temple of Roma there.

*

Temples of the imperial cult of the Koinon of Asia were set up in other cities: Smyrna, Sardes, Ephesus, Miletus, Cyzicus, and elsewhere [58]. Some of these temples may have been dedicated to Roma, but some certainly were not, such as the temple to Tiberius, Livia and the Senate at Smyrna. So we cannot include them in a discussion of the temples of Roma.

In other areas, Roma may have been introduced only with the cult of either Julius Caesar or Augustus. After his victory at Pharsalus, the dictator followed Pompey to Egypt and subsequently spent some time in the East. The Kaisareion founded at Alexandria is perhaps the most famous of Caesar's foundations. It excluded Roma and placed Caesar squarely in the Pharaonic-Ptolemaic tradition of ruler-worship [59].

Antioch — The other Kaisareion founded by the dictator was established in Syrian Antioch in 47 BC [60]. SJÖQVIST has studied Malalas' rather confused descriptions of the building and made them intelligible by comparison with archaeological evidence from other Kaisareia [61]. Malalas' word $\beta\alpha\sigma\iota\lambda\iota\kappa\acute{\eta}$ is obviously incorrect—the Kaisareion was rather a quadri-porticus open to the sky that contained a statue of Caesar in a central apse of one portico and a statue of Roma [62]. It is the temenos and the architectural unit rather than the temple proper, although the complex included a temple.

Cyrene — One side of a Kaisareion at Cyrene is identified by an inscription as a "porticus Caesarei" [63]. This inscription records the restorations carried out on the southeast and southwest porticos in the last decade or so of Augustus' reign, and the original building should

---

[56] *BMC Pontus* 105 #10; 108 #32.
[57] Cassius Dio 51, 20, 6–9.
[58] See p. 81 above.
[59] See pp. 96–97 above; SJÖQVIST *OR* 1 (1954) 95ff.
[60] Malalas p. 216, 17–21 (ed. DINDORF).
[61] *OR* 1 (1954) 91–95.
[62] See p. 153 below.
[63] *CIL* III 10; REYNOLDS *PBSR* 26 (1958) 160.

probably be dated no later than the first half of the reign of Augustus [64]. New trenches have verified SJÖQVIST's suggestion that the basilica was a later addition. The plan of the original monument is still uncertain but seems to have been some form of quadri-porticus [65] based on the Kaisareion at Alexandria, the apparent prototype for such buildings throughout the Roman empire [66].

A fragment of a dedication in monumental letters of the early first century AD has been found in this Kaisareion [67]. The words [ὑ]πὲρ Ῥώμας have been variously restored but must certainly refer to Roma [68]. It certainly recalls Malalas' statement that Caesar placed a statue of Roma in the Kaisareion at Antioch. Surely Roma also played a role in this Kaisareion of Cyrene.

WARD-PERKINS has brought together other references to Kaisareia in the East—at Gythium, Messene, Smyrna, Palmyra, and Phanagoria on the Bosporus [69]. The text from Palmyra shows that a Kaisareion (as opposed to Sebasteion) cannot be connected with Julius alone, but the term was used for buildings erected long after his death [70].

Caesarea and Sebaste — Herod the Great of Judaea founded the city of Caesarea, and rebuilt Samaria (rededicated as Sebaste) in honor of his new patron Augustus. In each city a temple was dedicated to the emperor and, Josephus tells us, monumental statues of Roma and Augustus were erected in the Caesarea temple which stood on a hill overlooking the port [71]. These cult statues show that this temple was dedicated to Roma as well as to Augustus and the same can perhaps be said for the contemporary temple at Sebaste [72]. The temple at Sebaste was built on a great artificial platform constructed on a hill top, not unlike Herod's temple in Jerusalem [73]. The temple was approached through an enormous enclosed forecourt supported arti-

---

[64] WARD-PERKINS *PBSR* 26 (1958) 165. What follows is based on the work of WARD-PERKINS, BALLANCE and REYNOLDS contained in the article "The Caesarea at Cyrene and the Basilica at Cremaia" *PBSR* 26 (1958) 137–194. Other Kaisareia include Thera (*IG* XII 3, 326); Hypaepa (KEIL-PREMERSTEIN *Denkschr. Oesterr. Akad* 57 (1915) 76 #107).

[65] SJÖQVIST *OR* 1 (1954) 100f.; WARD-PERKINS *PBSR* 26 (1958) 192.

[66] WARD-PERKINS *Ibid.* 183.

[67] REYNOLDS *Ibid.* 159 #1.

[68] *Ibid.* ὑπὲρ Ῥώμας αἰωνίας διαμονᾶς or ὑπὲρ Ῥώμας καὶ Σεβαστῶν διαμονᾶς. Cf. also GASPERINI *QAL* 6 (1971) 13.

[69] WARD-PERKINS *Ibid.* 177–178. On Caesarea in general, cf. Philo *Legatio* 150f.

[70] *Syria* 17 (1936) 277–282. The Καισαρῆον at Smyrna (*CIG* 3276) probably does not refer to a sanctuary of the dictator—if so, it would have been mentioned by the Smyrnaean embassy of 26 AD. See n. 3 above.

[71] *BJ* 1, 21, 7; *AJ* 15, 9, 6.

[72] See pp. 94–95 above.

[73] CROWFOOT-KENYON-SUKENIK *The Buildings at Samaria* (London, 1942) 123ff.

ficially by subterranean corridors and vaults. Herod built these temples to persuade the Romans that he was a Hellenistic princeling rather than a barbarian tribal leader. His own people clearly gave scant worship to the imperial cult, and it is doubtful that he was so foolish as to pressure them in this direction. These temples are purely a diplomatic act between Herod and the Romans.

Ancyra — The most famous of all the temples of Roma and Augustus is the temple at Ancyra in Galatia where the principal extant text of the *Res Gestae* was engraved on the walls of the pronaos. Of all the temples discussed, only this actually survives. The cella walls and the pronaos with the great entrance door into the cella remain. But excavations have clarified the plan of the temple: eight by fifteen columns of the Ionic order [74]. There was a prostyle of four Corinthian columns before the pronaos, and two columns in antis at the entrance to the episthodomos.

The date of this temple, or dates of its component parts, have provoked disagreement. Though the excavators KRENCKER and SCHEDE dated the ur-temple—cella [75], pronaos and episthodomos—to the second century BC, the decoration and detail have now convinced scholars of its Augustan origins [76]. The temple was probably built by the Galatian Koinon in 25–20 BC [77]. Its orientation to the West suggests that it was built on the site of an older temple to the Anatolian gods Men and Kybele.

The coins of Ancyra show temples with four, six and eight column facades. The version with eight columns was minted from the reign of Marcus Aurelius to that of Caracalla [78]. An earlier version with a four column prostasis and no peristyle appears again on coins of Nero. Although four and six column temples could be abbreviations of an eight column facade, SCHEDE prefers to see two stages in the building of this temple [79].

*

Now and again other buildings have been identified as temples of Roma and Augustus. RAMSAY was particularly fond of finding or imagining such temples. He argues that the building in the forum at Antiochia where the Latin text of the *Res Gestae* was carved was a temple of "Roma (?) and Augustus" [80]. This is at least possible, but

---

[74] KRENCKER-SCHEDE *Der Tempel in Ankara* (Berlin, 1936) 14 Abb. 9.
[75] *Ibid.* 50.
[76] BOETHIUS-WARD-PERKINS *Etruscan and Roman Architecture* (London, 1970) 389; AKURGAL *Ancient Civilizations and Ruins of Turkey* (2nd edition, Istanbul, 1970) 243.
[77] AKURGAL *Ibid.* 245.
[78] KRENCKER-SCHEDE *op. cit.* 40–42; plate 45.
[79] *Ibid.* 42.
[80] *JRS* 6 (1916) 105.

his assertion that such temples existed in other Phrygian cities—Eumenia, Apamea, Acmonia—merely because priests of Roma were found in those cities is untenable [81]. The worship of Roma did not require a temple; often an altar of Roma was simply placed in the sanctuary of another divinity.

II. Statues

Though only a single statue and several reliefs of Roma have survived from the Greek world, there must have been hundreds of statues of the goddess. Every temple of Roma would have contained a cult statue ($ἄγαλμα$) which was destined to receive cultus [82]. In addition, numerous other statues ($εἰκόνες$) were erected either "for" or "to" the goddess, to use NOCK's terminology for homage and worship [83]. The former were honorific statues like those dedicated to any mortal benefactor; the latter were votive offerings only appropriate to a divinity. Though a temple is evidence that a cult existed, a mere statue is not since $εἰκόνες$ usually had no connection with cultus [84]. Thus Josephus calls the cult image of Roma and Augustus at Caesarea an $ἄγαλμα$, whereas the statue dedicated to Roma on Melos or the statuette which C. Vibius Salutaris left to Ephesus in his will is described as an $εἰκών$ [85]. In this Roma follows the pattern of Hellenistic kings who were treated both as gods and as benefactors and were thereby honored both with $ἀγάλματα$ and $εἰκόνες$ [86].

The earliest surviving statue of Roma was found, and still stands, in the college of the Poseidoniasts on Delos. The casual tourist would hardly look twice at this headless, weather-ravaged figure standing amidst a jumble of stones. She can be identified only by the inscription on the pedestal on which the goddess once stood: $θεὰ Ῥώμη Εὐεργέτις$ honored by the Poseidoniasts for Rome's kindness toward their association and toward their homeland, Berytus [87].

Though the statue is mutilated, its drapery testifies to its Hellenistic conception and execution [88]. The college of the Poseidoniasts existed

---

[81] *CB* 377; 467; 479.   [82] HABICHT 142f.

[83] NOCK *HSCP* 41 (1930) 23; 48 (= *Essays* I 220; 239f.); *JRS* 47 (1957) 115 (= *Essays* II 833f.). The dative can be used in either circumstance; the accusative refers only to the statue itself.

[84] NOCK *HSCP* 41 (1930) 3 (= *Essays* I 204). For an exception where an $εἰκών$ receives cultus, cf. *Ibid.* 9 (= *Essays* I 208).

[85] Josephus *AJ* 15, 9, 6; *IG* XII 3, 1097; *Ephesos* II 27.

[86] HABICHT 143.

[87] *ID* 1778. MARCADÉ 128ff. convincingly connects the statue and pedestal. Contra, PICARD *EAD* VI 56f.

[88] MARCADÉ 280; plate lxv; HORN *Stehende weibliche Gewandstatuen in der hellenistischen Plastik MDAI(R)* Ergänzungsheft 2 (Munich, 1931) 77.

by 150 BC, and at some later time architectural modifications were carried out to accommodate the altar and statue of Roma[89]. On stylistic grounds, this statue of Roma has been associated with a statue of Cleopatra which was sculpted on Delos about 130 BC[90]. The Cleopatra may have influenced Menandros, the Athenian sculptor of the Roma, and it seems best to date the Roma to the latter part of the second century BC[91].

This statue of Roma reflects Menandros' interest in, and perhaps even research into, the effects of transparency on drapery and the depiction of layers of fabric[92]. Similar concerns can be detected on other Delian statues: the Cleopatra as well as a Diodora and two Polymnias in the Rhodian style[93]. MARCADÉ has rightly emphasized both the Hellenistic characteristics of the Roma and the prominent "Rhodian" traits in the treatment of the drapery[94]. But he is much less convincing when he speaks of the statue's Athenian characteristics[95]. Perhaps, having established that the sculptor was the Athenian Menandros, MARCADÉ felt compelled to place the statue in the "Athenian school". But the archaizing tendencies of the Athenian school do not appear on this statue, and MARCADÉ's attempt to find them is unpersuasive[96]. By the second century, Athenian sculptors were no longer confined to this formulaic, archaic style; rather, their increasing mobility had gained them a widespread knowledge of and expertise in various styles[97]. Menandros could certainly work within the stylistic orbit of the Rhodian school.

The Delian statue of Roma is not the warlike, Amazonian Roma. What would be the model for a peace-loving Roma? The Tyche of Antioch by Eutychides of Sicyon has often been suggested as the intellectual and visual model for the goddess Roma[98]. The Tyche was pacific and, since its erection about 300 BC, it had become the most famous and widely copied symbolic statue of the Hellenistic East[99].

---

[89] Date before 150 BC: *ID* 1520 and MARCADÉ 289 n. 4; later modifications: PICARD *BCH* 44 (1920) 289ff.
[90] PICARD *EAD* VI 61.
[91] MARCADÉ 131; cf. also chapter 2 n. 254.
[92] BIEBER *The Sculpture of the Hellenistic Age* (2nd ed., New York, 1961) 129 comments that this use of *Coae vestes* is typical of the Rhodian style.
[93] *Ibid.* 131; MARCADÉ 489.
[94] MARCADÉ 289; 337; 489f.
[95] MARCADÉ 286: "atticisme mitigé," "marque de l'atticisme" or still less convincing: "elle s'inscrit sans peine dans la lignée des grandes figures drapées créées par Praxitèle." (MARCADÉ 133).
[96] KLEINER *Tanagrafiguren JDAI* Ergänzungsheft 15 (Berlin, 1942) 232 rejects Attic influence in this statue.
[97] ASHMOLE *CAH* VIII 668; 672.
[98] See chapter 1 nn. 40–43 above.
[99] For a copy of Eutychides' statue, cf. *CAH* Plates III 124.

But her actual attitude—Tyche formed part of a group being crowned by Antiochus and Seleucus—could not have influenced this Delian statue of Roma. I have already rejected Tyche as an intellectual or religious model for Roma[100]; likewise she seems to have had no influence on this earliest depiction of Roma in the East. Only later, when Roma was syncretized in the West with the Fortuna Populi Romani, did she inherit the iconography of Tyche on Roman coinage[101].

In the aftermath of Pydna, the Rhodians erected a statue of the Roman People some fifteen meters high. That mini-colossos—Polybius describes this statue as κολοσσός—was set up in the temple of Athena on Rhodes[102]. The mercantile Poseidoniasts could easily have seen it and decided to erect a similar one on Delos. Since the Delians imitated the style of the Rhodian school, they might well adopt Rhodian compositions and figural attitudes as well[103]. Still, we do not know whether the statue at Rhodes was warlike or pacific.

Another possible model for Roma is Athena[104]. A connection between the patron goddess of Athens and the deification of Roma had already been made on Athenian coinage, and the association later became popular among the Romans themselves[105]. The Athenians undoubtedly deemed it the highest form of flattery; the Romans a source of vicarious pride and respectability. Though this later connection of Athena and Roma is clear enough, the origin of it remains uncertain. We would expect the earliest portrayals of Roma in the Greek world of the late third and early second century to depict a warlike goddess[106]. Perhaps this image together with the close association of Athens with Roman policy during this period led to the adoption of Athena as the pictorial model for Roma. Later, as propaganda attributed Rome's power to the arts of peace (*fides*) rather than the arts of war (*virtus*), Roma may have taken over a more pacific mien from Pallas. Athens' prominence after Pydna may have led the Rhodians to use Athena as the model for their Roma who, after all, was placed in Athena's temple. And the model would have been even

---

[100] Cf. p. 20 above.
[101] HOMMEL *Die Antike* 18 (1942) 139 f.
[102] Polybius 31, 4, 4.
[103] MARCADÉ 490.
[104] A connection often mentioned by scholars; e.g. OLIVER *Demokratia* 163; WEINSTOCK *DJ* 100; VERMEULE *Goddess Roma* 65 f.; MATTINGLY *BMCRE* III cxxxviii; etc. Most of these discussions are concerned with representations of Roma with the attributes of Athena on coins or gems. See my discussion on pp. 103 f. above.
[105] See chapter 2 nn. 485–486.
[106] Roma appears armed on the earliest Greek coin which depicts her: the didrachm from Locri Epizephyrii in Magna Graecia issued about 204 BC. See pp. 109–110. But other portraits of Roma or Rhome on Roman coinage in the third or even second century BC should not concern us; there was no copying from Italian models in the Greek East. Cf. CALZA *Dedalo* 7 (1926) 663 f.

more appropriate to the Delians who were but cleruchs from Athens[107]. This is speculation, but since Athena eventually influenced the depiction of Roma in statues, on gems and on coins, it seems reasonable to trace that influence back to the second century when Athens was most closely identified with the policies and propaganda of the Roman Republic.

Not long after Menandros completed his statue of Roma on Delos, a temple dedicated to Hecate was completed by the Carian city of Stratonicea[108]. The temple, which was situated in the nearby deme of Lagina, contained a frieze with both mythological and political scenes (though even the political scenes were depicted in a mythical way). As SCHOBER has arranged the panels, the north side portrays an alliance concluded between cities; in the center, the goddess Hecate looks on while two female figures seal the oath with a handshake[109]. The female figure in armor has been identified as Roma[110]; she clasps the hand of a more conventional Amazon with bared breast and a helmet. Whether this latter figure represents Stratonicea or Asia cannot be determined[111].

Since the temple was built in the late second century BC, the reference is probably to the organization of Asia after the defeat of Aristonicus. The Greek cities of Asia (of which a number are personified on this north side) opposed Aristonicus and would have been sincerely grateful for his defeat[112]. Moreover, the city of Stratonicea owed an earlier debt of gratitude to Rome. Between 188 and 167 Stratonicea and almost all Caria were subject to Rhodes. The goddess Rhodos was even included in the worship of Hecate in Stratonicea[113]. After Pydna, the city was freed from Rhodes by the Roman Senate[114], and her consequent gratitude was probably reflected in the replacement of Rhodos by Roma in the joint cult with Hecate. It may be this municipal devotion to Roma that is recalled in the frieze of the temple.

---

[107] In the second century BC a great marble table was dedicated jointly to Athena Nikê and the Demos of the Romans (*ID* 1807). Since there was about the same time a cult and priesthood of Roma and the Demos of the Athenians on Delos (*ID* 1877), there is a temptation to see both the goddesses functioning as proxies for the personification of their respective Demos.

[108] On the date, cf. BIEBER *op. cit.* 165.

[109] SCHOBER *Der Fries des Hekateions von Lagina Istanbuler Forschungen* 2 (Vienna, 1933) 63f.; block 223; plate xi.

[110] VERMEULE *Goddess Roma* 101 #1; SCHOBER *op. cit.* 74; BIEBER *op. cit.* 165.

[111] SCHOBER *op. cit.* 75f. prefers Asia Minor.

[112] *Ibid.* 72f. For a survey of scholarly opinion on the date of this temple, see BERG *Numen* 21 (1974) 132 n. 19.

[113] FOUCART *BCH* 14 (1890) 365 #4. BERG 134 n. 25 suggests that the Hecate-Helios-Rhodos triad is replaced by Hecate-Caesar-Roma.

[114] Polybius 30, 21, 3; cf. pp. 48f. above.

After the Mithridatic wars the Stratoniceans founded a pentaeteric festival dedicated to Hecate and Roma. The senatus consultum granting freedom to Stratonicea and the text establishing this festival were both inscribed on the cella wall of the temple of Hecate at Lagina [115]. The connection of these two goddesses in the festival thus seemed traditional: they were already present in the center of the north frieze of the temple.

At Aphrodisias in 1937, an Italian archaeological expedition excavated an Ionic portico dedicated to Aphrodite, Divus Augustus-Zeus, Tiberius, Livia and the Demos [116]. The unusual feature of this portico is a series of heads spaced above the colonnade: gods, heroes, monsters, the imperial family, personifications and theatrical masks [117]. The portico seems to have been dedicated by local citizens during the reign of Tiberius.

JACOPI has identified one lovely head as the goddess Roma [118]. It is a beautiful face with hair parted in the center and slightly separated lips. The figure wears a helmet like that worn by Roma on late Republican coinage, and it seems a successful amalgam of the Amazonian and pacific aspects of Athena. The identification is plausible, since Roma would customarily appear on such a monument of early imperial date, especially when characters as diverse as Paris, Agrippina Maior, Heracles and Hera are included. Roma had been mentioned as one of the guarantors of a second century treaty involving Aphrodisias, and another text implies the existence of a cult of the Demos of the Romans in the city [119]. So Roma must have been present among the portraits on the portico, and the head identified by JACOPI seems the most likely. She retains here the loveliness of a Greek divinity, not yet burdened with the dour matronliness which the Romans themselves would eventually impose upon her.

In the Antonine period, a huge altar was erected at Ephesus on the model of the altar of Zeus at Pergamum. Perhaps such a monument does not belong in my survey of depictions of the Greek personification of Rome, since by this period the imperial style had become uniform throughout the Empire. Yet the frieze from this altar is of considerable interest, even if it does not reflect purely Greek attitudes toward Roma.

---

[115] *OGIS* 441 (= *RDGE* 18).

[116] JACOPI *MA* 38 (1939) 74ff.; text of dedication is found on 87. Cf. also VERMEULE *RIA* 54–55.

[117] JACOPI *op. cit.* 96ff.

[118] JACOPI *op. cit.* 135–138; VERMEULE *RIA* 54; VERMEULE *Goddess Roma* 105 #37.

[119] Treaty: see chapter 2 n.142. Fines: REINACH *REG* 19 (1906) 234 #138b. 16–17.

The frieze, now in Vienna, has an integrated sculptural program which has been plausibly restored by VERMEULE[120]. The military figure of the emperor presides at the end of the right projecting wing; along the right side occur scenes of combat; the long rear side contains scenes of the imperial family including the apotheosis of Trajan, Hadrian, Antoninus and Marcus Aurelius. The left side portrays various gods and goddesses and the projecting left wing depicts the figure of Roma[121]. Roma, here a seated Athena type, looks back on the events portrayed behind her as though she were a witness. The altar should be dated soon after the death of Hadrian when this style was prevalent throughout the Empire[122].

Perhaps Roma also appears on the cuirass of Hadrian in several Eastern statues of that emperor[123]. The central figure on these cuirasses varies between the more common Palladium and the rarer Roma crowned by Victoriae who is portrayed, for example, on the cuirass of the statue of Hadrian found at Knossos[124].

*

Only this handful of statues of Roma from the East actually survives. Another slightly larger group are mentioned in epigraphical or literary sources. Of course there must have been hundreds, even thousands, of statues of Roma. But here I merely assemble literary and epigraphical evidence for statues of Roma set up in the Greek East.

One of the earliest statues of Roma was erected by the Cibyrates. A decree of Cibyra gives the terms of a mutual assistance treaty with the Romans[125]. The final clause provides that the treaty be inscribed on bronze tablets and set up both at the temple of Jupiter Capitolinus in Rome and on the base of the gold statue of Roma in Cibyra. The treaty, and therefore the statue, should be dated between Apamea and Pydna (167)[126]. A gold statue could not have been very large and it is

---

[120] VERMEULE *RIA* 95–123, plates 34–52.   [121] *Ibid.* 119 plate 50.

[122] There are real similarities between this Roma and the one on the base of the column of Antoninus Pius now found in the Vatican. There the goddess witnesses the apotheosis of Antoninus and Faustina (NASH *Pictorial Dictionary of Ancient Rome* (2nd ed., London, 1968) I 272 plate 322). VERMEULE *RIA* 95; 123 regards these reliefs as the "apogee of Roman art in Asia."

[123] This general type of cuirassed statue has been studied by VERMEULE in his monograph "Hellenistic and Roman Cuirassed Statues" *Berytus* 13 (1959) 1–82. On these statues of Hadrian, cf. pp. 55–57.

[124] TOYNBEE *Essays in Roman Coinage presented to H. Mattingly* (Oxford, 1956) 213 n. 2.

[125] *OGIS* 762.

[126] See pp. 39–40 above. SCOTT *TAPA* 62 (1931) 101 ff. argues that statues of precious metals were linked with divine honors during the Hellenistic era. HERRMANN *MDAI(I)* 15 (1965) 87 n. 49a correctly challenges SCOTT's view in publishing the base of a gold statue of the second century Milesian politician, Eirenias.

likely that the statue—since it had a base large enough to bear bronze tablets—might itself have been bronze, plated with gold. A statuette seems improbably modest; and anything else would be far too expensive for such a small federation.

A text from the island of Melos mentions the erection of an honorific bronze statue of Roma[127]. This statue was further honored with a gold crown, following the common convention of voting crowns of precious metal to statues in marble or bronze[128]. It was cast about 150 by the sculptor Polianthes of Cyrene who had worked at Delos in the 160's, notably on a statue of Masinissa[129].

We have already discussed the statue of Roma on Delos set up by the Koinon of Poseidoniasts. But that was not the only statue of Roma on Delos. Another of the private associations of Delos, the Competaliasts who at first were largely Italian, also erected a statue of Roma. The base was found in the agora of the Competaliasts and the dedication of the statue in 94 is precisely dated by the consuls of the year[130]. The statue shares a small chapel with a statue of Fides built a few years before. Again we have the recurrent connection of Roma to Jupiter and Fides—the guarantors of oaths and treaties[131].

The statues of both the Competaliasts and the Poseidoniasts were for private cults, but there was probably also a statue of Roma for public worship: most likely in the prytaneum where she shared a cult and three chapels with the Demos of the Athenians and Hestia[132]. But statues of Roma may have stood elsewhere as well, even in the sanctuary of Apollo as ROUSSEL has suggested[133]. In 140/139 the Athenian administrators compiling the inventory of the temple of Apollo recorded a silver crown there (στέφανον ἀργυροῦν τὸν τῆς Ῥώμης) which seems to indicate a crown associated with a statue rather than a crown dedicated to the goddess[134]. Still, the statue is not explicitly mentioned and the crown could have been placed in the treasury of Apollo merely for safekeeping.

There are three other texts, largely undatable, which seem to have been bases of statues of the goddess Roma. The clearest is from Olympia: [Ἡ πόλις ἡ τῶν] Ἠλείων Ῥώ[μ]ην ἀν[έθηκ]εν[135]. This statue was

---

[127] *IG* XII 3, 1097. Though ἄγαλμα is the usual term for a statue destined for cultus, εἰκών can nevertheless be used for a votive statue of the god; cf. NOCK *HSCP* 41 (1930) 4; 9; 21 (= *Essays* I 204; 208; 218).
[128] SCOTT *TAPA* 62 (1931).
[129] MARCADÉ 131 n. 3; 336; MARCADÉ *Recueil des Signatures des Sculpteurs Grecs* (Paris, 1953–1957) II 105. Also cf. LIPPOLD *RE* XXI 1362f.
[130] *ID* 1763; cf. p. 66 above.
[131] Cf. pp. 130f. above.
[132] *ID* 1877; 2605; ROUSSEL *DCA* 222; BRUNEAU 444.
[133] ROUSSEL *DCA* 222 n. 7; BRUNEAU 445.
[134] *ID* 1450 A. 119.   [135] *Olympia* 317.

dedicated to Olympian Zeus. Until recently, a statue of Roma at Assus had been attested only by WADDINGTON's restoration of a very fragmentary text [136]. MERKELBACH has now joined this fragment with another from Assus to form a nearly complete dedication of a statue of Roma by Assus and the Romans resident there:

ὁ δῆμος καὶ [οἱ] πραγματευόμενοι Ρω[μαῖοι]
θεὰ[ν Ρώ]μην [τ]ὴν εὐεργέτιν τοῦ κόσμ[ου] [137]

Finally, a brief text from the city of Julis on the island of Ceos dedicates a statue to Roma: Ὁ δῆμος ὁ Ἰουλιητῶν θεᾶι [Ρώ]μηι Σωτείραι [138]. The text is certain, but of course the statue was not necessarily of Roma; the Elaeans had dedicated a statue of Roma to Zeus [139]. This one might have represented only a local dignitary or a Roman benefactor, but we would expect some identification of the honored person. I would therefore identify this as a statue of Roma.

Early in the second century AD a wealthy Roman equestrian, G. Vibius Salutaris, bequeathed a number of gifts to Ephesus. In his testament three silver statuettes—the size is unclear but the one of Artemis weighed seven pounds—were dedicated to Artemis and the Gerusia of the Ephesians. The statuettes were of Artemis, of the Demos of the Romans, and of the Gerusia [140]. In the bequest, Vibius requests that nine pedestals be set up to carry the statues in each group. The base which carried the three statuettes dedicated to Artemis and the Gerusia is preserved. A bilingual dedication describes the statues thus [141]:

7. Dianam argenteam, item imagines duas, unam urbis Ro-
8. manae et aliam Gerusiae

17. Ἄρτεμιν ἀργυρέαν καὶ εἰκόνας ἀργυρᾶς [β], μίαν ἡγεμονίδος Ῥώμης καὶ {ἄλλην τῆς} φιλοσεβάστου γερουσίας

Both the will and the dedication clearly refer to the same group of statuettes. In the former the statuette is called ὁ δῆμος ὁ Ῥωμαίων, in the latter *urbs Romana* and ἡγεμὼν Ῥώμη. The figure must have been feminine, and the texts illustrate the potential for confusion between the goddess Roma and the personification of the Roman people. I think the visual representations of the two must have been indistinguishable [142].

---

[136] LE BAS-WADDINGTON *Voyage Archéologique en Grèce et en Asie Mineure* (Paris, 1847–1870) V 1727: [ἡ βουλὴ καὶ] ὁ δῆμος καὶ [ἡ γερουσία?] θεὰ[ν Ῥώ]μην. KIEPERT *Annali Ist. Arch.* 14 (1842) 146 #30 restored it differently.
[137] MERKELBACH *ZPE* 13 (1974) 280.
[138] *IG* XII 5, 622. [139] *Olympia* 317.
[140] *Ephesos* II 27.164. On these texts, cf. OLIVER *The Sacred Gerusia* *Hesperia* Supplement VI (Athens, 1941) #3–4 with good bibliography.
[141] *Ephesos* II 28.7–8; 17–18. [142] Cf. pp. 25f. above.

Both names are used for statues set up by eastern cities and kings on the Capitol. There the Lycian League set up an inscription announcing the dedication of a statue of Roma to Jupiter Capitolinus[143]. This inscription, which was set up soon after 167 BC, refers to the statue as τὴν Ῥώμην since it was probably the only such statue on the Capitol at that time[144]. Other dedications were added, with Laodicea and King Mithridates of Pontus adding statues of the Demos of the Romans[145]. These statues and dedications formed part of a group that were rebuilt as a single monument after the Capitoline fire of 83 BC[146]. It was an appropriate location for Jupiter himself—according to the dream of Catulus, the rebuilder of the temple—to entrust a statuette of Roma to the boy Octavius. Here too the names of the statuette in different sources—*signum rei publicae*; εἰκόνα τῆς Ῥώμης—betray the possible confusion of names[147].

Finally, several statues of Roma are attested in the literary sources, though they are described in different ways. Polybius reports that in 164 the Rhodians built a κολοσσός of the Demos of the Romans[148]. But we know nothing else about it save that it was built in the temple of Athena at Rhodes.

More than a century later Julius Caesar founded the Kaisareion in Antioch and there set up a bronze statue to the Tyche of Roma[149]. Of course the statue was not necessarily one of Roma, but statues of gods or mortals which are dedicated to another divinity as votive offerings were usually placed in the sanctuary of that divinity; thus a statue of Roma was dedicated to Zeus at Olympia. In the Kaisareion of Antioch, the statue was almost certainly of Roma or the "Tyche of Roma". What is this "Tyche of Roma"? That is the term used by our source, the sixth century Byzantine historian Johannes Malalas, but it is possible that he or his local source is simply interpreting the statue in terms familiar to Antioch. But there is also the strong possibility that Caesar, always responsive to local practice, had cloaked this statue of Roma in the iconography of Tyche: the mural crown, cornucopia, etc. There is no evidence for this statue other than the passage in Malalas.

In his newly founded city of Caesarea, Herod placed monumental statues of Roma and Augustus in the temple which he dedicated in

---

[143] CIL I² 725.
[144] LARSEN *CP* 51 (1956) 169 n. 30.
[145] CIL I² 728; 730.
[146] See Additional Note.
[147] Suetonius *Augustus* 94, 8; Cassius Dio 45, 2, 3.
[148] Polybius 31, 4, 4.
[149] Malalas p. 216 17–21 (ed. DINDORF). In interpreting στήλη as a statue, I follow SJÖQVIST *OR* 1 (1954) 90 and DOWNEY *A History of Antioch in Syria* (Princeton, 1961) 154; cf. *Patristic Greek Lexicon* (Oxford, 1961ff.) s.v. στήλη.
[150] Josephus *AJ* 15, 9, 6.

their honor in 10 BC[150]. These were cult statues and the statue of Roma, says Josephus, rivalled the great statue of Hera at Argos[151].

*

Other temples of Roma also held cult statues of the goddess, but there is no reliable evidence for the iconography of these statues. It is true that coins depicting temples often follow a convention of bringing the divinity outside, or on the porch, of the temple[152]. While such coins can be useful in confirming hypotheses formed from other evidence, of themselves they are far too unreliable to provide firm evidence for a pose or attributes of the cult statue.

III. Altars

In cities where there are cults of Roma, there must have been altars (βωμοί) to provide the focal point for cult celebrations. Altars were necessary to a cult; temples an expensive option[153]. The existence of an altar certainly does not preclude a temple, since all temples had altars within the precinct to serve the cult of the divinity who dwelt in the temple. But the mention of only an altar in the sources probably indicates the absence of a temple, since one would expect mention of the most distinctive and important monument in the temenos. Since our evidence for altars of Roma consists both of the altars themselves as well as literary and epigraphical mentions of altars, we should keep this dichotomy in mind.

*

Four altars of Roma actually survive. In none of these has the goddess been joined with the imperial cult. All carry the name of Roma in the genitive, a common identification of the god to whom an altar is dedicated[154].

Delos — Two of the altars of Roma are located on the sacred island of Delos. From the sanctuary of the Egyptian gods is a marble fragment (2′ × 1′ × 1′) with the simple inscription: Ῥώμης[155]. This may have been set up by the θεραπευτής in gratitude for the decree of the Senate of 164 BC that permitted the practice of the cult of Serapis[156].

---

[151] Josephus *BJ* 1, 21, 7.
[152] TRELL *NC* 4 (1964) 241 f.
[153] For altars in the ruler cult, cf. HABICHT 141 f.
[154] BENJAMIN-RAUBITSCHEK *Hesperia* 28 (1959) 68; RAUBITSCHEK *TAPA* 77 (1946) 150. For a discussion of the dative on altars, cf. NOCK *HSCP* 41 (1930) 47 f. (= *Essays* I 239 f.).
[155] *ID* 2484.
[156] Decree: *ID* 1510; ROUSSEL *DCA* 223.

At the establishment of the Poseidoniasts in the little court before the sacellum erected to Roma, there stood an altar of the goddess. The dedication remains [157]:

> Τὸ κοινὸν Βηρυτίων
> Ποσειδωνιαστῶν
> ἐμπόρων καὶ ναυκλή-
> ρων καὶ ἐγδοχέων
> Ῥώμης
> ἀρχιθιασιτεύοντος
> Διονυσίου τοῦ Σωσιπάτρου

Here the genitive identifying the altar is placed in the center of the text and should simply be excluded in reading the text. This text was carved about 100 BC. Though the altar could have replaced an earlier one [158], it was more likely part of the same program which remodelled the sacellum and set up Roma's statue late in the second century BC. There is no evidence of an earlier cult of Roma in the Koinon.

Teos — At Teos there is an altar of Zeus Ktesios, Zeus Kapetolios, Roma and Agathos Daimon [159]. Zeus appears both in his domestic guise as protector of the home and in his public guise as the protector of treaties, and is thus an early example of the Greek awareness of Jupiter Capitolinus [160]. This altar, like the cult of Roma and Πίστις at Teos, probably reflects some alliance with Rome after Teos received her freedom in 167 [161]. We see here that Roma differed from deified kings who were rarely joined with gods on altars [162].

Maronia — A few years ago, a white marble altar of Roma and Zeus was found at Maronia in Thrace [163]. The cult at Maronia had already been known from an inscription which mentions a priest of Zeus and Roma in the second century AD [164]. Cults of Roma often survived in Thrace and Macedon independently of the imperial cult [165].

*

Only these four altars survive, though inscriptions mention three other altars of Roma.

Astypalaea — We know an altar of Roma existed on Astypalaea because the treaty between Rome and Astypalaea was set up on that

---

[157] Dedication: *ID* 1779. HOLLEAUX *REA* 19 (1917) 96.
[158] MARCADÉ 131.
[159] *IGR* IV 1556. BOECKH *CIG* 3074 calls it an altar.
[160] For other examples of Eastern knowledge of Jupiter as protector of treaties, see p. 130 above.
[161] *Syll.* 656. See p. 55 f. above.
[162] HABICHT 142.
[163] BABRITSAS *Arch. Del.* (1965) 484 #4 (plate 610A) = *SEG* XXIV 636.
[164] *IGR* I 831.   [165] See pp. 195f. below.

altar in the temple of Athena and Asclepius[166]. There is a lacuna in the text: πρὸς τῷ βωμῷ ... τῆς Ῥώμης which must be completed with the name of another divinity associated with Roma. BOECKH's old suggestion of [τοῦ Διὸς καί] seems reasonable, given the association of Zeus with Roma in matters of treaties[167]. But any prominent local divinity might have been linked with Roma on the altar.

Thyatira — An inscription copies the dedication from an altar of Roma, Augustus and the local Demos set up by a local notable, Alexandros, with his own money[168]. The stone was found near Hierocaesarea, but on prosopographical grounds it should probably be placed at Thyatira[169]. It was dedicated between 27 BC and 14 AD.

Xanthos — METZGER has recently reported the discovery of a large stele with a list of victors of the Romaia of the Koinon of the Lycians[170]. His report mentions that the text includes mention of an altar of Roma. L. ROBERT has taken responsibility for the future publication of this text.

IV. Sacrifices

Sacrifices to Roma must have been performed all over the Greek world, not merely in those cities with cults of the goddess. Sacrifices required neither cults nor priests; they were honors voted frequently by Greek cities and could be performed by archons or other magistrates[171]. Sacrifices could be voted for specific occasions or permanently endowed to be celebrated annually, monthly or even more frequently[172]. The evidence for sacrifices to Roma is scant and provides few details.

The most detailed description of sacrifices to Roma comes from the regulations for the cult placed on one anta of the temple of Roma in Miletus in the second century BC[173]. These regulations concern the priesthood, the Romaia, and the sacrifices to be performed by the priests or others. Each year the priest in Miletus took 600 drachmas from the treasury, presumably to recompense him for the sacrifices of the year. On the first day of Taureon at the beginning of the Milesian year, he sacrificed a sheep to the Demos of the Romans and to Roma[174]. On the eleventh of Taureon the new gymnasiarchs took office and

---

[166] *IG* XII 3, 173 (= *RDGE* 16).
[167] Ad *CIG* 2485.
[168] *IGR* IV 1304.
[169] ROBERT *Hellenica* VI 71 n. 2.
[170] *RA* (1970) 321.
[171] On sacrifices in the ruler cult, cf. *OGIS* 222.31 f.; HABICHT 138 f.
[172] ROBERT *EA* 175 #29.
[173] *Milet* I 7, 203.
[174] SAMUEL *Greek and Roman Chronology* (Munich, 1970) 115.

together with the ephebes sacrificed to the Demos of the Romans and Roma, as did the retiring gymnasiarchs who were required to give a certain portion to the priest of the Demos and Roma. The priest sacrificed a sheep on the first of each succeeding month (for which he received ten drachmas from the treasury of the prytanies). In these regulations (which cover only the first six months of the Milesian year), other officials also conducted other sacrifices to the Demos and Roma. On the 7th day of the second month (Thargelion), the eponymous αἰσυμνήτης sacrificed a bull to the divinities, as he did in the fifth month (Metageitnion). In both cases a certain portion of the sacrifice was reserved to the priest. (If Apollo held the eponymous magistracy, his προσέταιροι who represented the Milesian tribes performed both these sacrifices.)[175] Finally, a pig was sacrificed to the Demos of the Romans and to Roma by the fifty archons on the 18th of Boedromium—the sixth month of the year[176]. Here the text breaks off, having recorded the monthly sacrifice by the priest and four additional ones by other officials in the first half of the year.

About 130 BC a treaty was concluded between Pergamum and Rome. As was customary, the treaty was set up in the temple of Jupiter Capitolinus in Rome as well as in the temple of Demeter in Pergamum[177]. And the Pergamenes decreed that a special sacrifice (θυσίαν ὡς καλλίστην) be performed to Demeter and Kore and other protective goddesses of Pergamum, as well as to Roma and all other gods and goddesses. These sacrifices were intended to secure and celebrate the alliance. Roma was thus invoked as a protector of Rome, and also as a guardian of oaths and treaties.

Roma's name is mentioned in a list of sacrifices from Erythrae[178]. The first part of the text is missing but sometime early in the second century BC the Koinon of the Ionians provided twenty-four drachmas for a sacrifice to Roma.

In 69 BC Aegina honored one of its notable citizens, Diodoros Heraclidas, with a crown and also decreed that sacrifices be performed on his behalf to Apollo and to Roma[179].

The final mention of sacrifices performed by the Koinon of Asia to Augustus and Roma occurs in the time of Hadrian[180]. An inscription specifies that each candidate on entrance to the college of hymnodes will have to pay as part of his entrance fee one hundred denarii for the sacrifices of Augustus and Roma as well as thirty denarii to the treasury of the two gods[181]. This text was probably set up in the precinct of the temple of Augustus and Roma.

---

[175] *LSAM* 133. [176] Cf. REHM *Milet* I 7, p. 295.
[177] *Syll.* 694; cf. chapter 2 n. 334.
[178] *LSAM* # 26 [179] *IG* IV 2.
[180] *Pergamum* II 374. [181] *IBID.*

In 189 BC, sacrifices, together with an ἀγὼν γυμνικός, were established by the Delphians in gratitude for the senatus consultum granting them freedom and autonomy. The response of the consul C. Lucius Salinator recounts that the Delphic embassy bringing thanks for the senatus consultum announced, ἀγῶνα τὸν γυμνικὸν καὶ τὴν θυσίαν ὑπὲρ ἡμῶν συνετελέσατε [182]. Though ὑπέρ usually means "on behalf of" in such contexts [183], this festival must have been Romaia since no other god is named. The sacrifices must therefore also have been to Roma. The city furnished the sacrifice in the prytaneum—and an inscription from the 150's shows the prominence of these sacrifices, all other sacrifices in the city were merely lumped together [184].

After Sulla's conquest of Athens, he took some interest in Greek affairs and the city of Oropus gained immunities and privileges from him [185]. He joined Romaia to the traditional festival of the Amphiaraia. A letter from the consul of 74 records the words of Sulla, saying that the games and sacrifices which the Oropians had celebrated to Amphiaraus should now also be celebrated ὑπὲρ τῆς νίκης καὶ τῆς ἡγεμονίας τοῦ δήμου τοῦ Ῥωμαίων [186]. The festival became the Amphiaraia-Romaia; presumably sacrifices to Roma or the Demos of the Romans continued as well.

V. Dedications

Dedications to Roma appeared in a wide variety of guises: on temples, altars, and statues or more simply as the record of a small gift to the goddess. The religious monuments of Roma have already been discussed; here, I will deal only with the remaining, and somewhat rag-bag, collection of dedications.

A number of these dedications concern crowns—a traditional way of honoring both gods and men. These honorific crowns were not the ascetic laurel bestowed on the occasion of festival victory, they were crowns of precious metal intended to adorn the local statue of Roma or to be sent to Rome. During and after the war with Perseus, gold crowns seem to have flooded into Rome and, whether dedicated to Roma or to Jupiter, were kept on the Capitoline together with various other dedications to Roma [187]. For some donors, these crowns were sureties of their fidelity; for others a desperate attempt to secure Roman favor or indulgence. In this latter spirit, Rhodes voted a gold

---

[182] *Syll.* 611 (= *RDGE* 38).

[183] Nock *HSCP* 41 (1930) 23 (= *Essays* I 220).

[184] *IDelphes* 1, 152; *SGDI* 2680: ἐν τὰν θυσίαν τῶν Ῥωμαίων καὶ ἐν τᾶς λοιπὰς θυσίας ἐν ἇς ἁ πόλις συντέλει πάσας.

[185] See p. 106 above.

[186] *IG* VII 413 (= *RDGE* 23).

[187] E.g. the crowns from Alabanda and Lampsacus; Livy 43, 6, 5f.

crown to Roma in 167[188], and a decade later rivals for the throne of Cappadocia—King Ariarathes V, Orophernes his brother, and King Demetrius of Syria—all did so as well[189].

About 150 BC the citizens of Melos honored Roma with a gold crown, presumably to be placed on the bronze statue which the same dedication records[190]. A silver crown belonging to Roma is mentioned a decade later on a Delian inventory list from the temple of Apollo and this may have adorned a statue of Roma placed in that temple[191]. Finally, METZGER reports that an unpublished Lycian text of the second century mentions that a crown not awarded in the Romaia was deposited on Roma's altar[192]. But this was probably an ordinary laurel crown, rather than an honorific one in precious metal.

There were other dedications to Roma in the second century BC— arms dedicated after the Romaia at Miletus[193], some unspecified votive offerings on Chios[194], as well as dedications placed on the Capitol in Rome[195]. In the reign of Claudius, a gold statue of the Pax Augusta Claudiana was, by imperial command, dedicated instead to the goddess Roma[196].

After Roma was joined in the imperial cult, various kinds of dedications were made. These might be simply to Roma and Augustus (or one of his successors)[197] or more comprehensively to the Senate[198] or the imperial family both living and dead: γένος Σεβαστοῦ[199], οἶκος Σεβαστοῦ[200], θεοὶ Σεβαστοί[201]. In Exarchos in Phocis the priest of the emperor Caligula dedicated a statue of that emperor to the goddess Roma[202].

The object dedicated often remains unspecified, though we know the portico from Cyrene was dedicated to Zeus, Roma and Augustus[203], and the priests of Roma and Augustus of the Galatian Koinon list on their temple at Ancyra specific gifts dedicated to the patron divinities[204].

---

[188] Polybius 30, 5, 4.   [189] Polybius 31, 32, 3; 32, 10, 4; 32, 2, 1.
[190] *IG* XII 3, 1097.
[191] *ID* 1450 A 119; ROUSSEL *DCA* 222 n. 7; BRUNEAU 445
[192] *RA* (1970) 321.   [193] *Milet* I 7, 203.
[194] KONTOLEON *Akte* 192f. (Cf. chapter 2 n. 215)
[195] CIL I² 725 (= CIL VI 372); see Additional Note.
[196] BELL *Jews and Christians in Egypt* (London, 1924) #1912. 34f.
[197] *IGR* IV 971 + 978; *IGR* IV 1534; *IG* XII 5, 1013; *IG* XII Supp. 9.
[198] *OGIS* 479.
[199] JAMOT *BCH* 26 (1902) 298 #17.
[200] PLASSART *BCH* 50 (1926) 394 #14.
[201] LAUMONIER *BCH* 58 (1934) 379 #43; *IG* IX 2, 32.
[202] KLAFFENBACH *SB Berlin Akad.* (1935) 705–706.
[203] *SEG* IX 127.
[204] *OGIS* 533 (= ROBERT *Gladiateurs* #86).

Dedications to the Demos of the Romans are not necessarily to a divinity. The crowns voted to the Demos and the Senate, for instance, need hardly have religious implications [205]. On the other hand, the table which the Delians set up to Athena Nike and the Demos of Romans was a cult object and the deified Demos thus resembles Roma.

VI. Calendars

The honors bestowed on Hellenistic princes encompassed every possible adulation; even calendars were changed to incorporate new honorific months named after the ruler or his family [206]. This should not surprise us; our own calendar still retains months named after Julius Caesar and Augustus. These honors, like so many others, descended from the ruler cult to Rome.

Demetrius Poliorcetes was probably the first to have been honored in this way, when the Athenians renamed the month Munychion as "Demetrion" in 307 BC [207]. The practice was then adopted by other cities, especially those dependent upon the Seleucid or Attalid dynasties [208]. And, like other honors of the ruler cult, it was later applied to Roma, Caesar, Augustus and his successors. Such an honor was surely considered a divine honor in Rome [209]. As so often, the Romans tried to justify this action by precedent: the month of Junius was attributed to the liberator M. Junius Brutus [210]. That precedent was specious: the month, like the gens Junia itself, was named after Juno [211]. The true precedent was in the East. The Hellenistic model perhaps first caught Roman attention when the Mytileneans named a month after their benefactor Pompey [212]. But it was a serious matter to transfer such practice to Rome. The divine honors so easily accepted by Roman proconsuls in the East were far from acceptable in the capital. Yet after Caesar's assassination and the appearance of the comet, the Senate's decrees of 45 were put into effect: the month of "Quintilius" became "Julius" [213]. The outrage expressed by Cicero in his letter of

---

[205] *ID* 465.

[206] On the honorific month, SCOTT *YCS* 2 (1931) 199–278 remains the basic work and my discussion owes much to it. HABICHT 155f. treats not only honorific months, but even honorific days in the cults of Hellenistic kings.

[207] Plutarch *Demetrius* 12, 2; SCOTT *Ibid.* 201.

[208] SAMUEL *Greek and Roman Chronology* (Munich, 1970) 284f. lists the names of months, including honorific ones. On festivals to kings held during the honorific months of those kings, cf. HABICHT 155.

[209] Suetonius *Divus Julius* 76, 1.

[210] Macrobius *Sat.* 1, 12, 31.

[211] SCOTT *op. cit.* 219–221; WEINSTOCK *DJ* 153.

[212] *IG* XII 2, 59.18. Cf. SCOTT *op. cit.* 206; SAMUEL *op. cit.* 129 is less certain and merely reports this month as Ποµ[. . .].

[213] Dio 45, 7, 2; SCOTT *op. cit.* 221–224.

July 44 shows that this was a particularly offensive act; Suetonius calls it a divine honor [214]. But the same honor was granted to Augustus in 27 BC—a rare divine honor voted to him by the Senate during his lifetime [215].

The honorific month also passed from the ruler-cult to the cult of Roma. The calendar of Pergamum may have included a month Ῥωμαῖος—though it is attested only by roof-tiles [216]. The Pergamene calendar remains confused: there are names for too many months. SAMUEL's hypothesis seems plausible: the calendar changed during the regal period to allow the introduction of honorific months such as Philetaireios and Eumeneios. Though SCHUCHHARDT suggests that the month Romaios may have been introduced in the reign of Attalus I to celebrate his Roman alliance [217], I doubt that such honors were voted to Roma while the Attalids still ruled Pergamum. There is still no evidence for the worship of Roma in Attalid dominions [218]. The introduction of Romaios belongs in the long Pergamene tradition of honorific months but occurred only after the bequest of Attalus.

Of the two calendars from Paphos in Cyprus [219], the first contains the months Sebastos, Agrippaios, Libaios, Oktabios, [Julaios], Neronaios, Drusaios, Aphrodisios, Ankisaios, Romaios, Aeneadaios, Kapetolios [220]. These months were named after Augustus and members of his family, the gens Julia, Roma and Jupiter Capitolinus. The calendar must be dated after the marriage of Julia and Agrippa in 21 BC, most likely in the aftermath of the Paphian earthquake of 15 BC when Augustus sent funds for relief and the citizens renamed their city "Augusta" [221]. In this calendar only the months Romaios and Kapetolios are named in honor of the Roman state; the others all honor Augustus.

But this calendar quickly became obsolete; the deaths of Agrippa (12 BC), Octavia (11 BC) and Drusus (9 BC) were followed by the self-exile of Tiberius (6 BC) and the disgrace of Julia (2 BC). Exactly when

---

[214] *Ad Att* 16, 1, 1; 16, 4, 1. Suetonius *Divus Julius* 76: *ampliora humano fastigio*.

[215] Dio 55, 6, 6; Suetonius *Augustus* 31; SCOTT *op. cit.* 224–227.

[216] *Pergamum* II 689–691 and p. 398; SAMUEL *op. cit.* 126; SCOTT *op. cit.* 205–206. BOEHRINGER-KRAUSS *Altertümer von Pergamon* IX *Das Temenos für den Herrscherkult* (Berlin, 1937) 80f. is doubtful about a month Ῥωμαῖος at Pergamum.

[217] *Pergamum* II p. 398.

[218] See p. 58 above.

[219] For a full discussion, cf. SCOTT *op. cit.* 207–219. SAMUEL *op. cit.* 183ff. agrees with the attribution of this calendar to Cyprus; LAFFI *SCO* 16 (1967) 45 is uncertain of its origin, and provides an extensive bibliography.

[220] BOLL *Cat. cod. astrol. Gr.* II 139f.; cf. chapter 2 n. 432.

[221] Dio 54, 23, 7; cf. CHAPOT *Mélanges Cagnat* (Paris, 1912) 75; SCOTT *op. cit.* 207–208.

the Paphians adopted their new calendar is uncertain, but it must have been introduced after Augustus became pontifex maximus (12) and before the title of pater patriae (2 BC) was given to him. The new calendar completely eliminated the imperial family, and honored only Augustus, his ancestry and his titles, together with Vesta and Roma: Aphrodisios, Apogonikos, Aineios, Julos or Julios, Kaisarios, Sebastos, Autokratorikos, Demarchexousios, Plethypatos or Pleisthypatos, Archiereus, Hestios or Hestiaios, Romaios [222]. Both Vesta and Roma were closely connected with Augustus: Vesta's cult had been brought to the Palatine, and Roma was joined in cults with Augustus throughout the Eastern Empire. But among the living, only Augustus was honored—a sad reminder of his loneliness in power during this period of his reign.

VII. Coins and Gems

The goddess Roma is perhaps most widely known from her frequent depiction on Roman coinage, and scholarly interest in Roma has largely been restricted to numismatists [223]. These types have been extensively discussed and in any case we are not here concerned with Roma in the West. I do not believe that Roma appeared on Roman coins before the second century BC when her cults had already been established in the Greek world [224]. Since Roma came from the East to the West, the eastern conception of Roma may well have influenced her depiction on some Roman coins, and I will briefly note these types. Otherwise I will restrict this discussion to a survey of Greek coins portraying Roma.

The earliest of these is the didrachm from Locri Epizephyrii, which has already been discussed [225]. It portrays a seated Roma, dressed in a chiton and peplon, with a shield. This Amazonian figure is being

---

[222] KUBITSCHEK *JÖAI* (1905) 111–116. In a hemerologium preserved in several mss. the month Ῥωμαῖος is replaced by Λῷος—which is probably an error; cf. SCOTT *op. cit.* 214.

[223] RICHTER 145ff.; THOMSEN *Early Roman Coinage* (Copenhagen, 1957–1961) II 153ff.; WEINSTOCK *DJ* 42f.; 93ff.; 100f.; 297; VERMEULE *Goddess Roma* with many additional references.

[224] I do not believe the case for Roma's presence on Roman coinage of the third century has been proven; cf. MATTINGLY *BMCRE* III cxxxvii. For a complete discussion of previous scholarship, see THOMSEN *op. cit.* who would place Roma's entrance in years soon after 216 BC (vol. II 138). Since the goddess is not identified by a legend (THOMSEN *op. cit.* II 155 n.115), it seems a futile exercise to identify this head as Roma, Ilia, Roma/Bellona, Diana of Aricia. I am sceptical about what can be proved until the typology of gods and heroes is better established. Cf. KNOCHE *Gymnasium* 59 (1952) 326f.

[225] See above pp. 109; 132f.; cf. also CALZA *Dedalo* 7 (1926) 664 who sees on this coin the pictorial representation of the Roma honored at Smyrna in 195 BC.

crowned by another female figure which can be identified as the personified Fides from the legend: *Ρώμα* and *Πίστις*. The coin was issued about 204 BC and, given Rome's political activity at that time, the military emphasis seems quite appropriate.

Soon after Perseus' defeat at Pydna, coins were issued throughout Macedon bearing a head of Roma [226]. The striking similarities of these issues from Pella, Amphipolis, Thessalonika and elsewhere seem to demonstrate a coordinated attempt on the part of the defeated Macedonians to appeal for clemency. This formed part of a propaganda campaign which included the establishment of cults of Roma and Zeus Eleutherios in various cities of Perseus' domains [227].

Elsewhere in the Greek world, the early numismatic representations of Roma draw on the typology of the Amazon, Athena or a combination of the two [228]. In Athens, as we might expect, the head of Roma on Athenian silver coinage clearly resembles Athena [229]. We have already discussed this association of Roma with Athena, culminating in the dedication of a temple of Roma just beside the Parthenon, and concluded that it would have been a matter of pride for Romans and Athenians alike [230]. But Athena's influence on Roma-types was hardly confined to Athens. The Phidian type of Athena Nikephoros was widely known outside of Athens [231]. It provided the model for the portrayal of Roma on coins issued by some Bithynian and Pontic cities just after Pompey's settlement there [232]. But here the goddess, who is seated on shields and holds the miniature Nike, is not only Athena but an Amazon as well. Some later coins would further stress the Amazonian element by portraying Roma armed, with a bared breast; others stress the relation to Athena Polias [233].

In the notes to Part I, I have listed the Greek coins depicting Roma which can be found in the major numismatic corpora. Even a cursory mention of them all here would entail a long chapter and be of relative-

---

[226] *BMC Macedon* 18 #72f.; 19 #79; 46 #21; 90 #3; 108 #2. MACKAY *Museum Notes* (1968) 5–13 argues convincingly that these coins must be dated just after Pydna, rather than twenty years later.

[227] Cf. pp. 107f.

[228] STRONG *JRS* 1 (1911) 3; VERMEULE *Goddess Roma* 29ff.; 51; WEINSTOCK *DJ* 100.

[229] THOMPSON *The New Style Silver Coinage of Athens* (New York, 1961) 359–362 #1110–1124.

[230] See p. 104 above.

[231] Athena Nikephoros appears on a fourth century coin from Side in Pamphylia: *BMC Lycia* 145 #15.

[232] *BMC Pontus* 117 #1 (Bithynium); 152 #2f. (Nicaea); 179 #1f. (Nicomedia); 21 #83 (Amisus); WADDINGTON *Recueil Général* I² 169 #22 (Amastris); II 249 #29 (Apamea); IV 617 #5 (Tios); *SNG-DEN* 18 #583 (Prusa). On these monetary issues and the settlement of Bithynia-Pontus by Pompey, cf. pp. 84f.

[233] MATTINGLY *BMCRE* III cxxxviii.

ly little usefulness. During the Empire a new Western conception of Roma became widespread and was reflected in numismatic types found throughout the Roman imperium. Such transformations, effected by the moneyers in Rome, lie beyond the scope of this study.

It is possible, of course, that Roman coinage of the late republic can tell us something of Greek depictions of Roma. It is possible that the seated Roma with her foot on a globe derives from a Greek work of art, but that type appeared first on the Roman coinage of the 70's BC [234]. The mural crown is worn by Roma on Greek coins of the Empire, but it seems to go back to a Roman type based on Cybele [235]. The origins of such types are difficult, or impossible, to determine, and even more conventional types were merged so that Roma, Virtus and Minerva became virtually indistinguishable [236]. For this reason I have tended to shun numismatic evidence, except where the type is clearly identified by a legend.

Roma also appeared on engraved gems in the type of Athena Nikephoros, but it is difficult to ascertain the origin of most gems. One of the most famous gems from antiquity, the Gemma Augustea, may have been the work of a Greek artist [237]. It depicts Roma and Augustus in the guise of Athena and Zeus Eleutherios. Whatever its origin, this stone and its elaborate symbolism is indicative of the new propaganda aims of the imperial court: Dea Roma in the literature and art of the Roman Empire served a different function from the Greeks' own θεὰ Ῥώμη [238].

---

[234] WEINSTOCK *DJ* 42 ff.

[235] On Cybele in Rome, cf. BÖMER *MDAI(R)* 71 (1964) 130 ff.

[236] VERMEULE *Goddess Roma* 65 ff.; GRANT *Roman Imperial Money* (London, 1954) 269.

[237] For an excellent reproduction of the Gemma Augustea, cf. RICHTER *Engraved Gems of the Romans* (London, 1971) #501. On the Greek origin and the complex symbolism of this stone, see OLIVER *Demokratia* 163 ff.

[238] On Dea Roma in the West, see my Princeton dissertation *DEA ROMA: The Development of the Idea of the Goddess Roma* (Ann Arbor, 1967). The relation between Roma and Vesta, treated there pp. 105 ff., will appear as a separate study.

Chapter 5

Romaia

The worship of Roma included sacrifices, athletic games, cultural competitions; all these were included in the term Romaia, a πανήγυρις dedicated to Roma¹. Although πανήγυρις originally meant any sort of assembly, it later came to apply more specifically to a religious assembly—usually convened to celebrate the festival of a divinity². Since our evidence for Romaia consists largely of honorific dedications and victory lists, few general allusions to the festival and its non-agonistic components survive. πανήγυρις appears only in the long decree of Araxa recording the institution of the Romaia of the Lycian Koinon and its second celebration four years later³.

Every πανήγυρις was a religious festival and therefore included certain religious ceremonies, however devoid of true religious content the cult of Roma might be⁴. Obviously there were sacrifices, though these were certainly not restricted to quinquennial or even annual occasions; they might occur as often as several times a month⁵. It was a frequent practice to make a meal of the beasts sacrificed to the god, as was done after sacrifices to Roma at Miletus⁶.

A noteworthy part of any Greek festival was the πομπή—perhaps the most famous example was the Panathenaic procession⁷. The πομπή enabled all the citizens to participate in the festivities. Such processions were part of most Greek religious celebrations, were transmitted

---

¹ HABICHT 147. For a necessary addition to the L-S-J entry Ῥωμαῖα, see DREW-BEAR *Glotta* 50 (1972) 218.

² ZIEHEN *RE* XVIII 581.

³ BEAN *JHS* 68 (1948) 46 #11. πανήγυρις in honor of Roma seems to have been celebrated on Chios; cf. KONTOLEON *Akte* 192ff. For πανήγυρις as the place for festivals, cf. ROBERT *Gladiateurs* #86. 27–28 (= *OGIS* 533).

⁴ HABICHT 236.

⁵ *Milet* I 7, 203. Other sacrifices in Romaia, cf. *SGDI* 2680; *Syll.* 611 (= *RDGE* 38) (Delphi); ROBERT *Gladiateurs* #86 (= *OGIS* 533) (Ancyra); *Akte* 192 (Chios); *JHS* 68 (1948) 46 #11 (Lycian Koinon).

⁶ *Milet* I 7, 203; cf. NILSSON I 142f.; 829f.

⁷ NILSSON *Opuscula Selecta* (Lund, 1951) I 166f.

to the Romaia[8] and later became a standard feature of honors paid to the Emperor[9]. θεωροί from various cities paraded and brought gifts[10]; paeans were sung to the god.

But the Romaia are best known for their agonistic features. Our texts sometimes merely refer to the ἀγὼν γυμνικὸς τῶν Ῥωμαίων[11]. In Latin they are simply called *Ludi*[12], though *certamen* is once used in a text referring to a municipal celebration at Pergamum in honor of Roma and the Emperor[13]. This text also refers to the competition as εἰσελαστικός—a contest whose victor merits a formal honorific entry into his native city. Pliny's correspondence with Trajan at this time shows that this title could only be conferred by the emperor himself[14]. But the generic term ἆθλος only occurs once in reference to Romaia[15]. The agonistic events are nearly always designated by their technical names.

Competitors in many Romaia, as in most Greek festivals, were from nearby towns. One must not be misled by the great panhellenic celebrations. The great majority of festivals offered neither prizes nor prestige sufficient to draw competitors from afar, especially in athletic contests where the competitors remained amateurs[16]. For example, the athlete Zeuxis triumphed at Samos, Miletus, Priene and the Romaia at Ephesus[17]. We can reasonably conclude that Zeuxis lived in Ionia, especially since he ran at Samos in a race for boys. Young men rarely travelled. A victory list of the Romaia celebrated by the Lycian Koinon lists almost exclusively Greeks from Asia Minor—often from Lycia itself[18]. A successful athlete would travel far for major panhellenic festivals, but much of his experience would first have been gained in victories in his own or neighboring cities. So Leon the

---

[8] For processions in the ruler cult, see HABICHT 152. E.g. ROBERT *Gladiateurs* #86.50 (= *OGIS* 533).

[9] BELL *Jews and Christians in Egypt* (London, 1924) #1912.38 and note.

[10] Cf. the decree from Araxa: BEAN *JHS* 68 (1948) 46 #11.

[11] *Syll.* 611 (= *RDGE* 38) (Delphi); *IG* XII 9, 899 (Euboean Koinon); *OGIS* 458 (Asian Koinon).

[12] Livy 43, 6, 5. Of course these should not be confused with the Ludi Romani—a Roman festival in honor of Jupiter which was translated into Greek as Ῥωμαῖα. This festival had nothing whatever to do with the goddess Roma and, since the only text cited in LSJ under Ῥωμαῖα refers to these Ludi Romani, the lexicon adds to the confusion. DREW-BEAR *Glotta* 50 (1972) 218 corrects the LSJ entry.

[13] *Pergamum* II 269. Whether this refers to a single event (Pliny *Ep.* 10, 118) or many events (Suetonius *Caligula* 20) is difficult to determine.

[14] Pliny *Ep.* 10, 118–119.

[15] *Milet* I 7, 203.

[16] RINGWOOD *Agonistic Features of Local Greek Festivals, Chiefly from Inscriptional Evidence* (Poughkeepsie, 1927) 7.

[17] ROBERT *Hellenica* IX 73–76.

[18] Report by METZGER *RA* (1970) 321.

Olympic victor was probably a Rhodian with most of his victories not so very far from home[19]. Occasionally a special relationship existed between certain cities. Athenians abound in the fourth century victory lists at the Amphiaraia in Oropus[20], but by the first century the Thebans are pre-eminent in the musical and dramatic contests in the same Amphiaraia-Romaia[21].

There may have been more than one Romaia in a single city. Such principal Asian cities as Sardes, Smyrna and Pergamum had municipal celebrations in honor of Roma but also periodically hosted the Romaia-Sebasta of the Koinon of Asia[22]. The Romaia of the Hekatombaion on Delos certainly seem distinct from the ordinary Romaia there[23]. Delos is a likely place for the duplication of festivals. For example, two Antigoneia, two Demetreia and two Ptolemaia were celebrated at Delos: the first local and the second for the League of the Islanders[24]. Such independent colleges as the Competaliasts and Poseidoniasts honored Roma and might sponsor festivals quite independent of the Demos[25]. There were clearly separate cults of Roma on Delos; separate festivals were surely possible. Likewise, since there were two cults of Roma in Athens—one with Augustus on the Acropolis and another with Demos at the foot of Kolonos Agoraios—separate Romaia in Athens were also possible[26].

Just as the festivals in honor of Hellenistic kings[27], Romaia could be held at various intervals. Most of the local festivals were annual[28], and the texts specifically indicate if they were quinquennial, as was the traditional Olympiad[29]. Texts specify πενταετηρίς as the period for the Romaia of the Lycian Koinon, the Romaia-Letoia in Caria, the Romaia-Hekatesia in Stratonicea, the Romaia in Citium on Cyprus, and the Aphrodisia-Romaia in Oropus[30]. But the Romaia-Sebasta of

---

[19] *SEG* XXII 350. See chapter 2 n. 46 and *ZPE* 12 (1973) 259ff.

[20] *IG* VII 414; on special relationship, cf. p. 172 below and RINGWOOD 44 n. 221.

[21] *IG* VII 419–420.

[22] See above p. 81ff.

[23] *ID* 2596. See above p. 65 n. 243. There are several festivals to Apollo on Delos; cf. BRUNEAU 86f.

[24] BRUNEAU on Antigoneia: 558f.; 564f.; on Demetrieia: 563f.; on Ptolemaia: 519f.; 531.

[25] On Competaliasts and Competalia, cf. BRUNEAU 617f.

[26] See pp. 102ff. above.

[27] HABICHT 151–152.

[28] HABICHT 151.

[29] WEINSTOCK *DJ* 314f.

[30] BEAN *JHS* 68 (1948) 46 #11 (Lycia); BEAN *JHS* 73 (1953) 32 #13 (Caunus); *OGIS* 441 (Stratonicea); HOGARTH *Devia Cypria* 109 #28 (Citium); *IG* VII 4253 (Oropus). Some scholars interpret *IG* XII 1, 730 to affirm the quinquennial nature of Romaia in Rhodes; see chapter 2 n. 45.

the province of Asia could hardly have been quinquennial, even though it is described as pentaeteric [31]. The Koinon of the cities of the province of Asia met annually [32], not least because the high priesthood was held for only one year [33]. The avowed purpose of this gathering was religious: to worship Roma and the emperor. The festival was the means to do so. It is difficult to imagine this annual meeting without its essential religious component. Whatever the original situation when the temple and cult of the Asian Koinon was first established in Pergamum, by the reign of Tiberius the Romaia-Sebasta of the Koinon were celebrated in a number of major Asian cities. Perhaps the festival was pentaeteric in each of eight cities and two festivals a year were held [34]. Similarly, the Bithynian Koinon, whose festival is also called pentaeteric, probably rotated among Nicaea, Nicomedia, and other cities where a local festival also took place yearly [35]. The date of this annual meeting varied: in Gaul it was celebrated on August 1; in Lycia around October 1 [36]. But whatever the schedule of the formal festivals, other events connected with the cult of Roma occurred between festivals. The regulations from Miletus make it clear that the priest had many events to organize: sacrifices, contests, and a ritual torch race. The ὑμνῳδοί of Roma and Augustus in Pergamum presumably were not restricted to the quinquennial festivals at Pergamum [37]. They were certainly performed on the emperor's birthday, and probably also on other days on which the imperial family was honored [38]. The evidence from Miletus and Pergamum, when combined with what is known of other cults of the Hellenistic age, indicate significant activity in the cult of Roma even between the annual or pentaeteric Romaia [39].

Our knowledge of Romaia and the cults of Roma depends almost entirely on inscriptions. In studying the evidence for Romaia, we see how haphazard this evidence can be. Some festivals are known through a single dedication to a victor in his homeland far from the site of the festivals. It is impossible to imagine how many of these festivals are forgotten and will remain so until new evidence is unearthed. But we know enough to realize that Romaia must have blanketed the Greek

---

[31] MORETTI *IAG* 65.
[32] DEININGER *Provinziallandtage* 144.
[33] *Sardis* 8.
[34] MORETTI *RFIC* 32 (1954) 276f.; DEININGER *Provinziallandtage* 55.
[35] MORETTI *IAG* p. 177–178; DEININGER *Provinziallandtage* 61.
[36] DEININGER *Provinziallandtage* 145.
[37] *IGR* IV 353; see pp. 192f.
[38] *IGR* IV 1608c; BELL *Jews and Christians in Egypt* (London, 1924) 32 ad #1912.38.
[39] Monthly sacrifices to Hellenistic kings: *OGIS* 56.33 (Ptolemy III); *OGIS* 383. 132f. (Antiochus I of Commagene).

world and, once established, they remained. Smyrna celebrated Romaia for 350 years and there is little reason to think that city unique. Romaia must have lasted, as Roma herself did, until the end of paganism.

I. Athletic Contests

Romaia included the athletic events which Greeks had contested for centuries. We are fortunate in having extensive victory lists from the Amphiaraia-Romaia in Oropus to supplement evidence from dedications to individual victors in various Romaia [40]. The evidence does not distinguish local peculiarities in the athletic sphere and most events (excluding equestrian events) listed in the Oropus texts are confirmed by other texts. The events attested cover the entire range of foot-races (στάδιον, δίαυλος, ἵππιος, δολιχός) and the race in armor (ὁπλίτης). Other attested events are contests in boxing and wrestling (πάλη, πυγμή, παγκράτιον) and of course the pentathlon. Events often included in the pentathlon — discus, javelin and jumping — are not found in the Romaia at Oropus or elsewhere. As was common at Greek festivals, separate events were held for boys, youths and men.

Since Boeotia was under Athenian control when the Amphiaraia were organized in the late fourth century BC, the Amphiaraia may have been modeled on the Panathenaia [41]. The Panathenaia shared a number of events with the Amphiaraia which were rare: equestrian events in armor and with special ceremonial chariots [42]. Both the northern Greeks (especially the Thessalians) and the Athenians were traditionally fond of horses and equestrian competitions, so we cannot distinguish direct influences from merely parallel traditions [43]. For example, the Amphiaraia-Romaia included the ἀπόβασις, a strange contest (ἀγὼν ἀποβατικός) in which the competitors used horses for the approach. The obvious military origin of this event can be traced back to the Homeric practice of coming to battle in chariots, dismounting to fight, and remounting to withdraw. The nature of the ἀπόβασις is unclear but it must be similar to the Olympic κάλπη — a race in which a rider dismounted to finish on foot. The ἀποβάτης dismounted from a chariot to continue the race on foot. We are told by Harpocratian

---

[40] *IG* VII 416; 417; 420. Other texts also mention athletic events at Romaia: *IG* II² 3153 [+ Hesperia 15 (1946) 224 #51]; *IG* IV² 1, 629; *IG* VII 48; ROBERT *EEP* 128 #3; *Syll.* 1064–1066; *ID* 1957; MAIURI *NS* #34; *IGR* IV 1262; ROBERT *BCH* 49 (1925) 232f. xi.

[41] RINGWOOD *op. cit.* 44 n. 221 has a discussion with bibliography.

[42] RINGWOOD *op. cit.* 46; PREUNER *Hermes* 57 (1922) 80–94.

[43] GARDINER *Greek Athletic Sports and Festivals* (London, 1910) 235f. Cf. also Panathenaic victory lists *IG* II² 2311; 2314.

(citing Theophrastus) that only the Athenians and Boeotians celebrated this event [44]. And the event is clearly seen as neither athletic nor equestrian, but sui generis [45]. An equestrian contest was also included in the Romaia at Magnesia [46], which is hardly surprising since the major local festival—the Leukophryêna honoring Artemis—also included equestrian contests as well as the usual musical and athletic games [47]. Local custom determined all.

One athletic contest not included in the Romaia-Amphiaria but attested in other Romaia was the torch race-λαμπαδηδρομία. This was usually a relay race in which a torch was passed instead of a baton. Most of the evidence deals with races for teams of boys. In later times individual competitions seem to have been held and both relay and individual torch races coexisted in Hellenistic Delos [48]. The Alexandrian Protogenes won the torch race for the ephebes in the Romaia there in the first year of the Athenian domination [49]. His origin makes it likely that he competed individually rather than as part of a team. The regulations for the cult of Roma at Miletus speak of the torch race, held in the boys' palestra [50]. Here too it seems to be an event for the young—appropriate enough when we recall the lines of Lucretius [51]:

> Augescunt aliae gentes, aliae minuuntur
> inque brevi spatio mutantur saecla animantum
> et quasi cursores vitai lampada tradunt.

At times the torch-race was detached from more ordinary celebrations and became a ceremonial duty rather than a true athletic event [52]. Thus was it singled out in the regulations for the cult of Roma at Miletus.

II. Musical and Dramatic Events

Greek agonistic festivals included musical events as well as athletic and equestrian contests. "Musical" here is used in its widest sense— ἀγὼν μουσικός included events under the special patronage of the

---

[44] Harpocratian p. 45. 4–10 (ed. DINDORF). Cf. REISCH RE I 2814–2817.
[45] IG VII 4254.
[46] IMagn. 127.
[47] IMagn. 22; 41; 61; etc.
[48] MORETTI IAG p. 146–148; JÜTHNER RE XII 569–577.
[49] ID 1950 (167–166 BC).
[50] Milet I 7, 203.
[51] 2, 77–79. For other uses of this image, see BAILEY's Commentary ad. loc.
[52] Cf. GARDINER op. cit. 292f. The torch race on horseback seems to have been rarer; Plato Resp. I 328a has Socrates say when he hears of such a race: Ἀφ' ἵππων; καινόν γε τοῦτο. λαμπάδια ἔχοντες διαδώσουσιν ἀλλήλοις ἁμιλλώμενοι τοῖς ἵπποις.

Muses. So the ἀγὼν μουσικός celebrated by the Carian city of Stratonicea in honor of the goddess Roma included not only competitions on musical instruments but also contests in poetry, dramatic composition, acting, singing and declamation.

By the third century BC the Greeks had begun to distinguish these events according to the place where they were performed: ἀγὼν σκηνικός denoted events that took place on the stage building, and ἀγὼν θυμελικός denoted events (musical performances, singing, declamation) that took place in the orchestra where the altar (θυμέλη) of Dionysus stood[53].

Nearly all our evidence for thymelic contests in Romaia come from the long victory lists from Oropus. The Amphiaraia-Romaia included a dozen events: musical performance (flute; cithara; trumpet); accompanied song; poetic composition of various kinds (epic; lyric; dramatic); recitation; and declamation[54]. The nature of some of these events is obvious, though the standards of excellence applied in a few of them may seem bizarre to modern taste. For example, both the herald (κῆρυξ) and the trumpeter (σαλπιστής) were originally military offices that had come to be used in civilian assemblies. Not until the second century were these events included in festivals[55]. We are dependent on Pollux to provide some indication of the criteria on which these competitions were judged. The herald should have not only vocal power and clear enunciation but also such excellent breath control that his breathing was not noticeable and the flow of his speech perfectly smooth[56]. Perhaps it was just as well that the term ἀγὼν μουσικός was less frequently applied to these late Hellenistic festivals. It would have profaned the name of the Muses to associate it with contests in vocal and pulmonary stamina!

Outside Oropus only a single text attests a thymelic event in a festival to Roma[57]. It honors a flautist whose victories are astonishing. The Delphic inscription lists 57 victories in festivals ranging from Rome and Naples to Tarsus, including three Pythian victories. One of the victories of this musician, whose career must have lasted into the third century AD, was at the Romaia held at Smyrna.

---

[53] J. FREI *De Certaminibus Thymelicis* (Basel diss., 1900) 5–15.

[54] *IG* VII 416–420. I omit the εὐαγγέλια τῆς Ῥω[μαίων νίκης] listed in *IG* VII 417 with Euphanes of Oropus given as victor. While MOMMSEN *Hermes* 20 (1885) 274 (= *GS* V 501) accepted it as a contest, DITTENBERGER ad *IG* VII 416 and FREI *op. cit.* 37 interpreted it as a special announcement of victory. I think it best to regard it as a ritualized announcement which was allotted to a local favorite, in this case Euphanes who appears as agonothete in *IG* VII 419. Whether a genuine announcement or a ritualized re-enactment, it could hardly have been a competitive event.

[55] FREI *op. cit.* 66 with evidence.

[56] Pollux IV 91f.; FREI *op. cit.* 44.   [57] DELPHES 1, 550

For dramatic competitions in Romaia, most of our evidence again comes from Oropus. Victories for poets and actors in both tragedy and comedy are recorded. One text even distinguishes actors who win in a new play from those in a classic one, and we must regret that we do not know which plays were revived for this Boetian audience in the first century BC[58]. The multiplicity of dramatic contexts at the Amphiaraia-Romaia clearly resulted from Athenian influence. But since these competitions are not attested in the original inscriptions from the fourth century, they may have been introduced under subsequent Athenian influence. Or was perhaps this elaborate musical and dramatic program which engaged Sulla's interest in the festival; his weakness for stage entertainers was notorious.

Many other Romaia undoubtedly incorporated dramatic contests, but the evidence is limited. The most interesting text is a dramatic victory list from Magnesia on the Maeander which lists the poets who triumphed in new tragedies, comedies and satyr plays[59]. This monument attests at least five celebrations of the Romaia at Magnesia— probably between 150 and 100 BC. Even then it was common for the tragic poet also to write the satyr play—since in several instances the same poet won in both the tragic and stayric competitions. The text also provides the names of the dramas which won the prize. The subjects of tragedies and satyr-drama had hardly changed since the fifth century: we find a *Clytemnestra* and a *Hermione*[60]. The satyr plays also treated standard themes from the epic cycle: Ajax, Protesilaus, and Palamede. But the comedy which flourished in Magnesia in the late second century was almost certainly modeled on comedy of the fourth century: Metrodorus won at Magnesia with his *Homoioi* (a title employed by several fourth century poets)[61] and Agathenor's successful *Milesia* may have had some relation—if only in the characteristics of the title role—to earlier productions with the same title[62]. We will never know the precise relationships of all these plays but world literature (and popular entertainment even more) is studded with examples of a successful plot, character or theatrical device which is imitated, re-imitated and imitated again.

What was the nature of such a dramatic competition in the late Hellenistic age? Surely the poets and actors were usually members of the guilds of artists dedicated to Dionysos[63]. They were therefore

---

[58] *IG* VII 420. [59] *Syll.* 1079 (= *IMagn.* 88).
[60] Cf. NAUCK *TGF* p. 176; p. 204.
[61] Poseidippus (KOCH *CGF* III 34); Ephippos (KOCH *CGF* II 258); Antiphanes (KOCH *CGF* II 82). Cf. WEBSTER *Studies in Later Greek Comedy* (London, 1953).
[62] Alexis (KOCH *CGF* II 351); Philemon (KOCH *CGF* III 357).
[63] SIFAKIS *Studies in the History of Hellenistic Drama* (London, 1967) 137ff.; PICKARD-CAMBRIDGE *The Dramatic Festivals of Athens* (2nd ed., Oxford, 1968) 279–305.

professionals who received a fee as well as the opportunity to win the prize. Perhaps these troops gave the same "new play" at one, then another festival—taking their Athenian triumphs on a provincial tour [64].

Two poets named as victors at Magnesia are attested from other sources. The tragedian Theodoros is probably the tragic poet Theodoros mentioned by Diogenes Laertius [65]. But more important are the references to Diomedes. In 105 BC he participated in the Athenian $\vartheta\varepsilon\omega\varrho\acute{\iota}\alpha$ to Delphi as a tragic synagonistes—a supporting actor [66]. But this Athenian's career was to move upward: he became a successful writer of comedies to whom statues were erected in Epidaurus and the theater of Dionysos in Athens [67]. When Diomedes' play was performed at the Romaia in Magnesia, he had already been honored by the Pergamenes with honorary citizenship [68]. So Diomedes was a well-known and popular comic poet on the festival circuit. Whether he actually wrote a new play for the Romaia at Magnesia, adapted one, or simply sent over an old one is impossible to say.

The tragic poet Polyxenos who was twice victorious in the Romaia-Letoia celebrated quinquennially in Caunus was honored by a statue set up in Caunus [69]. And a small fragment from Paros has been restored to refer to actors victorious in unspecified Romaia [70]. Though the restoration is possible, it is too doubtful to merit further discussion.

III. *Gladiators and Beasts*

Roman emperors were deeply involved in the casual entertainments of the amphitheater: gladiatorial contests and wild beast hunts. The emperors often gave the shows, presided over them, and in the bizarre case of Commodus, actually participated in the shows. The amphitheater was the acceptable form of festival entertainment in Rome and throughout the West for both the mob and the aristocracy, including senators and the emperor himself.

But the Greeks, we have been told, were different. A popular view butressed by eminent scholars held that the Greeks, an altogether more spiritual and philosophical people, had no interest in such Roman

---

[64] Plays could hardly have been always "new"; perhaps "modern" would be a better term. SIFAKIS *Ibid.* 24 doubts that competition existed at Dionysia at Delos due to the small number of names of poets as compared with actors; yet *Syll.* 424 shows three tragic teams at a third century Soteria.

[65] Diogenes Laertius 2, 104.
[66] *IDelphes* 2, 49.
[67] *IG* IV² 626; *IG* II² 4257.
[68] *Syll.* 1079; on special awards to artists, cf. SIFAKIS *op. cit.* 99.
[69] BEAN *JHS* 73 (1953) 32 #13.
[70] *IG* XII 5, 139.

barbarities[71]. Where gladiatorial shows appeared in Greek-speaking lands, they were put on for the rabble[72]; or they were put on in areas where the local population was not wholly hellenized and thus retained that mindless oriental craving for cruelty that has for thousands of years figured in European mythology[73]. Unhappily, the myth of the spiritual Greeks is just that — pure myth.

It is true that gladiatorial contests did not find acceptance in the East during the Republic. The Romanized Syrian king Antiochus Epiphanes brought them to Antioch[74], but aside from that rather personal production, gladiatorial contests in the East seem to have been presented by Romans (Lucullus at Ephesus)[75] or Italians (the Competaliasts at Delos)[76]. But during the Empire gladiatorial contests could be found throughout the East. If they were rare in mainland Greece, this was due to the poverty prevalent in mainland Greece during the Empire. There were few Greeks with sufficient private wealth to give such expensive shows[77]. The railing of such moralists as Plutarch and Dio Chrysostom only confirms the extent to which Roman practices had been adopted in the Greek world by the second century AD[78]. By the time of Domitian, gladiatorial contests occurred even in the theater of Dionysus at Athens[79]. Of course there were exceptions: Dio tells us that the ever-independent Rhodians did not introduce such games[80]. But elsewhere gladiators and beast-hunts were widely accepted by the end of the first century AD.

These gladiatorial contests were intimately linked with the municipal and provincial worship of the emperor[81]. Gladiatorial events formed no part of the Romaia celebrated to honor the goddess Roma during the Republic, but after Roma was joined with the cult of the emperors, blood sports were certainly included in the games. Eusebius tells us that in the second century AD, a Christian, Germanicus, was thrown to the beasts at the festival of the Koinon of Asia celebrated at

---

[71] ROBERT *Gladiateurs* 240f. is invaluable in citing at length and criticizing attitudes of CHAPOT, LAFAYE and FRIEDLÄNDER.

[72] So CHAPOT.

[73] So LAFAYE.

[74] Livy 41, 20, 11.

[75] Plutarch *Lucullus* 23.

[76] *ID* 1961; BULARD *La religion domestique de la colonie italienne de Délos* (Paris, 1926) 124f.; 158f.; 149f.; ROBERT *Gladiateurs* 264 n. 4.

[77] ROBERT *Gladiateurs* 247. This may be overstated; cf. ROSTOVTZEFF *SEHRE* 652.

[78] ROBERT *Gladiateurs* 249f. It is amusing to read contemporary Romans such as Tacitus *Ann.* 14, 20 denouncing the depravity caused by the introduction of Greek festivals into Rome.

[79] Dio Chrysostomus XXXI 121; Lucian *Demonax* 57.

[80] Dio Chrysostomus XXXI 121.

[81] GRANT *Gladiators* (London, 1967) 56.

Smyrna[82]. The men who gave the gladiatorial combats—the munerarii—were everywhere the priests or high-priest of the imperial cult[83]. These men not only presented the annual festival for the entire province, but may also have given some games at local celebrations, as did the municipal priests of the imperial cult. Roma remained for a time the co-recipient of these festivals, though her name was eventually dropped[84]. The inscription on the antae of the temple of Roma and Augustus in Ancyra in the reign of Tiberius lists the many events presented by the priests of Roma and Augustus of the Galatian Koinon: μονομάχων; κυνήγιον; ζευγητριάκοντα; ταυρομαχία; ταυροκαθάψια (horsemen pursuing bulls and tiring them before wrestling them down by the horns, like an American rodeo)[85]. The text lists many other benefactions: sacrifices, public banquets, grain distributions, as well as the more general procession and πανήγυρις. The festivals celebrated during the Empire in honor of the imperial cult (and Roma) went far beyond gymnastic, equestrian, musical and thymelic contests—the traditional components of a Greek festival which had earlier made up the Romaia[86].

IV. Joint Festivals

Greek religion was essentially local religion. Olympia, Delphi and Delos were always far more remote than the local cults of familiar gods and heroes. Even today, the local saint or divinity remains enormously important in the religions of Mediterranean peoples. So it was for the Greeks, both in their cults and their festivals. Of course the great panhellenic celebrations captured the attention of the Greek world and the winners were showered with honors on their return home—but few Greeks ever attended such a festival. They could only appreciate the victory vicariously through the poems or statue commissioned to honor the victor. Except on the rare occasion when a city's favorite won a panhellenic crown, local festivals aroused far more enthusiasm. Greek athletics, like Greek religion, demanded participation—unlike the spectator-performer structure of both Roman athletics and Roman state religion. Some of the Greek local festivals were truly local, such as the Leonidea at Sparta (honoring Leonidas who led the Spartan resistance at Thermopylae) in which only Spartan citizens could partici-

---

[82] *HE* 4, 15.
[83] ROBERT *Gladiateurs* 270f.
[84] See above p. 82.
[85] ROBERT *Gladiateurs* 135 #86 (= *OGIS* 533). On the date, ROBERT is followed by MAGIE 1318 n. 27.
[86] *IG* XII 2, suppl. 9 seems to concern wild beasts from Moesia being secured for a festival to Roma and Tiberius. But the text is fragmentary.

pate⁸⁷. Other festivals were not so restricted, but the prizes and honors were hardly sufficient to draw athletes from afar. So many of the festivals, though open to all, retained their local character.

Local festivals were sometimes held in honor of Olympian gods in their local guise, sometimes in honor of purely local divinities or heroes⁸⁸. Before the Roman period, joint festivals honored local deities together with Hellenistic rulers⁸⁹. Such an honor could be paid with little financial burden to the city. When Rome established her hegemony in the Greek world, local festivals were broadened to honor this new power. At first Romaia were added to local festivals, and Roma to local cults. With the Empire came an explosion of renamed and completely new festivals to honor the emperor and his family — Sebasteia Kaisareia — or later, to honor individual emperors — Traianeia, Adrianeia, Kommodeia, Severeia⁹⁰. But the true nature of such changes is often difficult to determine — perhaps Σεβαστεῖα and Καισάρεια do not really indicate a joint festival but have no more force than "Imperial"⁹¹. At times these additions to the original festival are omitted on later inscriptions⁹². It is difficult to imagine a city deciding to eliminate the name of Roma or an emperor, unless it were to replace it with a more current form of flattery. Possible explanations suggest themselves for the disappearance of these titles:

1) the texts are inexact; they provide only the distinctive local name and sometimes omit the widespread Ῥωμαῖα or Σεβαστά⁹³.

2) Words like Ῥωμαῖα and Σεβαστά were sometimes used as epithets rather than as genuine parts of the titulature of the festival⁹⁴;

3) only a single celebration of a local festival was dedicated to Roma or the emperor, joining them with the god to whom the festival was dedicated. Afterwards, the festival was celebrated as before.

All of these may sometimes be true, though there is no direct evidence for the last, and perhaps too simple, explanation which would force us to revise our notions of Greek festivals to include such occasional and impermanent changes. But since the gods included in civic

---

⁸⁷ Pausanias 3, 14, 1.
⁸⁸ RINGWOOD *Agonistic Features* (n. 16 above) 7.
⁸⁹ HABICHT 149–150.
⁹⁰ Cf. MORETTI *IAG* Index II p. 275–279.
⁹¹ NOCK *HSCP* 41 (1930) 59 (= *Essays* I 248); ROBERT *RP* 84 (1958) 25.
⁹² Stratonicea: Hekatesia Romaia (*OGIS* 441 = *RDGE* 18) in 81 BC, but Hekatesia (*Syll.* 1066) in 5 AD; Laodicea: Deia Sebasta (*IBM* 605) but Deia in a later text (*IBM* 615).
⁹³ Cf. chapter 2 n. 138 above and below p. 179.
⁹⁴ See note 91 above. Σεβαστά can more easily be seen as an epithet than Ῥωμαῖα, which only occurs in this sense in Naples (*IG* XIV 748).

sacrifices were easily changed, temporary transformations of local festivals should not be discounted.

At Caunus a festival was dedicated to Roma and Leto [95]. But by the early Empire the name of the festival had been altered to Letoia Kaisareia [96]. Here Roma was actually replaced by the emperor; elsewhere, as in the provincial festival of Asia, she simply faded away [97]. Leto, who was quite popular in southwestern Asia Minor [98], was also associated with Roma in the festival celebrated by the Lycian League [99]. It is difficult to know whether this festival is to be distinguished from the quinquennial festival celebrated by the Lycians from 189 [100]. In any case, at least one celebration of the Letoia between 167 and 146 was also dedicated to the goddess Roma [101].

After its loyalty during the Mithridatic wars, the Carian city of Stratonicea had freedom and autonomy restored by a senatus consultum and the city established a festival to Hecate and Roma at the sanctuary of Hecate just outside the city [102]. It was at that same sanctuary that Hecate had once been associated with Rhodos, but now the goddess was joined with the deification of the new power, Roma [103]. The foundation seems to have been intended as a permanent quinquennial festival dedicated to both divinities. Why then do we find on an Augustan text from Cos a reference only to the Hekatesia in Stratonicea [104]? The explicit nature of the senatus consultum makes it clear that the festival to Hecate and Roma had been established on a permanent basis and it seems difficult to imagine Roma being voted out, unless she was replaced by the emperor. I can only suggest that this Coan victory list which makes several references to the Romaia on Cos, identified the Stratonicean festival by its more traditional name in order to distinguish it from the many Romaia around the Aegean [105].

Romaia were joined in the Sullan period to the Amphiaraia of Oropus. A text that records Sulla's privileges to the Oropians—that all revenue from towns and harbors of Oropus should be devoted to the festival celebrated in honor of the local hero Amphiaraus—indicates

---

[95] BEAN *JHS* 73 (1953) 32 #13.
[96] PUGLIESE-CARRATELLI *PP* 5 (1950) 77 #5; see also ROBERT Ἀρχ. Ἐφ. (1966) 116.
[97] See p. 82 above.
[98] See above p. 39; 48 n. 128; also cf. WEHRLI *RE Suppl.* V 555f.
[99] *SEG* XXII 350; J. & L. ROBERT *BE* 1962 #153; DUNST *ZPE* 3 (1968) 141.
[100] BEAN *JHS* 68 (1948) 46 #11.
[101] See my note on the date of *SEG* XXII 350: *ZPE* 12 (1973) 259ff.
[102] *OGIS* 441. 133f. (= *RDGE* 18).
[103] FOUCART *BCH* 14 (1890) 365 #4; see p. 24 n. 64 above.
[104] *Syll.* 1066.
[105] HECKENBACH *RE* VII 2779f. Though there were other Hekatesia, those celebrated at Lagina were the most famous.

that games and sacrifices on behalf of Rome's victory and power were to be joined to the Amphiaraia [106]. But in the Severan period epigraphic texts refer to this festival once again solely by its original name [107]. The reasons for the change away from Amphiaraia-Romaia are unclear; texts bearing that nomenclature all date between Sulla and Actium so the change could have come at any time between Augustus and the Severans [108]. Since the Severan texts are all from Athens, perhaps the Athenians with their own Romaia used only the traditional and distinctive name for the festival. But uncertainty remains.

These particular inscriptions have an additional interest. The texts make clear that, though the games were dedicated both to Amphiaraus and Roma with a single agonothete administering them, Roma was not joined to the cult of Amphiaraus. The priesthood of Amphiaraus alone remained one of the three eponymous magistracies at Oropus even after Sulla brought Roma into the festival [109].

Another Boetian festival to which Romaia were joined was the Erotidea celebrated by Thespiae on the slopes of Mount Helicon. Plutarch says that the quinquennial festival of music and athletics also honored the Muses (who traditionally dwelt on Mount Helicon), and epigraphical evidence confirms a connection of the Mouseia with the Erotideia [110]. Lest we draw a scandalous picture of this festival, Athenaeus solemnly assures us that the festival to Eros had no sexual overtones, but merely honored him as the god of φιλία and ὁμόνοια [111]. A second century text from Megara still mentions the Erotideia alone, before an Athenian text joins Romaia to the festival later in the century [112]. Later, some imperial texts of the first century AD join Kaisareia with the Erotideia-Romaia [113]. Whether Kaisareia was simply used as an epithet at Thespiae is difficult to ascertain—the title Kaisarea Sebasteia Mouseia seems to confirm it [114]. But there are other texts of

---

[106] *IG* VII 413 (= *RDGE* 23); cf. MOMMSEN *Hermes* 20 (1885) 274.

[107] *IG* II² 2193; 2196–7; 2237; 2242.

[108] *IG* VII 419; 420; *Syll.* 1064; *Priene* 232; 233 (?).   [109] *IG* VII 419; 420.

[110] Plutarch *Amatorius* 1–2; Pausanias 8, 31, 3. JAMOT *BCH* 19 (1895) 369 interprets the passage in Pausanias to state that there were only musical contests at the Mouseia, only athletic ones at the Eroditeia. ROBERT *Hellenica* II 11 follows this interpretation. For epigraphical texts, see n. 115 below.

[111] Athenaeus 13, 561 C–E.

[112] *IG* VII 48 and *IG* V 1, 656, 659; *IG* II² 1064. ROESCH *Thespies et la Confédération Béotienne* (Paris, 1965) 226 believes that the Erotideia were only established in the second century.

[113] *IG* VII 2517–2518; perhaps also PLASSART *BCH* 82 (1958) 158 #9; PLASSART *BCH* 50 (1926) 447 #87.

[114] *IG* VII 1774–1776; on epithets cf. JAMOT *BCH* 26 (1902) 299. If, however, the dedication *BCH* 26 (1902) 298 #17 is correctly restored: Γένει Σεβ[αστοῦ] καὶ Ῥώμηι καὶ [Ἔρωτι?] it would argue that there was really a triple festival and Καισαρεία was more than a mere epithet.

the first century AD in which Ῥωμαῖα is omitted[115]. It would be convenient to assume that these texts are later than the preceding, and that our texts constitute a logical continuum in the development of the Erotideia of Thespiae: first alone (or with Mouseia); then Romaia added; then Kaisareia; and finally Romaia dropped from the title. Whether such a neat pattern reflects the reality, or whether the titles changed more frequently, the evidence cannot tell us. But there is little doubt that the Romaia Erotideia of Thespiae was a single joint festival[116].

There is epigraphical evidence for other festivals in which Roma may have been joined to the pre-existing celebrations, but it is often difficult to determine whether it is a single joint festival or two (or more) discrete festivals. For example, the runner Socrates of Epidaurus won victories in the Pythaeia and Romaia at Megara, Dia, Aianteia and Romaia at Opus, and Poseidaia and Romaia at Antigoneia[117]. The text implies that each of these is a single festival, but there is no indication that these festivals recurred in this form. In fact the phrasing, especially for the Megarian festival, leaves open the possibility that there were actually separate celebrations. The Pythaeia of Megara are attested without Roma both in the second century BC and in several imperial texts[118]. This single text joining Pythaeia and Romaia is hardly enough to indicate a permanent change in the nature of the festival[119].

There is even less evidence for the festivals in Opus and Antigoneia separate from the Romaia—no evidence at all for a festival of Zeus and Ajax in Opus, and only a supposition that the Poseidaia mentioned in some texts were celebrated at Antigoneia[120]. There is no other evidence for Romaia in these cities.

On Chios, Romaia seem to have been joined with Theophania. Here too it is difficult to fix any progression. The early second century text from Chios joins a πομπή to Roma with the Theophania[121]. Yet two later victory lists from the first century BC still list Theophania alone[122]. No sufficiently clear evidence for Theophania Romaia on Chios survives. One final text, which mentions [γυμνα]σιαρχήσας καὶ ξ[υσταρ-

---

[115] JAMOT BCH 26 (1902) 298f. #18–19.   [116] ROBERT RP 70 (1944) 20.
[117] IG IV 1², 629 (c. 100 BC).
[118] Second century BC: IG VII 48; Hesperia 15 (1946) 222f. #51 with L. & J. ROBERT BE 1946–1947 #81. Imperial texts: IG VII 106 (not before Hadrian); IG V 1, 659. Πυθάεια in Megara also restored in IG IV 673 by ROBERT RP 56 (1930) 36 n.10.
[119] It is implied by MORETTI IAG p. 140 and ROBERT EEP 76 n.3 that the festivals are permanently united. The evidence is insufficient to prove it.
[120] ROBERT RP 56 (1930) 36 lists the texts.
[121] KONTOLEON Akte 192.
[122] Syll. 1064; ROBERT EEP 126f. #3.

χήσας] τῶν θεοφανικῶν [Σεβαστῶν] Ῥωμαίων, is tantalizing but it remains too fragmentary [123]. The θεοφανικά was not the festival and ROBERT has suggested that it refers to the funds for the festival [124]. But there is no clear evidence for a merging of Theophania with Romaia on Chios. Perhaps the safest interpretation of the early text is that celebrations to Roma were incorporated as part of the Theophania, which was a general festival capable of making room in any given year for the σωτήρ or θεὸς ἐπιφανής of the hour [125].

Other epigraphical attestations of Romaia joined with local festivals, do not permit us to determine whether there is any intrinsic connection between the festivals. Romaia were joined with Poseidonia and Halieia on Rhodes [126], with Dionysia and Aiakeia on Aegina [127], with Asclepieia [128], with Didymeia in Didyma [129]; perhaps Romaia also appear on a difficult Magnesian text [130]. But whether joint festivals or not, these Romaia are clearly celebrations to honor Roma. Even that is doubtful for the Italika Romaia Sebasta celebrated in Naples. This festival was founded in 2 AD and was principally intended to honor Augustus—the terms Ῥωμαῖα and Ἰταλικά were no more than honorific epithets [131]. These games, the only Greek games in Italy, were modeled on the games of the Koinon of Asia held at Pergamum, but they honored only Augustus.

---

[123] *IGR* IV 950.
[124] ROBERT *BCH* 59 (1935) 465.
[125] *SEG* XV 532 from Chios has the restoration Ἡρα[κλήων καὶ Ῥωμ]αίων καὶ Καισαρήων. ROBERT *BE* 1956 #213 approve of the restoration, but it remains doubtful.
[126] MAIURI *NS* #18.
[127] *IG* IV 2.
[128] *SEG* XXIII 212—perhaps at Chios where Romaia are already attested: ROBERT *EEP* 126f. #3.
[129] *Didyma* 339.
[130] *IMagn.* 192: Λευκοφρύνηα Ἴσθ[μια Πύ]θια Ἀρεσανταδ[ι]ά[νεια] Ῥωμαίων. Ῥωμαῖα listed in index p. 231 under "Spiele" but KERN says "Name des Festes unverständlich" and seems to think it refers to Romaia. ROBERT *Hermes* 65 (1930) 117 restores more plausibly: ἀρέσαντα δήμ[ωι] Ῥωμαίων.
[131] *IG* XIV 748 and MITTEIS-WILCKEN *Grundzüge und Chrestomathie der Papyruskunde* (Leipzig, 1912) I 2 #156. On date of this festival, cf. GEER *TAPA* 66 (1935) 216. On the importance of these games dedicated to Augustus, cf. ROBERT *CRAI* (1970) 9; *AC* (1968) 408; *Epigramme Grecque* 286; BOWERSOCK 83.

Chapter 6
Officials of Roma

Municipal Priests

Much of the evidence for the municipal cult of Roma consists of honorific dedications to officials of this cult. Priesthoods of Roma are attested in dozens of Greek cities, and there must have been many more. But not every city necessarily had a priesthood, even if it occasionally sacrificed to the goddess. Sacrifices could be performed by priests of other cults or by civic officials[1]. The administration of a temple or a cult of Roma would certainly require a priesthood, but dedications and sacrifices to Roma are not sufficient evidence for a local cult of the goddess[2].

Officials of the municipal cult of Roma were almost without exception men: priests, high-priests or agonothetes. This is somewhat surprising since it is generally the case in Greek religion that priests serve the cults of gods and priestesses the cults of goddesses[3]. The single priestess of Roma known to us is a very special case: Caecilia Tertulla was priestess of Julia Augusta and Roma in Attalia[4]. Priestesses normally administered the cults of the empresses just as they had administered the cults of the Hellenistic queens in Asia[5]. To find a priestess in this imperial cult is hardly startling; but it is the exception that proves the rule. No other priestesses of Roma are attested[6]. Is

---

[1] *OGIS* 11.18f.   [2] HABICHT 145–146.

[3] FARNELL *The Cults of the Greek States* (Oxford, 1896–1909) I 320; II 639f.; HABICHT 147 n.30.

[4] *SEG* II 696; J. & L. ROBERT *BE* 1948 #229.

[5] Priestess of Hestia, Livia and Julia in Athens: *IG* II² 5096; Berenice and Laodice: WELLES *Royal Correspondence in the Hellenistic Period* (New Haven, 1934) #36–37.

[6] There are several texts which might be thought to attest a municipal priestess of Roma:

1) BEAN-MITFORD *Journeys in Rough Cilicia in* 1962 *and* 1963 *Denkschr. Öster· Akad. Wiss.* 85 (Vienna, 1965) #36 = J. & L. ROBERT *BE* 1967 #623:

Τειμοκράτην ῥητῆρα θεᾶς Ῥώμης ἱερῆα
στῆσε φίλη θυγάτηρ, χρηστότατον πατέρα.

Neither BEAN-MITFORD nor the ROBERTS indicate whether ἱερῆα replaces ἱερέα or ἱέρεια. Both are possible variants in Cilician texts; cf. LAMINGER-PASCHER

181

this simply an accident of preservation? Possibly, but on closer reflection the absence of priestesses in the cult of Roma should not surprise us. Although Roma was in form a goddess, she was in fact the deification of the power of the Roman state. She was the descendant of Hellenistic kings who exercised power; she was no consort. Not, that is, until the Empire when she became the divine consort of Augustus[7]. Then we would expect priestesses of Roma, and then we find them in the provincial cult.

To examine the social and political importance of the priests of Roma, we must turn to epigraphical evidence, however slender the information it provides[8]. In the Western provinces the local priesthood of the imperial cult of Roma and Augustus was the very summit of the municipal cursus[9]. The Greek cities were more idiosyncratic in their priesthoods and offices, yet even in the Republic the priesthood of Roma had attained considerable prominence in a large number of cities. Most notably, the priest of Roma was designated as eponymous magistrate, by whose name the year was identified on decrees and documents of the city.

Index Grammaticus zu den Griechischen Inschriften Kilikiens und Isauriens I— SB. Öster. Akad. Wiss. 284, 3 (Vienna 1973). But the index of BEAN-MITFORD lists the word under ἱερεύς. The context seems to demand that the masculine be understood.

2) HERRMANN *Neue Inschriften zur historischen Landeskunde von Lydien und angrenzenden Gebieten* — Denkschr. Öster. Akad. Wiss. 77, 1 (Vienna, 1959) #3 = SEG XIX 709. The beginning is missing from this text and HERRMANN would supply στεφανηφορούσης to modify the fragmentary female name. He suggests the possibility that the priesthood of Roma might also be linked, as in *Ibid.* #6 (= SEG XIX 710): στεφανηφόρου δὲ καὶ ἱερέως τῆς Ῥώμης is the eponymous official. But the restoration remains hypothetical and more evidence is required to restore a female eponymous official than a single parallel text referring to a priest.

3) The wife of Q. Trebellius Rufus is identified in an Athenian text as a priestess of Roma, but she served in Toulouse in Gaul; OLIVER *Hesperia* 10 (1941) 72f. = AE 1947 #69.

4) *Sardis* 119; cf. chapter 2 n. 291. Here too there is no firm evidence of a priestess; on στεφανηφόρος, cf. RE III A 2345; IPriene 208.

The priestess of the imperial cult does appear at the provincial level, though perhaps merely as the consort of the high priest; cf. TAM II 188 and DEININGER *Provinziallandtage* 76 n. 1.

[7] As on the Gemma Augustea: FURTWÄNGLER *Die antiken Gemmen* (Leipzig-Berlin, 1900) I plate 56; RICHTER *Engraved Gems of the Romans* (Princeton, 1971) 104 #501 with plate. For other gems with Roma and Augustus, cf. RICHTER #484–485. Cf. also OLIVER *Demokratia* 163ff.

[8] A discussion of provincial priests is unnecessary here since they have recently been treated by DEININGER *Provinziallandtage* 148ff.

[9] ÉTIENNE *Le culte impériale dans la péninsule ibérique d'Auguste à Dioclétien* (Paris, 1958) 223f.

The best known eponymous officials are the archons of Athens and the consuls of Rome. But this model can be misleading since those offices remained eponymous for many centuries; in other cities the eponymous magistrate or priesthood might be changed to conform to a new political situation. So in the second century BC the priesthood of Roma became eponymous in various Greek cities in Asia, often in connection with another office as well. This is an obvious sign of the prominence of the cult: any eponymous office will attract distinguished citizens who naturally wish to see their names perpetuated on all the documents of the city.

A treaty concluded between the Sardians and the Ephesians at the beginning of the first century BC is dated by their respective priests of Roma[10]. Sometime after the death of Attalus III, the priest of Roma became eponymous in these and other cities in the former kingdom of Pergamum[11]. These priesthoods must have all been established about the same time, just after the defeat of Aristonicus or during the Roman organization of the province of Asia. Then priests of Roma replaced, or were joined with, the στεφανηφόρος or πρύτανις as the eponymous offices[12].

Though priests of Hellenistic kings seem to have served as eponymous officials only in cities actually founded by the object of the cult[13], eponymous priests of Rhodos, Roma and the emperors were under no such constraints. The Samian colony at Minoa on Amorgos is hardly a Rhodian foundation nor are Ephesos and Sardes Roman ones. In fact, the connection between eponymous priests of kings and foundations may be more apparent than real, an illusion caused by the paucity of the evidence. In the Empire when priests of Roma and Augustus or even of the emperor alone served as eponymous, there is no discernable connection between such priesthoods and imperial foundations[14].

Some officials were occasionally co-eponymous; elsewhere the same men held several offices simultaneously as eponymous official, as at Side where the eponymous official was both δημιουργός and priest of Roma[15]. In these cases the priesthood of Roma was simply added to the eponymous δημιουργία which was widespread in Asia and on the islands[16].

---

[10] *OGIS* 437 (= *RDGE* 47).
[11] Tripolis: *MAMA* VI 53; Thyatira: *IGR* IV 1304 (+ ROBERT *Hellenica* VI 71 n. 2); Nysa: *Syll.* 781; Cyme: *IGR* IV 1302; (N)akokome: *SEG* XIX 710; Pergamum: MIONNET Suppl. V 446 #1040; *MDAI(A)* 32 (1907) 432 #282 (as interpreted by ROBERT *Hellenica* IX 77). Cf. above p. 71ff.
[12] Cf. above p. 73f. See preceding note on Tripolis and Thyatira.
[13] HABICHT 146.
[14] Priene: *IPriene* 222; Cos: *IGR* IV 1087; see note 11 above for Cyme, Nysa, and Pergamum.
[15] BEAN *The Inscriptions of Side* (Ankara, 1965) #111.
[16] SCHÖFFER *RE* IV 2858f.; ROBERT *Noms Indigènes dans l'Asie Mineure gréco-romaine* I (Paris, 1963) 478–479.

Changes of the eponymous official sometimes seem surprisingly rapid. Sardes, where there is considerable evidence, illustrates this well. In the second century the eponymous official was the στεφανηφόρος [17]; later the στεφανηφόρος also held the priesthood of Roma [18]; by the beginning of the first century the priests of Zeus Polieus and of Roma were co-eponymous [19]; and finally a text is dated by the priest of Roma alone [20]. The priest of Roma soon became so well established as eponymous that the full title was no longer necessary [21]. Marc Antony's tenure as eponymous priest of Roma at Sardes shows that the office might even be used to honor a non-resident; the administrative duties would then be undertaken by a substitute.

Ephesus also changed its eponymous officials over the same period. There the πρύτανις was probably eponymous until the bequest of Attalus III; soon after the πρύτανις and priest of Roma appear as co-eponymous [22]. Between 51/50 and 40/39 the situation is less clear; the πρύτανις certainly eponymous and the priest of Roma was probably also retained [23]. But after 39/38 it is clear that the priest of Roma was no longer eponymous in Ephesos, perhaps the result of a misguided attempt to demonstrate loyalty to Antony who used the city as a base.

At Priene the πρύτανις is the earliest known eponymous magistrate. But in 333 BC the πρύτανις disappeared and, as a result of the arrival of Alexander, the στεφανηφόρος became eponymous [24]. Texts for Priene continue to be dated in this way into the first century BC [25]. But an inscription dated by the local high priest of Roma and Augustus shows that at some point a change was made [26].

Not all eponymous priesthoods of Roma were immediately transferred into eponymous priesthoods of Roma and Augustus. In Sardes priests of Roma remained eponymous during the reign of Augustus and an imperial text from Abdera in Thrace is dated by a priest of Zeus Eleutherios and Roma [27]. But usually, where the priest of Roma had been eponymous, the distinction passed to the priest of Roma and Augustus.

---

[17] *Sardis* 21.

[18] *Sardis* 93—exact date unknown. Though the text could be first century BC, a second century date provides a more reasonable progression.

[19] *OGIS* 437 (= *RDGE* 47).   [20] *Sardis* 112; 113; 114; 115.

[21] *Sardis* 116ff.; Marcus Antonius: *Sardis* 129.

[22] *OGIS* 437 (= *RDGE* 47).

[23] *Ephesos* II 30. For the precise date, now see J. &. L. ROBERT *BE* 1972 #388. *Ephesos* III 4 shows as eponymous prytany a man listed in the second part of Ephesos II 30.

[24] *IPriene* 2–3. Since the texts were inscribed only months apart, the change is clearly datable.

[25] Cf. *IPriene* Index IV 4.   [26] *IPriene* 222.

[27] AVEZOU-PICARD *BCH* 37 (1913) 138f. #42.

The status of priests of Roma is noteworthy in other ways. In Athens the earlier cult of Roma, Demos and the Charites continued even after the new cult of Roma and Augustus had been established. A seat in the theater of Dionysius was reserved for the priest of this cult, while another seat was reserved for the priest of Roma and Augustus [28]. But these remain only two seats among dozens and hardly indicate any special position for either priest. Yet the two known Athenian priests of Roma and Augustus suggest the cult's particular importance, for both were hoplite generals [29]. Though the eponymous archonship was a more prestigious post, the fact that it could be held for only a single year considerably diminished its political importance. So the office of hoplite general, which could be held repeatedly, became the most important magistracy of Athens [30]. The hoplite general served the imperial cult in other ways: as agonothete for the Sebasteia [31]; as priest of the empress [32]; and as priest of Tiberius-Apollo [33]. The evidence is not sufficient to establish whether the priest of Roma and Augustus was always a general or to trace changes from reign to reign in the Julio-Claudian period [34]. However, it is clear that the priesthood of Roma and Augustus and other offices in the imperial cult were held by the most powerful men in Athens. They were aristocratic and probably possessed enormous wealth, since the costs of public service were substantial [35].

Pisidian Termessus boasts a dozen dedicatory inscriptions listing priests of Roma. The texts are brief but testify to the importance of the priesthood of Roma in Termessus in the late second century AD [36]. At Termessus the priesthood of Roma was a life office held by men who also served in other important priesthoods or as the eponymous πρόβουλος [37]. In the cursus honorum, the priesthood of Roma precedes

---

[28] *IG* II² 5047; 5114. *IG* II² 3547 identifies a former eponymous archon as ἱερέα συγκλή[του Ῥώμης] καὶ Δήμου καὶ Χαρίτω[ν]—but the restoration has no parallel. MAAS *Die Prohedrie des Dionysostheaters in Athen* (Munich, 1972) does not accept it; cf. chapter 2 n.479.

[29] *IG* II² 3173; 3242 (much improved by DINSMOOR *Hesperia* 30 (1961) 188).

[30] OLIVER *Athenian Expounders* 84; GRAINDOR *Athènes sous Auguste* (Cairo, 1927) 115ff.

[31] *IG* II² 3270.   [32] *IG* II² 3266B (Messalina?).

[33] *IG* II² 3274. OLIVER *Athenian Expounders* 87 suggests the restoration ἱερεὺς αὐτοῦ [καὶ Ῥώμης] for this text.

[34] OLIVER *ibid.* 84–101 attempts to do this, but the evidence is too sketchy to carry conviction.

[35] On Tiberius Claudius Novius, cf. GRAINDOR *Athènes de Tibère à Trajan* (Cairo, 1931) 141–143.

[36] See above pp. 86f.

[37] Priest of Augustus: *TAM* III 1, 110; priest of Dionysus: *TAM* III 1, 108–110; priest of Zeus Solymeus: *TAM* III 1, 113–114; πρόβουλος: *TAM* III 1, 153; 156.

other priesthoods, taking second place only to the πρόβουλος. Although after the promulgation of the Constitutio Antoniniana (212) all the priests of Roma were naturally Roman citizens, the two known late second century priests of Roma were not. It is peculiar that this important cult was then served by distinguished non-citizens, when other priesthoods in the same period were occupied by Roman citizens. Perhaps the conservative nature of the cult of Roma at Termessus, which remained independent of the imperial cult even in the third century AD, was responsible. Cults of Roma were originally intended for non-Roman citizens, and at Delos colleges of non-Romans administered these cults. An analogous dual standard lies behind Augustus' permission to establish separate temples of the imperial cult for citizens and non-citizens. Perhaps a similar taboo remained attached to the cult of Roma in Termessus for centuries after Romans elsewhere were permitted to honor the goddess Roma.

The priest of Roma in Eumenia, Epigonos Philopatris, was honored by his fellow citizens as σωτήρ and εὐεργέτης and his name appears on local coinage in the reign of Augustus [38]. When Roma was included in the imperial cult, the joint priesthoods were naturally held by distinguished local citizens. The first priest of Roma and Augustus in Pergamum was M. Tullius Cratippus, scion of a distinguished line of philoromans [39]: his father had been priest of Roma and Salus and his grandfather, M. Tullius Cratippus, had been a friend and client of Cicero [40]. Caecilia Tertulla, who was priestess of Livia and Roma at Attalia, had a son who became a provincial governor under Claudius [41]. Local priests of Roma and Augustus were sometimes called ἀρχιερεύς, like Diophenes of Mytilene whose father had led the city's embassy to Caesar in 45 BC [42]. This inflated title presumably gained the local priest enough added distinction to secure his precedence over the numerous other ἱερεῖς serving the various municipal cults [43]. Where evidence is available, it indicates that in the East as in the West municipal priesthoods of the imperial cult (and earlier of Roma) occupied a high place in the local cursus and attracted the local aristocracy.

In the Greek world, priesthoods were most commonly filled by election, though there is no direct evidence for the election of priests of Roma [44]. Yet where the priesthood of Roma was combined with such

---

[38] *IGR* IV 741; BABELON *Coll. Wadd.* #6027; IMHOOF-BLUMER *GM* #680.
[39] HABICHT *Pergamum* III p. 165.
[40] *CIL* III 399; O'BRIEN-MOORE *YCS* 8 (1942) 23f.
[41] *SEG* II 696.   [42] *IG* XII 2, 656. See above p. 67.
[43] Other local high priests of Roma: HAUVETTE-BESNAULT *BCH* 5 (1881) 191f. #14 (Bargylia); LAUMONIER *BCH* 58 (1934) 300–303 (Alabanda).
[44] ABBOTT-JOHNSON *Municipal Administration in the Roman Empire* (Princeton, 1926) 93.

important municipal offices as the eponymous πρυτανεία, δημιουργία or στεφανηφορία, the incumbent must have been elected.

Priesthoods were also sold to the highest bidder, a practice castigated both by Romulus and in the New Testament[45]. Nonetheless, sale of priesthoods was practiced in a great number of cults during the Hellenistic period[46]. This does not seem to have been a chronological development, but rather a difference in attitude between Ionia (where sale was used) and mainland Greece (where it was infrequent)[47]. Only at Miletus is the sale of the priesthood of Roma attested. The Milesian regulations even permit the purchaser of the office to register someone else as priest in his stead. Priesthoods sold in this way would hardly be regarded as honors but rather as liturgies[48].

Inheritance was another method of filling priesthoods. In primitive societies, religious functions were frequently reserved to certain families and this continued in some Greek cults. Though this practice was more commonly found in the tradition-oriented cities of mainland Greece[49], several priests of Roma in Asia also held office by heredity. At Pergamum M. Tullius Cratippus was priest of Roma and Augustus διὰ γένους. Although he was the first priest of Roma and Augustus there[50], his father had served as priest of Roma and Salus. Cratippus' title thus testifies to the continuity between cults of Roma and those of Roma and Augustus[51].

Two other local priests of Roma served in the office by ancestral right (διὰ προγόνων): Epigonos Philopatris, a priest of Roma in Eumenia; and a priest of the cult of Roma, Drusus and Tiberius at Attalia[52].

Details of the requirements for the priesthood of Roma[53] survive only in a lengthy inscription from Miletus. There the priest must be at least twenty years old. The cult regulations permit the priest to resign in favor of another. Whether a priesthood was passed around among members of a prominent family is unknown; it must have seemed attractive to pool family resources and acquire a priesthood. Whoever served as priest in this cult had to be consecrated to Zeus Telesiourgos.

The term of the priesthood of Roma varied from city to city. Though most Greek municipal priests held office for life[54], only a few priesthoods of Roma are so attested. Perhaps the reason is that the priest-

---

[45] Dion. Hal. *AR* 2, 21, 3.
[46] NILSSON II 77–78, with ample documentation.
[47] *Ibid.* 81.
[48] The legal writers sometimes classed a priesthood as an *honor* (*Cod. Theo.* 12, 1, 75), sometimes as a *munus* (*Cod. Theo.* 12, 1, 103).
[49] NILSSON II 81 n. 7.
[50] *IGR* IV 473 as revised by HABICHT *Pergamum* III p. 165.
[51] *CIL* III 399.
[52] *IGR* IV 741; *SEG* XVII 582.
[53] *Milet* I 7, 203. [54] NILSSON II 78.

hood of Roma often became eponymous and was thus, by definition, a one-year term⁵⁵. However, the priests of Roma at Termessus all served for life (διὰ βίου)⁵⁶. Though we have four names from a period of sixty years, other priests may also have served during this period, thus making any attempt to determine their length of service futile. The high priest of Roma and Augustus at Mytilene also held office for life⁵⁷, as would presumably any priest who achieved his office by inheritance. Other priests of Roma served for a fixed term of years, such as the four-year term for priests of the Lycian League⁵⁸. There the priest simply served for the period between the quinquennial festivals celebrated in honor of Roma by the cities of Lycia⁵⁹. At Miletus the priest also served four years. The regulations give his term as 3 years 8 months beginning in Metageitnion. But since Metageitnion was the fifth month of the Milesian year, it is likely that only the first priest was to serve 3 years 8 months and that the next priest began a full four-year term on the first day of Taureon, the beginning of the Milesian year⁶⁰.

There is very little evidence for iteration of municipal priests of Roma. Where the priesthood is eponymous, repetition is unlikely. But Sextus Valerius Flaccus served twice as priest of Roma in Attalia during the second century AD. And if the hoplite general in imperial Athens always served as the priest of Roma⁶¹, then abundant evidence for iteration exists since T. Claudius Novius held the hoplite generalship eight times⁶².

Other Municipal Officials

Though the priest was the essential religious functionary in the cult of Roma, other officials also existed. The priest took overall responsibility for the organization of the festival, but specialists usually handled the detailed preparations. At Miletus the responsibility for Romaia was shared between the priests, the gymnasiarchs, and the παιδονόμοι who presumably took care of particular areas⁶³. But elsewhere special gymnasiarchs were appointed or elected to administer

---

[55] See above pp. 182ff.
[56] *TAM* III 1, 16; 90; 108; 787.
[57] *IG* XII 2, 656.
[58] *OGIS* 556.
[59] *JHS* 68 (1948) 46 ⧧ 11
[60] SAMUEL *Greek and Roman Chronology* (Munich, 1970) 115; REHM *Milet* I 7, p. 197 (three *or* four years).
[61] OLIVER *Athenian Expounders* 93.
[62] See note 35 above.
[63] *Milet* I 7, 203.

the Romaia⁶⁴. After the development of the guilds of Dionysiac artists in the third centry, the administration of major festivals obviously entailed an enormous amount of patient labor: negotiations with the guilds, contracts with individual artists and, unhappily, subsequent lawsuits against defaulting competitors⁶⁵. In addition, various local arrangements must be made for the accommodation of artists and visitors, the provision of areas for competition, the scheduling of events, the designation of judges, and the provision of prizes⁶⁶. If an eminent man held this title, as Hadrian did at the city Dionysia of Athens⁶⁷, there must have been a staff to handle such extensive preparations. These festivals could not be arranged overnight. It is not surprising to find that in various cities of Asia where festivals of Roma and Augustus were celebrated, agonothetes were appointed for life⁶⁸.

Aristotle in his *Politics* says that in smaller cities priests may be able to administer a cult alone, but larger cults require additional officials to carry out their more extensive religious administration. He mentions the ἱεροποιοί among these⁶⁹. The title was well known at Athens in classical times⁷⁰, and a college of ἱεροποιοί took over the administration of the Romaia at Athens. An inscription of the midsecond century lists dozens of ἱεροποιοί for the Romaia and Ptolemaia⁷¹. The Athenian colony carried this office to Delos where twenty-two men are named as ἱεροποιοί for the Romaia around 127 BC⁷². How honorific or how practical this task was is impossible to say. Even before the Empire and the provincial cults of Roma and Augustus, the cities sent ambassadors to the communal celebrations in honor of the goddess. Early in the second century Araxa honored Orthagoras for, among other services, having led the delegation from the city as θεωρός to the first celebration of the Romaia by the Lycian Koinon⁷³. Four years later he served again, this time providing the expenses from his own resources—always welcome to a small city.

Another official of the cult is the νεωκόρος θεᾶς Ῥώμης καὶ θεοῦ Αὐγούστου⁷⁴. The sources do not agree on the nature of this office⁷⁵.

---

⁶⁴ *IG* XII 1, 46 (Rhodes); *IGR* IV 454 for the Romaia Sebasta of the Asian Koinon.
⁶⁵ SIFAKIS *Studies in the History of Hellenistic Drama* (London, 1967) 137–139.
⁶⁶ PICKARD-CAMBRIDGE *The Dramatic Festivals of Athens* (2nd edition, Oxford, 1968) passim.
⁶⁷ *IG* II² 1105 Bb line 15.   ⁶⁸ *Sardis* 8.99–100; *OGIS* 470; *IGR* IV 1608c.
⁶⁹ *Politics* 1322b.   ⁷⁰ *Ath. Pol.* 54, 6.
⁷¹ *IG* II² 1938.   ⁷² *ID* 2596.
⁷³ BEAN *JHS* 68 (1948) 46 #11 = *SEG* XVIII 570.
⁷⁴ *Pergamum* III 29; cf. *IGR* IV 454: νεωκόρος θεᾶς Ῥώμης καὶ θεοῦ Σεβαστοῦ Καίσαρος.
⁷⁵ BÜCHNER *De Neocoria* (Giessen, 1889) 2–21 remains the standard collection and discussion of passages from the lexicographers and elsewhere. Also cf. HANELL *RE* XVI 2423–2424.

Were these officials simply minor functionaries charged with the care of the temple [76]: protection, maintenance and provision? Or were these more prestigious and important positions [77]? The variety of usage in the lexicographers and inscriptions precludes a single definition of the function and status of a νεωκόρος. The νεωκορία in Pergamum (we must not confuse the office of νεωκόρος with the honorific epithet conferred on cities) [78] was certainly an important position given to quite eminent citizens. Although this νεωκόρος was not an official of the Koinon [79], he was concerned with the temple of Roma and Augustus of the province of Asia [80]. Pergamum's responsibility for such a temple (or temples) is demonstrated in its own epithet νεωκόρος. A distinguished local citizen was appointed by the Pergamenes to fill this office. Of course many νεωκόροι are attested, but it is appropriate to comment on two who carry Roma in their titles. In the reign of Tiberius, the college of youths (νέοι) at Pergamum set up a text honoring the G. Julius Sacerdos who had been municipal priest of Tiberius before his accession and gymnasiarch of the Romaia Sebasta of the Koinon of Asia [81]. The νεωκόρος T. Claudius Nicomedes was even more distinguished. He was an equestrian whose military career is recorded on an honorific text of Pergamum which also testifies that he reached the highest rank in the Koinon of Asia [82]. In Pergamum at least the office of νεωκόρος was far from a menial job of housekeeping the temple—it was the delegation of the city's own important political and religious responsibility of νεωκορία to one of its eminent Roman citizens.

Provincial Officials

The provincial concilia of the Roman Empire were religious assemblies, convened to worship the cult of Roma and Augustus. The extent to which these concilia exercised political, administrative and even governmental functions remains a matter for discussion and investigation [83]. The older Greek leagues and the cities of Ionia and Asia originally met, long before the accession of Augustus, to honor the

---

[76] HOMOLLE *BCH* 8 (1884) 287.
[77] BÜCHNER *op. cit.* 12f.
[78] *Ibid.* 22f.; HANELL *RE* XVI 2425; ROBERT *RP* 93 (1967) 45f.
[79] DEININGER *Provinziallandtage* 50–52 does not mention it.
[80] *Pergamum* III 29; 31.
[81] *IGR* IV 454.
[82] *Pergamum* III 29; 30: ἀρχιερέα Ἀσίας; ἀγωνοθέτην δι' αἰῶνος τῶν σεβαστονεικηφορίων κοινῶν τῆς Ἀσίας. DAUX *REG* 84 (1971) 366f. corrects σεβαστονεικηφορίων to Σεβαστῶν Νικηφορίων.
[83] LARSEN *Representative Government in Greek and Roman History* (Berkeley, 1955) passim; BRUNT *Historia* 10 (1961) 212; DEININGER *Provinziallandtage* 156f.; 161f.; 180f.; MILLAR *CR* 16 (1966) 388–390.

Hellenistic princes and later Roman generals[84]. Such meetings naturally turned to matters of common concern. And so in some areas, for example Lycia, the seeds of communal action had been sown long before the end of the Republic[85].

The provincial concilia of the East at first concerned themselves with issues related to the imperial cult, issues which included many aspects of the relationship between the cities and the central government. In addition to the annual selection of a provincial priest of Roma and Augustus[86], the Koinon of Asia undertook such projects as the revision of the calendar of Asia[87]. The Koinon was also responsible for the publication of important documents, usually its own decrees concerning the cult, but occasionally documents from Rome. The Galatian Koinon set up Augustus' *Res Gestae* in the temple of Roma and Augustus at Ancyra and perhaps elsewhere in Galatia[88].

These religious assemblies came to have a significant impact on provincial political administration. The distress displayed by the Senate in 62 AD at the *novam provincialium superbiam*, manifested in voting or withholding thanks for the proconsul, shows that such votes must have had some impact in Rome[89]. More directly, the assembly could bring charges of extortion against imperial officials, something frequently done by the Bithynian Koinon[90]. These were probably brought by a majority vote, though the Koinon would be unlikely to pursue a case unless there was considerable agreement in the province. A prudent governor would obviously curry the favor of at least one city or faction and thus, in the event of charges, be in a position to produce local testimonials. That such prosecutions were sometimes successful is a tribute to provincial persistence[91].

In other cases the provincials used their Koinon as a forum to bring their views to the attention of the central government. An amusing example occurred when Domitian published an edict requiring that half the vines in the provinces be uprooted. The Asian cities met and voted to send their high priest, the sophist Scopelianus, to Rome to plead their case. He plead the case so successfully that Domitian completely reversed his edict and encouraged increased viniculture. The

---

[84] DEININGER *Provinziallandtage* 7f.; on Asia, cf. *OGIS* 438 and above p. 80; on Ionia, cf. *LSAM* #26 and BOWERSOCK 115f.

[85] DEININGER *Provinziallandtage* 70; MORETTI *Ricerche sulle Leghe Greche* (Rome, 1962) 190.

[86] DEININGER *Provinziallandtage* 150f.

[87] *Ibid.* 53–54; *OGIS* 458; cf. LAFFI *SCO* 16 (1967) 1–99.

[88] *Ibid.* 67–69; see above p. 90.

[89] Tacitus *Ann.* 15, 20–22.

[90] BRUNT *Historia* 10 (1961) 212–213; 224f.

[91] *Ibid.* 213–217.

sophist even amassed a devoted following in Rome who accompanied him back to Asia [92].

With their expanding activity, the Koina acquired officials and a bureaucracy. Since the assemblies were religious institutions, the chief official was the high priest of Roma and Augustus who in Asia was also called the Asiarch [93]. (This dual titulature also prevailed in the other Anatolian Koina where the priests were called Galatarchs, Lyciarchs, Bithyniarchs, etc.) [94] These officials were elected annually by the Koina for one-year terms [95]. In Asia, there were eventually several high priests, each serving at one of the provincial temples of the imperial cult [96]. The priest serving at the temple which hosted the annual Romaia was presumably the presiding official of the Koinon for that year.

The provincial priesthood of the imperial cult was the highest honor a provincial could attain, unless he was summoned to Rome and the Senate. The appointments were genuinely federal, with priests serving far from their native cities [97]. Since DEININGER's recent book on the provincial assemblies has discussed these priesthoods in some detail [98], I will restrict myself to a single example of their prestige: Pylaimenes, son of the former king of Galatia, served as high priest of Roma and Augustus for the Galatian Koinon [99].

By the time of Claudius, special officials (ὑμνῳδοὶ θεοῦ Σεβαστοῦ καὶ θεᾶς Ῥώμης) were appointed by the Koinon for imperial celebrations [100]. Other officials served the Koinon, either at the temples (σεβαστοφάντης), at the celebration of the annual festival (γυμνασίαρχος τῶν Σεβαστῶν Ῥωμαίων; ἀγωνοθέτης θεᾶς Ῥώμης καὶ Αὐτοκράτορος Σεβαστοῦ), or simply in general administration (γραμματεύς; ἀργυροταμίας)[101].

The college of Hymnodes is first mentioned in a letter sent to Claudius [102]. Their full title ὑμνῳδοὶ θεοῦ Σεβαστοῦ καὶ θεᾶς Ῥώμης appears on a Hadrianic text [103]. This text discusses entrance into the college in rather crude detail [104]: each new hymnodes had to pay an entry fee of

---

[92] Suetonius *Domitian* 7; Philostratus *VS* 520.
[93] DEININGER *Provinziallandtage* 43–50; BOWERSOCK 117.
[94] DEININGER *Provinziallandtage* 49; LARSEN *Rep. Gov.* 119–120; 222 n. 35.
[95] *Sardis* 8.
[96] DEININGER *Provinziallandtage* 43–50.
[97] *Ibid.* 37–38.   [98] *Ibid.* 148 f.
[99] *OGIS* 533 = ROBERT *Gladiateurs* #86.
[100] *Pergamum* 374; *IGR* IV 1608c. On hymnodes, cf. ROBERT *REA* 62 (1960) 341 f.; MAGIE *RRAM* 1297 n. 58.
[101] νεωκόρος: *IGR* IV 454; σεβαστοφάντης: *IGR* IV 1410; γυμνασίαρχος: *IGR* IV 454; ἀγωνοθέτης: *OGIS* 470; γραμματεύς: *Ephesos* III 40; ἀργυροταμίας: DEININGER *Provinziallandtage* 50–52.
[102] *IGR* 1608.
[103] *Pergamum* 374A. Roma seems to have been dropped from the title of this college after 176 AD; cf. FRAENKEL *ad loc.* and RICHTER 137.
[104] *Pergamum* 374D.

over seven hundred denarii—one hundred denarii for the sacrifices of Roma and Augustus; thirty denarii for the sacred treasury; sixty-two and a half denarii for wine and bread for the college and their sons; and finally 15 denarii to each of the other thirty-five hymnodes. If the entrance rules resemble those of certain London clubs, the elitist aura is not accidental. Nearly all the hymnodes (32 of 36) were Roman citizens, and the college served as a "Romanized and Romanizing association"[105]. The hymnodes celebrated the accession of the emperor (*Dies Imperii*)[106], the third of January and other occasions connected with the imperial cult[107]. But the college was also a particularly distinguished form of liturgy, since the hymnodes were assessed to support the imperial cult; for instance, non-resident members of the college had to pay fifty denarii to provide for statues of the emperor. Non-resident membership, of course, can often be a sign of an elite society. While they celebrated the imperial mysteries and festivals, they were to be wined and dined by their own president and by the priest of the imperial cult. This single text gives a vivid picture of a select, highly Romanized group of Asians cultivating their imperial connections through celebrations, ritual banquets and song.

Another official of the cult in the provinces was the σεβαστοφάντης— but it is difficult to see any connection here with Roma[108]. This official obviously played an important role in the imperial mysteries—especially in the public display of images of the ruling house in the temple of the imperial cult[109]. The σεβαστοφάντης was more than a single agonothete to the Romaia-Sebasta[110], and so had no real connection with Roma. If cult statues of Roma were carried on display, there is no evidence for it.

Though the Koina grew in power and influence, their essential function remained the annual festival to honor Roma and Augustus. And they arranged honors of other kinds to the emperor and his family. Oaths of loyalty were taken annually on January 3 and Pliny once took these *cum provincialibus*, apparently at a meeting of the Bithynian Koinon[111]; the *Dies Imperii* was also an occasion for festivities[112]; and the birthdays of members of the imperial family were celebrated.

---

[105] ROBERT *REA* 62 (1960) 342.
[106] Pliny *Epistulae* 10, 53–54; 102–103; Trajan's *dies imperii* was January 28.
[107] Details of all that follows are found in *Pergamum* 374.
[108] The only text is *IGR* IV 1410 as restored by ROBERT *RP* 56 (1930) 26.
[109] LE BAS-WADDINGTON *Voyage Archéologique en Grèce et en Asie Mineure* (Paris, 1847–1870) 1178; ROBERT *REA* 62 (1960) 321 f. argues this case forcefully.
[110] NILSSON II 371.
[111] On the date of the *vota*, cf. Plutarch *Cicero* 2; Pliny *Epistulae* 10, 35–36; 100–101.
[112] See note 106 above.

On birthdays the college of hymnodes performed in Pergamum, and at games given to honor the birthday of Geta at Carthage, Saint Perpetua was martyred early in the third century [113]. Such was the final stage of the provincial cult of Roma and Augustus.

---

[113] *Passio Sanctarum Perpetuae et Felicitatis* 7, 9 in MUSURILLO *Acts of the Christian Martyrs* (Oxford, 1972); on the date, cf. BARNES *Tertullian* (Oxford, 1971) 263 ff.; PERGAMUM 374

Chapter 7

Roma Alone

Roma was worshipped in the Greek world for two centuries before the rise of Augustus. Though her cults had sometimes been joined with cults of other gods and her festivals with other festivals, these connections reflected local conditions and traditions. The cult of Roma remained essentially independent. Roma herself, the bastard offspring of the Hellenistic ruler cult, became the model for the worship of the Roman emperors. Roma was the transmitter; through her the forms of the ruler cult were kept alive between the fall of the Hellenistic dynasties and the deification first of Roman proconsuls and later of Roman emperors. Epithets like ἐπιφανής passed from the kings to Roma and thence to Julius Caesar and his successors [1]. Roma was not only a bridge across time, but the goddess also helped span the vast cultural gap between East and West. The cult of Roma and the succeeding cults of the Senate and Roman benefactors made the worship of Augustus less unexpected and therefore more acceptable to a Rome which had recently been inundated with anti-oriental propaganda [2].

When the Asian and Bithynian Koina first established the imperial cult in the East in 29 BC, the cult of Roma was incorporated into it and the goddess was joined with Augustus. Suetonius tells us that this marriage was required in provincial cults by imperial command, but a similar pattern filtered down to the municipal cults as well [3]. Roma, as the deified embodiment of the power of Rome, had replaced the Hellenistic kings. But now the power of Rome could be more appropriately embodied in the emperor and his family; the cult of Roma had lost its political *raison d'être*. After Roma's presence had smoothed the introduction of the imperial cult, the goddess was ignored and began to fade away. Her name tended to disappear from the titles of priests, from the names of festivals, from the dedications of temples. When later authors describe temples and cults of the Augustan age, she is

---

[1] Cf. pp. 111 ff.
[2] SCOTT *MAAR* 11 (1933) 36 f.
[3] Suetonius *Augustus* 52.

often forgotten. Cassius Dio omits Roma in his discussion of the foundation at Pergamum in 29, and Dio, Suetonius and Strabo all leave her out of their accounts of the altar founded at Lugdunum in 12 BC[4] — though in both cases Roma's presence is amply attested by contemporary numismatic and epigraphical evidence[5]. The goddess no longer served any political purpose and so the historians overlooked her, though her name sometimes continued to survive in local titles and formulas.

Some scholars have quite logically insisted that all cults of Roma, once they lost their political rationale, would have been merged into the imperial cult; and they have sometimes attempted to date inscriptions on this assumption. Unhappily, rigorous logic is not always respected in religious practice and in this instance, what is logical is unfortunately untrue. Some priesthoods (and so presumably cults) of Roma survived independent of the imperial cult until the third century AD. Though some of these late priests of Roma also held priesthoods of the imperial cult at some point in their careers, there was no necessary link between the two[6]. And it can hardly be maintained that the independent cult of Roma survived only in a few "remote places", since priests are attested in more than a dozen cities over a wide area from Greece and Thrace to Asia and Cyprus[7]. There is no easy explanation for Roma's survival. It is clear, however, that the rationale for the cult of Roma given above must be somehow incomplete; it does not explain the motivation of these cities in continuing independent cults to the goddess.

In some of these cities Roma had acquired a special position. In Termessus the priest of Roma was exceeded in prestige only by the eponymous πρόβουλος, and the priests were among the elite of the city[8]. The Lycian Koinon had founded a cult of Roma early in the second century BC and priests of Roma still can be found in the third century

---

[4] Pergamum: Dio 51, 20, 6–9 for which Tacitus *Annals* 4, 37 mentions Roma. Lugdunum: Dio 54, 32, 1; Strabo 4, 3, 2; Suetonius *Claudius* 2, 1.

[5] Pergamum: *IGR* IV 454; *SNG-DEN* 34 #419. Lugdunum: *CIL* XIII 1036 (Augustan), 1042 (Claudian), 1706 (Trajanic); *BMCRE* I #528f. On this, cf. my *DEA ROMA: The Development of the Idea of the Goddess Roma* (Princeton diss., 1967) 24f.; 41ff. which deals with the evidence for the altar and temple of Roma and Augustus at Lugdunum.

[6] For example, in Anazarbus L. Valerius Varus Pollio was priest of Roma and priest of Titus, but his contemporary L. Valerius Niger was only priest of Roma: KEIL *JÖAI* 18 (1915) Beiblatt 55. At Sparta however, the priesthood of Roma may have been linked with that of Augustus: *IG* V 1, 500; 525.

[7] BUCKLER-ROBINSON *AJA* 17 (1913) 44–45 relegate the cult of Roma alone to "remote places" and also say "we are bound to assume that in so important a city as Sardes the cult of Roma alone ceased soon after 27 BC."

[8] See pp. 185f. above.

AD⁹. Priests of Roma also survived in Lycia on the local level, since a distinguished citizen of Aperlae who had served three times as πρύτανις is recorded as a municipal priest of Roma¹⁰. In several other cities where the priest of Roma was co-eponymous the priesthood remained independent of the imperial cult: Thyatira in Lydia, Side in Pamphylia, and Anazarbus in Cilicia. Though the evidence from Thyatira is Augustan and hardly proves any prolonged survival of Roma there, it does show that the priest of Roma remained independent at least for a time after the establishment of the imperial cult there¹¹. In Side and Anazarbus, the priest of Roma and the δημιουργός remained eponymous at least until the Flavian era¹². In both cities the priest of Roma sometimes also held a priesthood in the imperial cult, but the connection was not mandatory. Elsewhere eponymous priests of Roma usually gave way to eponymous priests of the imperial cult.

T. Flavius Polybius served as a priest of Roma in the Peloponnesus in the third century AD; whether in Messene or for the Achaean League remains uncertain¹³. Several cities of Thrace and the Black Sea littoral also had priests of Roma in the third century AD, but it is unclear why these late independent cults of Roma clustered in Thrace¹⁴. The province of Thrace was not organized until the middle of the first century AD; perhaps the delay in the introduction of a provincial cult allowed the local cults of Roma to grow more entrenched since no provincial model of the imperial cult was offered to the cities¹⁵.

Several other cities have independent priests of Roma attested only for the Julio-Claudian period. Olympichos served as priest of Roma in Phrygian Apollonia during the reign of Tiberius, and his son held the same office toward the middle of the century¹⁶. In Cyprus, the evidence rests upon restored inscriptions but it does seem that Citium and Kourion had high priests of Roma in the early Empire, though in Citium the priesthood was merged into the imperial cult¹⁷. But the evidence is insecure and generalizations on the nature of Cyprus' devotion to Roma should remain very tentative¹⁸.

---

[9] *IGR* III 474; 490; 595.
[10] *IGR* III 692.
[11] *IGR* IV 1304; cf. chapter 2 n. 376 above.
[12] BEAN *The Inscriptions of Side* (Ankara, 1965) #111; 112; 127. Also cf. n. 6 above.
[13] *Olympia* 486; 487.
[14] Maronia: *IGR* I 831; Nicopolis: *IGR* I 589; Odessus: *IGR* I 1439.
[15] DEININGER *Provinziallandtage* 96f.
[16] *MAMA* IV 142; *IGR* III 320.
[17] HOGARTH *Devia Cypria* (London, 1889) 109 #28 (+ MITFORD *BSA* 42 (1947) 229 n. 118). Cf. MITFORD *OA* 6 (1950) 74 n. 7 which is acceptably restored. On Kourion, cf. MITFORD *The Inscriptions of Kourion* (Philadelphia, 1971) #77.
[18] MITFORD *OA* 6 (1950) 74 n. 7.

The evidence for late cults of Roma hardly conforms to any pattern. Statements about the "disappearance" of Roma are clearly unsupported and until the cults mentioned can be explained as "exceptions" we must be prepared to accept the continued existence of cults and priesthoods of Roma beside the imperial cult[19]. Since the political *raison d'être* for Roma had disappeared, we must conclude that this provided only a partial explanation for loyalty to the cult of Roma. Although the motivation behind the introduction of Roma was political, her worship nonetheless included religious forms and institutions. Perhaps the innate conservatism of religious practice gave the cult an existence independent of its origin and political significance. Local conditions, whether a specific political relation with Rome or the exceptionally high position of the priest of Roma in that society, may have given the cult a particular importance in certain eastern cities. The fact remains that priests of Roma did survive at least for a time in sixteen cities and must have survived in many others. Until we can explain this phenomenon we must confess that a certain part of the impact of Roma on the citizens of the eastern Empire remains beyond our understanding.

---

[19] Cf. n. 7 above.

Epilogue

The goddess Roma had always played a political role. She had been invented when the Greek cities first became aware of Rome's power in order to enable the Greeks to deal with this new political force by the familiar methods of Hellenistic diplomacy. Just as Rome replaced the Seleucids, Attalids and the Rhodians, so Roma replaced the cults of the kings and of Rhodos. Through the goddess the Greeks honored that rather inaccessible body—the Roman people. Roma was the deification of the *populus Romanus*; she should never be confused with obscure eponymous heroines who give their names to so many ancient cities. To appreciate that Roma was the deification of the *populus Romanus* is to understand why Roma could not easily be worshipped in Rome itself. Roma existed solely as a divine embodiment of the Romans themselves and thus would not be honored by them. So when a "Roma" appears on the coinage of the Roman Republic, she is not the θεὰ Ῥώμη we have been discussing in this study. She is merely some symbol for the Roman state: most probably derived from the Rhome invented by Greek historians and mythographers to explain the name of the city on the Tiber.

Until the last decades of the Republic the word "Roma" meant nothing else in Latin than the physical city itself[1]. The Romans knew of the Greek usage since there had been statues and dedications on the Capitol for over a century. But it was only late in the Republic that "Roma" came to be used as a collective for the inhabitants of the city and later as a personification[2]. She does not appear as a goddess until the poetry of the Augustan age[3]. But this goddess was hardly a Roma imported directly from the East after Augustus had just tried to unify Italy against Antony on a platform of anti-orientalism. This Roma was more than the deified Roman People; she, like *patria*, symbolized Rome past as well as Rome present. This use of Roma enabled the destinies of the imperial house to be linked with those of

---

[1] KNOCHE *Gymnasium* 59 (1952) 327. One of the few exceptions is Ennius *Scipio* frag. 6.

[2] Collective: described in *Rhetorica ad Herennium* 4, 32, 43; personification: Cicero *In Pisonem* 52. On all this, see KNOCHE *op. cit.* 330 ff.

[3] E.g. Vergil *Aeneid* 6, 781 ff.

the state—the title *pater patriae* is one expression of this and the association of Roma and Augustus is another. The goddess was represented as a traditional divinity. Sometimes a warrior, sometimes a mother-figure, she had always to draw on the attributes of other gods since she herself had no history, no myth[4]. On the Ara Pacis she became the germinal force of Rome, an apt maternal symbol for the fertile new golden age. For all her political utility, this Roma is far more symbolic, more remote from political reality than the $\vartheta\varepsilon\grave{\alpha}\ \text{Ῥώμη}$ of the East.

Roma was first linked with Augustus at Pergamum in 29 BC, though this union had been forshadowed by cults of Roma and Roman proconsuls in the Republic. Thus the worship of Roma came to the West already linked with Augustus in the imperial cult. As in the province of Asia, in the West the imperial cult was celebrated in provincial assemblies which eventually came to have administrative and even political importance. Cults of Roma and Augustus were also established by municipalities throughout Italy and the western provinces, and their priests were local nobles who often moved on to positions in the imperial administration. These cults were not only established in the highly Romanized areas, but even in recently pacified areas where the army constituted the only Roman presence[5]. Here the cults of Roma and Augustus were a showing of the flag to both the soldiers and the restive barbarians.

During the reign of Augustus official cults of Roma and Augustus were founded by imperial emissaries and celebrated on a provincial or regional basis, such as the festivals celebrated at the provincial temple at Lugdunum and the more local cults established for groups of cities among the Liburnians, the Lingones and in Northwest Spain[6]. The municipal cults of Roma and Augustus could be found everywhere. How was Roma understood by the Roman legionaries and recently pacified barbarians for whom these cults were intended? The eastern conception of Roma would have been inappropriate since so many of those involved were in fact Roman citizens. It would seem that, in the manner common to ancient religion, Roma was identified with a familiar divinity. I believe that divinity was Vesta, and I hope to argue this in a forthcoming study[7]. The idea of the eternity of the city had become widespread in the last decades of the Republic. Cicero accepts the *aeternum imperium* of Rome, while Varro and Sallust also speak of

---

[4] Warrior: Horace *Odes* 3, 3, 44. Mother: Propertius 2, 22, 39.
[5] KRASCHENINNIKOFF *Philologus* 53 (1898) 147–189.
[6] *DEA ROMA: The Development of the Idea of the Goddess Roma* (Princeton diss., 1967) 24–50 has a discussion of Augustan cult centers in the West.
[7] *Ibid.* 105–117.

the eternity of the Republic[8]. This idea passes directly to the Augustan writers who speak of the eternity of the city and of its *imperium*[9]. Vesta and Jupiter had been the *pignora imperi Romani*. Roma had been associated with Jupiter Capitolinus in the dedications on the Capitol and this association was also expressed in poetry[10]. But gradually the emperor replaced Jupiter, and Roma and Augustus became the new *pignora*. It was Roma and the emperors whose *aeternitas* was so often heralded in poems and on coins[11]. And as the emperor is frequently syncretized with Jupiter-Zeus in depiction and cult, so Roma takes on the trappings of Vesta[12].

But Roma was still not worshipped in Rome itself—there was no temple, no altar and no cult. Perhaps the remembrance of the Greek worship of Roma as a deification of the people of Rome had some deterrent effect. But the Empire was changing, and so was Rome's place in it. After the civil wars of 69, the emperors came first from Italy and later from the provinces. And these provincial emperors, Trajan and especially Hadrian, brought a renewed devotion to Roma. The Empire was more truly cosmopolitan: the inhabitant of Rome may be no more "Roman" than a Gaul or Spaniard. Rome was no longer a commonwealth, but the capital of a great Empire[13].

Hadrian brought the cult of Roma to Rome. The emperor himself was the primary force in the conception of the temple of Venus and Roma, and personally drew up the first plans[14]. On April 21, 121, Hadrian celebrated the *Natalis Romae* and consecrated the temple, or rather the idea of the temple[15]. Finally in 137 he dedicated the temple to Roma Aeterna and Venus Felix. He selected *aeterna* from many available epithets for Roma, and it now became the most popular epithet of the goddess[16]. And he seems to have founded a college of twelve priests to tend the cult[17]. Roma now became *the* most important divinity of Roman state religion and even the emperor-cult was subordinated to the worship of the city.

---

[8] *Pro Rabirio* 33; Varro *De Vita Populi Romani* (ed. Riposati) frag. 66; 114; 123; Sallust *Catilina* 53, 5.

[9] Livy 4, 4, 4: *in aeternum urbe condita*; Vergil *Aeneid* 1, 279f.: *imperium sine fine dedi*.

[10] Horace *Odes* 3, 5, 12 where Vesta is also mentioned.

[11] On *aeternitas*, cf. CHARLESWORTH *HTR* 29 (1936) 123ff.; *BMCRE* II 372 #346.

[12] Emperor as Jupiter-Zeus: BUCKLER *RPh*. 9 (1935) 177–188; Roma with palladium appears frequently on coins: *BMCRE* II 260 #188.

[13] WISSOWA 341.   [14] Cassius Dio 69, 4, 3.

[15] GAGÉ *Mélanges Cumont* (Brussels, 1936) 155.

[16] MOORE *TAPA* 25 (1894) 45.

[17] *CIL VI* 500 and MOMMSEN *ad loc.*; also cf. *CIL VI* 2136; 2137; 12230; *Ephemeris Epigraphica* IV 856.

This goddess, *Roma Aeterna*, has come a long way from our ϑεὰ Ῥώμη. She is no longer a deification of the Roman people; she is now a symbolic embodiment of the capital of the Empire and of the Empire itself. The city of Rome itself had become the *caput mundi*—something far more important than the sum total of the human population of the physical city. The civilizing force which that city brought to the ancient world—at least through the rose-colored glasses of official history—now transcended the city and had become eternal. So *Roma Aeterna* remained the primary symbol even after the effective government had moved to Milan or even to Constantinople. Through these centuries the divinity of Roma became less important as her symbolic force increased. With the growing insecurity of the late Empire in the face of rebellion, invasion, inflation, and social desintegration, *Roma Aeterna* took on a desperate tone: she symbolized what stood between late antique man and chaos. As such she was used by Christians and transmitted through the Middle Ages to the Renaissance. A Greek deification of a distant barbarian people constructed for rather narrow political aims had become intertwined with imperial propaganda, first serving the emperor's own political purposes, but eventually transcending politics ironically to become for more than a millenium the symbol of civilization itself.

Additional Note

The Dedicatory Inscriptions on the Capitoline Hill

As the Roman Republic extended its power in the eastern Mediterranean, the Greek cities voted honors to Roma and to the Roman People. They also dispatched embassies to Rome to announce these honors, bring gifts and arrange that their homeland's devotion be memorialized in the capital. Copies of treaties were deposited on the Capitol, since Jupiter Capitolinus was for the Romans the securer of oaths and treaties. So it is likely that gold crowns sent to Rome for dedication to Roma were also placed on the Capitol.

Therefore it is hardly surprising that some Greek states chose to honor the Roman people by erecting dedications and statues on the Capitoline Hill. MOMMSEN had noticed the physical similarities of some of these dedications, and DEGRASSI's work confirms that certain texts form a homogeneous group; dedications set up by eastern cities and kings, inscribed in roughly similar letter forms on travertine blocks of the same size (c. 57 cm. in height) with the same molding[1]. These physical similarities are so striking as to demand that the texts were roughly contemporary and probably even formed part of the same monument.

The date of these texts has been the source of controversy from MOMMSEN's day to the present. But in this debate scholars have used, as J. & L. ROBERT have noted, different kinds of arguments[2]. It might be useful to examine these arguments. MOMMSEN suggested that the texts were erected on the Capitol soon after Sulla's defeat of Mithridates and the peace of Dardanus (84 BC). This view, which is followed by DEGRASSI and MORETTI, rests on the fact that one of these texts *CIL* I² 731) was dedicated by a king Ariobarzanes of Cappadocia, and the first Ariobarzanes was elected to the throne in 95 BC. And a dedication by the Tabaeans (*CIL* I² 730) seems most likely on historical grounds to have been erected after the Mithridatic Wars. Since all

---

[1] MOMMSEN *Zeitschrift für Numismatik* 15 (1887) 207 ff. (= *Gesammelte Schriften* IV (1906) 69 ff).; DEGRASSI *BCAC* 74 (1951–1952) 38 ff. (= *Scritti Vari* (Rome, 1962) 434 ff.).

[2] J. & L. ROBERT *Carie* 97 n. 5.

texts in the group seem to be physically contemporary, MOMMSEN-DEGRASSI-MORETTI have argued that the other texts should also be dated after the Mithridatic Wars and have so interpreted those inscriptions.

On the other hand, some of the other texts lend themselves more easily to interpretation if placed in the second century. The dedication (*CIL* I² 725) of a statue of Roma by the Lycian League in gratitude for the restoration of freedom certainly seems to derive from the aftermath of Pydna when Rhodian rule in Lycia and Caria was ended by Rome[3]. Both the phrasing and tone of this dedication indicate a date soon after 167, though Lycia was again freed by Sulla and a post-Sullan date is possible[4].

Laodicea-on-the-Lycus dedicated a statue of the Roman People (*CIL* I² 728) for Roman benefactions. Since Laodicea surrendered the Roman praetor, Q. Oppius, to the Pontic armies, they could have expected few Roman benefactions except pardon and there is no evidence of it after the war[4]. On historical grounds, I would favor a date not long after the bequest of Attalus: either after the defeat of Aristonicus (131) or at the time of the organization of the province of Asia (129). Since the Greek cities were implacably opposed to Aristonicus, the text could be a sincere expression of Laodicean feeling at that time. Additionally, the clumsy Latin of the translation would have been far less likely in 83, after a half century under Roman rule.

The Ephesians dedicated a statue (*CIL* I² 727) in gratitude for the restoration of their freedom and scholars have debated at length possible dates for such a text. MAGIE suggested that Ephesus was already free from Attalid control as early as the 160s, but his evidence is weak[5]. It is far more likely that the city obtained its freedom as a result of the bequest of Attalus or by the action of the Roman commissioners who organized Asia soon thereafter.

The text which can most securely be dated in the second century was erected by king Mithridates Philopator Philadelphus who, as REINACH has shown by numismatic evidence, was a son of Mithridates III and came to the throne soon after 160[6]. Thus this text should be dated to the short reign of Mithridates IV in the 150s, the same period when dynastic wars in Cappadocia led the rival claimants to the throne to send gold crowns dedicated to Roma to be placed on the Capitol. MOMMSEN had suggested that this text was dedicated by an otherwise unknown Mithridates, a son of Eupator, who was given the kingdom of Paphlagonia by Sulla. DEGRASSI, while unwilling to

---

[3] See above pp. 36ff.; LARSEN *CP* 51 (1956) 156ff.
[4] Appian *Mithr*. 20, 79.   [5] See above p. 57.
[6] REINACH *RN* (1902) 52ff.

rebut REINACH, cannot quite bring himself to abandon MOMMSEN's Mithridates [7]. He dates the text after the peace of Dardanus relying on epigraphical, rather than historical, considerations: travertine is rare before the first century BC; the letter forms seem first-century; physical similarity between this and the other texts once on the Capitol which he believes to be post-Sullan.

After this examination of the most important texts dedicated by eastern cities and kings to Jupiter Capitolinus and the Roman People, there are several questions which must now be answered: where were these texts set up? how were they set up? when were they set up? On the first two questions I see no reason to challange the picture drawn by DEGRASSI. MOMMSEN once thought (and others have long accepted) that there were two sets of texts, one set up on the Capitol and the second on the Capitolium Vetus on the Quirinal. But that theory was largely based on the fact that two of the four texts then known had been found on the Quirinal. But as additional, similar texts were discovered elsewhere in Rome, even MOMMSEN agreed that the texts must all have once stood on the Capitol.

These texts have long been associated with the temple of Jupiter Optimus Maximus Capitolinus where so many documents were deposited and displayed. But DEGRASSI is probably correct in positing a separate monument on the Capitol for these texts. The temple of Jupiter was destroyed by fire on July 6, 83 BC, and was not rededicated until 69 BC. DEGRASSI sees the destruction of the temple as the reason why this separate monument was constructed for the dedications and statues in the period immediately following Sulla's return to Rome. Since the known texts and fragments demand a perimeter of at least sixty feet, a single monument would be reasonable.

Though I do not wish to dispute DEGRASSI's attribution of most of these texts to a single monument on the Capitol, we must question the date he suggests for the monument (soon after 83 BC). On historical grounds, we have seen that, with only two exceptions, all the texts belonging to the monument best pertain to historical circumstances in the second century. The exceptions are the Ariobarzanes text which must be dated after 95, and the text from Tabae which is best dated after 81. Both DEGRASSI and LARSEN candidly admit the difficulties of either position: whether one dates the texts after Sulla or, with LARSEN and MAGIE, dates many of them in the second century [8]. The historical evidence seems to demand texts from a period of almost a century, while the epigraphical evidence clearly points to a single monument.

---

[7] DEGRASSI *BCAC* 74 (1951–1952) 28; 44; MOMMSEN *op. cit.*
[8] DEGRASSI *Ibid.* 44; LARSEN *CP* 51 (1956) 158.

The solution to this dilemma lies in the process of reinscription: the recarving of texts from earlier periods to preserve them. The Romans did this, and since we know from Livy that on occasion dedications and offerings on the Capitol were consolidated or removed, it is not difficult to imagine the reinscription of older texts on a new monument together with recent dedications of the same type [9]. Since the temple of Jupiter was destroyed by fire in 83, this rather large monument may have formed part of the rebuilding program—probably a rather high priority since Sulla's return to Rome in 82 brought dedications and offerings from various eastern cities and princes.

Of course such a monument could have actually been constructed on the Capitol any time after the accession of Ariobarzanes in 95. Perhaps there is something to be said for this earlier date, since the letter forms of the Tabaean text (which is best dated to 81) seem slightly later than others on the monument [10]. A date late in the 90s would explain this difference. In any event, the process of reinscription can help to explain the conflict between epigraphical and historical evidence and will allow scholars to avoid the tortured and tangled explanations heretofore necessary to date all the texts either to the mid-second century or to the post-Sullan era.

---

[9] 40, 51, 3. The inscription on the entablature of the porch of the Pantheon is a good example of reinscription.

[10] J. & L. ROBERT *Carie* 97 n. 5.

Appendix

Inscriptional Evidence for Roma in the Greek World

This appendix collects the epigraphical evidence for Roma in the Greek world. Only the specific reference to Roma has been quoted; economy permits no other course. Nevertheless, I hope the appendix will allow scholars to check rapidly the restorations and state of preservation of the texts. References are usually made to standard editions, except where additions or new restorations necessitate additional references. On many texts, there is additional discussion in the text or notes of the book and, though there are no cross-references between the notes and this appendix, the Index of Inscriptions should enable the reader to find such additional treatment.

Not all these texts actually refer to Roma. There are a number which earlier scholars had incorrectly connected with Roma: 19; 34; 78; 122; 134; 166; 187. 9 is a Greek text concerning the worship of Dea Roma in the West. For the sake of completeness, I have included these texts as well as others where the restoration of Roma is speculative.

The arrangement of this appendix follows roughly the geographical order of J. & L. ROBERT's *Bulletin épigraphique*, though within each general area the cities are listed alphabetically.

ATTICA

Athens

1) *IG* II² 1054
   Romaia at Thespiae
   ...] τῶν Ἐρωτιδείων καὶ Ῥω[μα]ίων ...
2) *IG* II² 1938
   Romaia in Athens
   ... οἵδε ἱεροποίησαν Ῥωμαῖα ...
3) *IG* II² 2336
   Priests of Roma on Delos (Pythilaos; Demetrios; Demetrios, son of Asklepides)
   45: ἱερεὺς Ῥώμης ...; 124: ἱερεὺς Ῥώμης; 261: ἱερεὺς Ῥώμης
4) *IG* II² 3173
   Dedication of the temple of Roma and Augustus on the Acropolis
   [ὁ] δῆμος θεᾶι Ῥώμηι καὶ Σ[εβασ]τῶι Καίσαρι ...
   ἱερέως θεᾶς Ῥώμης καὶ Σεβαστοῦ Σωτῆρος ἐπ' ἀκροπόλει.
5) *IG* II² 3153 (+ *Hesperia* 15 (1946) 224 #51)
   Romaia at Chalcis
   [Ῥωμαῖα τὰ ἐν] Χαλκίδι ...; Ῥωμ[αῖα] τὰ ἐν Χ[αλκίδι]

6) *IG* II² 3179
   Dedication to Roma and Augustus preserved only by a questionable copy
   ὁ δῆμος θεᾶι Ῥώμηι καὶ Σεβαστῶι Καίσαρι
7) *IG* II² 5047
   Priest of the Demos, the Graces and Roma at Athens (reserved seat in the theater)
   ἱερέως Δήμου καὶ Χαρίτων καὶ Ῥώμης
8) *IG* II² 5114
   Priest of Roma and Augustus at Athens (reserved seat in the theater)
   ἱερέως θεᾶς Ῥώμης καὶ Σεβαστοῦ Καίσ[αρος]
9) *Hesperia* 10 (1941) 72 #32; *AE* 1947 #69
   Priestess of Roma at Toulouse in Gallia Narbonensis
   ... Τρε[βελλίου Ρο]ύφου [γυναῖκα ἱ]έρειαν [ἐν Τ]ολώσῃ θεᾶς [Ῥώμης]
10) *Hesperia* 40 (1971) 308 #9
    Sacrifices to the Demos of the Romans (?)
    ... [τῶι δήμω]ι τῶι Ῥωμαί[ων ...

Eleusis

11) *IG* II² 3404
    Priest of Roma and Demos (?) — name fragmentary
    ... ὁ ἱερε[ὺς Ῥώμης? καὶ δή]μου ...
12) *IG* II² 3547
    Priest of the Senate, Roma, Demos and the Graces (?) = Meandros, son of Asklepiodoros
    τὸν ἱερέα συγκλή[του Ῥώμης] καὶ Δήμου καὶ Χαρίτω[ν ...]
    I suggest (chapter 2 n. 479) σύγκλη[ρον for συγκλή[του.

Rhamnus

13) *IG* II² 3242 (revised in *Hesperia* 30 (1961) 188)
    Priest of Roma and Augustus at Athens — Demostratos, son of Dionysios
    ... ἱερέως θεᾶς [Ῥώμη]ς κ[α]ὶ Σεβασ[τ]οῦ Καίσαρος ...

PELOPONNESUS

Aegina

14) *IG* IV 2
    Sacrifices to Roma; mention of Romaia and victor, Diodoros Heraclidas
    ... εἶν τ[ε] τοῖς Διο[νυσίοις καὶ Αἰαχ]είοις καὶ [Ῥ]ωμαί[οι]ς
    [κα]ὶ θ[ύ]εσθ[αι ὑπὲρ αὐτοῦ τῶι τ]ε Ἀπόλλωνι [καὶ] τᾶι Ῥώμα[ι].

Epidaurus

15) *IG* IV i² 629; MORETTI *IAG* 53
    Romaia in Megara; Romaia in Opus; Romaia in Antigonia (Victor: Sokrates)
    ... Πυθαεῖα καὶ Ῥωμαῖα τὰ ἐμ Μεγάροις ... Δῖα καὶ Αἰάντει[α κα]ὶ
    Ῥωμαῖα τὰ ἐν Ὀποῦντι ... Ποσείδαια [καὶ] Ῥωμαῖα τὰ ἐν Ἀντιγονείαι

Laconia. Gythium

16) *IG* V 1172 and p. 348 Index s.v.
    Priest of Roma (?) — C. Julius Eurycles Herculanos
    ... ἱερέα (θεᾶς Ῥώμης) κ[αὶ ἀρχιερέα] τοῦ τῶν [Σ]εβαστῶν [οἴκου] ...

Laconia. Sparta

17) *IG* V 525
Priest of Roma — Tiberius Claudius Spartiaticus
... ἱερέως θεᾶς Ῥώμης, ἀρχιερέως δὶς τῶν Σεβαστῶν ...
18) *IG* V 500
Priest of Roma — Tiberius Claudius Spartiaticus
... ἱερέα [θεᾶς Ῥώ]μης, ἀρχιερέα [τῶν τε Σ]εβαστῶν ...

Messenia

19) *IG* V 1417 (as restored by Tod *JHS* 25 (1905) 41 #1)
Priest (?) of the Romans; the restoration of Tod is incorrect
... [ἱερε]ὺ[ς]? Ῥωμαίων ... [ἱερέ?]ως Ῥωμαίων ... RATHER: [ἱππεὺς]
20) *SEG* XXIII 212; ORLANDOS *Prak. Arch. Et.* (1958) 178 (editio princeps)
Romaia
Ἁ πόλις Λυσικράτη Λυσιδάμου νικάσαντα Ἀσκλαπιεῖα καὶ Ῥωμαῖα

Olympia

21) *Olympia* 56
Italika Romaia Sebasta of Naples restored in this text
... τῶν Ἰτα[λικῶν καὶ Ῥωμαίων Σεβαστῶν ἰσολυμπίων ...]
22) *Olympia* 317
Base of a statue of Roma
[Ἡ πόλις ἡ τῶν] Ἠλείων Ῥώ[μ]ην ἀν[έθηκ]εν ...
23) *Olympia* 486; *Syll.* 893
Priest of Roma
... ἡ πόλις ἡ Μεσσηνίων Τι. Φλά. Πολύβιον ἱερέα θεᾶς [Ῥ]ώμης ...
24) *Olympia* 487
Priest of Roma
... Τίτον Φλάβιον Πολύβιον ... ἱερέα θεᾶς Ῥώμης ...
25) *SEG* XXII 350; HABICHT *Olympia VII Bericht* (1961) 218f.
Romaia Letoia of the Koinon of the Lycians (cf. ROBERT *BE* 1962 #153)
Romaia in Lindos (?) (cf. MELLOR *ZPE* 12 (1973) 259f.) (Victor: Leon)
... Ῥωμαῖα Λητῶα τοῦ [κοινοῦ] τῶν Λυκίων ... Ῥωμαῖα ἐν Λ[ίνδῳ].

CENTRAL & NORTHERN GREECE

MEGARIS

Megara

26) *IG* VII 48
Romaia in Chalcis—the victor's name is unknown
... Ῥωμαῖα ἐν Χαλκίδι ...

BOEOTIA

Thebes

27) *IG* VII 2517
Agonothete of the Kaisareia Erotideia Romaia at Thespiae—Lysandros
... ἀγωνοθετήσαντα Καισαρήων Ἐρωτιδίων Ῥωμαίων ...
28) *IG* VII 2518

Agonothete of the Kaisareia Erotideia Romaia (?) at Thespiae—the name is lost
[... ἀγωνοθετ]ήσαντα ... [καὶ Καισαρ]ήων Ἐρωτιδή[ων Ῥωμαίων ...]

Thespiae

29) *BCH* 26 (1902) 298 #17
Dedication to the Imperial Family and to Roma
Γένει Σεβ[αστοῦ] καὶ Ῥώμηι καὶ [Ἔρωτι?]
30) *BCH* 50 (1926) 394 # 14
Dedication to the Imperial House and Roma (restored)
θεοῖς Σεβαστοῖς καὶ τῶι Οἴκωι Σεβαστο[ῦ καὶ Ῥώμηι? ...]
31) *BCH* 50 (1926) 447 # 86
Fragmentary text with the name "Roma"
...]κη Ῥώμη
32) *BCH* 50 (1926) 447 #87
Fragmentary text; either a dedication to the emperor and Roma or a mention of Kaisareia Romaia
...] καὶ Και[σαρήων? ... κ]αὶ Ῥω[μαίων? ...
33) *BCH* 82 (1958) 158 #9 (with comments of ROBERT's *BE* 1959 #184)
Fragmentary victory list; Romaia included in title of festival
καὶ Ῥωμαίων [...]

Thisbe

34) *IG* VII 2234 (cf. Index p. 757 where *polis* is interpreted as "Thisbe")
Dedication to the Imperial Family and the *polis* (almost certainly Thisbe)
Γένει Σεβαστῶν καὶ τῇ πόλει ...

Oropus

35) *IG* VII 413; *RDGE* 23; *Syll.* 747
Records words of Sulla adding Romaia to Amphiaraia of Oropus
47: ... εἰς τοὺς ἀγῶνας καὶ τὰς θυσίας, ἃς Ὠρώπιοι συντελοῦσιν θεῷ Ἀμφιαράῳ, ὁμοίως δὲ καὶ ἃς ἂν μετὰ ταῦτα ὑπὲρ τῆς νίκης καὶ τῆς ἡγεμονίας τοῦ δήμου τοῦ Ῥωμαίων συντελέσουσιν, ...
36) *IG* VII 416
Agonothete of Amphiaraia Romaia (restored)—Alexidemos
[... ἀγωνοθετοῦντος τὰ Ἀμφιαρᾶα καὶ Ῥωμαῖα ...]
37) *IG* VII 419
Victory lists of Amphiaraia Romaia—prologue; agonothete: Euphanos
... ἀγωνοθετοῦντος τῶν Ἀμφιαρᾶων καὶ Ῥωμαίων Εὐφάνου ...
38) *IG* VII 420
Victory lists of Amphiaraia Romaia—prologue; agonothete: Eubiotos
... ἀγωνοθετοῦντος τὰ Ἀμφι[α]ρᾶα καὶ Ῥωμαῖα Εὐβιότου ...

LOCRIS

Opus

39) *IG* IX i 282
Fountain dedicated to the Demos of the Romans and to the emperor
... δήμῳ Ῥωμαίων καὶ θεῷ Σεβαστῷ Καίσαρι καὶ δήμῳ Ὀπουντίων ...

PHOCIS

Exarchos

40) KLAFFENBACH *SDAW* (1935) 705–706; text not yet published
    Report of a text dedicating a statue of Caligula to Roma

Delphi

41) *IDelphes* I 152
    Sacrifices for the Romans (for Roma?)
    ... ἐν τὰν [θ]υσίαν τῶν Ῥωμαίων·
42) *IDelphes* I 549
    Fragmentary text; mention of Romaia restored
    ... Βαρσιλλ[ῆα ἐν Ἐφέσῳ .... ἐ]ν Ἀθήναις· Ῥω[μαῖα ...]
43) *IDelphes* I 550; MORETTI *IAG* 81
    Romaia in Smyrna; name of the victor is lost
    27: Ῥωμαῖα ἐν Σμύρνῃ
44) *Syll.* 611; *RDGE* 38
    Sacrifices and games on behalf of the Romans (= Romaia)
    6: ... τόν τε ἀγῶνα τὸν γυμνικὸν καὶ τὴν θυσίαν ὑπὲρ ἡμῶν συνετελέσατε·
45) *SGDI* 2680
    Sacrifices on behalf of the Romans
    10: ... ἐν τὰν θυσίαν τῶν Ῥωμα[ί]ων ...

THESSALY

Demetrias

46) *IG* IX 2, 1135; cf. also OLIVER *GRBS* 8 (1967) 237; ROBERT's *BE* 1968 #313.
    Fragmentary verse inscription addressed to Roma (text of OLIVER)
    [γί]νατο μ[ὲν Δει]διός σε, δαΐ[κ]ράντειρα δὲ Ῥώμ[α]
    [ἤ]ρεν ἐπ[ὶ κλεινὸν μ]υριοτευχὲς ἕδος, ["Ω]λιε, ...

Hypata

47) *IG* IX 2, 32
    Dedication to Roma and the Divi
    [... καὶ θεᾷ Ῥ]ώμῃ[δὲ κα[ὶ] θεοῖς Σεβαστοῖς ...

MACEDON

Petres

48) Saloniki Museum #1281, reported by EDSON *HSCP* 51 (1940) 131 n. 6
    Cult of Roma and Zeus Eleutherios

Thessalonika

49) *IG* X 2, 1, 31; EDSON *HSCP* 51 (1940) 127f. #1
    Priest of Roma and the *Romaioi Euergetai*—fragmentary name: Neik...
    10: ... Ῥώμης δὲ κ[αὶ τῶν Ῥωμαίων] εὐεργέτων· ...
50) *IG* X 2, 1, 32; *HSCP* 51 (1940) 129f. #2
    Priest of Zeus Eleutherios and Roma (?); priest of Roma and *Romaioi Euergetai* (?)
    5: ... [ἱερέ]ως Διὸς Ἐλευθε[ρίου καὶ Ῥώμης Ζ]ωΐλου ...
    8: ...]ς Ῥώμης καὶ Ῥω[μαίων ...]

51) *IG* X 2, 1, 133
    Priest of Roma and the *Romaioi Euergetai*—the priest's name is lost
    7: ... Ῥώμης δὲ καὶ Ῥωμαίων εὐεργετῶν· ...
52) *IG* X 2, 1, 226
    Restored; priest of Roma (?) and the *Romaioi Euergetai*—Asklepas
    7: ... [.. Ῥώμης δὲ] καὶ Ῥωμαίων εὐ[εργε]τῶν· ...
53) *RA* 24 (1894) 213 #38, restored by ROBERT *EA* 448 n. 3
    Small fragment, restored as priest of Roma (?) and the *Romaioi Euergetai*
    ... [ἱερέως δὲ Ῥώμης καὶ Ῥω]μαίων εὐε[ργετῶν ...]

THRACE

Abdera

54) *BCH* 37 (1913) 138f. #42
    Eponymous priest of Zeus Eleutherios and Roma—priest's name is lost
    [Ἐπὶ ἱερέως Διὸ]ς Ἐλευθερίου καὶ Ῥώ[μης ...]

Aenos

55) *BE* 1972, 275 (from TAŞLIKLIOĞLU *Trakya'da epigrafya araştirmalari* II
    p. 3) The local gerusia honors the priest of Zeus and Roma—Athenodoros
    ... τὸν ἱερῆ τοῦ Διὸς καὶ τῆς Ῥώμης ...

Maronia

56) *IGR* I 831
    Priest of Zeus and Roma—M. Aurelius Tarsas
    Ἱερεὺς Διὸς καὶ Ῥώμης, ...
57) *Arch. Deltion* 20B (1965) 484 #4; *BCH* 92 (1968) 926; *SEG* XXIV 636
    Altar of Zeus and Roma
    Διὸς καὶ Ῥώμης

Nicopolis

58) *IGR* I 589; *IGB* II 701
    Priest of Roma—Q. Jul .... (?)
    ... ἱερεὺς Ῥώμ[ης ...]

Odessus

59) *IGR* I 1439; *IGB* I 48
    Priest of Roma—C. Flavius Theophilos
    5: ... ἱερέως θεᾶς Ῥώμης ...

AEGEAN ISLANDS

Astypalaea

60) *IG* XII 3, 173; *RDGE* 16
    Altar of Roma and ?
    49: ... πρὸς τῷ βωμῷ [...] τῆς Ῥώμης.

Ceos. Julis

61) *IG* XII 5, 622
    Base of a statue of Roma
    Ὁ δῆμος ὁ Ἰουλιητῶν θεᾶι [Ῥώ]μηι Σωτείραι

Chios

62) ROBERT *EEP* 126f. #3
 Romaia on Cos—victor: Demetrios, son of Diogenes
 4: Ῥωμαῖα τὰ ἐγ Κῷ
63) *IGR* IV 950; but see ROBERT *BCH* 59 (1935) 464.
 Theophanika Sebasta (?) Romaia on Chios; gymnasiarch: Athenion son of Symmachos
 ... [γυμνα]σιαρχήσας καὶ ξ[υσταρχήσας] τῶν θεοφανικῶν [Σεβαστῶν] Ῥωμαίων ...
64) *BE* 1956, 213; *SEG* XV 532
 Restored; agonothete of Romaia (?)—Claudia Hedea (?)
 ... ἀγωνοθετήσασαν τῶν Ἡρα[κλήων (καὶ) Ῥωμ]αίων καὶ Καισαρήων, ...
65) KONTOLEON *Praktika* 1953 (1956) 270f.; ROBERT's *BE* 1958 #384; *SEG* XVI 486; KONTOLEON *Akte* (1964) 192ff. I am grateful to Professor N. KONTOLEON for information on unpublished sections of the text and permission to mention them.
 3: ... κατὰ τὸμ πολεμὸν ἐπιφανείας ...
 5: .. [.. τῆς ἀγομένης τῆι Ῥώ]μηι μετὰ τὰ θεοφανία πομπῆς καὶ [θυσίας ..] ..
 7: .. [.. τὴν πανή]γυριν διὰ τὸ βούλεσθαι χάριν ἀποδιδό[ναι ..] ..
 25: ... ἀνάθημα τῇ Ῥώμῃ ...
66) *SEG* XIX 589
 Victory catalogue of M. Aurelius Heras; perhaps victor in Romaia of Asia
 [... Ῥωμαῖα?] κοινὰ Ἀσίας ... FORREST *SEG* doubts this restoration.

Cos

67) *Syll.* 1065; MORETTI *IAG* 60
 A victor in the Romaia Sebasta of Asia—the name is lost
 ... [Ῥ]ωμαῖα Σεβαστὰ τὰ τιθέμενα ὑπὸ τοῦ κοινοῦ τῆς Ἀσίας ...
68) *Syll.* 1066; MORETTI *IAG* 61
 A victor in the Romaia on Cos—the name of the victor, a son of Pythodoros, is lost
 7: ... Ῥωμαῖα τὰ τιθέμενα ὑπὸ τοῦ δάμου ...

Delos

69) *ID* 465 C 20
 Crowns voted to the Demos of the Romans and the Senate
 ... [εἰς τοὺς στεφ]άνους [δήμ]ωι τῶ[ι Ῥ]ωμαίων καὶ τεῖ συγκλ[ήτωι]
70) *ID* 1450
 Silver crown of Roma in the temple of Apollo
 A 119: ... στέφανον ἀργυροῦν τὸν τῆς Ῥώμης, ...
71) *ID* 1763
 Base of statue of Roma erected by the Competaliasts
 12: ... κομπεταλιασταὶ γενόμενοι τὴν Ῥώμην ἀνέθηκαν ...
72) *ID* 1778; *OGIS* 591
 Base of statue of Roma erected by the Poseidoniasts
 Ῥώμην θεὰν εὐεργέτιν τὸ κοινὸν Βηρυτίων Ποσειδωνιαστῶν ...
73) *ID* 1779
 Altar of Roma dedicated by the Poseidoniasts
 τὸ κοινὸν Βηρυτίων Ποσειδωνιαστῶν ... Ῥώμης ...
74) *ID* 1807
 Table dedicated to Athena Nike and to the Demos of the Romans
 ... τὴν τράπεζαν Ἀθηνᾶι Νίκη[ι καὶ τ]ῶι δήμωι τῶι Ῥωμαίων ἀνέθηκεν.

75) *ID* 1877
Priest of Hestia (?), Demos and Roma—name fragmentary
... ἱερεύς [Ἑστίας, Δή]μου, Ῥώμη[ς ...]

76) *ID* 1950
Victor in Romaia—Protogenes of Alexandria, the son of Diodotos
... τούς ἐφή[β]ους Ῥωμαῖα λαμπάδ[ι νική]σας, ...

77) *ID* 1957; MORETTI *IAG* 51
Victor in the Romaia in Chalcis—Menodoros of Athens
Ῥωμαῖα τὰ ἐν Χαλκίδι ...

78) *ID* 2296
"Romaia" (?) on a fragmentary text; perhaps merely the feminine of "Romaios"
... [Ῥ]ωμαῖα? [. ... Ἀ]ντιόχισσα

79) *ID* 2484
Marble altar dedicated to Roma
Ῥώμης

80) *ID* 2596
Officials of the Romaia in the month of Hekatombaion
... [οἵ]δε ἱερ[οποίη]σαν [τὰ] Ῥωμαῖα τὰ τ[οῦ Ἑκα]τομ[β]αιῶνος· ...

81) *ID* 2605
Priest of Hestia, Demos (?), and Roma
... [Ἑ]στίας [Δήμου Ῥ]ώμης, ...

Euboea. Chalcis

82) *IG* XII 9, 899b
Romaia celebrated by the Euboean League
12: ... ἐν τῶι ἀγῶνι τῶν Ῥωμαίων τῶι γυμνικῶι, [ὃν τίθησι τὸ κ]οινὸν τῶν Εὐβοιέων· ...

Ios

83) *IG* XII 5, 1013
Dedication to Roma and Augustus
Ῥώμηι [κα]ὶ Αὐτοκράτορι Καίσα[ρ]ι [θ]εῶι θεοῦ υἱῶι Σεβαστῶι.

Lesbos. Mytilene

84) *IG* XII 2, 25
Honors to Roma Nikophoros
... τᾷ Ῥώμᾳ τᾷ Νικοφό[ρῳ ...]

85) *IG* XII 2, 26 (+ supplementum ad 26)
Mention of Roma (?) Nikophoros on a fragment
15: ... [τὰν Ῥώμαν τὰν Νικ]όφορον ...

86) *IG* XII Supplementum 9 (+ Addenda (p. 208) ad 9)
Dedication to Roma and Tiberius
... τε καὶ Ῥώμᾳ καὶ Τε[βερίῳ Καίσαρι] ...

87) *IG* XII 2, 656
High priest for life of the goddess Roma and Augustus—Diaphenes, son of Potamon
[Ἀρ]χίρεως διὰ βίω θεᾶς Ῥώμας καὶ τῶ Σεβαστῶ Διὸς Καίσαρος ...

Melos

88) *IG* XII 3, 1097
Dedication of a bronze statue of Roma
Ὁ δᾶμος ὁ Μαλίων ἐτίμασεν τὰν Ῥώμαν εἰκόνι χαλκέαι καὶ στεφάνωι χρυσέωι ἀρετᾶς ἕνεκεν καὶ εὐεργεσίας τᾶς εἰς αὐτόν.

Paros

89) *IG* XII 5, 139
 Actors in a Romaia (?)
 [..... ὑπ]οκριτα[ὶ ἐνίκησαν τὰ Ῥωμ]αῖα

Rhodes. Camirus

90) *IG* XII 1, 730
 List of celebrations of Romaia
 7: [Ῥ]ωμαῖα ... 15: Ῥωμαῖα ... 19: Ῥωμαῖα ... 23: Ῥωμαῖα

Rhodes. Lindos

91) *Lindos* 229
 Very fragmentary; restored as Romaia (?)
 6: [... ἐπιδόντ]α [εἰς τὰ] Ῥωμα[ῖα] χρυ[σοῦς ...]
92) *Lindos* 482
 Agonothete of Romaia (?)—the name is lost
 10: ... ἀγωνοθετήσαντα Ῥω[μαίων ...]

Rhodes

93) *IG* XII 1, 46
 Gymnasiarch in the Romaia—Asklapiadas, son of Andronikos
 2: ... [γυμ]να[σίαρχο]ν πρεσβύτερον κατὰ Ῥωμαῖα ...
94) *ASA* 30–32 (1952–1954) 252 #3
 Romaia
 ... [τρι]ετηρὶς [Ῥ]ωμαῖα ...
95) *ASA* 30–32 (1952–1954) 256 #5
 Romaia
 3, 12, 22, 31, 42: Ῥωμαῖα
96) MAIURI *NS* 34
 Victor in Romaia—his name is lost
 ... νικάσας ... Ῥωμαῖα ...
97) MAIURI *NS* 18
 Victor in Poseidania and Romaia and Halieia—Polykles (?)
 ... νικάσαντα [Π]οσειδάνια καὶ Ῥωμαῖα καὶ Ἁλίεια ...
98) SEGRE *PP* 4 (1949) 73; *AE* 1951 #218
 Priest of Roma—the name is lost; his father was an Aristolochos (?)
 ... ἱερέως Ῥώμας ...
99) SEGRE *PP* 4 (1949) 81 #2
 Victor in Romaia; the victor's name is lost
 ... νικάσαντα παῖδας δίαυλον Ῥωμαῖα ...

Samos

100) *IGR* IV 971 + 978; *MDAI(A)* 49 (1924) 47; cf. HERRMANN *MDAI(A)* 75 (1960) 83 n. 42
 Dedication to Roma (?) and Augustus (text provided by G. DUNST)
 [θεᾶι Ῥώμη]ι καὶ Αὐτοκράτορι Κα[ίσαρι θ]εοῦ υἱῶι Σεβαστῶι ...
101) *IGR* IV 977
 Dedication to Roma and Augustus
 9: ... θεᾶι Ῥώμηι καὶ Σεβαστῷ Καίσαρι.

102) *IGR* IV 994; *MDAI(A)* 49 (1924) 47; HERRMANN *MDAI(A)* 75 (1960) 83 n. 42
Dedication to Roma (?) and Augustus (text provided by G. DUNST)
... θεᾶι [Ρώ]μηι καὶ Σ[εβαστῶι Καίσαρι] ...
103) HABICHT *MDAI(A)* 72 (1957) 242f. #65
Fine for infringement of treaty between Samos and Antiochia on the Maeander is to be paid to the goddess Roma
... ἀποτεῖσαι ἱερὰς τῆς Ῥώμης δραχμὰς δισμυρίας ...
104) HERRMANN *MDAI(A)* 75 (1960) 71 #1; DUNST by letter
Mention of the Romaion Sebaston: the sanctuary of Roma and the emperor
15: ... [παρὰ τῶι Ῥ]ωμαίωι Σεβαστῶι .. or DUNST: .. [ἐν τῶι Ῥ]ωμαίωι
105) HERRMANN *MDAI(A)* 75 (1960) 82 #2; DUNST by letter
A sanctuary (?) of Roma and Augustus (text of DUNST)
... [πρὸς τὸν ναόν τῆς θεᾶς] Ῥώμης καὶ τοῦ Σε[βαστοῦ ...]
106) *IGR* IV 975
Architrave dedication of the temple of Roma and Augustus
Ὁ δῆμος θεᾶι Ῥώμηι καὶ Αὐτοκράτορι Καίσαρι θεοῦ υἱῶι θεῶι Σεβαστῶι
107) *BCH* 49 (1925) 232f. xi
Victor in Romaia at Miletus—the name is lost
... νικήσαντα ... [Ῥω]μαῖα τὰ ἐμιλήτωι ...
108) HERRMANN *MDAI(A)* 75 (1960) 83 n. 42
Statue base of honorific statue dedicated to Roma and Augustus (?)
Ὁ δῆμος θεᾶι Ῥώμηι κ[αὶ Αὐτοκράτορι Καίσαρι Σεβαστῶι ...]
109) Unpublished texts; Dr. G. DUNST has kindly informed me of these texts:
Bases of statues set up in the temple of Roma and Augustus and dedicated to Roma and Augustus

Thasos

110) *IG* XII 8, 380
New pavement in the temple dedicated to Roma and Augustus
θεᾶι Ῥώμηι καὶ Αὐτοκράτορι Καίσαρ[ι θεοῦ υἱῶι] θε[ῶι] Σεβαστῶι ... τὸ μαρμάρινον στρῶμα τοῦ ναο[ῦ κατεσκεύασαν] ...

ASIA MINOR

MYSIA

Assus
111) *IGR* IV 247; STERRETT *PASA* I (1882–1883) 17f. #8 (a better edition)
A musical competition to Roma at Stratonicea in Caria
25: ... ἐν τῷ ἀγῶνι τῷ μουσικῷ συντελουμένῳ τῇ Ῥώμῃ ...
112) MERKELBACH *ZPE* 13 (1974) 280 which joins LE BAS-WADDINGTON *VA* 1727 + 1034a
Base of a statue (or votive gift) dedicated to Roma by Assus and resident Romans
ὁ δῆμος καὶ [οἱ] πραγματευόμενοι Ῥω[μαῖοι] θεὰ[ν Ῥώ]μην [τ]ὴν εὐεργέτιν τοῦ κόσμ[ου]

Elaea

113) *Syll.* 694; *IGR* IV 1692; *LSAM* 15
Sacrifices to Roma, as part of a treaty with Rome
50: ... [ὁμο]ίως δὲ καὶ τῆι [Ῥώμ]ηι καὶ τοῖς ἄλλοι[ς θεοῖ]ς ...

Pergamum

114) *CIL* III 399
 Priest of Roma and Salus
 ...M. TULLIO. M. F. COR. CRATIPPO. FRATRI. SUO. SACERDOTI. ROMAE. ET. SALUTIS ...
115) *Pergamum* 268 E. 34–36; *OGIS* 437
 Eponymous priests of Roma at Sardes and Ephesus
 ... ὡς μὲν Ἐφέσιοι ... ἱερέ[ως] δὲ τῆς Ῥώμης Ἀρτεμιδώρου, ... ὡς δὲ Σαρδιανοὶ ἐπὶ ἱερέω[ς] τῆς μὲν Ῥώμης Σωκράτου, ...
116) *Pergamum* 269
 Games in honor of Roma and Divus Augustus
 ... [EST CONST]ITUTUM εἰς ελαστικὸν ... QUOD IN HONOREM ROMAE [ET DIVI AUG ...]
117) *Pergamum* 374; *IGR* IV 353
 A.4–5: Hymnodes of Divus Augustus and of Roma
 D.14: Sacrifices of Divus Augustus and of Roma
 ... ὑμνῳδοὶ θεοῦ Σεβαστοῦ καὶ θεᾶς Ῥώμης ...
 ... εἰς θυσίας τοῦ Σεβαστοῦ καὶ τῆς Ῥώμης ...
118) *Pergamum* III 29
 Neokoros of the goddess Roma and of Divus Augustus
 ... Τι. Κλαύδιος Νικομήδης νεωκόρος θεᾶς Ῥώμης καὶ θεοῦ Αὐγούστου.
119) *Pergamum* III p. 165 which restores *IGR* IV 473
 Priest of the goddess Roma and of Divus Augustus—M. Tullius Cratippus
 ... [ἱερέα διὰ] γένους θεᾶς [Ῥώμης καὶ θεο]ῦ Σεβαστοῦ ...
120) *IGR* IV 454
 Neokoros of the goddess Roma and Divus Augustus
 Gymnasiarch of the Sebasta Romaia of Asia
 ... Γαίον Ἰούλιον Σακέρδωτα, τὸν νεωκόρον θεᾶς Ῥώμης καὶ θεοῦ Σεβαστοῦ Καίσαρος ... καὶ γυμνασίαρχον τῶν δωδεκάτων Σεβαστῶν Ῥωμαίων ...
121) *IGR* IV 498
 Sebasta Romaia—the name of the victor is lost
 10: ... τὰ μέγαλα Σεβαστὰ Ῥ[ω]μαῖα ...
122) *MDAI(A)* 37 (1912) 299 #25; *IGR* IV 1687
 This text does not refer to the goddess Roma, but to the city of Rome
 ... βασιλὶς τῶν ἐν Θεᾶι Ῥώμη(ι) ἱερῶν, ...

AEOLIS

Cyme

123) *IGR* IV 1302
 Eponymous priest of Roma and Augustus—Polemon, son of Zenon
 55: ... ἐπὶ ἱερέος τᾶς Ῥώμας καὶ Αὐτοκράτορος Καίσαρος ...

IONIA

Ephesus

124) *Ephesos* II 27; OLIVER *The Sacred Gerusia Hesperia Supplement* VI (1941) 55 #3
 Bequest of a silver statuette of the Demos of the Romans by G. Vibius Salutaris to be set up in Ephesus
 164: ... καὶ εἰκὼν ἀργυρέα τοῦ δήμου τοῦ Ῥωμαίων, ...

125) *Ephesos* II 28; OLIVER *The Sacred Gerusia Hesperia* Supplement VI (1941) 86 #4
Silver statuette (same as above) described as *urbs Romana* and as Ῥώμη
7: UNAM URBIS ROMANAE .... 17: μίαν ἡγεμονίδος Ῥώμης . . .
126) *Ephesos* II 30; on the dates, see J. & L. ROBERT *BE* 1972 #388
Twelve priests of Roma listed—Poseidonios; Seimos; Mousaios; Artemidoros; Badromios; Glaukon; Lucius Iunius Salvius; Alexandros; Timon; Aratos; Moschus; Athenagoras.
. . . ἱερεὺς γενόμενος τῆς Ῥώμης . . .
127) *Ephesos* II 31
Fragment restored on analogy with #126 to list a priest of Roma
. . . [γενόμενος ἱερεὺς Ῥώμης . . .]
128) *Ephesos* III 66
Priest of Roma and P. Servilius Isauricus—G. Licinius Maximus Julianus
. . . ἱερέα Ῥώμης καὶ Ποπλίου Σερουειλίου Ἰσαυρικοῦ, . . .
129) *JÖAI* 18 (1915) Beiblatt 281–282
Priest of Roma and P. Servilius Isauricus—T. Peducaeus Canax
. . . ἱερατεύσαντα τῆς Ῥώμης καὶ Ποπλίου Σερουειλίου Ἰσαυρικοῦ, . . .

Erythrae

130) *IGR* IV 1539; *LSAM* 26
Dedication to Roma by the Ionian League
11: . . . ἕκτηι, Ῥώμηι τε[λ]είου κδ κοινόν.
131) *IGR* IV 1534; but now *Inschriften von Erythrai und Klazomenai* (Bonn, 1972) 131
Dedication to Roma (?) and Augustus; *IEK* now restores the text differently
IGR: [θεᾶι Ῥώμηι καὶ Σε]βαστῶι Καίσαρι; *IEK*: [Γαίωι Ἰουλίωι Σε]βαστῶι

Magnesia

132) *IMagn.* 88
Victors in dramatic contests of the Romaia
. . . οἵδε ἐνίκων τὸν ἀγῶνα τῶν Ῥωμαίων ποιηταὶ καινῶν δραμάτων . . .
133) *IMagn.* 127
Athenagoras, victor in the Romaia
. . . νικήσαντα Ῥωμαῖα ἅρματι τελείωι.
134) *IMagn.* 192; ROBERT *RP* 65 (1930) 117
Fragmentary list of festivals; listed under Romaia in KERN's Index of festivals
. . . Ἰσθ[μια Πύ]θια Ἀρεσανταδρ[ι]ά[νεια] Ῥωμαίων . . .
But ROBERT's suggestion is superior: ἀρέσαντα δήμ[ωι] Ῥωμαίων

Miletus

135) *LSAM* 49; *Milet* 203
Regulations for the cult the Demos of the Romans and of Roma in Miletus
Sale of Office   A 1: ὁ πριάμενος τὴν ἱερωσύνην τοῦ Δήμου τοῦ Ῥωμαίων καὶ τῆς Ῥώμης . . .
Sacrifices   A 16: . . . θύσει τῶι Δήμωι τῶ(ι) Ῥωμαίων καὶ τῆι Ῥώμη . . .
Sacrifices   A 20: . . . θυέτωσαν οἱ εἰσιόντες . . . γυμνασίαρχοι . . . τῶι Δ. Ρ. καὶ τῇ Ῥώμη·
Romaia   B 20: . . . ἐν τοῖς Ῥωμαίοις . . .
Temple of Roma B 21: . . . ἐπ' ἂν δὲ συντελεσθῇ τὸ ἱερὸν τῆς Ῥώμης, ἐν τῶι Ῥωμαίῳ·

  Sacrifices   B 22: θυέτω δὲ καὶ ὁ ἱέρεως . . . τῶι Δ. Ρ. καὶ τῇ Ῥώμῃ . . .
  Sacrifices   B 27: . . . θυέτω ὁ αἰσυμνήτης τῶι Δ. Ρ. καὶ τῇ Ῥώμηι . . .
136) *Milet* 369
  Victor in the Romaia Sebasta of Asia—the name is lost
  12: . . . τὰ Σεβαστὰ Ῥωμαῖα τὰ τιθέμενα [ὑ]πὸ τοῦ κοινοῦ τῆς Ἀσίας.

Didyma

137) *Didyma* 201
  Fragmentary text seems to mention the Romaia Sebasta of Asia
  [. . . τὸν ἀγῶνα τῶν Σεβαστῶν Ῥω]μαίων τὸν τ[ιθέ]μενον [ὑπὸ τ]οῦ κο[ινοῦ τῆς
  Ἀσίας . . .]
138) *Didyma* 339
  Agonothetes at the Didymeia Kaisareia Romaia—Minnion; Claudius
  Menophilus
  9: . . . ἀγωνοθετ[η]{σάντων} Διδυμείων κα[ὶ Κα]ισαρείων καὶ Ῥωμ[αί]ων . . .
139) *Didyma* 377
  Fragmentary text may also refer to the Didymeia (?), Kaisareia (?),
  Romaia (?)
  . . . ων καὶ Ῥω[μαίων . . .]

Priene

140) *IPriene* 105; *OGIS* 458 (texts from Priene Apamea, etc.); now cf. LAFFI
  SCO 16 (1967) 1–98.
  Mention of Romaia Sebasta of Asia; temenos of Roma and Augustus in
  Pergamum
  58: . . . ἐν τῷ γυμνικῶι ἀγῶνι τῶι ἐν Περγάμωι τῶν Ῥω[μα]ίω[ν] Σεβαστῶν . . .
  63: . . . ἐν τῶι τῆς Ῥώμης καὶ τοῦ Σεβαστοῦ τεμένει.
141) *IPriene* 222
  Eponymous priest of Roma and Augustus—the name is lost
  Ἐπὶ ἀρχιερέως Ῥώμης καὶ Αὐτοκράτορος [Καίσαρος θ]εοῦ Σεβασ[τοῦ . . .]
142) *IPriene* 232
  Victor in the Amphiaraia Romaia
  Ὁ δῆμος Διονύσιον Μηνοδώρου νικήσαντα Ἀμφιαρᾷα καὶ Ῥωμαῖα.
143) *IPriene* 233
  Victor at Amphiaraia Romaia (?) in Oropus—the name is lost
  . . . [Ἀμφιαρᾷα καὶ Ῥωμαῖα τ]ὰ ἐν Ὠρωπῶι.

Smyrna

144) *IGR* IV 1410; cf. ROBERT *RP* 56 (1930) 26; BUCKLER *RP* 61 (1935) 181 f.
  Priest (or agonothete) of the goddess Roma and Divus Augustus—
  Ti. Claudius Herodes
  [. . . ἱερέως] θεᾶς Ῥώμης καὶ θεοῦ [Καίσαρος . . .]
  ROBERT and BUCKLER: [. . . ἀγωνοθέτου] κτλ.

Teos

145) *IGR* IV 1556
  Altar of Roma, Zeus Ktesios, Zeus Kapetolios and Agathos Daimon
  Διὸς Κτησίου, Διὸς Καπετωλίου, Ῥώμης, Ἀγαθοῦ Δαίμονος.
146) *BCH* 19 (1895) 554
  Priest of Roma and Pistis
  Ἱερεὺς ἀπεδείχθη Ῥώμης καὶ Πίστεως Στράτων Ἑστιαίου.

LYDIA

(N)akokome

147) *SEG* XIX 710; HERRMANN *Denk. Wien* 77, 1 (1959) 8-10 #6
Eponymous stephanephorus and priest of Roma—Apollonides, son of Aischrion
... στεφανηφόρου δὲ καὶ ἱερέως τῆς Ῥώμης ...

Apollonis

148) *SEG* XIX 709; HERRMANN *Denk. Wien* 77, 1 (1959) 6-7 #3
Perhaps dated in the same way as the preceding text, but no mention of Roma remains in this fragmentary text

Hierocaesarea

149) *IGR* IV 1304
Altar of Roma and Augustus at Thyatira; eponymous priest—Andronikos
... πρυτάνεως δ[ὲ καὶ ἱε]ρέως τῆς Ῥώμης ... τὸν Βωμὸν ἐκ τῶν ἰδίων [ϑ]εᾷ Ῥώμῃ καὶ Αὐτοκράτορι Καίσαρι ...
150) *IGR* IV 1309
Priest of Roma
Ἀθηνόδωρος Μιθρήους τοῦ Κράτητος ἱερεὺς γενόμενος Ῥώμης, ...

Hypaepa

151) *IGR* IV 1608
Fragmentary text; agonothete of Roma (?) and Augustus—Anaxagoras
... διὰ βίου ἀγων[οθέτου θεᾶς Ῥώμης κα]ὶ θεοῦ Σεβαστοῦ Κα[ίσαρος ...
152) *OGIS* 470; *IGR* IV 1611
Priest and Agonothete of Roma and Augustus of the Asian Koinon—C. Julius Pardalas
... ἀρχιερέως καὶ διὰ βίου ἀγω[ν]οθέτου θεᾶς Ῥώμης καὶ Αὐτοκράτορος

Sardes

153) *Sardis* 8; *IGR* IV 1756
Priests of Roma and Augustus of the Asian Koinon; agonothetes of Romaia — Charinos; Demetrios; Philistes; M. Antonius Lepidus
75, 83, 89: ... ὁ ἀρχιερεὺς θεᾶς Ῥώμης καὶ Αὐτοκράτορος Καίσαρος ...
99: ... τοῦ ἀρχιερέως καὶ ἀγωνοθέτου διὰ βίου τῶν μεγαλῶν Σεβαστῶν Καισαρήων θεᾶς Ῥώμης καὶ Αὐτοκράτορος Καίσαρος ...
154) *Sardis* 27
Priest of Roma—Iollas
... καὶ γενόμενον ἱερέα τῆς Ῥώμης ...
155) *Sardis* 93
Eponymous priest of Roma—Alexarchos, son of Stratippos
Ἐπὶ ἱερέως τῆς Ῥώμ[ης ...]
156) *Sardis* 112
Eponymous priest of Roma—Dionysios, son of Athenaios
Ἐπὶ ἱερέως τῆς Ῥώμης ...
157) *Sardis* 113
Eponymous priest of Roma—Kotobeos
Ἐπὶ ἱερέως τῆς Ῥώμης ...

158) *Sardis* 114
Fragmentary; restored as an eponymous priest of Roma (?)—the name is lost
[Ἐ]πὶ ἱε[ρέως τῆς Ῥώμης ..]
159) *Sardis* 115
Fragmentary; restored as an eponymous priest of Roma—Diodoros
[Ἐπὶ ἱερέως τῆς Ῥώμ]ης ...

Thyatira

160) *IGR* IV 1228
Priest of Roma—Asklepiades, son of Tryphon
... τὸν πρύτανιν καὶ ἱερέα τῆς Ῥώμης, ...
161) *IGR* IV 1262
Victor in the Romaia of Ephesus—Athenades, son of Pythodoros
... νικήσαντα Ῥωμαῖα τὰ ἐν [Ἐ]φέσωι παῖδας δίαυλον.
162) *IGR* VI 1276
Fragmentary text; high priest of Augustus (?) and Roma (?)—Zenon
... ἀρχιερεῖ τοῦ [Σ]ε[βαστοῦ Καίσαρος καὶ θεᾶς Ῥώμης ...]

CARIA

Alabanda
163) *BCH* 10 (1886) 306f. #2
High priest of Roma and Augustus—M. Antonius Meleagros
7: ... ἀρχιερατεύσαντα τῆς Ῥώμης καὶ το[ῦ] Σεβαστοῦ Καίσαρος ...
164) *BCH* 58 (1934) 300ff.
High priest in Alabanda of Roma and Augustus—Aristogenes, son of Meniskos
9: ... [ἀ]ρχιερατεύσαντα ἐν τῇ πατρίδι τῆς τε Ῥώμης καὶ τοῦ Σεβαστοῦ [Κ]αίσαρος ...

Aphrodisias

165) Unpublished text (courtesy of Professor K. ERIM and Miss Joyce REYNOLDS)
Dedication to Zeus, Homonoia and Roma contained in a treaty between Plarasa-Aphrodisias, Cibyra and Tabae from the 2nd century BC.
166) LE BAS-WADDINGTON *Voyage Archéologique* V 1620c; ROBERT *RP* 56 (1930) 30f.
Fragmentary text, restored by LE BAS-WADDINGTON to refer to a festival of Roma and Augustus; ROBERT has shown that the restoration was incorrect and that the text refers not to Roma, but to the city of Rome.
LE BAS-WADDINGTON: ... πρὸ τῆς εἰς Ῥώμην [καὶ Σεβαστὸν ἑορτῆς, ...]

Bargylia

167) *BCH* 5 (1881) 191f. #14
High priest of Roma and Augustus dedicates a statue of Titus—Exekestos Diodoros
... ὁ ἀπὸ τῆς πόλεως ἀρχιερεὺς θεᾶς Ῥώμης καὶ θεοῦ Σεβαστοῦ ...

Caunus

168) *JHS* 73 (1953) 32 #13; *SEG* XII 466
Base of a statue of Polyxenos, victor in the festival of Leto and Roma
... ἐν τοῖς τιθεμένοις ὑπὸ τοῦ δήμου Λητοῖ καὶ Ῥώμηι πενταετηρικοῖς ἀγῶσιν ...

Halicarnassus

169) *Syll.* 1064; MORETTI *IAG* 56; new reading of line 7 by Jeanne ROBERT
Victor in Romaia-Amphiaraia in Oropus; Romaia in Cibyra; Romaia in Chalcis. The victor was Drakontomenes, son of Hierokleos
5: Ἀμφιαρᾷα καὶ Ῥωμαῖα τὰ τιθέμενα ὑπὸ ’Ωρωπίων . . .
7: Ῥωμαῖα τὰ ἐν Κε[ρκύρ]αι; but now ROBERT: Κι[βύρ]αι
11: Ῥωμαῖα τὰ ἐν Χαλκίδι ἄνδρας ἵππιον, Ἀμφιαρᾷα καὶ Ῥωμαῖα τὰ τιθέμενα ὑπὸ ’Ωρωπίων . . .

170) *IBM* 894
Roma used in apposition to πατρίς in the emperor's titulature; mention of the temenos of Roma and Augustus at Pergamum.
5: . . . πατέρα μὲν τῆς [ἑαυ]τοῦ πατ[ρ]ίδος θεᾶς Ῥώμης, . . .
41: . . . [ἐν τῷ] τεμένει τῆς Ῥώμης καὶ τ[οῦ Σεβαστοῦ . . .]

Hyllarima

171) *BCH* 58 (1934) 379 #43
Dedication to the Augusti, the goddess Roma and the Demos
[θ]εοῖς Σεβαστοῖς [κ]αὶ . . . θεᾷ Ῥώμῃ καὶ Δήμῳ . . .

Lagina Cf. Stratonicea below.

Mylasa

172) *CIG* 2696
Dedication of the temple of Roma and Augustus
Ὁ δῆμος Αὐτοκράτορι Καίσαρι θεοῦ υἱῷ Σεβαστῷ . . . καὶ θεᾷ Ῥώμῃ

173) *BCH* 12 (1888) 15 #4
Priest of Roma (?) and Augustus—Aetion
. . . ἱερεὺ[ς θεᾶς Ῥώμης καὶ Αὐτοκράτορος] Καίσαρος Σεβαστοῦ . . .

Nysa

174) *Syll.* 781
Priest of Roma and Augustus, perhaps eponymous—Herakleides, son of Herakleides
[ἱ]ερέως Ῥώμης καὶ Αὐτοκράτορος Καίσαρος Σεβαστο[ῦ . . .]

Physcus

175) FRASER-BEAN 3 #3; also cf. MEYER *Gnomon* 26 (1954) 473
Dedication to the Demos of the Rhodians, or of the Romans (MEYER)
. . . καὶ τῷ δάμῳ τ[ῶν Ῥοδίων . . .]; or MEYER: τ[ῶν oder τ[ῷ Ῥωμαίων . . .

Stratonicea (found in the Stratonicean deme of Lagina)

176) *OGIS* 441
Pentaeteric festival to Hekate and Roma
132: . . . καὶ τὸν ἀγῶνα τὸν τιθέμενον κατὰ πενταετηρίδα Ἑκάτηι Σωτείραι Ἐπιφανεῖ καὶ Ῥώμηι θεᾶι εὐεργέτιδι . . .

Tralles

177) *MDAI(A)* 8 (1883) 326 #9
Fragmentary text, with an improbable restoration of Roma
10: . . . [τὰ κ]οινὰ Ἀ[σίας ἐν Σ]άρδεσιν [. . . . .]τον τῆς [Ῥώμης?]

LYCIA-CIBYRA

Aperlae

178) Priest of Roma, Zeus and Apollo—Hippolochos
11: ... ἱερατεύσαντα Ῥώμης καὶ Δι[ὸς] καὶ Ἀπόλλωνος ...

Araxa

179) *JHS* 68 (1948) 46 #11; *SEG* XVIII 570; POUILLOUX *Choix d'Inscriptions Grecques* (Paris, 1960) 32f. #4
Pentaeteric festival to Roma celebrated by the Lycian League
69: ... τοῦ τε κο[ι]νοῦ τῶν Λυκίων ἄγοντος πανήγυριν κατὰ πενταετηρίδα Ῥώμῃ θεᾷ ἐπιφανεῖ ...
75: ... ἔν τε τῇ δευτέρᾳ πανηγύρει τῇ ἀχθείσῃ ὑπὸ τοῦ κοινοῦ τῇ Ῥώμῃ.

Balbura

180) *IGR* III 474
Priest of Roma of the Lycian League—Thoantianos
19: ... ἱερασαμένου Λυκίων θεᾶς Ῥώμης ...

Cibyra

181) *OGIS* 762
Treaty between Roma and Cibyra inscribed on the base of a gold statue of Roma which had been decreed by the Cibyrates
15: ... ἐπὶ τῆς βάσεως τῆς Ῥώμης, ἣν ἐψηφίσαντο χρυσ[ῆν].

Oenoanda

182) *IGR* III 490
Priest of Roma of the Lycian League—M. Aurelius Onesiphorus
10: ... ἄρξαντα καὶ Λυκίων τοῦ κοινοῦ ἱερωσύνην θεᾶς Ῥώμης ...

Sidyma

183) *TAM* II 1, 223; *IGR* III 595
Priest of Roma of the Lycian League—M. Aurelius [... Nei]kolaos
7: ἱερατεύσαντα θεᾶς Ῥώμης Λυκίων τοῦ ἔθνους· ...

Tlos

184) *TAM* II 2, 583; *OGIS* 556; *IGR* III 563
Priest of Roma of the Lycian League—the name is lost
8: ... ἱερατεύσαντα Ῥώμης Λυκίων τοῦ κοινοῦ κατὰ πενταετηρίδα ...

Trysa

185) *IGR* III 687
Priest of Roma—Menekles, son of Menekles
... ἱερέα Ῥώμης ...

Xanthus

186) Unpublished, but reported by METZGER *RA* 1970, 321
Lycian festival to Roma; mention of an altar of Roma

PHRYGIA

Acmonia

187) RAMSAY *Social Basis* 18 #7; revised version of *CIG* 3858c
Very fragmentary; restored by RAMSAY to read ἀ[ρχιερέ]ως τῆς πό[λεως] ...; RAMSAY would see a priest of Roma here.
His restoration and interpretation are most improbable.

Apamea (cf. *IONIA* Priene #140 above)

188) *IGR* IV 793
Priest of Roma—Mutas, son of Diokles
... ἱερέα Ῥώμης ...

Apollonia

189) *IGR* III 320
Priest of Roma
... Δ[ημήτρι]ον Ὀλυ[μπίχ]ον, ἱερέα Ῥώ[μη]ς γενόμενο[ν ...]
190) *MAMA* IV 142; *IGR* III 322
Priest of Roma—Olympichos, son of Artemon
... [καὶ ἱερέα θε]ᾶς Ῥώμης γενόμ[ενον ...]

Dorylaïum

191) *OGIS* 479; *IGR* IV 522; also cf. BUCKLER *RP* 61 (1935) 187
Dedication to the Divi, Divae, Roma, the Senate and the Demos of the Romans
... [θεοῖ]ς Σεβαστοῖς καὶ θεαῖς Σεβασταῖς [καὶ Ὁμονοίαι Σ]εβαστῆι καὶ θεᾶι Ῥώμηι καὶ θεῶι Συνκλήτωι [καὶ τῶι] δήμωι Ῥωμαίων ...

Eumenia

192) *IGR* IV 741
Priest of Roma
Ὁ δῆμος Ἐπίγονον Μενεκράτους Φιλόπατριν τὸν ἱερέα τῆς Ῥώμης σωτῆρα καὶ εὐεργέτην διὰ προγόνων.

Tripolis

193) *MAMA* VI 53
Priest of Roma (?)—Apollonios, son of Dionysios
... ἱερατεύσας θεᾶς Ῥ[ώμη]ς ...

GALATIA

Ancyra

194) *Hellenica* IX 73–76
Romaia in Ephesus; Victor: Zeuxis
... Ῥωμαῖα τὰ ἐν Ἐφέσῳ
195) ROBERT *Gladiateurs* #86 (best text); *OGIS* 533
From temple of Roma and Augustus; gifts of priests to Roma and Augustus
Γαλατῶν ο[ἱ ἱε]ρασάμενοι θεῶι Σεβαστῶι καὶ θεᾶι Ῥώμηι ...
196) *CIL* III 281
The significance of this text is unclear
ROMA

PISIDIA

Termessus

197) *TAM* III 1, 16
Priest of Roma—Apollonios, son of Thoas
... ἱερεὺς θεᾶς Ῥώμης διὰ βίου ...
198) *TAM* III 1, 90; *IGR* III 446
Priest of Roma—M. Aurelius Meidianus Platonianus Varus
... ἱερεὺς θεᾶς Ῥώμης διὰ βίου ...
199) *TAM* III 1, 108
Priest of Roma and Dionysus—M. Aurelius Platonianus Otanes
... ἱερέα θεᾶς Ῥώμης καὶ Διονύσου διὰ βίου ...
200) *TAM* III 1, 109; *IGR* III 439
Priest of Roma and Dionysus—M. Aurelius Platonianus Otanes
... ἱερέα θεᾶς Ῥώμης καὶ Διονύσου διὰ βίου ...
201) *TAM* III 1, 110; *IGR* III 438
Priest of Roma and Dionysus—M. Aurelius Platonianus Otanes
Ἀρχιερασάμενον τοῦ Σεβαστοῦ, ἱερέα θεᾶς Ῥώμης καὶ Διονύσου διὰ βίου ...
202) *TAM* III 1, 112; *IGR* III 441
Priest of Roma—M. Aurelius Meidianus Platonianus Varus
Ἱερέα θεᾶς Ῥώμης Σεβαστῆς διὰ βίου ...
203) *TAM* III 1, 113; *IGR* III 440
Priest of Roma and Zeus Solymeus—M. Aurelius Meidianus Platonianus Varus
... ἱερέα θεᾶς Ῥώμης Σεβαστῆς καὶ Διὸς Σολυμέως διὰ βίου ...
204) *TAM* III 1, 114; *IGR* III 442
Priest of Roma and Zeus Solymeus—M. Aurelius Meidianus Platonianus Varus
Ἱερέα θεᾶς Ῥώμης Σεβαστῆς καὶ Διὸς Σολυμέως διὰ βίου ...
205) *TAM* III 1, 153; *IGR* III 437
Priest of Roma and Dionysus—M. Aurelius Platonianus Otanes
9: ... πρ(οβούλον), ἱ(ερέως) θεᾶς Ῥώμης καὶ Διονύσου διὰ βίου ...
206) *TAM* III 1, 156
Priest of Roma and Dionysus—M. Aurelius Platonianus Otanes
12: ... πρ(οβούλον), ἱ(ερέως) θεᾶς Ῥώμης καὶ Διονύσου διὰ βίου ...
207) *TAM* III 1, 176; *IGR* III 443
Priest of Roma—M. Aurelius Meidianus Platonianus Varus
Ἱερεὺς θεᾶς Ῥώμης διὰ βίου ...
208) *TAM* III 1, 787
Priest of Roma—Trokondas
Ἱερεὺς θεᾶς Ῥώμης διὰ βίου ...

PAMPHYLIA

Attalia

209) *SEG* II 696
Priestess of Julia Augusta and of Roma
... Καικιλίαν Τέρτυλ[λαν] ἱερασαμένην Ἰου[λίας] Σεβαστῆς καὶ θεᾶ[ς] ἀρχηγέτιδος Ῥώμ[ης] ...
210) BEAN *Belleten* 22 (1958) 32 #19; *SEG* XVII 577
Priest of Roma—S. Pacius Valerianus Flaccus
... ἱερασάμενον θεᾶς Ῥώμης δὶς ...

211) BEAN *Belleten* 22 (1958) 32 #20; *SEG* XVII 578
Sextus Pacius, twice priest of Roma
... ἱερατε[ύ]σαντα Ῥώ[μ]ης δὶς ...
212) BEAN *Belleten* 22 (1958) 34 #24; *SEG* XVII 582
Priest of Roma and Drusus Caesar—the name is lost
... ἱερασάμενον τῆς θεᾶς Ἀρχηγέτιδος Ῥώμης καὶ Δρούσον Καίσαρος ...

Perge

213) *SEG* VI 727; but now BEAN *Belleten* 22 (1958) 53f. and ROBERT *BE* 1959, 448
Restored as Amphiaraia Romaia (?); but BEAN prefers Amphiaraia on the basis of a new reading of the stone—the name of the victor is lost
16: ... Ἀμφιαρᾶα (κ)[αὶ Ῥωμαῖα ἐν 'Ωρωπῷ·]; BEAN: Ἀμφιαρᾶα ἄ[νδρας

Side

214) BEAN *The Inscriptions of Side* (Ankara, 1965) #111
Priest of Roma and demiourgos—M. Annius Afer
... ἱερεὺς θεᾶς Ῥώμης καὶ δημιουργός, ...
215) BEAN *Ibid.* 22 #112; *AE* 1966 #479
Priest of Roma (?) and demiourgos—Ti. ... Magnus (?)
... [ἱερεὺς] θεᾶς [Ῥώμης] καὶ δημιουρ[γός, ...]
216) BEAN *Ibid.* 35 #127; *AE* 1966 #465
Priest of Roma and demiourgos—D. Junius Zenodotos
Ἱερεὺς θεᾶς Ῥώμης καὶ δημιουργός ...
217) BEAN *Ibid.* 65 #183; *AE* 1966 #460
Fragmentary; priest (?) of the Divi and of Roma (?); this seems incorrect
12: ... [ἱερέω]ς τῶ[ν τε Σ]εβ[α]στῶν κα[ὶ] τῆς [Ῥώμης?] ...
218) BEAN *Ibid.* 68 #186.
Very fragmentary; priest (?) of Roma (?) and demiourgos (?)
[... ἱερεὺ]ς θεᾶ[ς Ῥώμης καὶ δημιου]ργός· ...
219) BEAN *Ibid.* 69 #189; *AE* 1966 #480
Line completely restored with mention of priest of Roma and demiourgos
[... ἱερεὺς θεᾶς Ῥώμης καὶ δημιου]ργός ...

CICILIA

Anazarbus

220) *JÖAI* 18 (1915) Beiblatt 55; *AE* 1920 #72
Two priests of Roma—L. Valerius Niger and L. Valerius Onarus Pollio
... δημιουργήσας καὶ ἱερασάμενος θεᾶς Ῥώμης καὶ ... ἱερασάμενος θεοῦ Τίτου Καίσαρος Σεβαστοῦ καὶ δημιουργήσας καὶ ἱερασάμενος θεᾶς Ῥώμης ...

Antiochia-ad-Cragum

221) BEAN-MITFORD *Denk. Wien* 85 (Vienna, 1965) 34 #36; ROBERT *BE* 1967 #623
Elegaic couplet (identified as such by ROBERT) honors priest of Roma
Τειμοκράτην ῥητῆρα θεᾶς Ῥώμης ἱερῆα
στῆσε φίλη θυγάτηρ χρηστότατον πατέρα.

SYRIA

Emesa

222) CUMONT *Syria* 7 (1926) 347
Intaglio with a text to the Tyche of Roma and of Ephesus
Μεγάλη Τύχη Ῥώμη[ς] καὶ Ἐφέσου

CYPRUS

Citium

223) HOGARTH *Devia Cypria* (London, 1889) 109 #28
High priest of Roma—the name is lost
... ἀρχιερέα τῆς Ῥώ[μης] ...
224) MITFORD *OA* 6 (1950) 74 n. 7; also MITFORD *BSA* 42 (1947) 204 n. 10
Fragmentary; high priest of the Divi Augusti (?) and of Roma (?)—
Ti. Claudius
[... ἀρ]χιερέα τῶν [Σεβαστῶν κα]ὶ τῆς [Ῥώμης?]

Paphos

225) MITFORD *JRS* 50 (1960) 75ff.; *SEG* XVIII 578
Oath of the Cypriots to Tiberius sworn by many deities including Roma;
also honors to Roma and the imperial family
7: τὸν ἔκγονον τῆς Ἀφροδίτης Σεβαστὸν θεὸν Καίσαρα καὶ τὴν ἀέναον Ῥώμην καὶ τοὺ[ς ...]
17: ... μετά τε τῶν ἄλλων θεῶν μόνοις Ῥώμῃ καὶ Τιβερίωι Καίσαρι ...

Kourion

226) MITFORD *The Inscriptions of Kourion* (Philadelphia, 1971) #77
High priest (?) of Roma restored on a fragmentary text—the name is lost
[... τὸν ἀρχιερέα] τῆς Ῥώμης [...]

Salamis

227) *IGR* III 961 as restored by MITFORD *OA* 6 (1950) 75 n. 1
High priest of the Augusti and of Roma (?)—Flavius Phi...
[... ἀρ]χιερα[σ]αμένου τ[ῶ]ν Σεβαστῶν [καὶ τῆς Ῥώμης] ?

CYRENE

228) REYNOLDS *PBSR* 26 (1958) 159 #1; GASPERINI *QAL* 6 (1971) 12ff. C 10
Monumental letters in Kaisareion; probable restorations concern Roma
[ὑ]πὲρ Ῥώμας [αἰωνίας διαμονᾶς]
or [καὶ Σεβαστῶ διαμονᾶς]
229) *SEG* IX 127; now GASPERINI *apud* STUCCI *L'Agora di Cirene* (Rome, 1965) 219
Dedication to Zeus, Roma and Augustus (?)
GASPERINI: Ζηνὶ σωτῆρι καὶ Ῥώμ[αι αἰωνίαι (?) καὶ ....]αι
καὶ Σε[βαστῶι θεῶι (?) Καίσαρι (?)]
230) Unpublished, by the courtesy of Miss Joyce REYNOLDS
Fragmentary text, with a mention of the goddess Roma and Tiberius
231) *SEG* IX 277 (+ Addendum)
Restoration of Roma here seems incorrect
Μ{ν}ησθνῖ [Ῥώ]μη

THE WEST (only texts in Greek, or pertaining to the Greek world)

Naples

232) *IG* XIV 748; *IGR* I 449
Victor in the Italika Romaia Sebasta celebrated in Naples—T. Flavius Euanthes
... νικήσαντι Ἰταλικὰ Ῥωμαῖα Σεβαστὰ ἰσολύμπια ...

233) *IGR* I 448
Very fragmentary; restored to refer to Italika (?) Romaia Sebasta (?)
[... Ἰταλι]κῶν Ῥωμαί[ων Σεβαστῶν ...]

Rome

234) *CIL* VI 372; *OGIS* 551; *IGUR* 5; Degrassi *BCAC* 74 (1954) 19 #1; *ILLR* 174; *CIL* I² 725
Lycian League dedicated a statue of Roma on the Capitol to Jupiter and to the Roman People
Λυκίων τὸ κοινὸν κομισάμενον τὴν πάτριον δημ[ο]κρατίαν τὴν Ῥώμην Διὶ Καπετωλίωι καὶ τῶι δήμωι τῶ[ι] Ῥωμαίων ...
... [LUCEI] ROMA(M) IOVEI CAPITOLIO ET POPULO ROMANO...

235) *CIL* VI 374; *CIL* I² 728; *IGUR* 6; Degrassi *BCAC* 74 (1954) 21 #3; *ILLR* 177
Laodicea dedicates a statue of the Demos of the Romans
POPULUS LAODICENSIS AF LYCO POPULUM ROMANUM, QUEI SIBEI SALUTEI FUIT, BENEFICI ERGO, QUAE SIBE[I] BENIGNE FECIT.
Ὁ δῆμος ὁ Λαοδικέων τῶν πρὸς τῶι Λύκωι τὸν δῆμον τὸν Ῥωμαίων ...

236) *CIL* VI 373; *CIL* I² 727; Degrassi *BCAC* 74 (1954) 23 #5; *ILLR* 176
Ephesus dedicates a statue of the Roman People (?); fragmentary
POPULUS EPHESIU[S POPULUM ROMANUM] ...

237) *CIL* VI 30922; *CIL* I² 730; *IGUR* 9; Degrassi *BCAC* 74 (1954) 27 #8; *ILLR* 180
Mithridates Philapator dedicates a statue of the Demos of the Romans
[REX METRADATES PILOPATOR ET PIL]ADELPHUS REGUS METRADATI F(ILIUS) [POPULUM ROMANUM ...]
[Βασιλεὺς Μιθραδάτης Φιλ]οπάτωρ καὶ Φιλάδελφος
[βασιλέως Μιθραδάτ]ου τὸν δῆμον τὸν
[Ῥωμαίων ...]

Index of Ancient Sources

In order to keep this index within reasonable limits, I have restricted it to texts dealing with Roma or her worship, and texts which I discuss or interpret. Texts cited in passing in the notes are not usually included.

A. AUTHORS

Agathocles — cf. *FGrHist* 472
Anth. Pal.
  IX 291: 127
  IX 518: 125
  IX 526: 124f.
Apocalypse 13ff.: 127f.
Appian
  Mac. 4: 30^{13}; 60^{212}
  Syr. 21: 99^{462}
Athenaeus 13, 561: 178

Cat. Cod. Astr. II 139f.: 93^{432}; 161^{220}
Cicero
  Amic. 91: 16
  Phil. XI 5: 20
  Rab. Post. 33: 200
Claudian *Cons. Hon.* 354ff.: 13

Dio Cassius
  45, 2, 3: 153^{147}
  51, 20, 6f.: 80; 140f.; 196
  54, 32, 1: 196
  69, 4, 3: 201^{14}
  76, 4: 119
Dionysius Hal.
  AR 1, 72: $17^{24\ 28}$
  4, 32, 1: 113
Dionysius Per. 353ff.: 127

Eusebius *HE* 4, 15: 174

Festus
  266: 18^{30}
  269: 18^{28}
FGrHist
  III B 472 F 5: 19^{36}; 132^{168}
  III C 840 F 13b; 40d: 17^{28}

Harpocratian 45. 4–10: 169
Heraclides — cf. *FGrHist* 840

Herodotus 1, 94: 17^{21}
Horace
  Odes 3, 5: 114; 201^{10}
  3, 3, 44: 200^{4}

Josephus
  AJ 15, 9, 6: 95; 143; 145
  BJ 1, 21, 7: 95; 143

Livy
  4, 4, 4: 201^{9}
  7, 6, 3: 22
  29, 18, 19: 109; 132^{173}
  33, 18, 22: 48^{129}
    30, 11: 49^{133}; 63^{232}
  34, 51: 99
  38, 14, 3–10: 40
  40, 51, 3: 206
  41, 6, 8f.: 28^{7}; 32^{25}
    12: 33
  42, 26, 8: 33^{31}
  43, 6, 5: 42; 166^{12}
  44, 14, 8–9: 33
    15, 1f.: 34^{37}
  45, 44, 4–20: 22^{51}
Lucretius 2, 77–79: 170

Malalas p. 216, 17–21: 94; 142; 153
Melinno (DIEHL *Anth. Lyr.*
  Gr. II 315–316): 67f.; 119; 121ff.

Nonnus *Dion.* 41, 389–391: 126

Oracula Sibyl. VII 108–113: 125

Pliny
  Ep. 7, 6, 1: 83^{362}
    10, 35–36: 193
    10, 118f.: 166
  Pan. 1: 114

Plutarch
   Amat. 1–2:   178
   Flam. 16: 21^{47}; 99ff.; 121; 131^{157}
   Q. R. 6: 18^{28}
Pollux *Onom.* IV 91f.:   171
Polybius
   16, 25–26:   101
   20, 9, 10f.: 32^{26}; 132^{174}
   21, 34:   40
   24, 10, 5:   16
   25, 4–6:   27; 28; 32^{25}
   27, 4, 5: 33^{33}
   28, 17, 4: 33^{33}
   30, 5, 4:   35; 159^{188}
      6–8:   29; 35^{42}
   30, 18:   22
      24:   34^{37}
   31, 4: 32^{27}; 34^{37}; 38^{61}; 47^{119}
      6:   48
   31, 4, 4: 26^{75}; 35^{44}; 147
      32, 3: 53^{168}; 91^{421}; 159^{189}
   32, 1, 1: 53^{168}; 91^{421}
      2, 1: 159^{189}
      10, 4: 159^{189}
      11, 10:   92
   33, 6: 53^{166}; 91
Propertius 2, 22, 39: 200^{4}
Sallust *Cat.* 53, 5:   200
[Scymnos] *GGM* I 205, 231–234:   126
Servius *Aen.* i, 273: 18^{30}
Strabo 4, 3, 2:   196
Suetonius
   Aug. 52: 21^{46}; 195
      94, 8: 153^{147}
      101:   90^{407}
   Claud. 2, 1:   196
Symmachus *Relat.* 3, 9:   13
Tacitus
   Ann. 4, 37:   80; 196
      56:   14; 51^{149}; 135^{8}
Varro *De Vita Pop. Rom.*
   66; 114; 123:   200
Vergil
   Aeneid 1, 279f.: 201^{9}
      6, 781ff.: 199^{3}

B. INSCRIPTIONS

Numbers in bold face refer to the Appendix. In some cases, the Appendix will list another edition by which a text is cited in the notes (and this index); eg. *IAG* 56 refers to Appendix **77** where *Syll.* 1064 is listed, and the index entry *Syll.* 1064 with provide the references to this text.

AE
   1920   72:   **220**
   1947   69:   **9**
   1951   218:   **98**
   1966   460:   **217**
            465:   **216**
            479–480:   **215**; **219**

Arch. Deltion
   18 (1963) A I 23 ≠ 39: 24^{63-64}
   20 (1965) B 484 ≠ 4:   **57**; 107^{507}; 155^{163}

Arch. Eph. (1966) 117: 48^{128}

ASA
   3 (1916) 149 ≠ 84: 119^{75}
   30 (1952) 252f. ≠ 3; 5:   **94–95**; 35^{45}
            292f. ≠ 66a: 48^{128}

BCH
   5 (1881) 191f. ≠ 14:   **167**; 45^{105}; 186^{43}
   10 (1886) 306f. ≠ 2:   **163**; 43^{93}
   12 (1888) 15 ≠ 4:   **173**; 44^{98}
   14 (1890) 365 ≠ 4: 24^{64}
   19 (1895) 554:   **146**; 56^{186}; 133^{179}
   26 (1902) 298 ≠ 17:   **29**; 107^{504}; 178^{114}
   37 (1913) 138f. ≠ 42:   **54**; 107^{507}; 184^{27}
   49 (1925) 232f. xi: **107**; 54^{172}
   50 (1926) 394 ≠ 14:   **30**; 107^{504}
            447 ≠ 86–87:   **31–32**
   58 (1934) 300f.:   **164**; 43^{91}; 186^{43}
            345f. ≠ 39: 25^{70}; 47^{117}
            379 ≠ 43:   **171**; 25^{70}; 47^{118}
   82 (1958) 158 ≠ 9:   **33**; 105^{495}
   92 (1968) 926:   **57**

BEAN
   Side   111:   **214**; 88^{392} ^{94}; 197^{12}
           112; 127:   **215**;**216**; 88^{392}
           183; 186; 189:   **217–219**; 88^{392}

CIG
  2485: **60**; 156^{167}
  2696: **172**; 44^{98}; 138^{26}
  3858c: **187**

CIL
  I² 589: 86^{381}
    725: **234**; 37; 153^{143}; 204
    727: **236**; 57^{194}; 204
    728: **235**; 26^{75}; 76^{321}; 204
    729: 76
    730: **237**; 84^{368}; 203f.
    731: 92^{426}; 203
  III 10: 142^{63}
    281: **196**
    399: **114**; 78^{340}; 187^{51}
  VI 372; 373; 374: cf. *CIL* I² 725; 727; 728
    500: 201^{17}
    30922: cf. *CIL* I² 730
  VII 370; 392: 20^{43}

Denkschr. Oesterr. Akad.
  77, 1 (1959) ǂ 3; 6: **148**; 147
  85 (1965) 34 ǂ 36: **221**; 88^{396}; 126; 181^6

Didyma 201; 339; 377: **137**; **138**; **139**

EHRENBERG-JONES 320b: 114^{27}

Ephesos
  II 27: **124**; 25^{73}; 59^{205}; 145^{85}; 152^{140}
    28: **125**; 25^{73}; 59^{205}; 116^{47}; 152
    30: **126**; 58^{200}; 184^{23}
    31: **127**
    53–56: 82^{355}
  III 66: **128**; 26^{77}; 58^{201}

FRASER-BEAN 3 ǂ 3: **175**; 50^{144}

GRBS 8 (1967) 237: **46**; 126

Hesperia
  10 (1941) 72 ǂ 32: **9**; 182^6
  15 (1946) 224 ǂ 51: **5**
  30 (1961) 188: **13**; 185^{29}
  40 (1971) 308 ǂ 9: **10**; 102^{472}

HOGARTH *Devia Cypria* 109   28: **223**; 93^{430}; 197^{17}

HSCP
  51 (1940) 127f. ǂ 1–2: **49–50**
    131 ǂ 6: 48; 107^{507}

IAG
  51: **77**
  53: **15**
  56: **169**
  60–61: **67–68**
  65: 168^{31}
  81: **43**

IBM
  522: 58^{204}; 138^{31}
  894: **170**; 50^{144}; 112^5

ID
  465 C 20: **69**
  1450: **70**; 66^{248}; 151^{134}; 159^{191}
  1555: 84^{370}
  1763: **71**; 66^{250}; 151^{130}
  1778: **72**; 113^{21}; 145^{87}
  1779: **73**; 66^{256}; 155
  1807: **74**; 66^{249}; 129^{139}
  1877: **75**; 23^{57}; 65^{245}; 151^{132}
  1950: **76**; 170^{49}
  1957: **77**; 99^{460}
  2296: **78**
  2484: **79**; 66^{247}; 154^{155}
  2596: **80**; 65^{243}; 167^{23}; 189^{72}
  2605: **81**; 65^{245}; 151^{132}

IDelphes
  1, 152: **41**; 101^{468}; 158^{184}
    549: **42**; 101^{468}
    550: **43**; 51^{150}

IEK 131: **131**; 55^{175}

IG
  II² 1054: **1**; 178^{112}
    1938: **2**; 102^{477}; 189^{71}
    2336: **3**; 67^{258}; 103^{479}
    3153: **5**; 99^{460}
    3169: 83^{363}
    3173: **4**; 139^{37}; 185^{29}
    3179: **6**
    3242: **13**; 185^{29}
    3404: **11**; 102^{479}
    3547: **12**; 102^{479}; 185^{28}
    4676: 23^{58}
    5047: **7**; 23^{57}; 102^{479}; 104^{487}; 140^{43}; 185^{28}
    5080: 101^{471}
    5114: **8**; 104^{487}; 140^{43}; 185^{28}
  IV 2: **14**; 105^{493}; 157^{179}
    i² 629: **15**; 105^{492}; 179^{117}
  V 1, 500; 525: **18–17**; 106^{503}
    1172: **16**; 106^{503}
    1417: **19**; 106^{500}

VII 48: **26**; 99⁴⁶⁰
413: **35**; 106⁴⁹⁶; 116⁴⁹;
158¹⁸⁶; 178¹⁰⁶
416: **36**; 106⁴⁹⁷; 169⁴⁰; 171⁵⁴
417: 169⁴⁰; 171⁵⁴
419: **37**; 106⁴⁹⁷; 171⁵⁴
420: **38**; 106⁴⁹⁷; 169⁴⁰;
171⁵⁴; 172⁵⁸
2234: **34**; 107⁵⁰⁴
2517–2518: **27–28**; 178¹¹³
IX 1, 282: **39**
2, 32: **47**; 107⁵⁰⁴
1135: **46**; 126
X 2, 1, 4: 108⁵¹²
31–32; 133; 226: **49–52**;
108⁵¹²; 129¹³⁶
XI 4, 751; 756: 64²³⁸
XII 1, 46: **93**; 35⁴⁵; 189⁶⁴
157: 24⁶³
730: **90**; 35⁴⁵
892: 24⁶⁴
2, 25–26: **84–85**; 67²⁵⁹; 116⁴⁴
656: **87**; 67²⁶⁰; 131¹⁵⁴; 186⁴²
Supp. 9: **86**; 67²⁶¹; 175⁸⁶;
3, 173: **60**; 24⁶⁶; 68; 156
1097: **88**; 68; 151¹²⁷; 159¹⁹⁰
5, 38: 24⁶⁷
139: **89**; 70²⁸²; 173⁷⁰
622: **61**; 69²⁷⁴; 112⁷; 152
1013: **83**; 69²⁷⁸
7, 245: 24⁶⁷
493b: 24⁶⁴
8, 380: **110**; 69²⁷⁹; 140⁴⁵
9, 899b: **82**; 99⁴⁶⁰; 166¹¹
XIV 748: **232**; 110⁵²⁴; 176⁹⁴;
180¹³¹

IGB

I 48: **59**
II 701: **58**

IGR

I 448–449: **233; 232**
589: **58**; 109⁵¹⁶; 197¹⁴
831: **56**; 197¹⁴
1439: **59**; 109⁵¹⁶; 197¹⁴
III 320: **189**; 75³¹⁵; 197¹⁶
322: **190**
437–443: **205; 201; 200; 203;
202; 204; 207**
446: **198**
474: **180**; 39⁶⁶; 196⁹

490: **182**; 39⁶⁶; 196⁹
563: **184**
595: **183**; 196⁹
687: **185**; 39⁶⁷; 119⁷¹
692: **178**; 39⁶⁷; 197¹⁰
785: 87³⁸⁷
961: **227**
IV 247: **111**; 49¹³⁵; 77³³¹
353: **117**
454: **120**; 189ff.
473: **119**; 79³⁴²; 187⁵⁰
498: **121**
522: **191**
741: **192**; 75³¹²; 186³⁸; 187⁵²
793: **188**; 74³¹⁰
950: **63**; 61²¹⁸; 179f.
971+978: **100**; 61²²⁰
975: **106**: 61²²⁰
977: **101**; 61²²⁰
994: **102**; 61²²⁰
1087: 46¹¹⁵; 183¹⁴
1228: **160**; 72²⁹⁸
1262: **161**; 57¹⁹⁷
1276: **162**
1302: **123**; 77³²⁸; 183¹¹
1304: **149**; 72²⁹⁹; 156¹⁶⁸; 183¹¹;
197¹¹
1309: **150**; 73³⁰³
1410: **144**; 192¹⁰¹; 193¹⁰⁸
1534: **131**; 55¹⁷⁵
1539: **130**
1556: **145**; 56¹⁸⁶; 155¹⁵⁹
1608: **151**; 189⁶⁸; 192¹⁰⁰
1611: **152**
1687: **122**; 79³⁴⁵; 112⁵
1692: **113**
1756: **153**

IGUR

5: **234**
6: **235**
9: **237**

ILLR

174: **234**
176–177: **236; 235**
180: **237**

IMagn

88: **132**
127: **133**; 52¹⁶⁰; 170⁴⁶
192: **134**; 52¹⁶⁰; 180¹³⁰
205f.: 23⁵⁹

I Priene
105: **140**
124: **23**⁵⁹
222: **141**; 53¹⁶²; 184²⁶
232–233: **142–143**; 106⁴⁹⁷

JHS
25 (1905) 41 ╪ 1: **19**; 106⁵⁰⁰
68 (1948) 46 ╪ 11: **179**; 37⁵⁶; 115³³; 165³; 189⁷³
73 (1953) 32 ╪ 13: **168**; 48¹²⁸; 173⁶⁹

JÖAI
18 (1915) Beiblatt 55: **220**; 88³⁹⁸; 196⁶
281f.: **129**; 58²⁰¹

JRS
50 (1960) 75f.: **225**; 93; 118⁶⁵
64 (1974) 195ff.: 86³⁷⁹

KONTOLEON *Akte* 192ff.: **65**;
60f.; 115; 159¹⁹⁴; 165³; 179¹²¹

LEBAS-WADDINGTON
1034a: **112**; 77³³⁰
1620: **166**; 50¹⁴²
1727: **112**; 77³³⁰; 152¹³⁶

Lindos
229: **91**; 35⁴⁶
482: **92**; 35⁴⁶

LSAM
15: **113**
26: **130**; 51¹⁴⁷⁻¹⁴⁸; 157¹⁷⁸
49: **135**

MAMA
IV 142: **190**; 75³¹⁵; 197¹⁶
143: 75³¹⁴
VI 53: **193**; 73³⁰⁶; 183¹¹

MDAI(A)
8 (1883) 326 ╪ 9: **177**
32 (1907) 432 ╪ 282: 78³³⁸; 183¹¹
37 (1912) 299 ╪ 25: **122**
44 (1919) 34 ╪ 19: 61²²¹
49 (1924) 47: **100**
72 (1957) 242ff. ╪ 65: **103**; 45¹⁰⁷; 62
75 (1960) 71ff. ╪ 1–2: **104–105**; 139³⁶
83 n. 42: **108**; 61²²⁰

Milet
203: **135**; 54; 135¹³; 156f.; 165⁵; 170⁵⁰; 187⁵³; 188
369: **136**

MITFORD *Kouroin* ╪ 77: **226**; 93⁴³¹; 197¹⁷

NS
18: **97**; 35⁴⁵
34: **96**; 35⁴⁵

OA 6 (1950) 74 n. 7: **224**; 92⁴²⁸; 197¹⁷
75 n. 1: **227**; 92⁴²⁸

OGIS
437: **115**; 71²⁸⁸; 80; 184¹⁹⁻²²
441: **176**; 49¹³⁷; 114; 149¹¹⁵
458: **140**; 141⁵⁰; 166¹¹; 191⁸⁷
470: **152**; 189⁶⁸; 192¹⁰¹
479: **191**; 25⁷⁴; 75³¹⁹
533: **195**
551: **234**
556: **184**
591: **72**
762: **181**; 24⁶⁶; 40⁷¹; 150¹²⁵
763: 54¹⁷³

Olympia
56: **21**
317: **22**; 151¹³⁵
486–487: **23–24**; 106⁵⁰⁰⁻⁵⁰¹; 197¹³

Olympia VII Bericht 218f.: **25**

PASA 1 (1882) 17f. 8: ╪ **111**

PBSR 26 (1958) 159 ╪ 1: **228**; 96⁴⁴⁴; 143⁶⁸

PP
4 (1949) 73f.: **98**; 35⁴⁵
81 2: ╪ **99**; 35⁴⁵

Pergamum
II 268: **115**
269: **116**; 79³⁴⁴; 166¹³
374: **117**; 157¹⁸⁰; 168³⁷; 192f.
689f.: 161²¹⁶
III 29: **118**; 189⁷⁴; 190⁸²
30–31: 190⁸²
p. 165: **119**; 79³⁴²; 187⁵⁰

POUILLOUX *Choix* ╪ 4: **179**

Prak. Arch. Et. (1953) 270ff.: **65**
(1958) 178: **20**

RA (1970) 321: **186**; 156^{170}; 159^{192}

RAMSAY *Social Basis* 18 ≠ 7: **187**; 75; 118^{71}

RDGE
16: **60**
18: **176**
23: **35**
38: **44**
57: 80^{349}

ROBERT *BE*
1967 ≠ 623: **221**; 88^{397}; 181^{6}
1972 ≠ 275: **55**; 107^{507}

ROBERT *EA* 448 n. 3: **53**

ROBERT *EEP* 126f. ≠ 3: **62**; 46^{115}

ROBERT *Gladiateurs* ≠ 86: **195**; 90^{412} ; 159^{204}; 165^{3}; 175^{85}; 192^{99}

ROBERT *Hellenica* IX 73ff.: **194**; 166^{17}

Sardis
8: **153**; 189^{68}; 192^{95}
27: **154**; 71^{289}
93: **155**; 71^{290}; 184^{18}
112–115: **156–159**; 71^{291}
116f.: 71^{291}; 184^{21}
119: 71^{291}; 182^{6}
129: 184^{21}

SDAW (1935) 705f.: **40**; 106^{502}; 159^{202}

SEG
II 696: **209**; 117^{54}; 181^{4}; 186^{41}
VI 727: **213**
IX 127: **229**; 96^{443}
277: **231**; 96^{445}
XII 466: **168**
XV 532: **64**; 61^{218f}; 180^{125}
XVI 486: **65**
XVII 577–578: **210–211**; 87^{389}
582: **212**; 87^{387}; 117^{54}; 187^{52}

XVIII 570: **179**
578: **225**
XIX 589: **66**
709: **148**; 72^{301}; 182^{6}
710: **147**; 72^{301}; 182^{6}; 183^{11}
XXII 350: **25**; 35^{46}; 39^{66}; 167^{19}; 177^{99}
XXIII 212: **20**; 46^{115}
XXIV 636: **57**

SGDI 2680: **45**; 101^{468}; 158^{184}

Syll.
611: **44**; 100; 158; 166^{11}
679: 53^{161}
694: **113**; 78^{334}; 130^{149}; 157^{177}
747: **35**
781: **174**; 73^{302}; 183^{11}
893: **23**
1064: **169**; 41^{74}; 106^{498}
1065: **67**; 81^{351}
1066: **68**; 46^{115}; 49^{138}; 177^{104}
1079: **132**; 52^{160}; 172^{59}; 173^{68}
1125: 123^{103}

Syria 7 (1926) 347: **222**; 59

TAM
II 1, 223: **183**: 39^{66}
2, 583: **184**; 39^{66}
III 1, 16: **197**; 87^{385}
90: **198**; 188^{56}
108: **199**; 86^{383}; 188^{56}
109–110: **200–201**; 86^{383}; 185^{37}
112: **202**
113–114: **203–204**; 86^{383}; 130^{141}; 185^{37}
153; 156: **205–206**; 86^{383}; 185^{37}
176: **207**
787: **208**; 87^{385}; 188^{56}

ZPE
8 (1971) 286f.: 81
13 (1974) 280: **112**; 77^{330}; 152

C. PAPYRI

BELL *Jews and Christians* ≠ 1912: 96^{449}; 159^{196}

BGU
III 887: 88^{393}
895: 97^{453}
937: 97^{452}

Fouad I Univ. Papyri ≠ 10: 97^{453}

Mit diesem Werk erhalten Sie
einen umfassenden Überblick
über die wichtigsten Religionen der Welt

Handbuch der Religionsgeschichte

Herausgegeben von
Prof. Dr. Jes Peter Asmussen und
Prof. Dr. Jørgen Læssøe in
Verbindung mit Prof. Dr. Dr. Carsten Colpe

3 Bände von zusammen 1639 Seiten, insgesamt
261 Abbildungen und 12 Kartenskizzen. Leinen.

Das Faszinierende an der Religionsgeschichte ist ihr weitgespannter kulturgeschichtlicher Hintergrund. In diesem Rahmen geht es dann um die einzelnen Religionen und ihre historisch bekannten Formen, die ihnen zugrunde liegenden religiösen Erfahrungen und die Wirkungen, die die Religionen aufeinander ausgeübt haben.

Ein abschließendes Kapitel des Herausgebers der deutschen Übersetzung, Prof. Dr. Dr. Carsten Colpe, faßt die über die klassische Ausprägung der einzelnen Religionen hinausgehende neueste Entwicklung unter dem charakteristischen Gesichtspunkt des Synkretismus zusammen.

Drei verschiedene Register erschließen das Werk zu handlicher Benutzbarkeit.

Aus dem Inhalt:
Band 1: **J. P. Johansen / V. Grønbech**, Primitive Religion / **E. Holtved**, Eskimo-Religion / **L. Honko**, Religion der finnisch-ugrischen Völker. Religion der slawischen Völker / **F. Le Roux Guyonvarc'h**, Keltische Religion / **L. Ejerfeldt**, Germanische Religion / **A. Hvidtfeldt**, Religionen der indianischen Hochkulturen / **H. L. Jansen**, Ägyptische Religion / **J. van Dijk**, Sumerische Religion / **J. Læssøe**, Babylonische und assyrische Religion.

Band 2: **S. S. Hartman**, Hethitische Religion / **J. Pedersen**, Kanaanäische Religion / **E. Nielsen**, Die Religion des alten Israel / **B. Salomonsen**, Das Spätjudentum / **R. Edelmann**, Das Judentum / **K. Barr**, Die Religion der alten Iranier / **C. Colpe**, Zarathustra und der frühe Zoroastrismus / **M. Boyce**, Der spätere Zoroastrismus / **F. Møller-Kristensen**, Indische Religionen: Die Vedareligion. Der Hinduismus. Der Buddhismus. Der Jainismus / **E. Haarh**, Der Lamaismus.

Band 3: **G. Malmquist**, Die Religionen Chinas / **H. Henne**, Die Religionen Japans / **P. J. Jensen**, Die griechische Religion. Die römische Religion / **S. Giversen**, Der Gnostizismus und die Mysterienreligonen / **J. P. Asmussen**, Der Mithraskult / **S. S. Hartman**, Der Mandäismus / **J. P. Asmussen**, Der Manichäismus / **J. Pedersen**, Der Islam und seine Vorgeschichte / **C. Colpe**, Synkretismus, Renaissance, Säkularisation und Neubildung von Religionen in der Gegenwart / **G. Chappuzeau**, Namen, Sach- und Quellenregister.

V&R **Vandenhoeck & Ruprecht** Göttingen und Zürich

DATE DUE

BL   34842
820
.R65   Mellor, Ronald
M44   The worship of the
1975   goddess Roma in the
          Greek world.

HIEBERT LIBRARY
Fresno Pacific College - M. B. Seminary
Fresno, Calif 93702